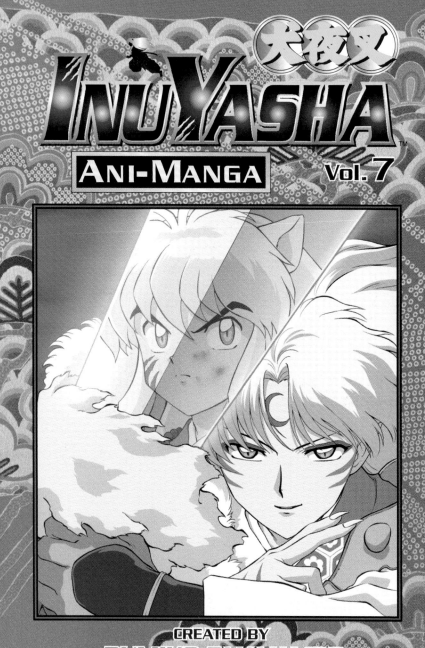

INUYASHA
ANI-MANGA
Vol. 7

**CREATED BY
RUMIKO TAKAHASHI**

Inuyasha Ani-Manga™
Vol. #7

Created by
Rumiko Takahashi

Translation based on the VIZ anime TV series
Translation Assistance/Katy Bridges
Lettering/John Clark
Cover Design & Graphics/Hidemi Sahara
Editor/Frances E. Wall

Managing Editor/Annette Roman
Editorial Director/Alvin Lu
Director of Production/Noboru Watanabe
Sr. Director of Licensing & Acquisitions/Rika Inouye
Vice President of Sales & Marketing/Liza Coppola
Executive Vice President/Hyoe Narita
Publisher/Seiji Horibuchi

Published by VIZ, LLC
P.O. Box 77010
San Francisco, CA 94107

10 9 8 7 6 5 4 3 2 1
First printing, January 2005

www.viz.com

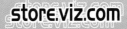

Story thus far

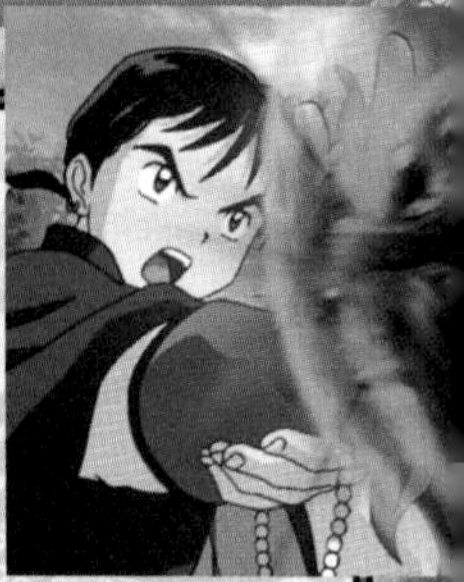

Kagome, a typical high school girl, has been transported into a mythical version of Japan's medieval past, a place filled with incredible magic and terrifying demons. Who would have guessed that the stories and legends Kagome's superstitious grandfather told her could really be true!?

It turns out that Kagome is the reincarnation of Lady Kikyo, a great warrior and the defender of the Shikon Jewel, or the Jewel of Four Souls. In fact, the sacred jewel mysteriously emerges from Kagome's body during a battle with a horrible centipede-like monster. In her desperation to defeat the monster, Kagome frees Inuyasha, a dog-like half-demon who lusts for the power imparted by the jewel, and unwittingly releases him from the binding spell that was placed 50 years earlier by Lady Kikyo. To prevent Inuyasha from stealing the jewel, Kikyo's sister, Lady Kaede, puts a magical necklace around Inuyasha's neck that allows Kagome to make him "sit" on command.

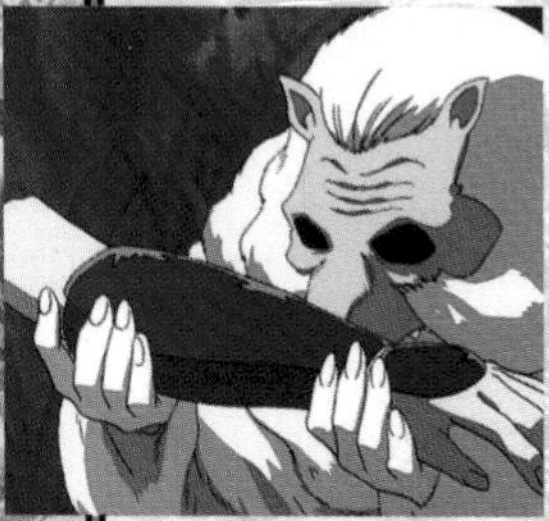

In another skirmish for possession of the jewel, it accidentally shatters and is strewn across the land. Only Kagome has the power to find the jewel shards, and only Inuyasha has the strength to defeat the demons who now hold them, so the two unlikely partners are bound together in the quest to reclaim all the pieces of the Shikon Jewel.

Inuyasha, Kagome, and Shippo have found a new friend and ally in Miroku, a lecherous monk with a family curse that makes his hand a powerful wind tunnel. But Inuyasha's half-brother Sesshomaru, his old nemesis, has returned and stolen their father's sacred sword, the Tetsusaiga. When Inuyasha and Sesshomaru clashed before, Sesshomaru—a full-fledged demon—was unable to touch the sword, for the Tetsusaiga's power can only be used to protect and defend humans. But with the help of nefarious, shape-shifting Naraku, Sesshomaru obtained a human arm with which he can wield the Tetsusaiga for his own gain!

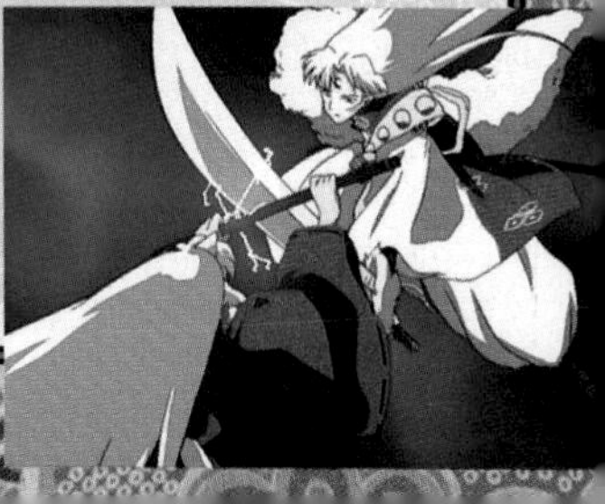

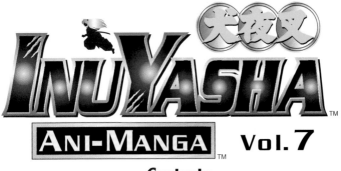

INUYASHA

ANI-MANGA Vol. 7

Contents

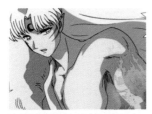
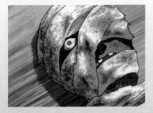
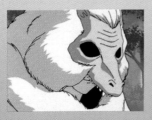

19
Go Home to Your Own Time, Kagome!

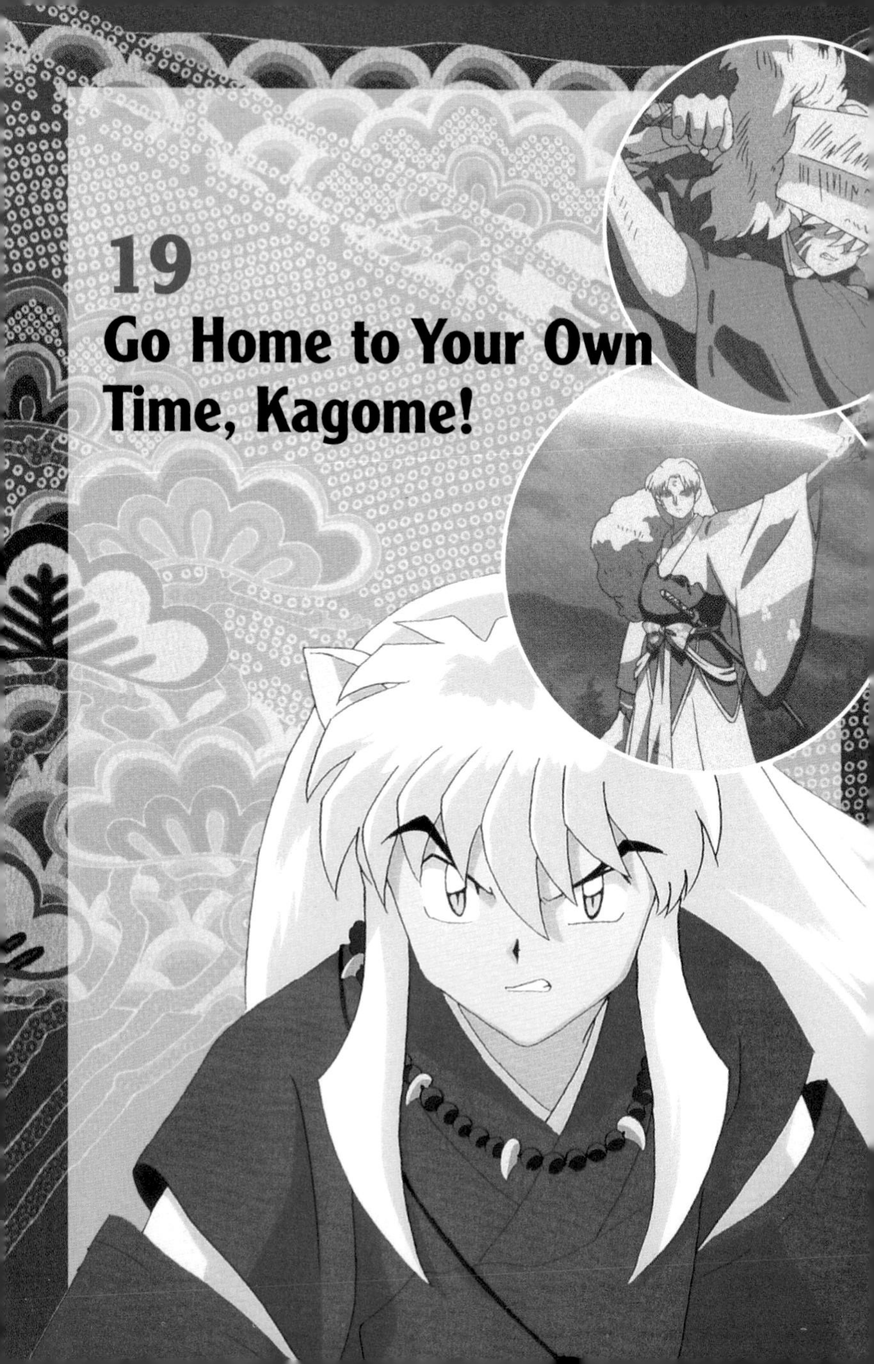

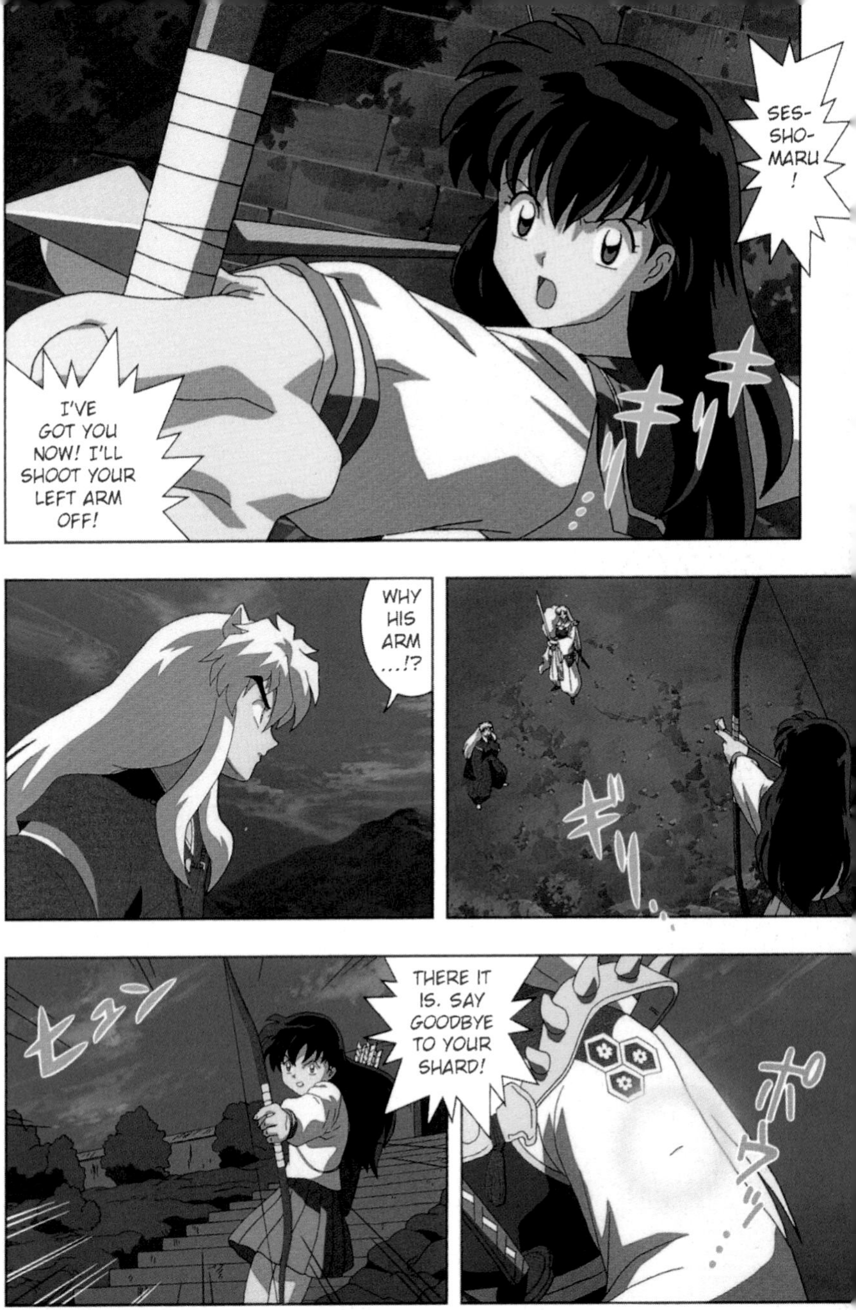
SES-SHO-MARU!
I'VE GOT YOU NOW! I'LL SHOOT YOUR LEFT ARM OFF!
WHY HIS ARM ...!?
THERE IT IS. SAY GOODBYE TO YOUR SHARD!

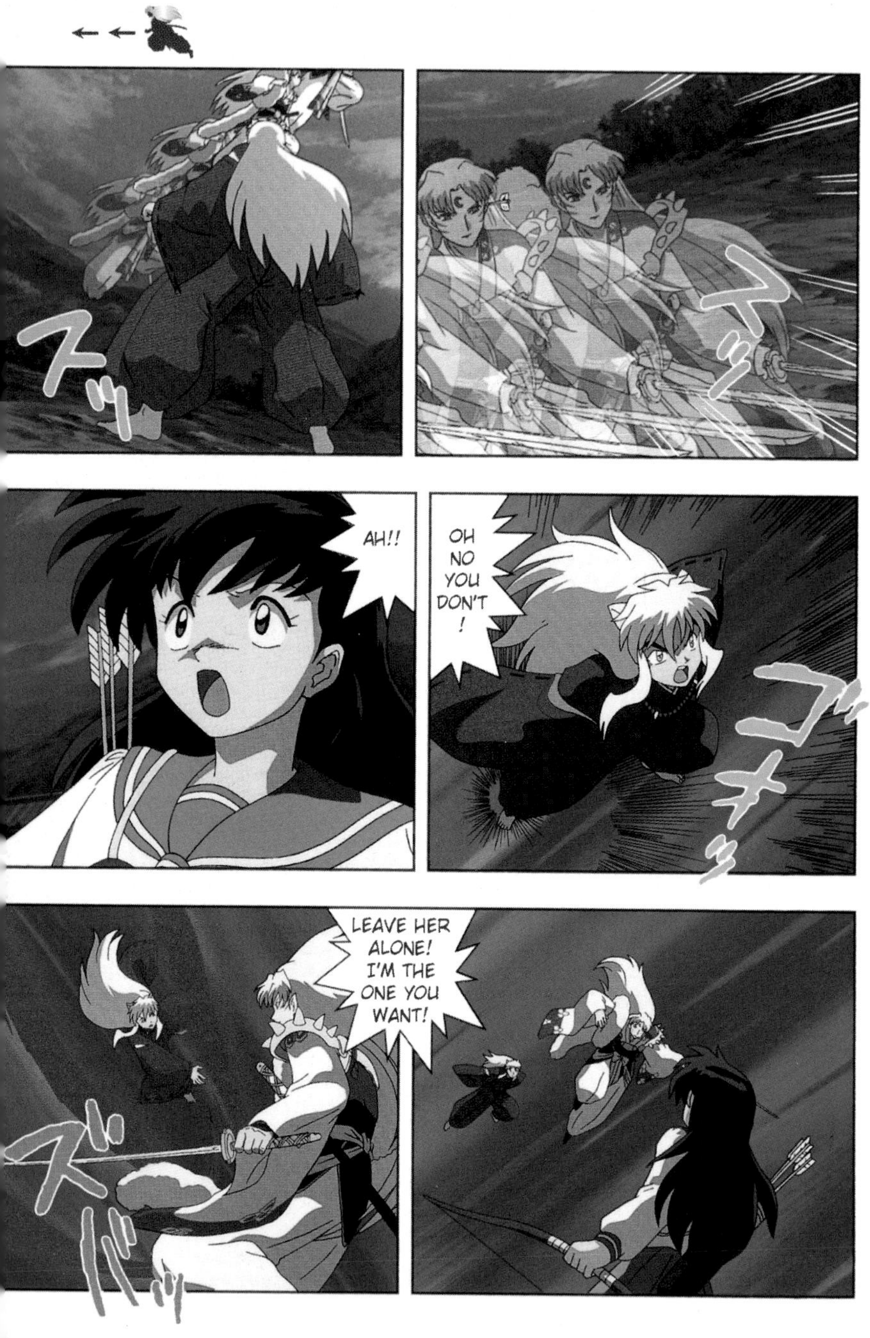
OH NO YOU DON'T!
AH!!
LEAVE HER ALONE! I'M THE ONE YOU WANT!

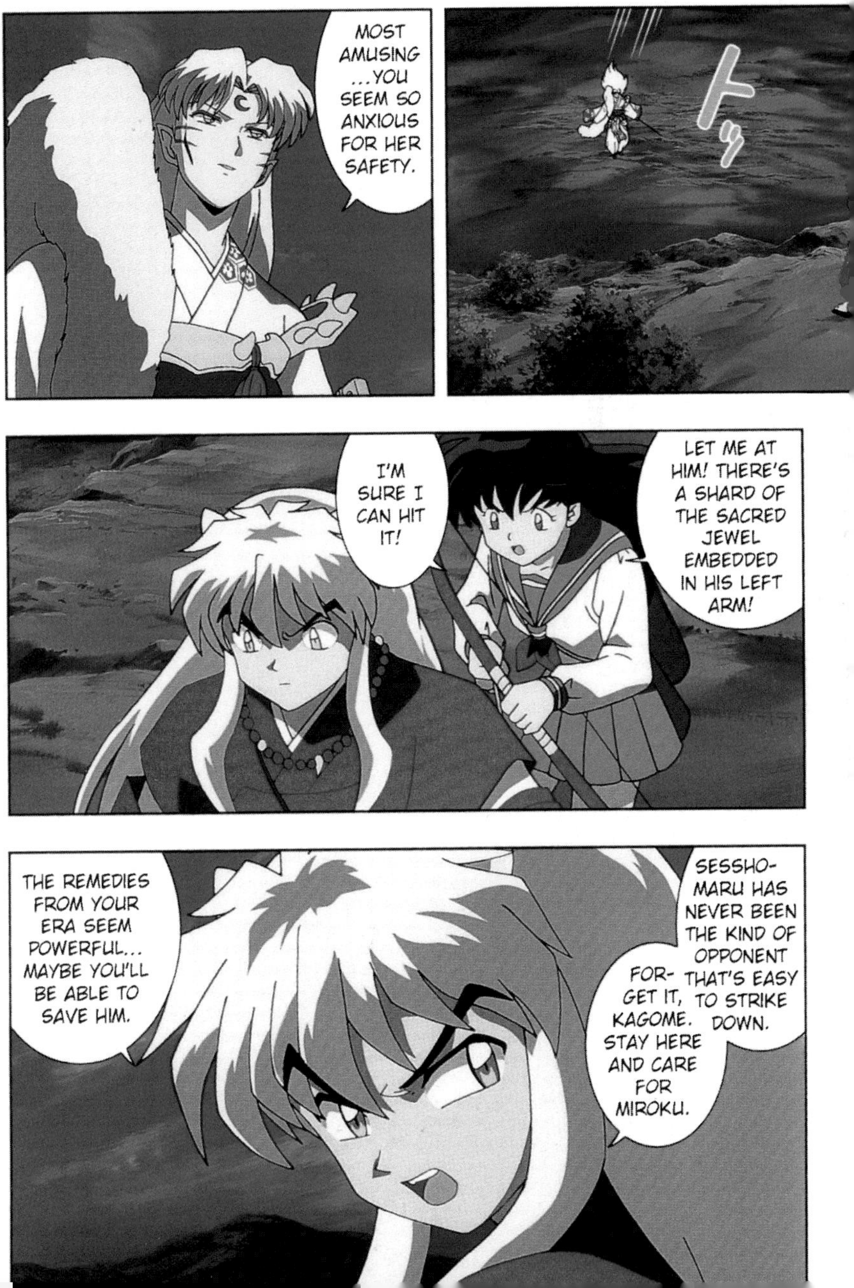

トッ
MOST AMUSING ...YOU SEEM SO ANXIOUS FOR HER SAFETY.
LET ME AT HIM! THERE'S A SHARD OF THE SACRED JEWEL EMBEDDED IN HIS LEFT ARM!
I'M SURE I CAN HIT IT!
SESSHO-MARU HAS NEVER BEEN THE KIND OF OPPONENT THAT'S EASY TO STRIKE DOWN.
FOR-GET IT, KAGOME. STAY HERE AND CARE FOR MIROKU.
THE REMEDIES FROM YOUR ERA SEEM POWERFUL... MAYBE YOU'LL BE ABLE TO SAVE HIM.

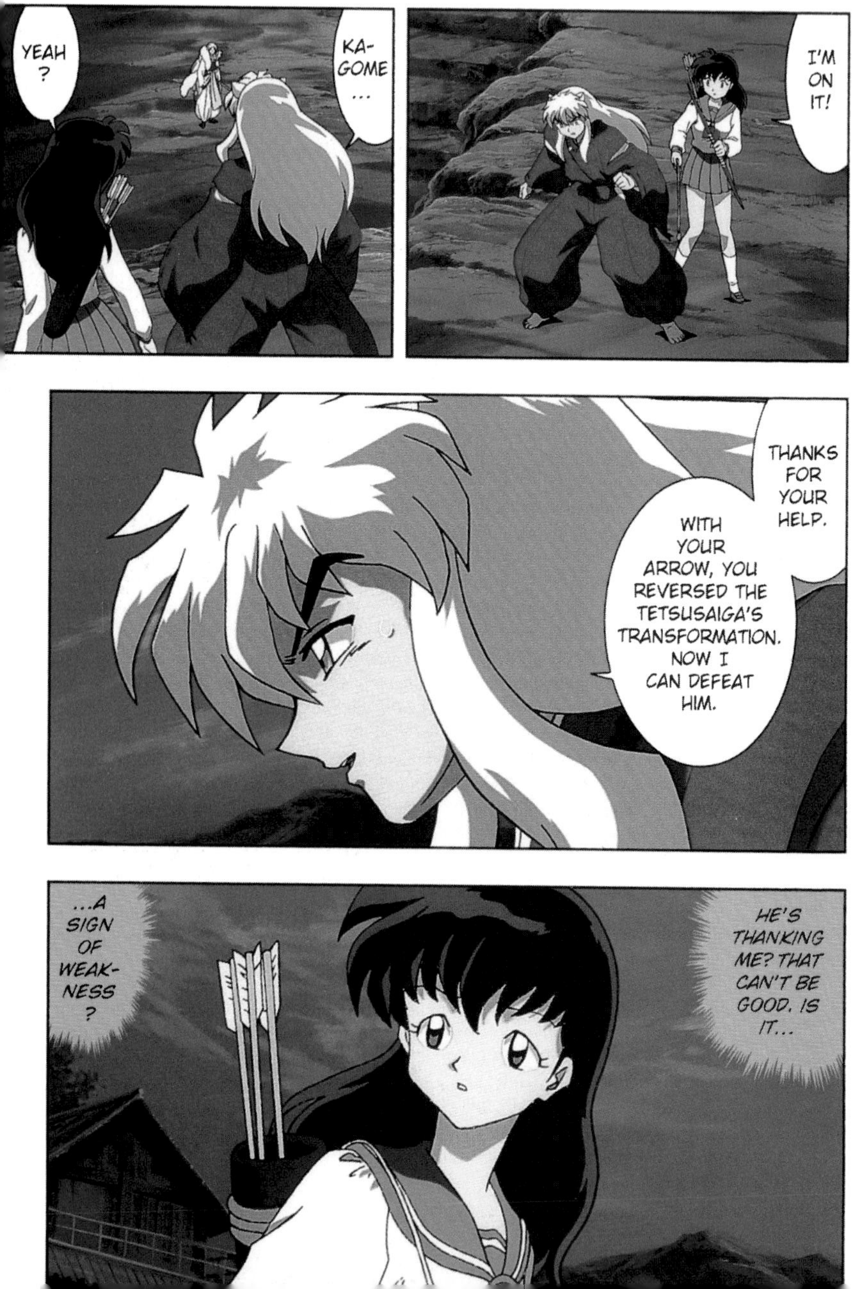
I'M ON IT!
KA-GOME...
YEAH?
THANKS FOR YOUR HELP.
WITH YOUR ARROW, YOU REVERSED THE TETSUSAIGA'S TRANSFORMATION. NOW I CAN DEFEAT HIM.
HE'S THANKING ME? THAT CAN'T BE GOOD. IS IT...
...A SIGN OF WEAKNESS?

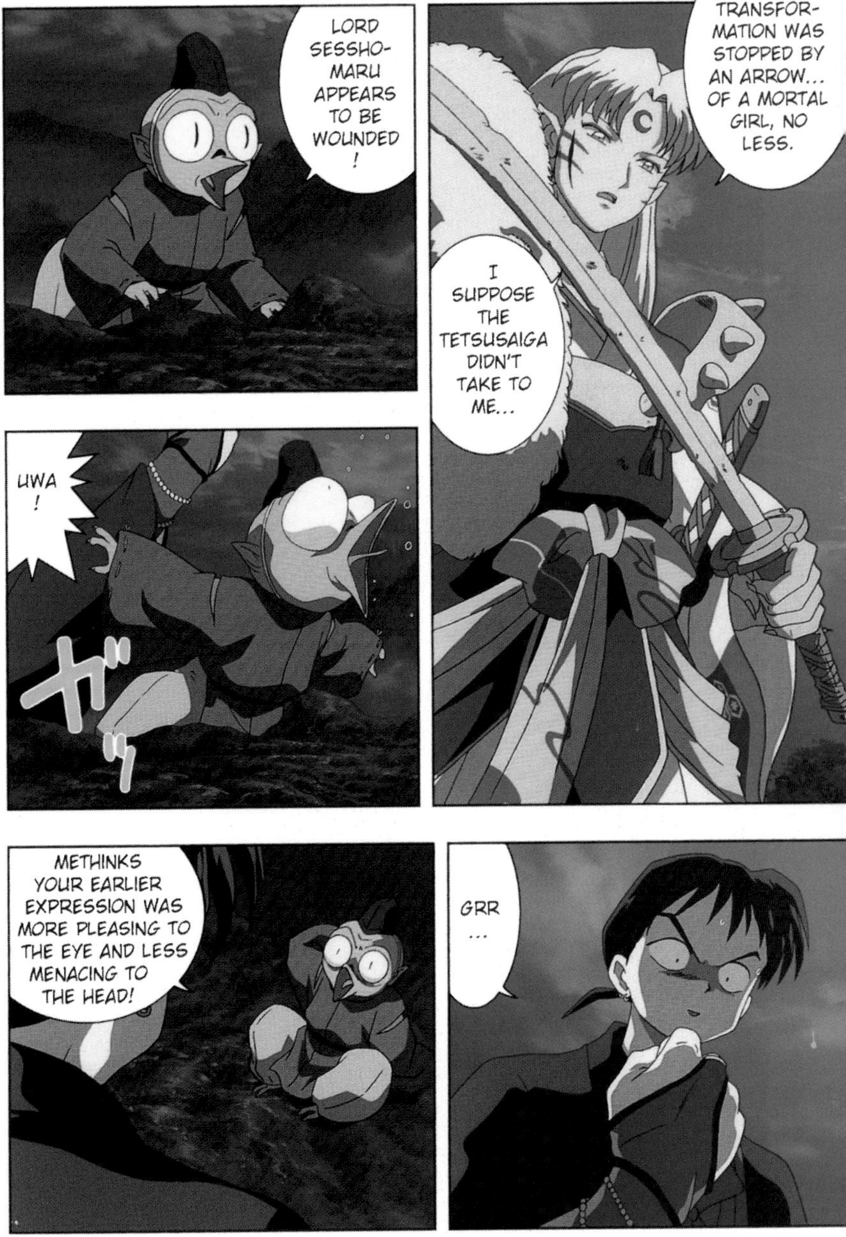
THE TRANSFORMATION WAS STOPPED BY AN ARROW... OF A MORTAL GIRL, NO LESS.
I SUPPOSE THE TETSUSAIGA DIDN'T TAKE TO ME...
LORD SESSHOMARU APPEARS TO BE WOUNDED!
UWA!
ガッ
GRR...
METHINKS YOUR EARLIER EXPRESSION WAS MORE PLEASING TO THE EYE AND LESS MENACING TO THE HEAD!

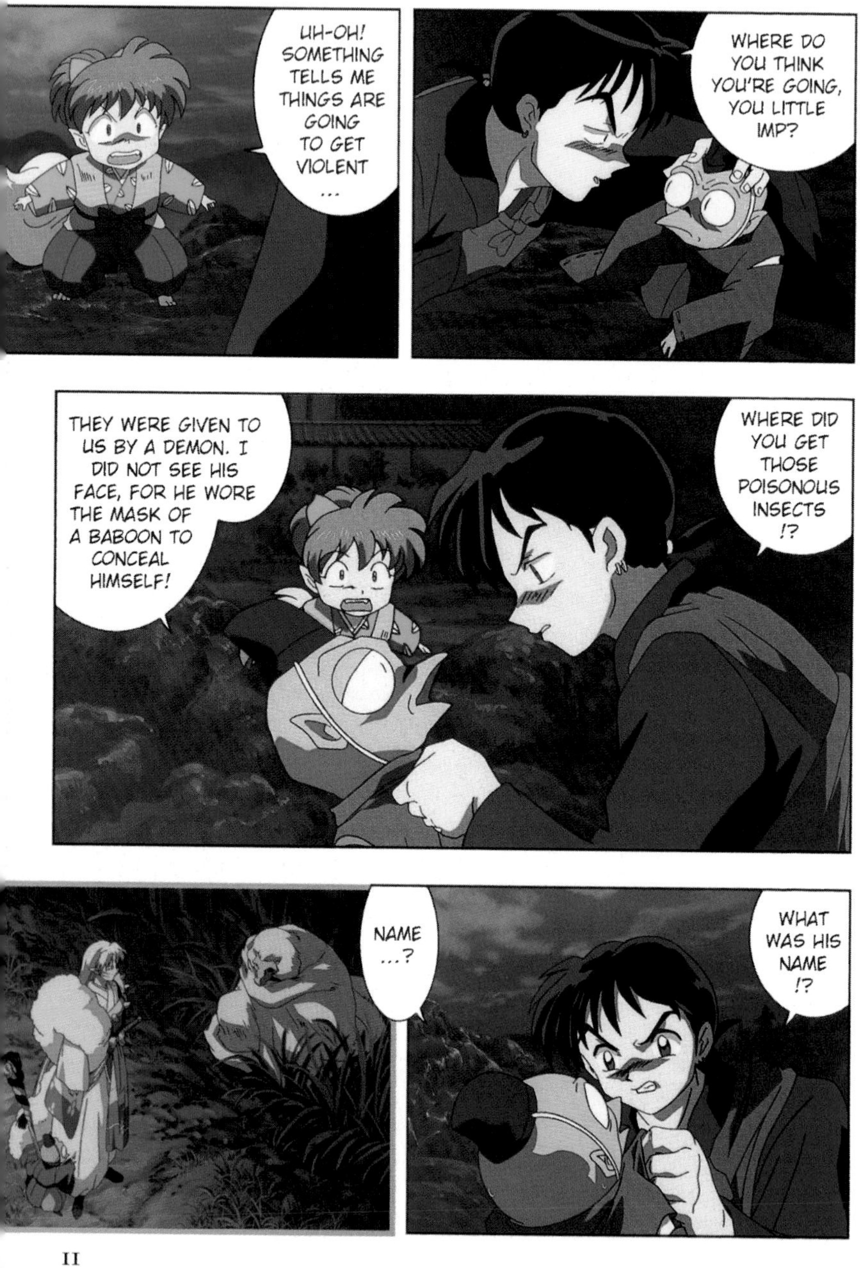
WHERE DO YOU THINK YOU'RE GOING, YOU LITTLE IMP?
UH-OH! SOMETHING TELLS ME THINGS ARE GOING TO GET VIOLENT ...
WHERE DID YOU GET THOSE POISONOUS INSECTS !?
THEY WERE GIVEN TO US BY A DEMON. I DID NOT SEE HIS FACE, FOR HE WORE THE MASK OF A BABOON TO CONCEAL HIMSELF!
WHAT WAS HIS NAME !?
NAME ...?

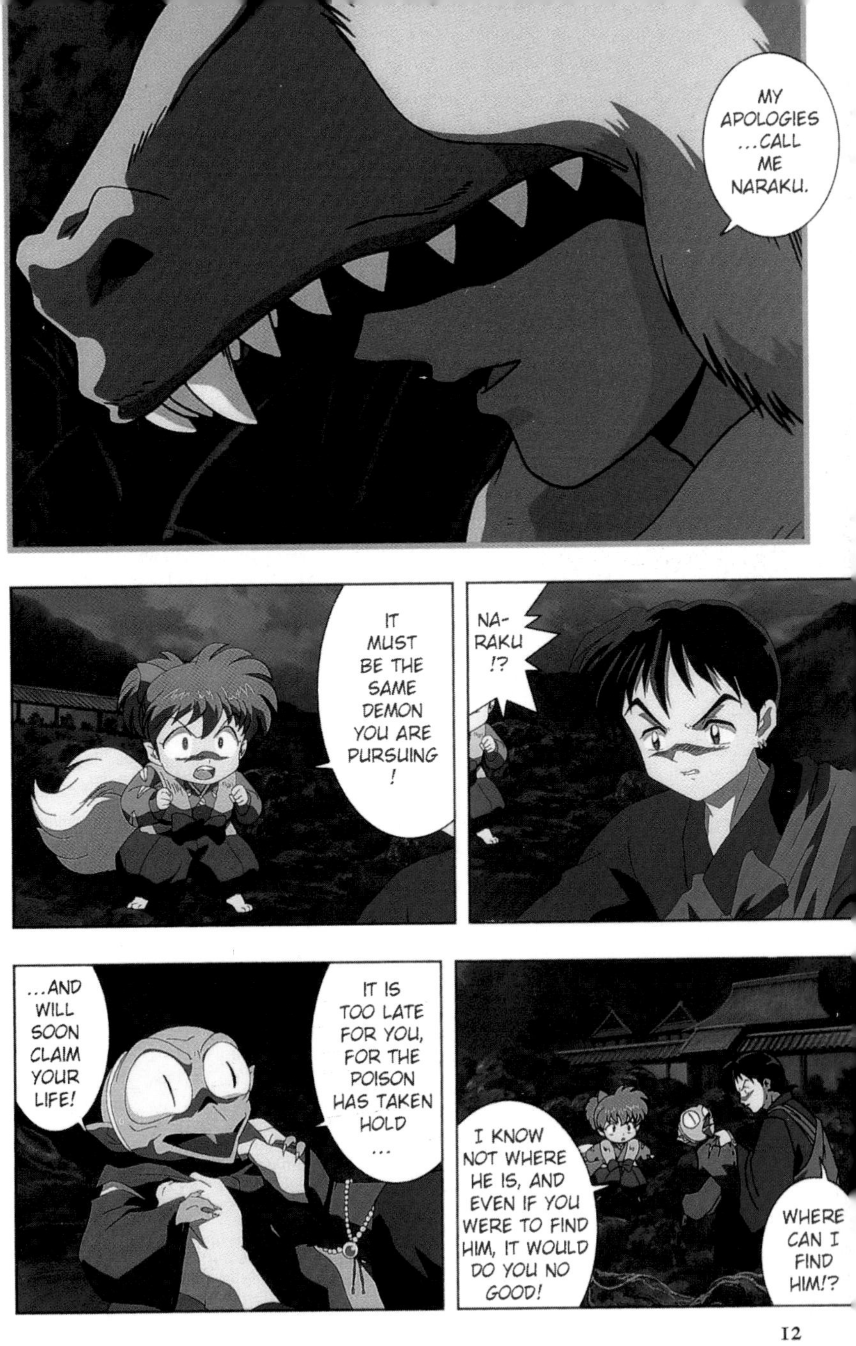
MY APOLOGIES ...CALL ME NARAKU.
NA-RAKU !?
IT MUST BE THE SAME DEMON YOU ARE PURSUING !
WHERE CAN I FIND HIM!?
I KNOW NOT WHERE HE IS, AND EVEN IF YOU WERE TO FIND HIM, IT WOULD DO YOU NO GOOD!
IT IS TOO LATE FOR YOU, FOR THE POISON HAS TAKEN HOLD ...
...AND WILL SOON CLAIM YOUR LIFE!

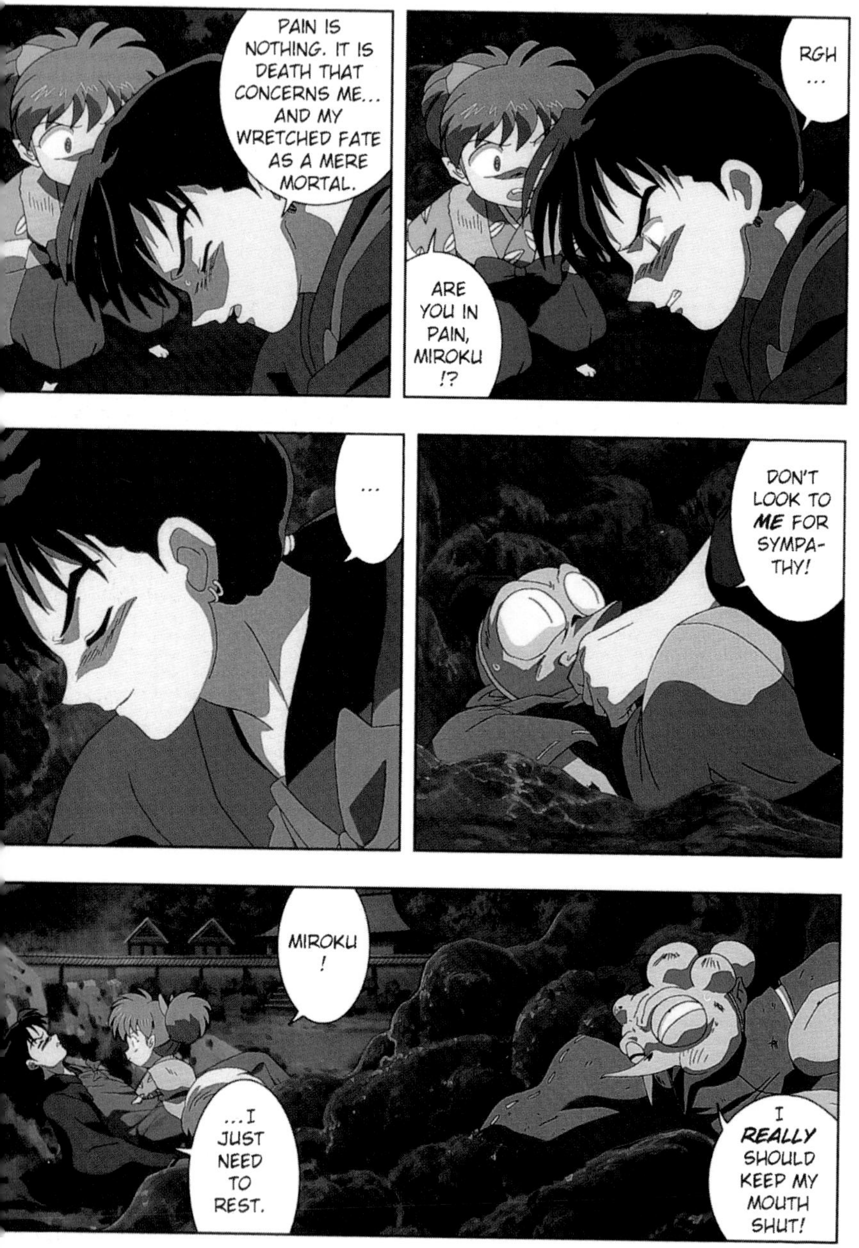
RGH ...
ARE YOU IN PAIN, MIROKU!?
PAIN IS NOTHING. IT IS DEATH THAT CONCERNS ME... AND MY WRETCHED FATE AS A MERE MORTAL.
DON'T LOOK TO *ME* FOR SYMPA-THY!
...
MIROKU!
I *REALLY* SHOULD KEEP MY MOUTH SHUT!
...I JUST NEED TO REST.

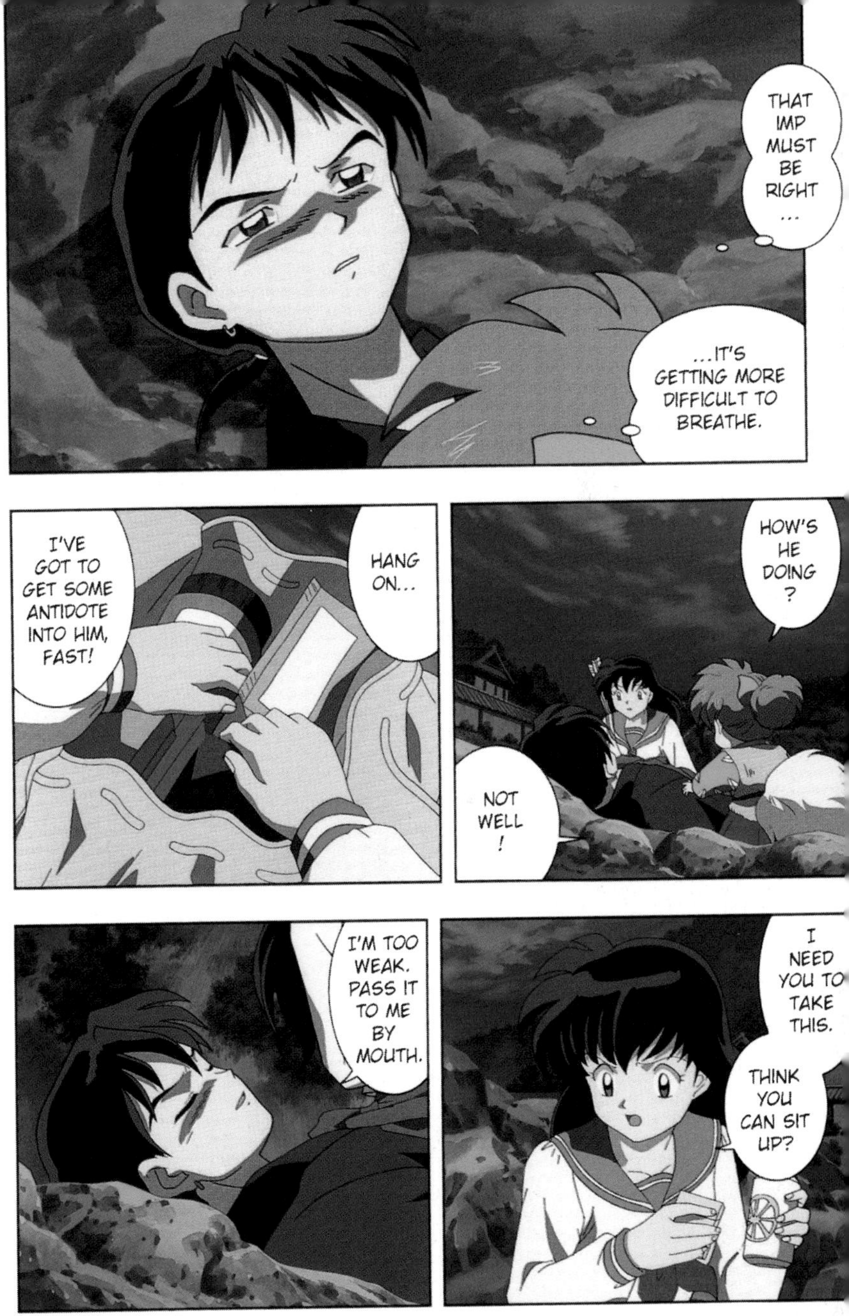
THAT IMP MUST BE RIGHT...
...IT'S GETTING MORE DIFFICULT TO BREATHE.
HOW'S HE DOING?
NOT WELL!
HANG ON...
I'VE GOT TO GET SOME ANTIDOTE INTO HIM, FAST!
I NEED YOU TO TAKE THIS.
THINK YOU CAN SIT UP?
I'M TOO WEAK. PASS IT TO ME BY MOUTH.

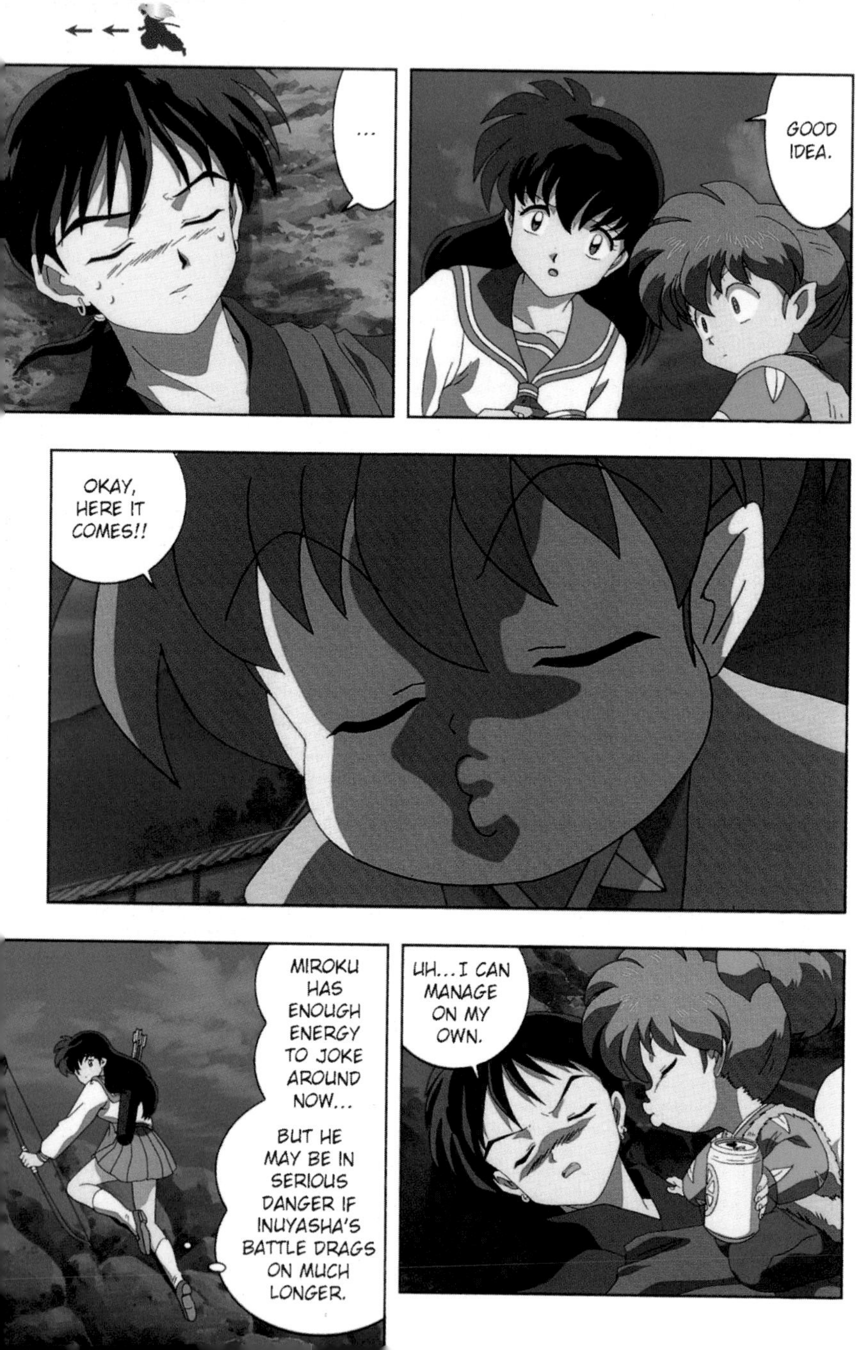
GOOD IDEA.
...
OKAY, HERE IT COMES!!
UH...I CAN MANAGE ON MY OWN.
MIROKU HAS ENOUGH ENERGY TO JOKE AROUND NOW...
BUT HE MAY BE IN SERIOUS DANGER IF INUYASHA'S BATTLE DRAGS ON MUCH LONGER.

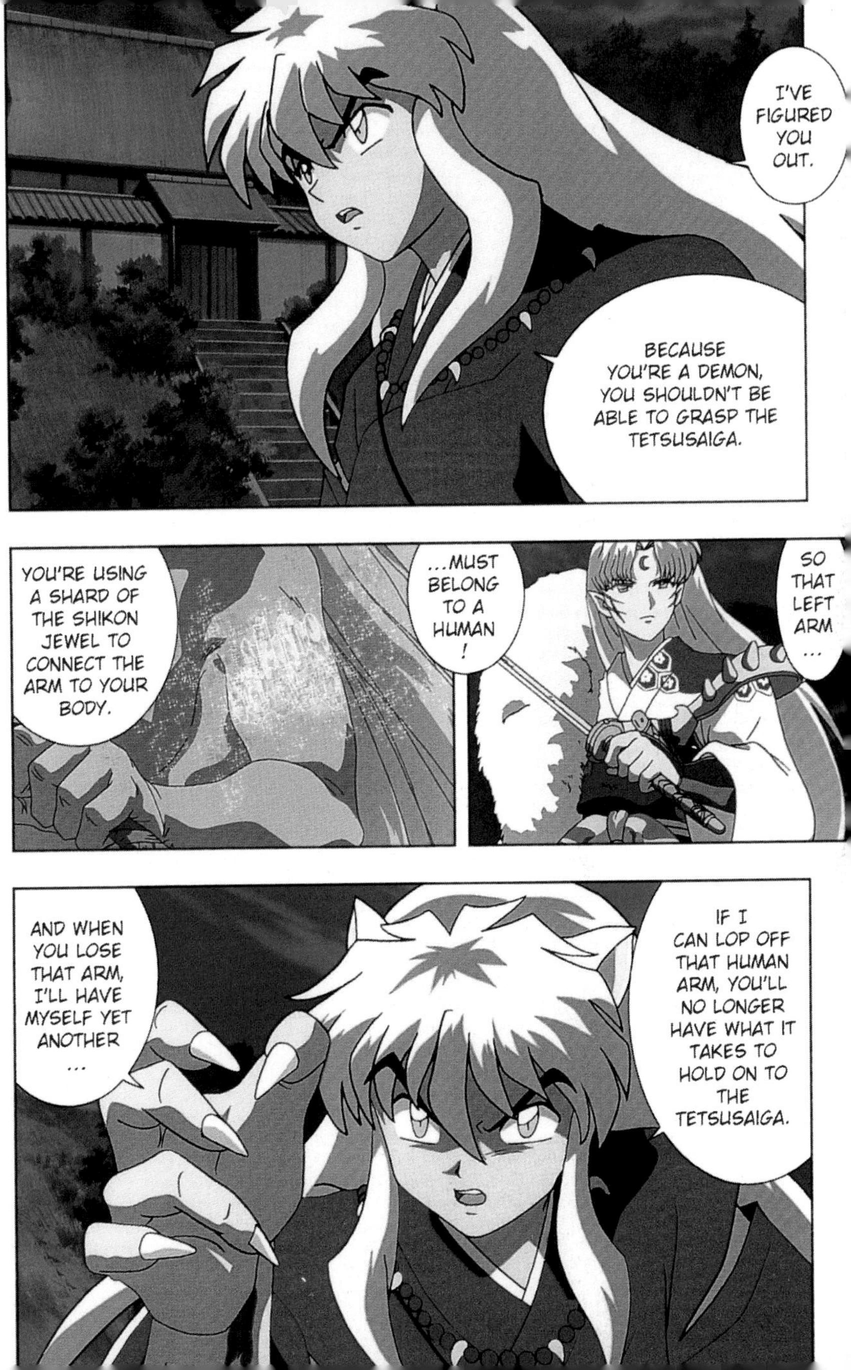
I'VE FIGURED YOU OUT.
BECAUSE YOU'RE A DEMON, YOU SHOULDN'T BE ABLE TO GRASP THE TETSUSAIGA.
SO THAT LEFT ARM ...
...MUST BELONG TO A HUMAN!
YOU'RE USING A SHARD OF THE SHIKON JEWEL TO CONNECT THE ARM TO YOUR BODY.
IF I CAN LOP OFF THAT HUMAN ARM, YOU'LL NO LONGER HAVE WHAT IT TAKES TO HOLD ON TO THE TETSUSAIGA.
AND WHEN YOU LOSE THAT ARM, I'LL HAVE MYSELF YET ANOTHER ...

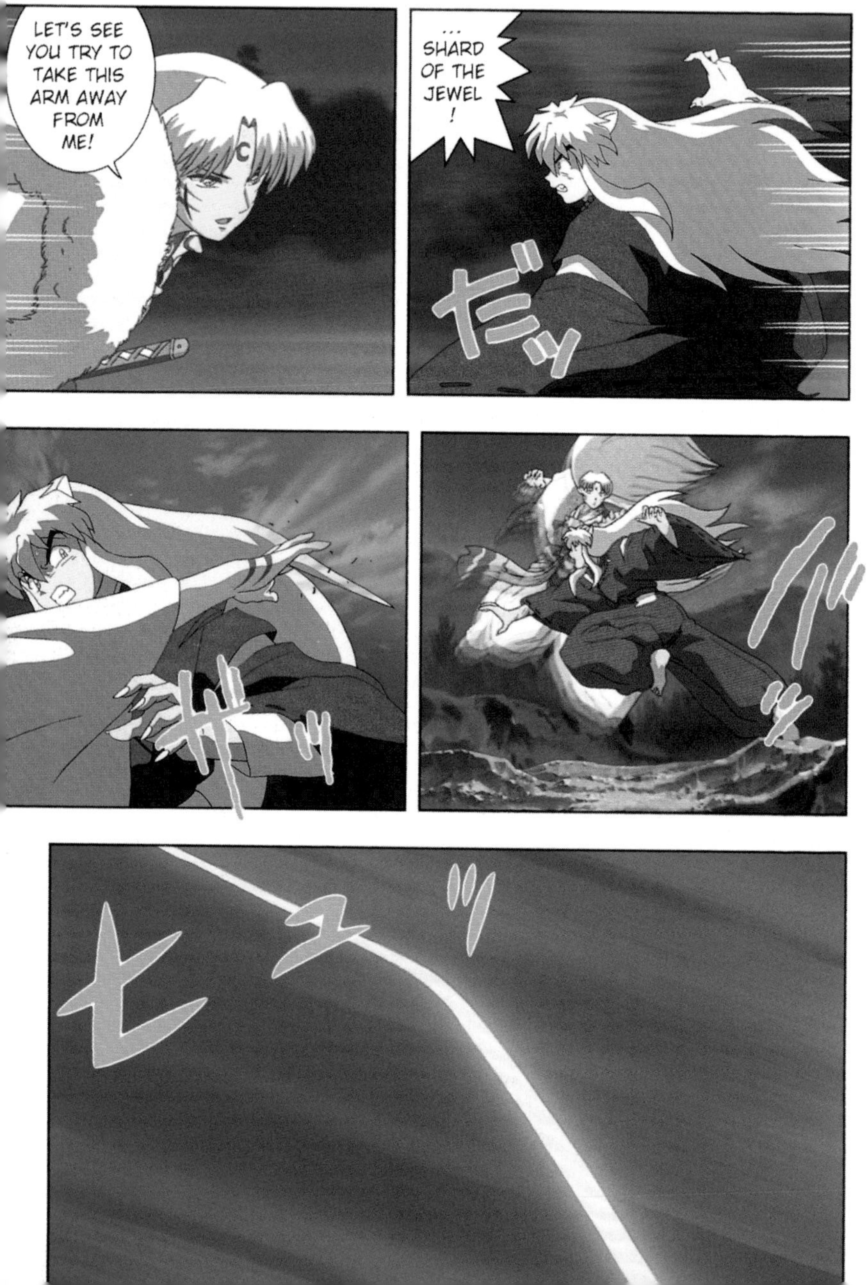
... SHARD OF THE JEWEL !
ダッ
LET'S SEE YOU TRY TO TAKE THIS ARM AWAY FROM ME!
ザッ
ヒュッ

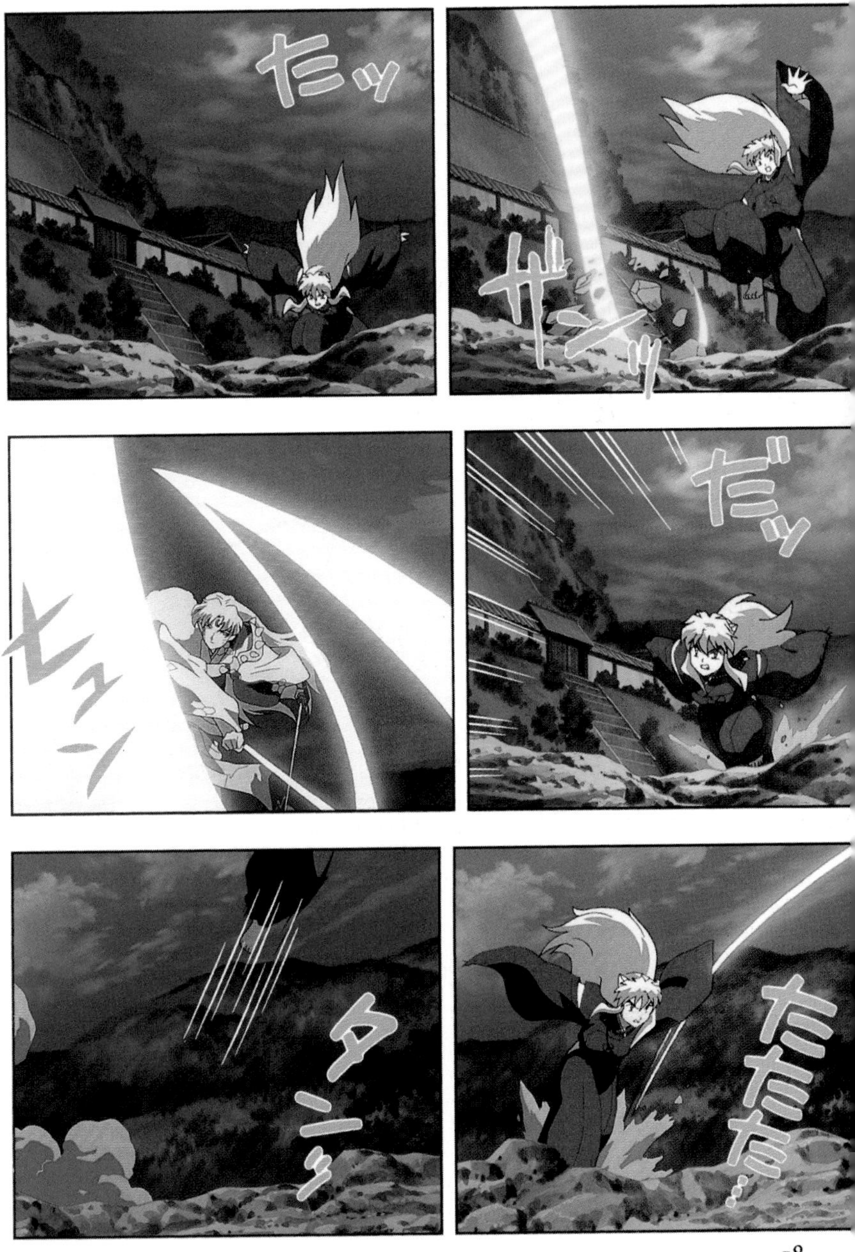

ザシッ
たッ
だッ
ヒュン
たたた…
タンッ

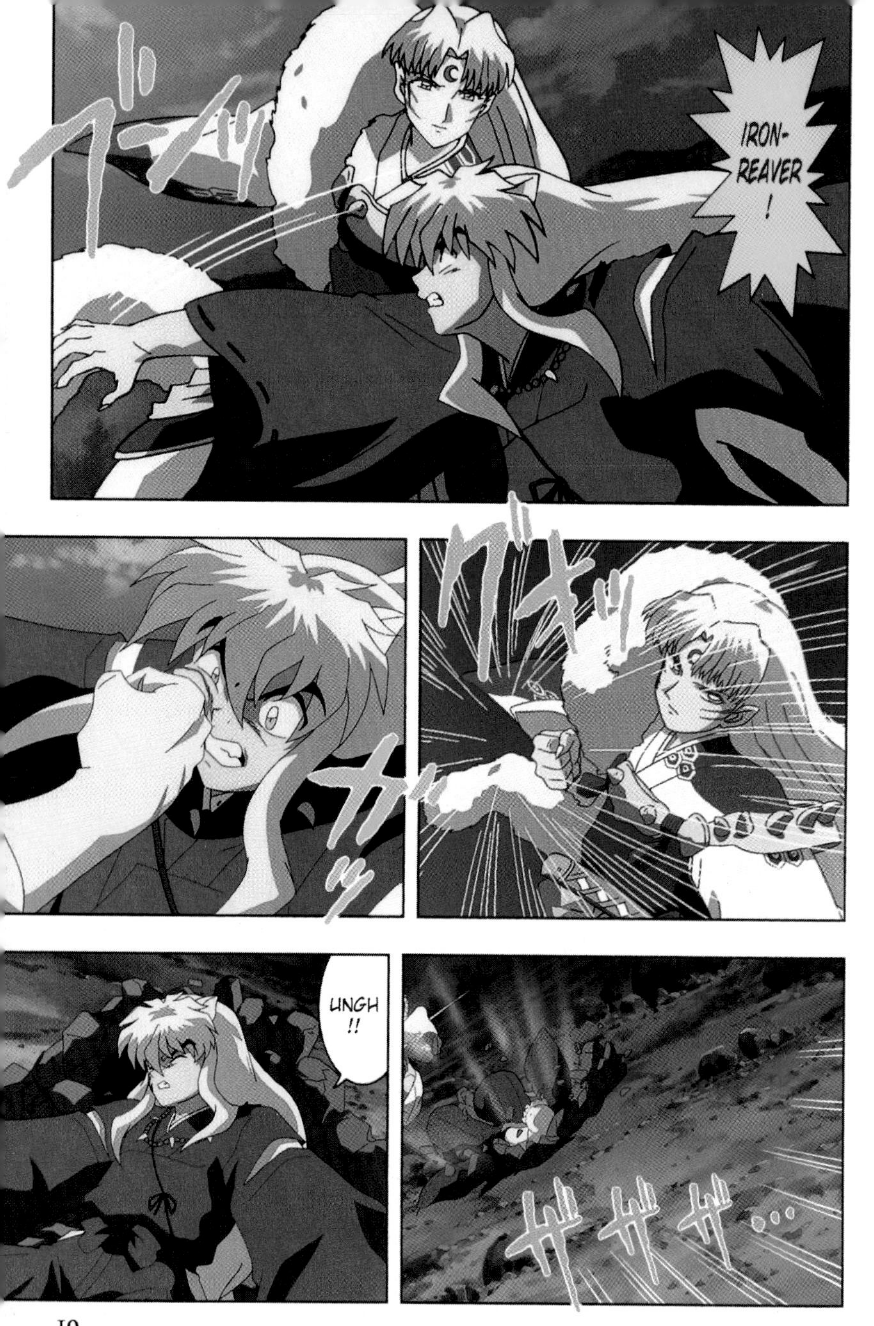
IRON-REAVER !
UNGH !!

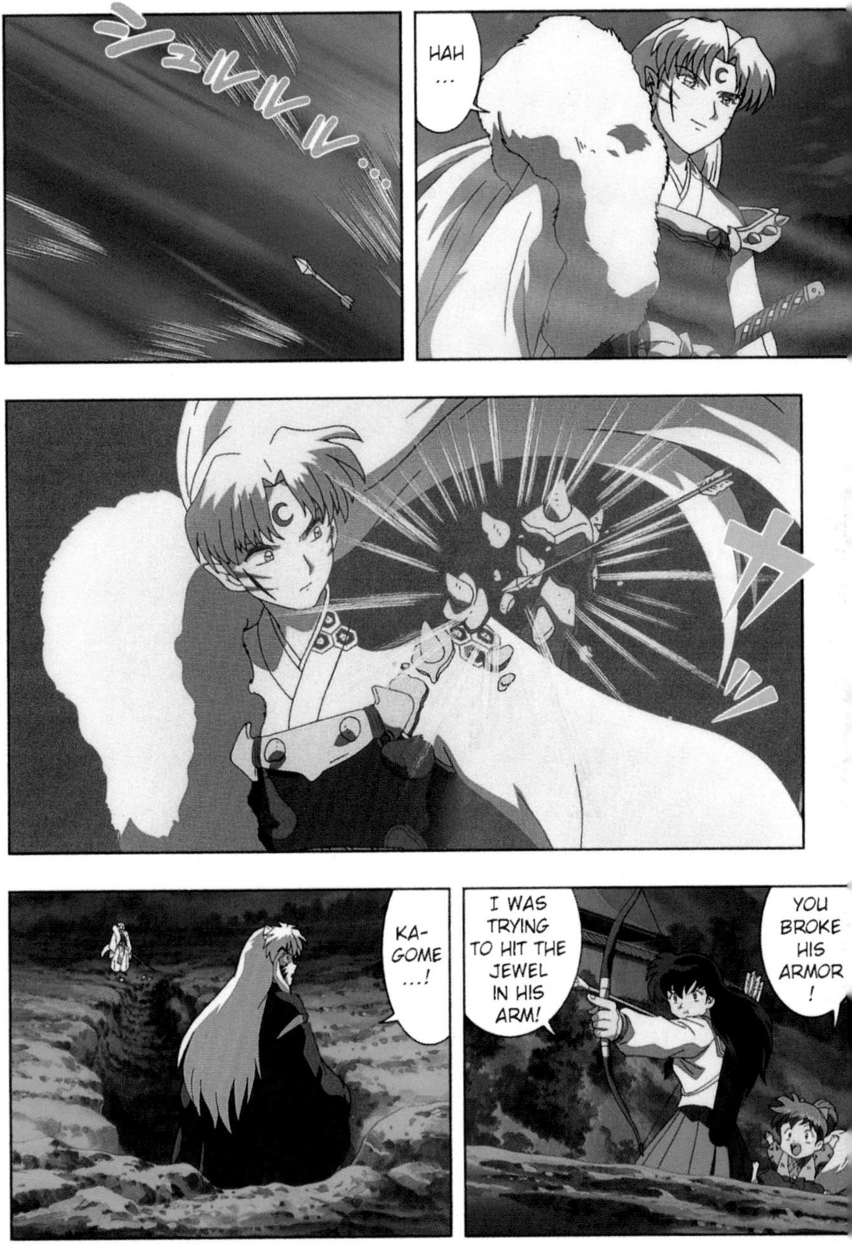
HAH ...
ジュルルルル...
YOU BROKE HIS ARMOR !
I WAS TRYING TO HIT THE JEWEL IN HIS ARM!
KA-GOME ...!

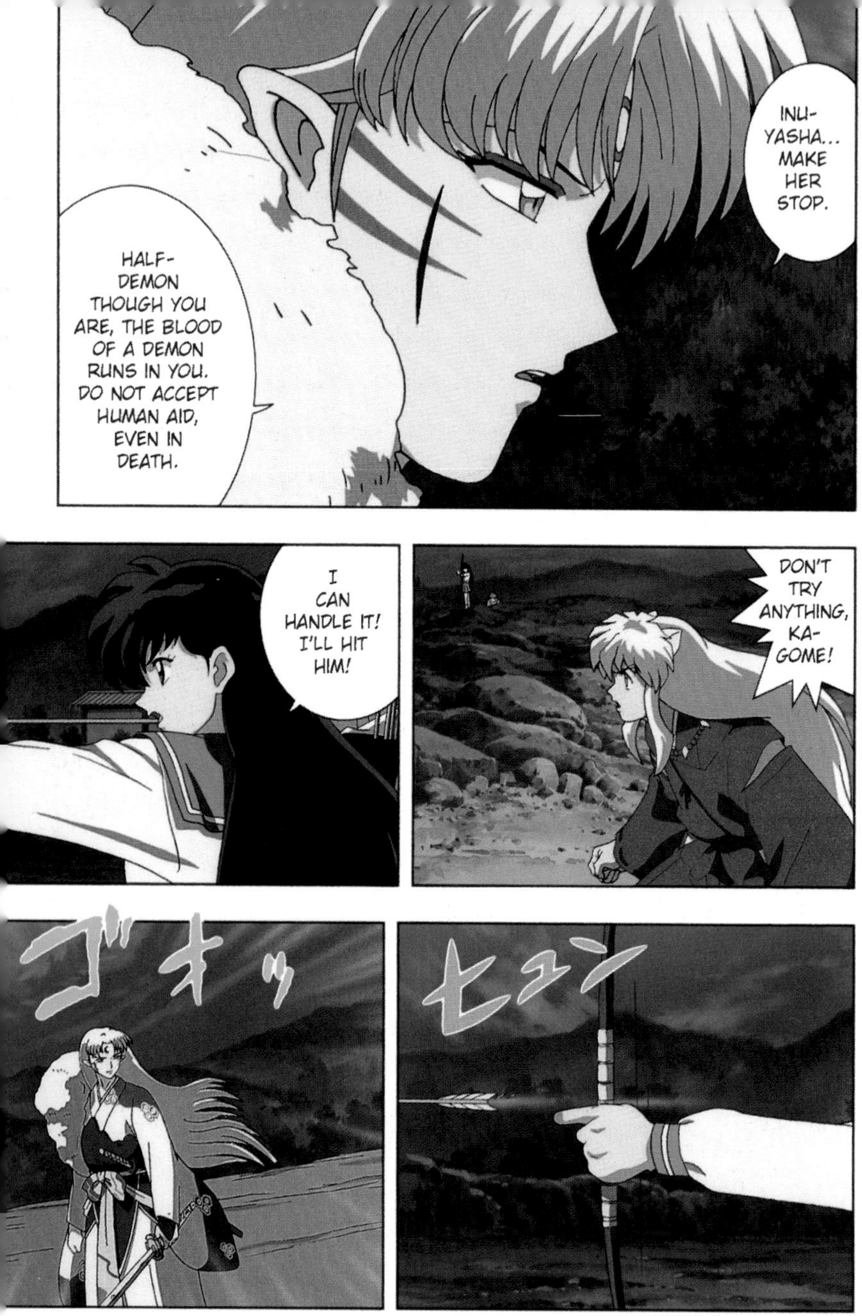
INU-YASHA... MAKE HER STOP.
HALF-DEMON THOUGH YOU ARE, THE BLOOD OF A DEMON RUNS IN YOU. DO NOT ACCEPT HUMAN AID, EVEN IN DEATH.
DON'T TRY ANYTHING, KA-GOME!
I CAN HANDLE IT! I'LL HIT HIM!
ヒュン
ゴオッ

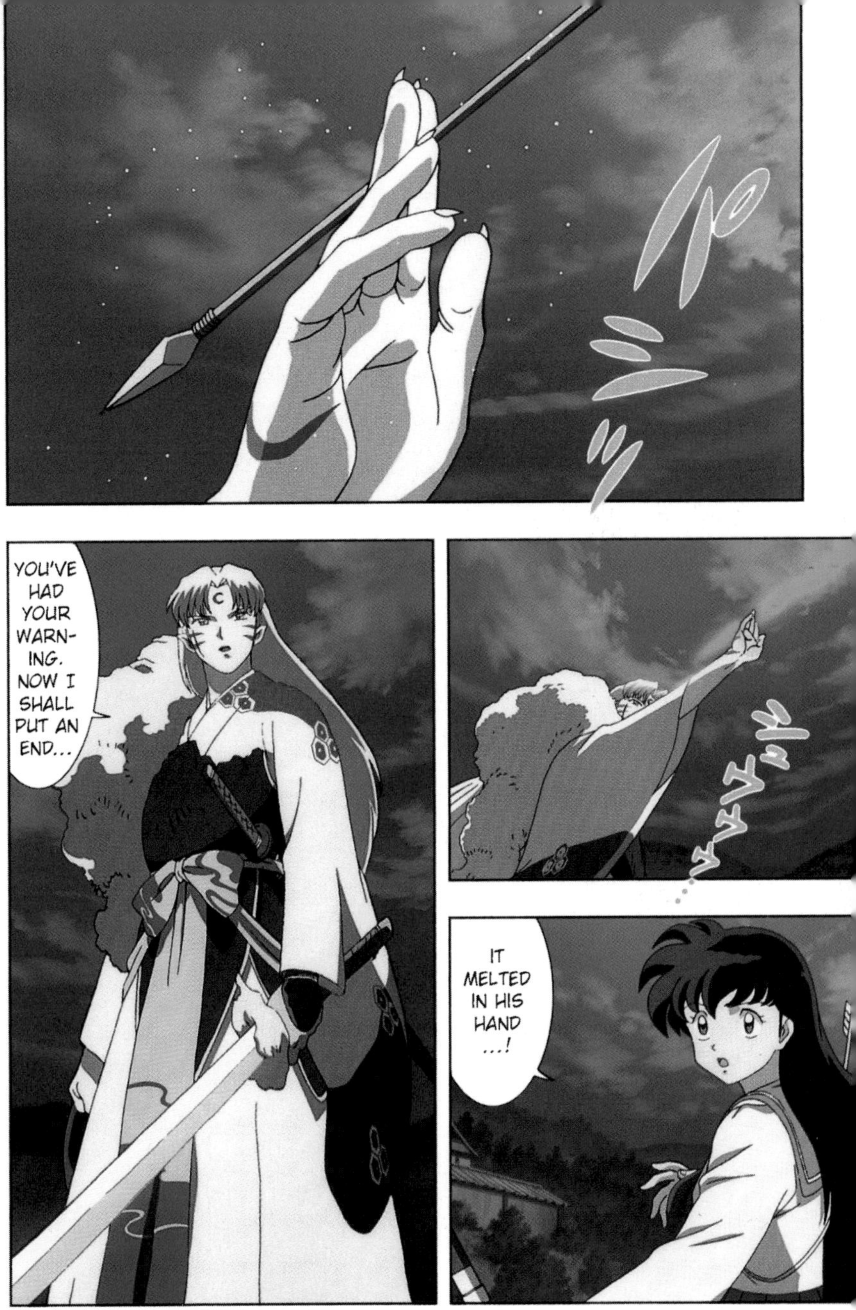
IT MELTED IN HIS HAND ...!
YOU'VE HAD YOUR WARN-ING. NOW I SHALL PUT AN END...

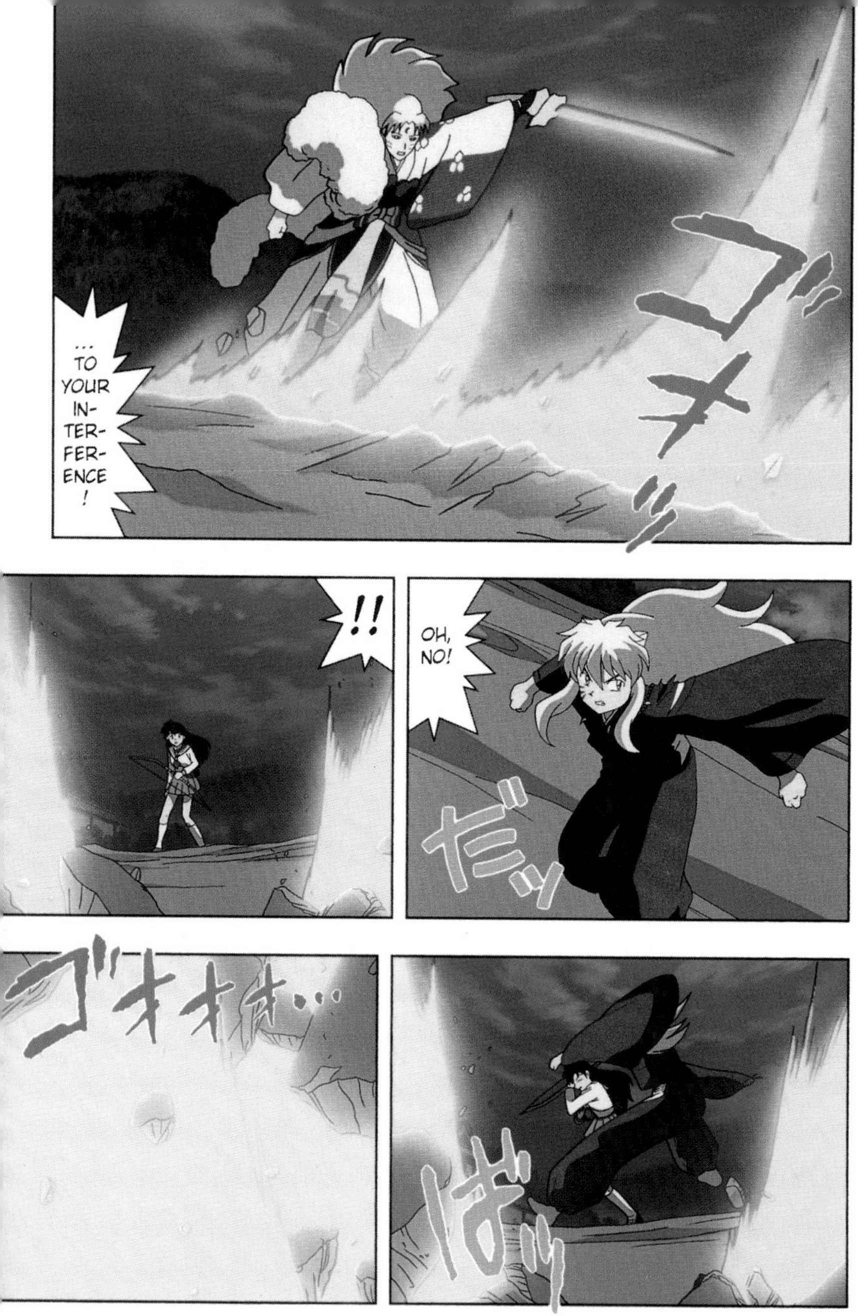
... TO YOUR IN-TER-FER-ENCE!
OH, NO!
!!

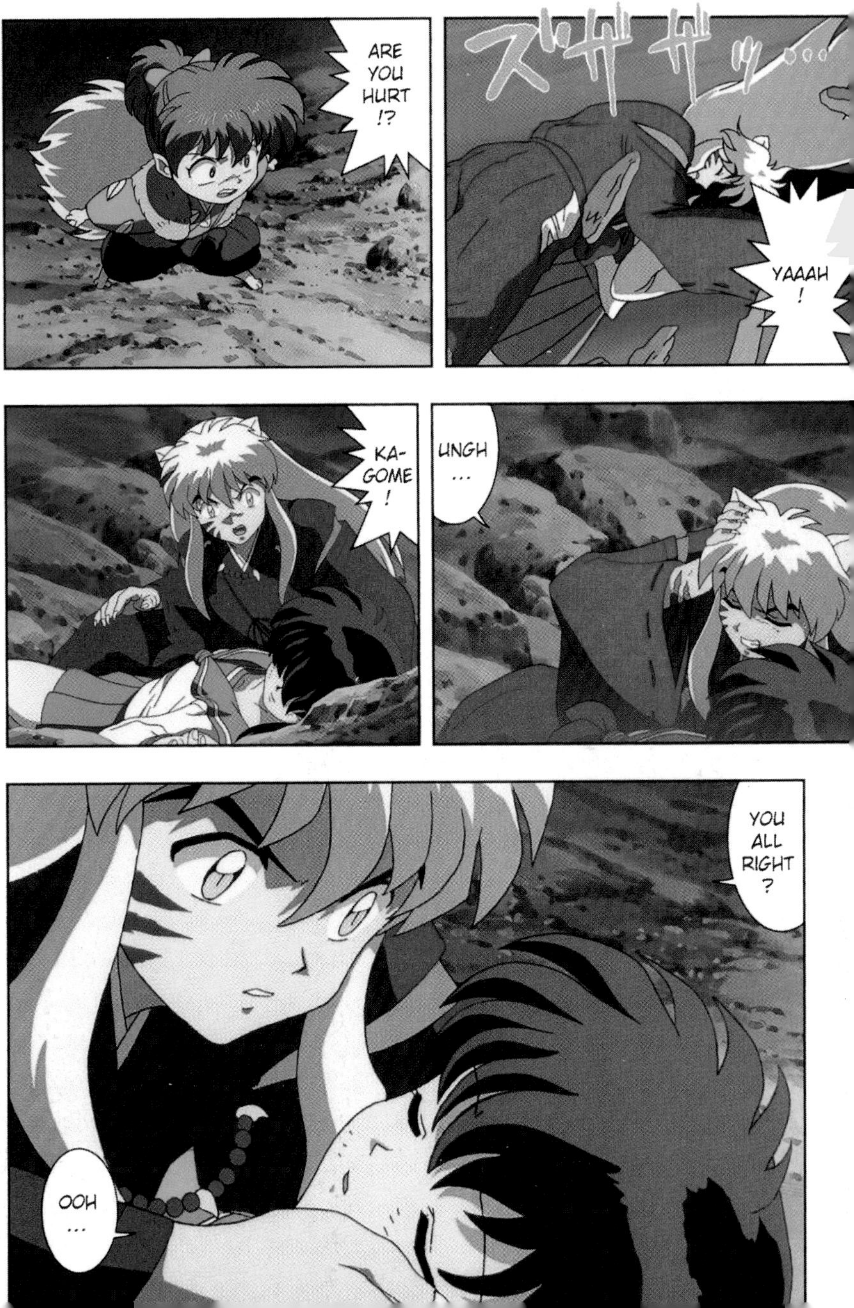
ズザザッ…
YAAAH!
ARE YOU HURT!?
UNGH...
KA-GOME!
YOU ALL RIGHT?
OOH...

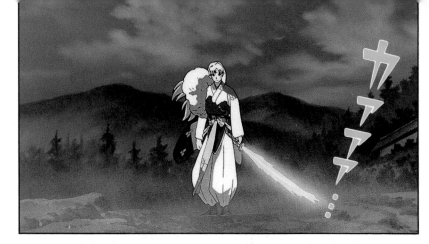

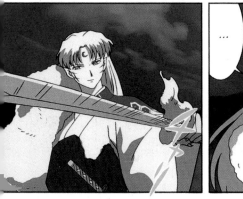

...

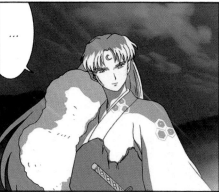

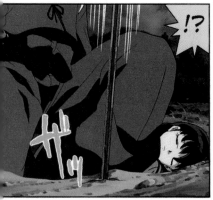

!?

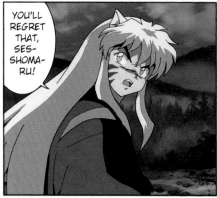

YOU'LL REGRET THAT, SES- SHOMA- RU!

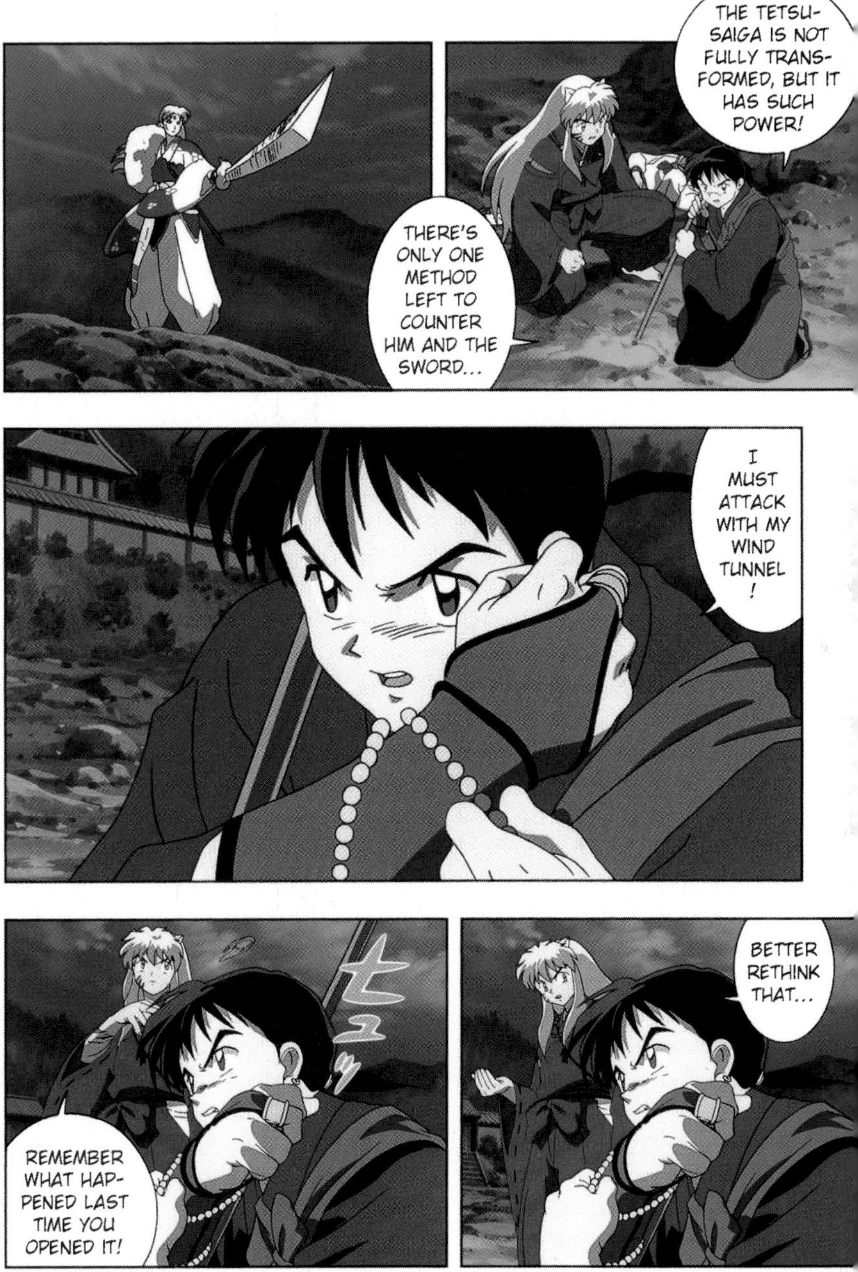
THE TETSU-SAIGA IS NOT FULLY TRANS-FORMED, BUT IT HAS SUCH POWER!
THERE'S ONLY ONE METHOD LEFT TO COUNTER HIM AND THE SWORD...
I MUST ATTACK WITH MY WIND TUNNEL!
BETTER RETHINK THAT...
REMEMBER WHAT HAP-PENED LAST TIME YOU OPENED IT!

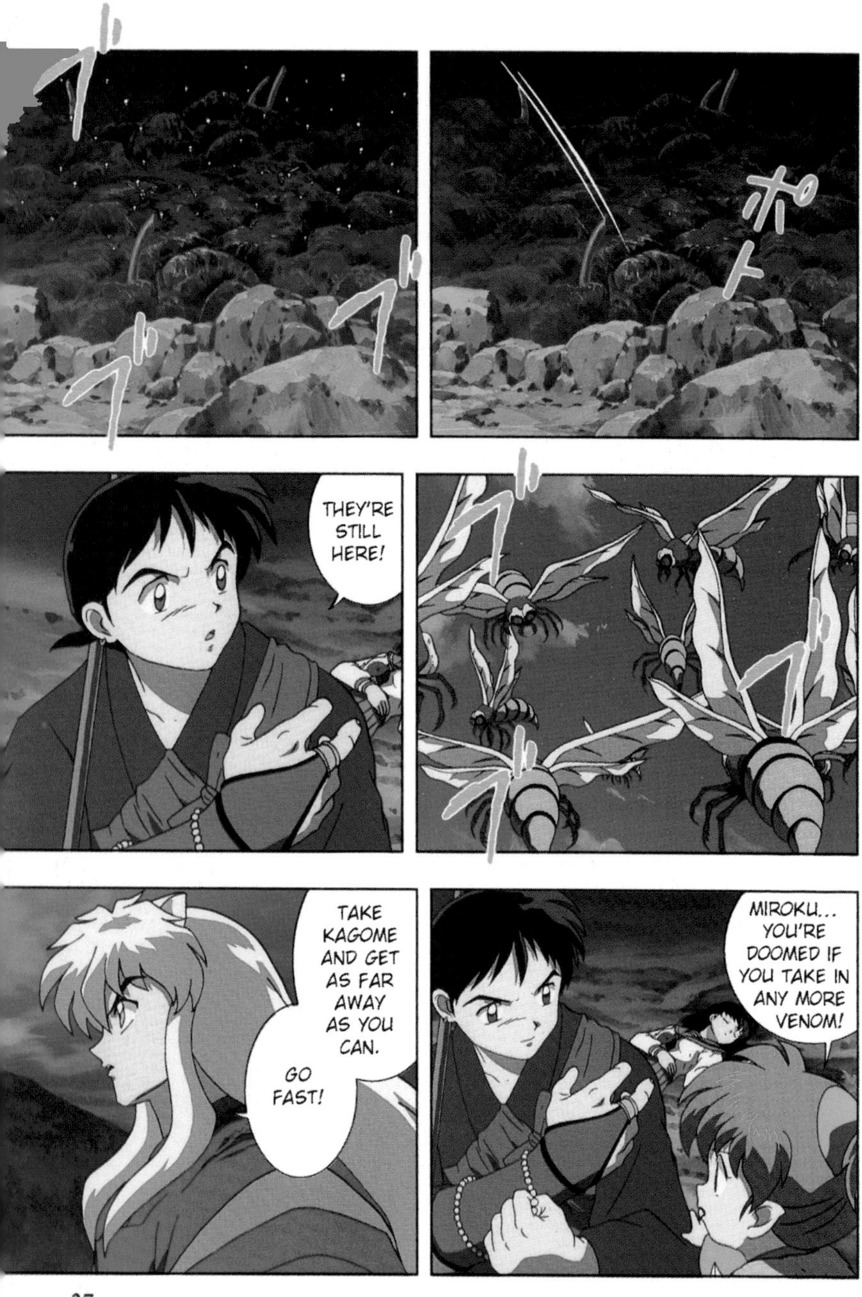
THEY'RE STILL HERE!
MIROKU... YOU'RE DOOMED IF YOU TAKE IN ANY MORE VENOM!
TAKE KAGOME AND GET AS FAR AWAY AS YOU CAN.
GO FAST!

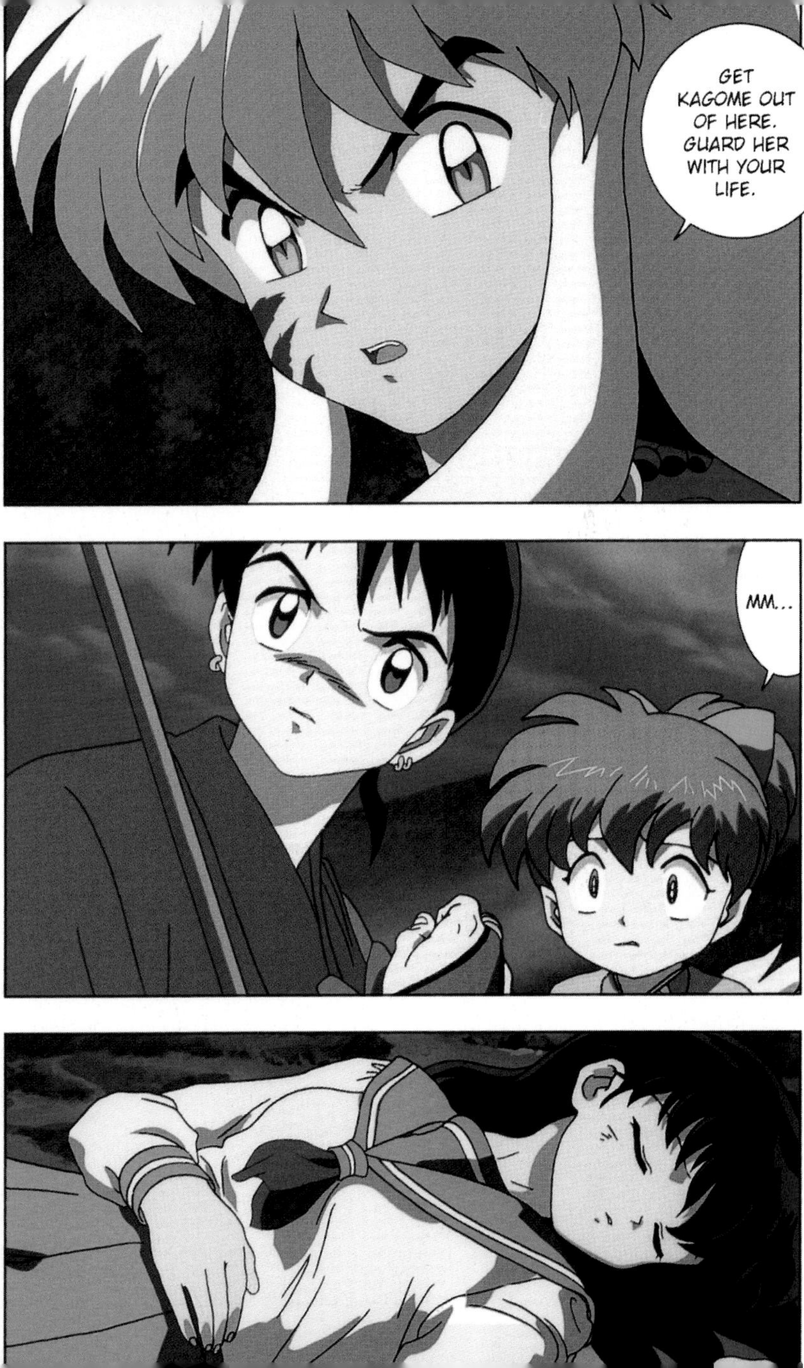
GET KAGOME OUT OF HERE. GUARD HER WITH YOUR LIFE.
MM...

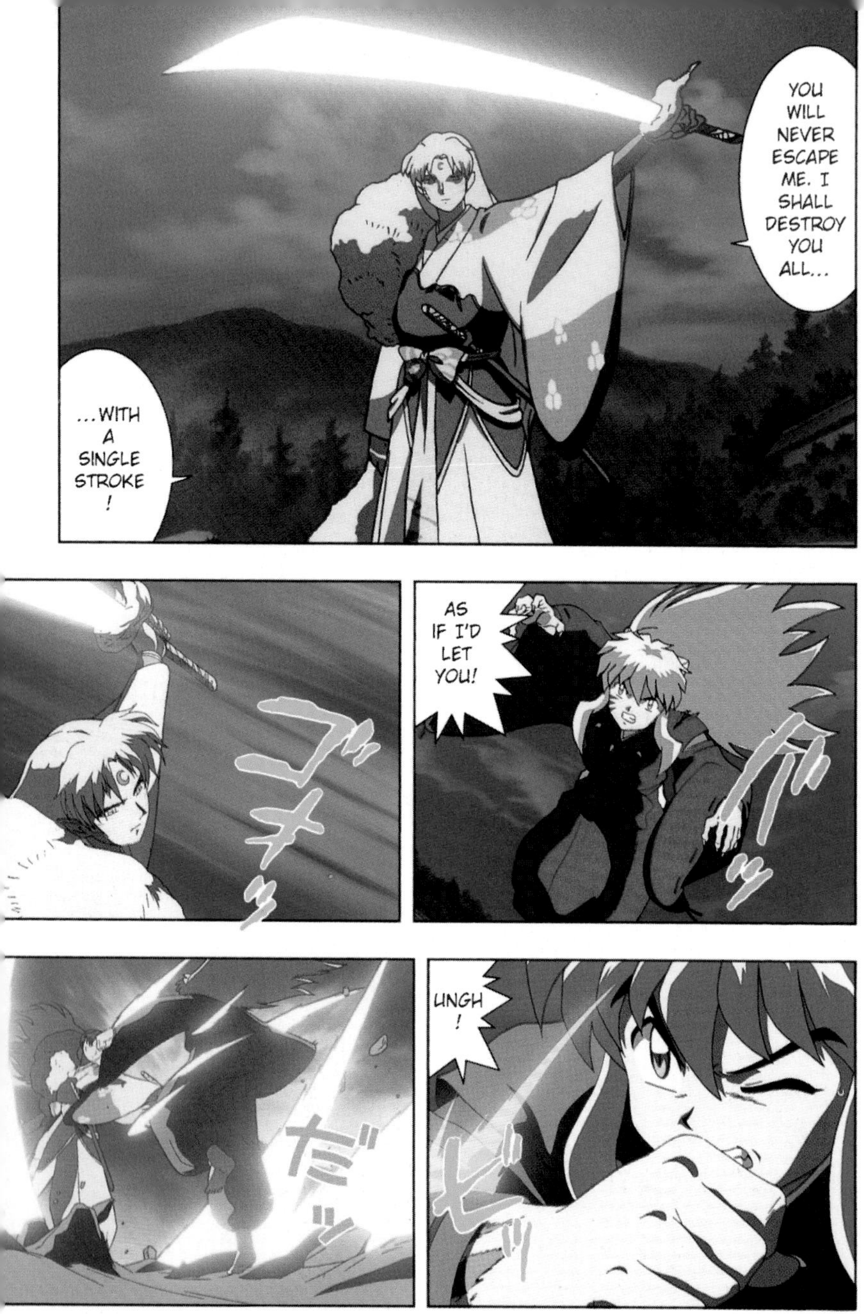
YOU WILL NEVER ESCAPE ME. I SHALL DESTROY YOU ALL...
...WITH A SINGLE STROKE!
AS IF I'D LET YOU!
UNGH!

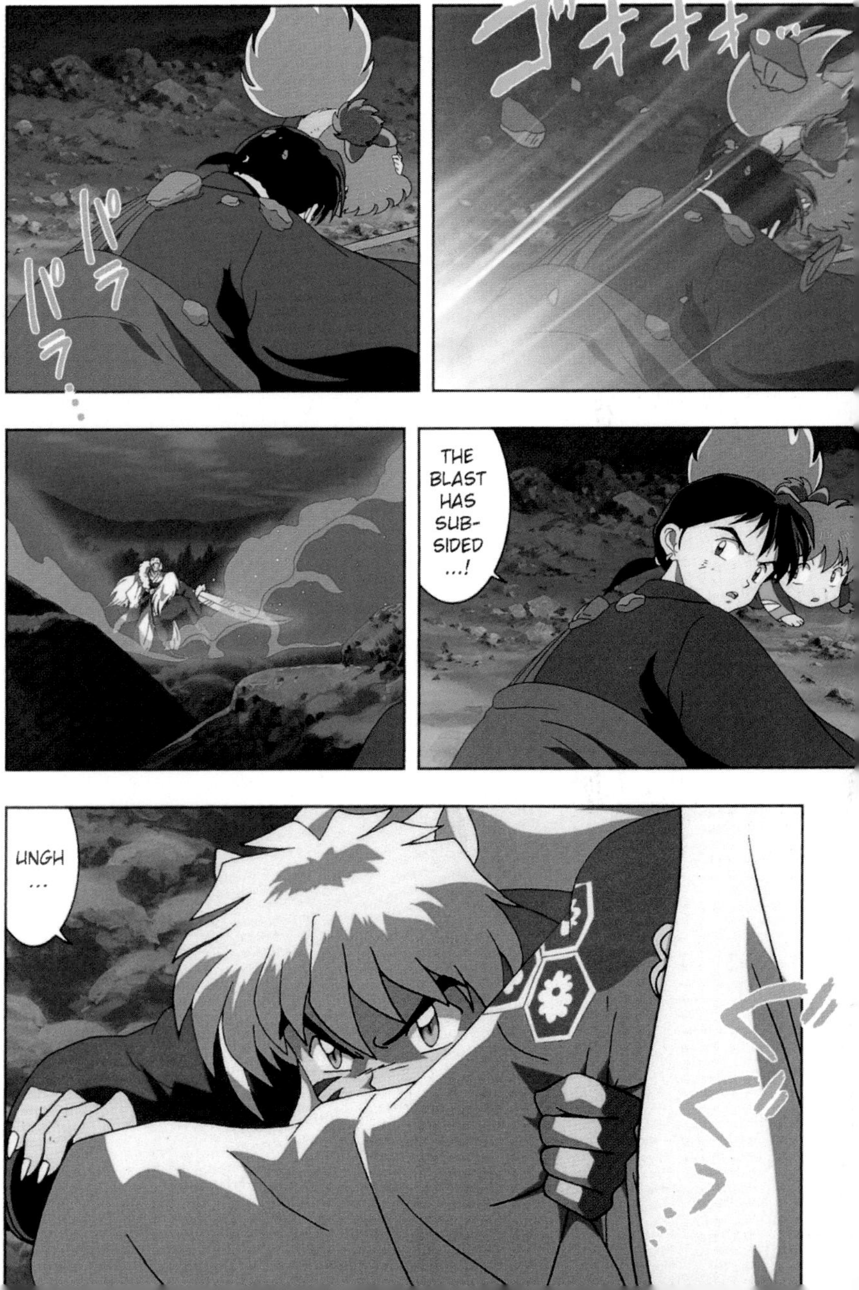
ゴオオオ…
パラパラ…
THE BLAST HAS SUB-SIDED ...!
UNGH ...

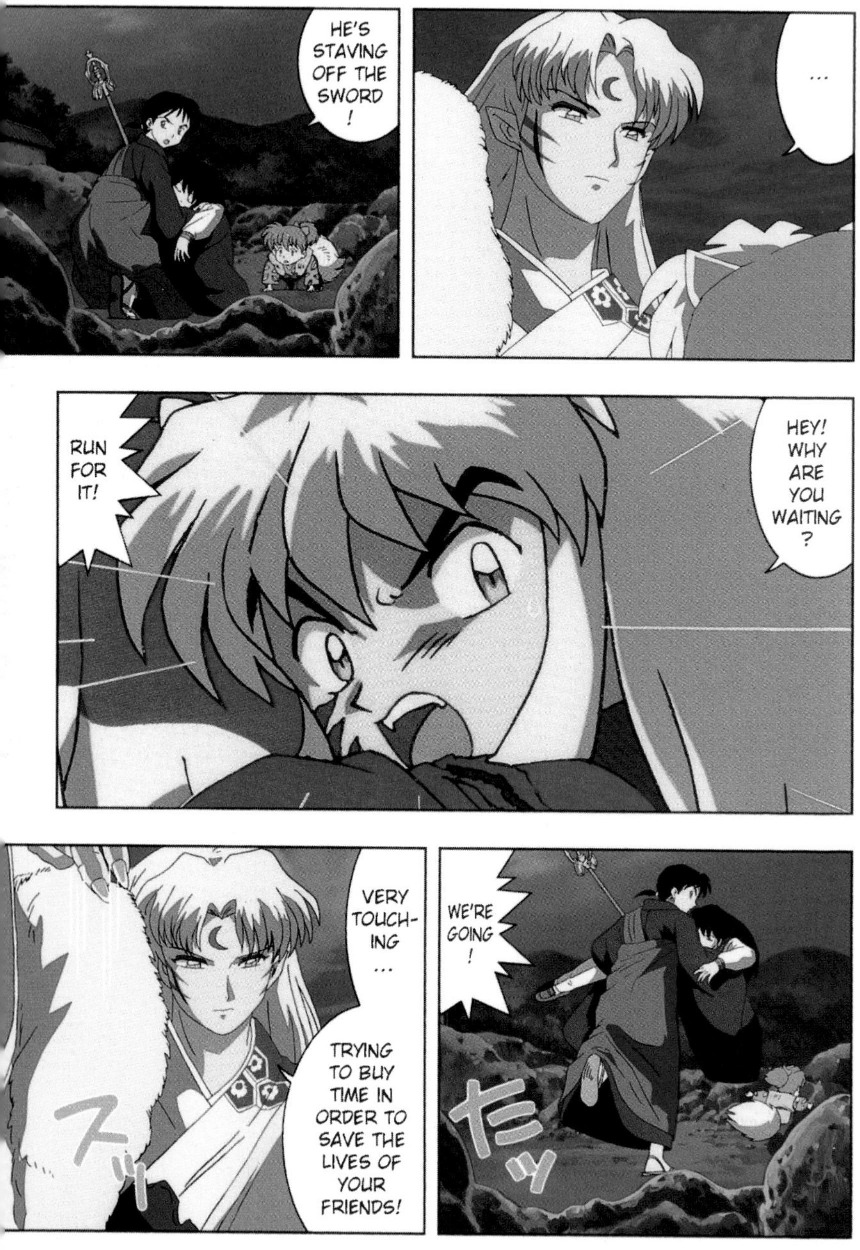
...
HE'S STAVING OFF THE SWORD!
HEY! WHY ARE YOU WAITING?
RUN FOR IT!
WE'RE GOING!
タッ
VERY TOUCHING...
TRYING TO BUY TIME IN ORDER TO SAVE THE LIVES OF YOUR FRIENDS!
スッ

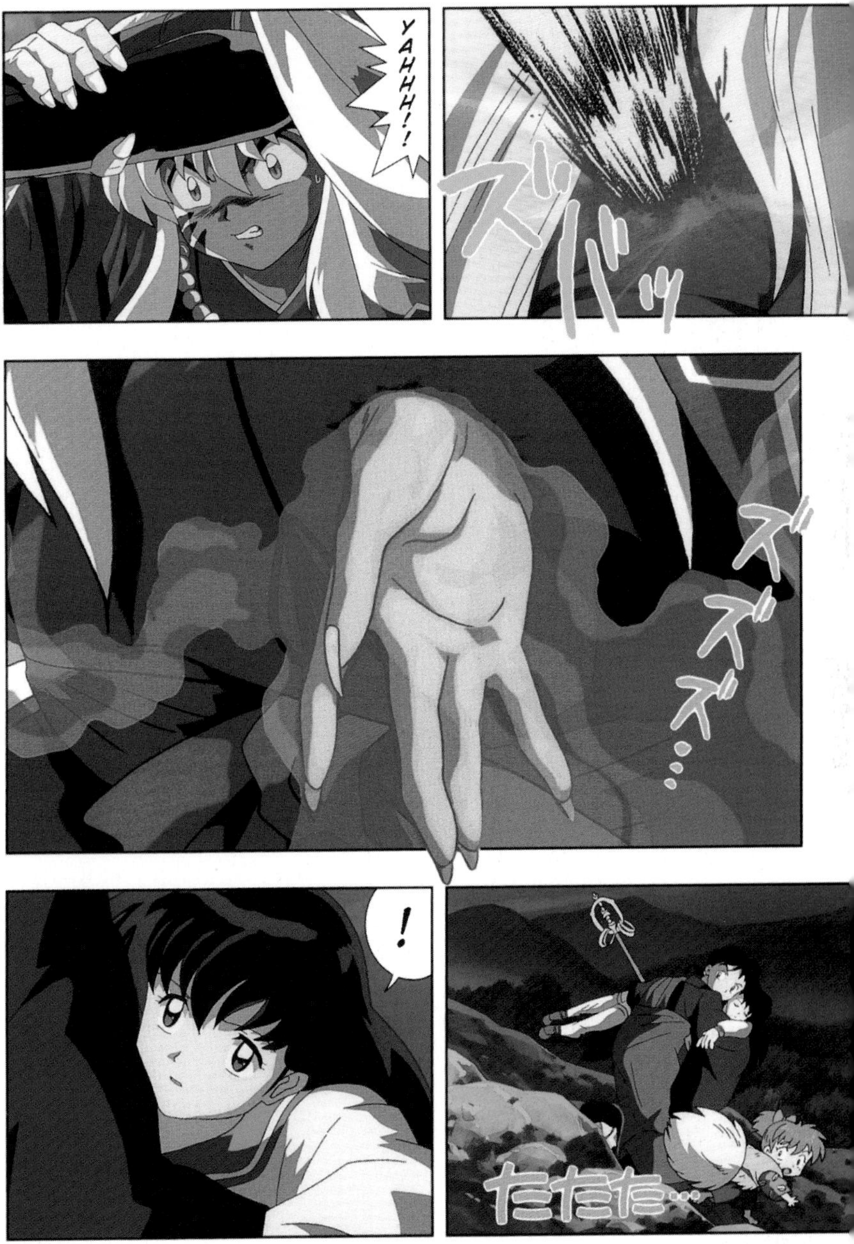
ズバッ
YAHHH!!
ズズズズ…
たたた…
!

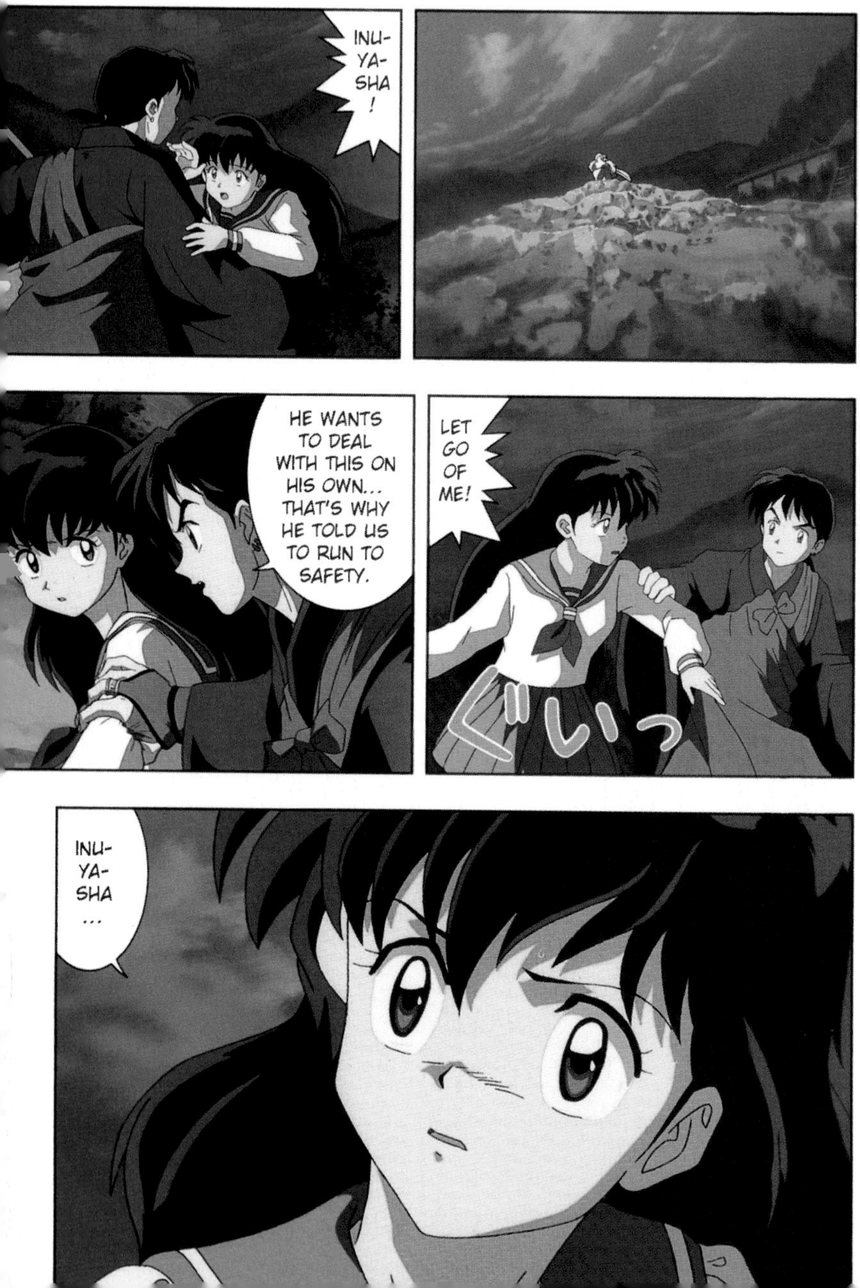
INU-YA-SHA!
LET GO OF ME!
ぐいっ
HE WANTS TO DEAL WITH THIS ON HIS OWN... THAT'S WHY HE TOLD US TO RUN TO SAFETY.
INU-YASHA...

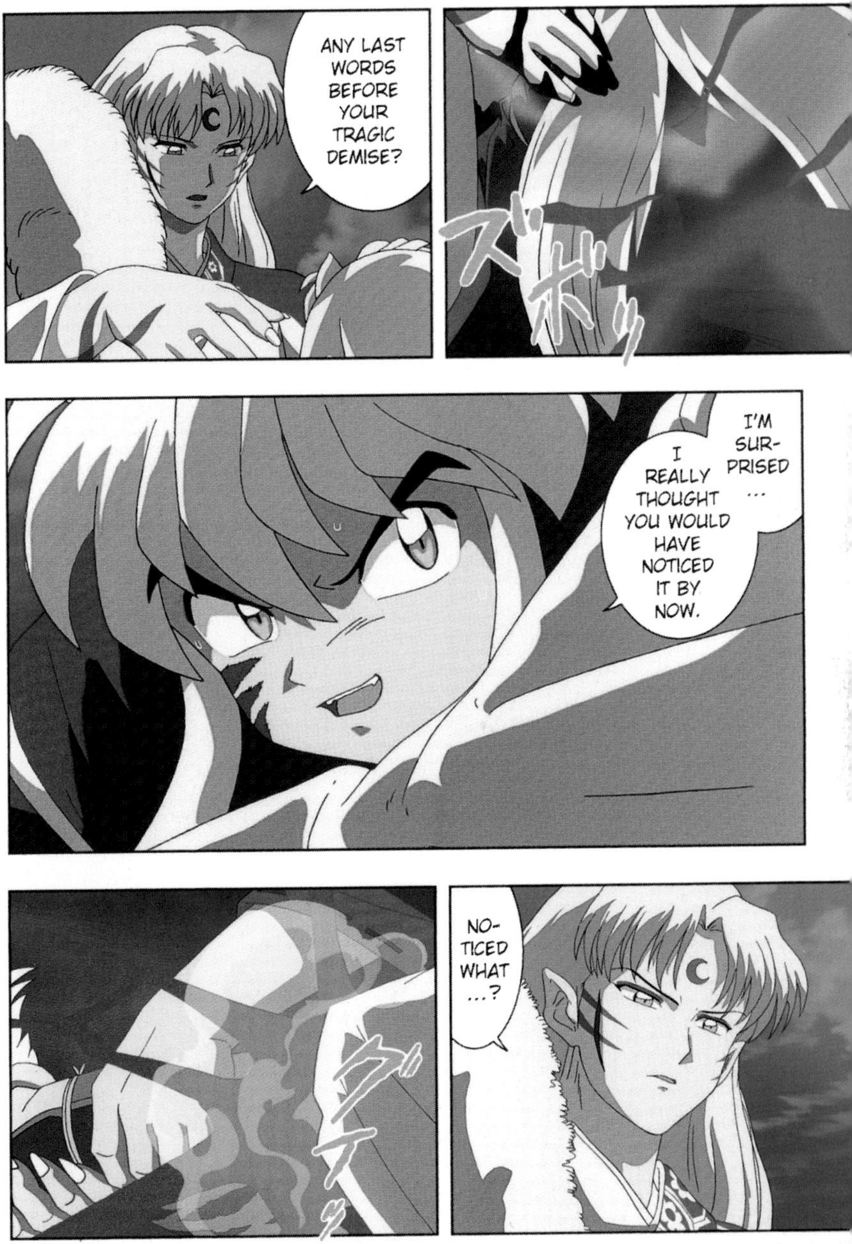
ズボッ
ANY LAST WORDS BEFORE YOUR TRAGIC DEMISE?
I'M SUR-PRISED...
I REALLY THOUGHT YOU WOULD HAVE NOTICED IT BY NOW.
NO-TICED WHAT...?

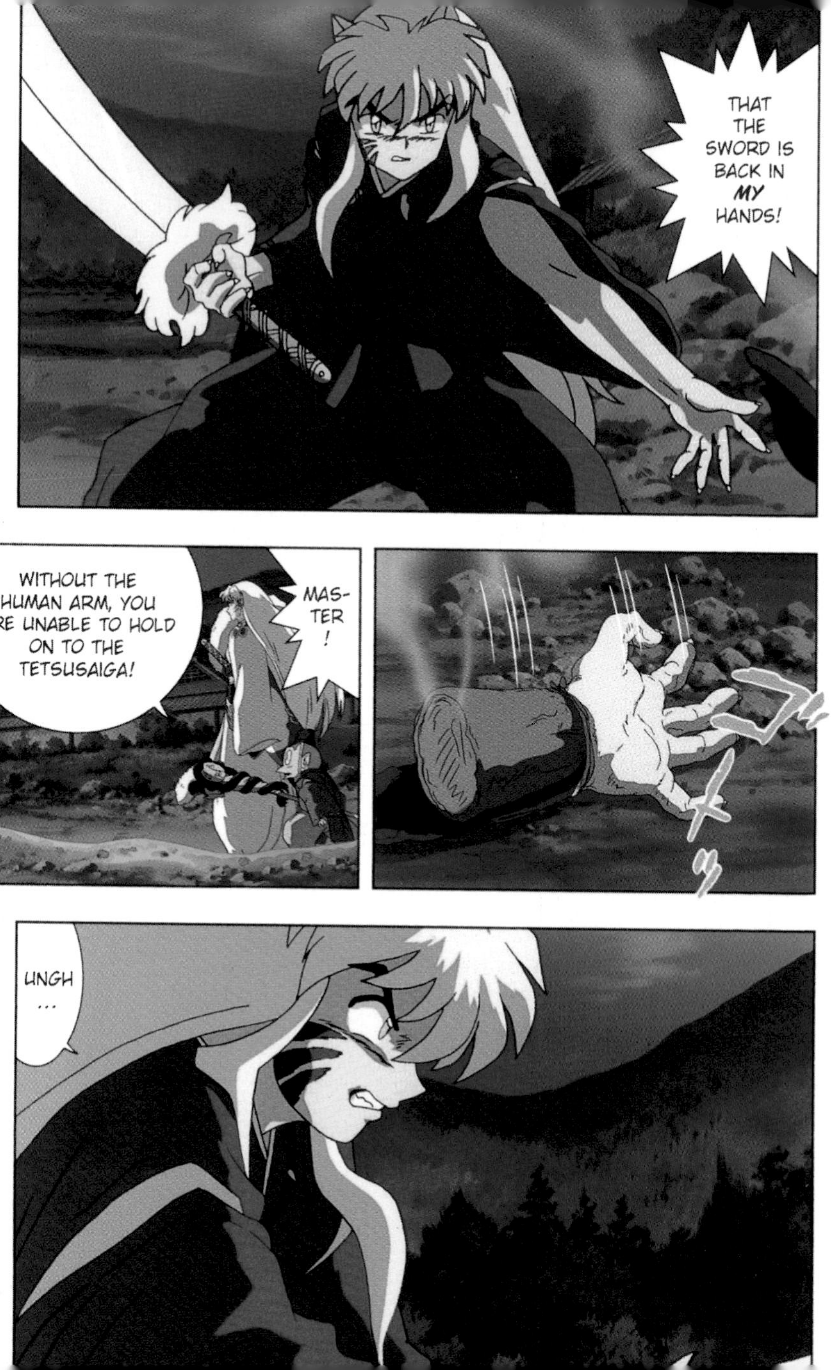
THAT THE SWORD IS BACK IN *MY* HANDS!
MAS-TER!
WITHOUT THE HUMAN ARM, YOU ARE UNABLE TO HOLD ON TO THE TETSUSAIGA!
UNGH ...

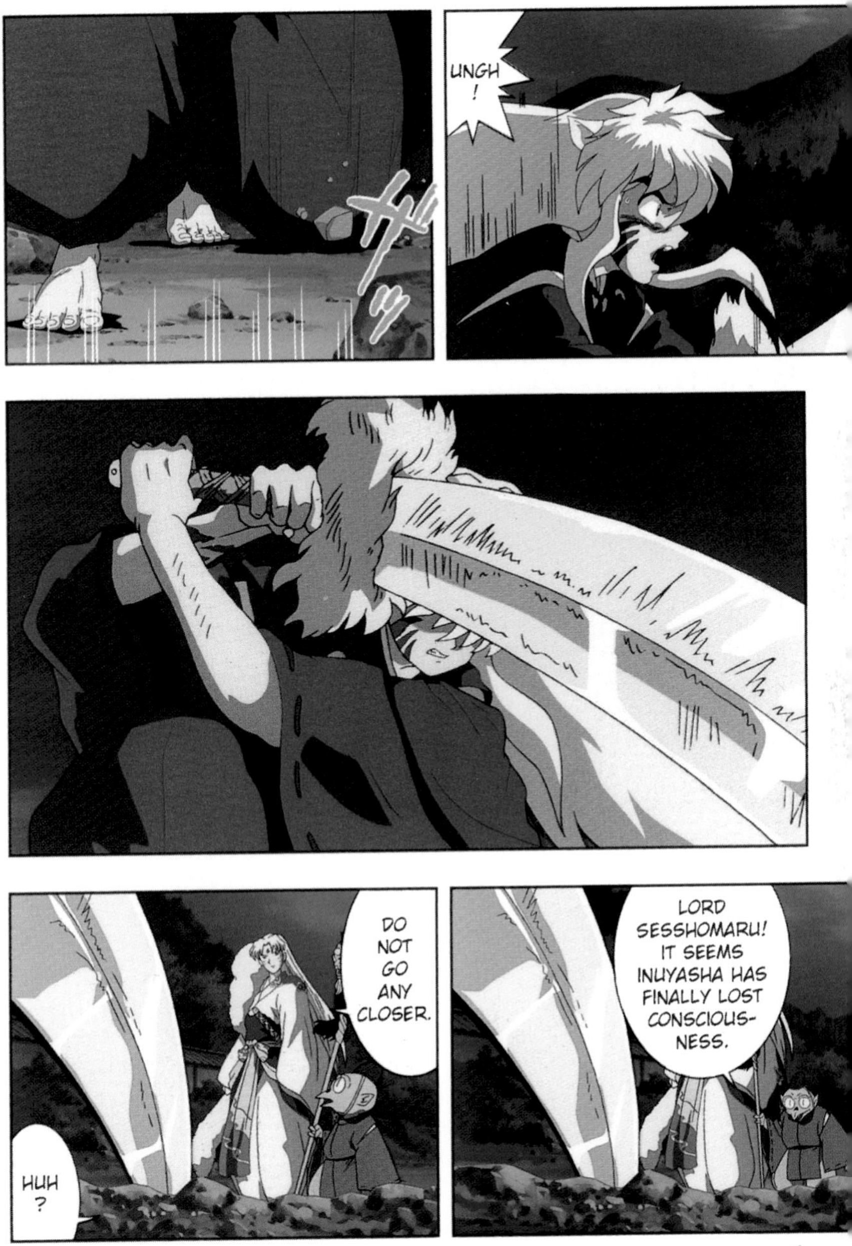
UNGH!
ザッ
LORD SESSHOMARU! IT SEEMS INUYASHA HAS FINALLY LOST CONSCIOUS-NESS.
DO NOT GO ANY CLOSER.
HUH?

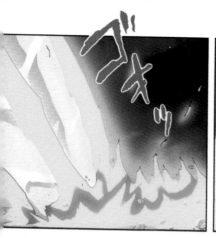

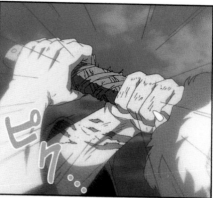

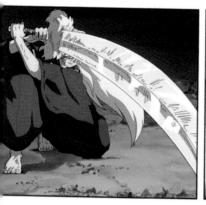

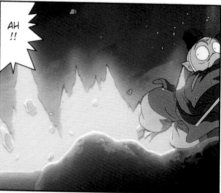

AH
!!

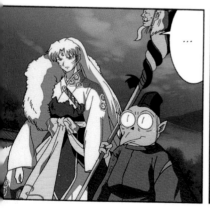

...

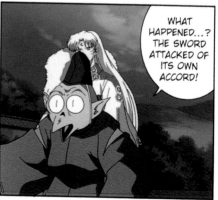

WHAT
HAPPENED...?
THE SWORD
ATTACKED OF
ITS OWN
ACCORD!

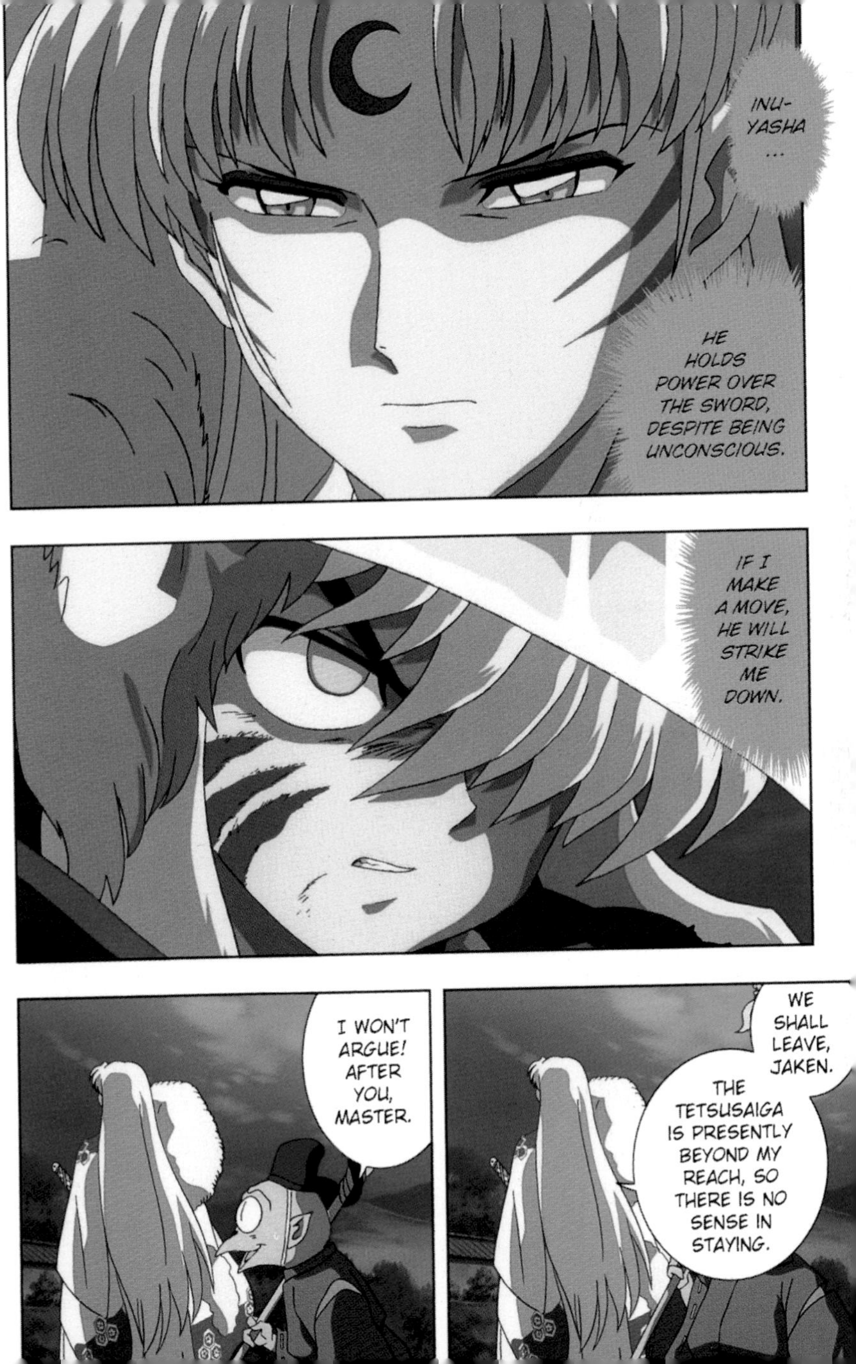
INU-YASHA ...
HE HOLDS POWER OVER THE SWORD, DESPITE BEING UNCONSCIOUS.
IF I MAKE A MOVE, HE WILL STRIKE ME DOWN.
WE SHALL LEAVE, JAKEN.
THE TETSUSAIGA IS PRESENTLY BEYOND MY REACH, SO THERE IS NO SENSE IN STAYING.
I WON'T ARGUE! AFTER YOU, MASTER.

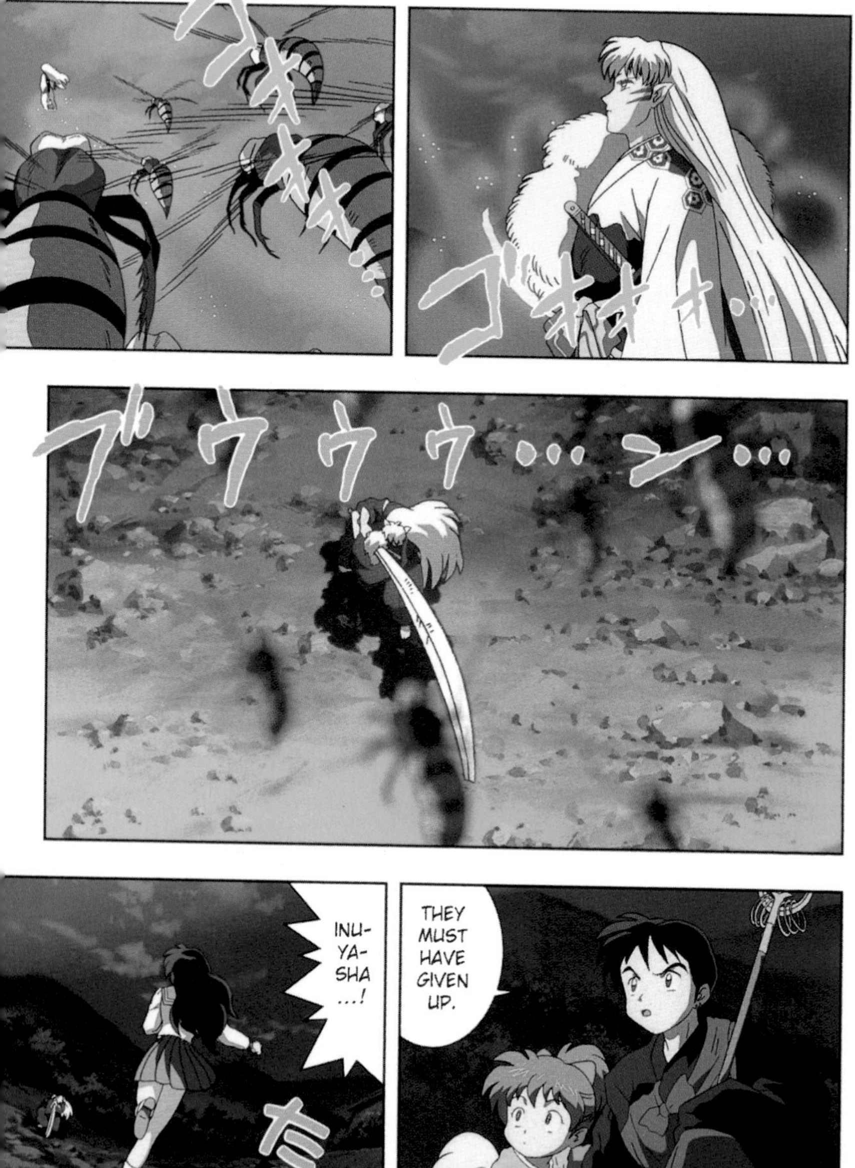
ゴオオオ…
ゴオオオ…
ブウウウ…ン…
THEY MUST HAVE GIVEN UP.
INU-YASHA…!
タッ

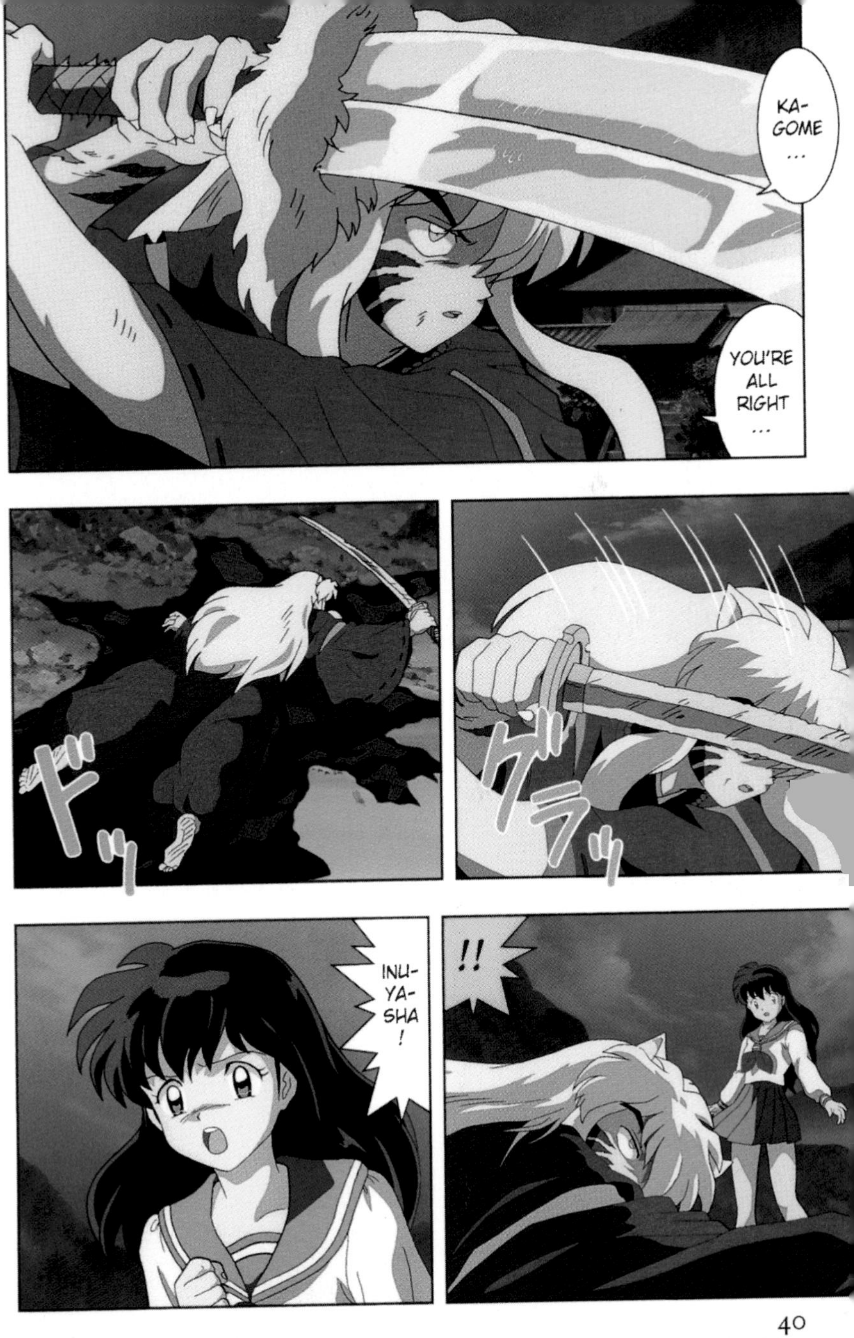
KA-GOME ...
YOU'RE ALL RIGHT ...
グラッ
ドッ
!!
INU-YASHA!

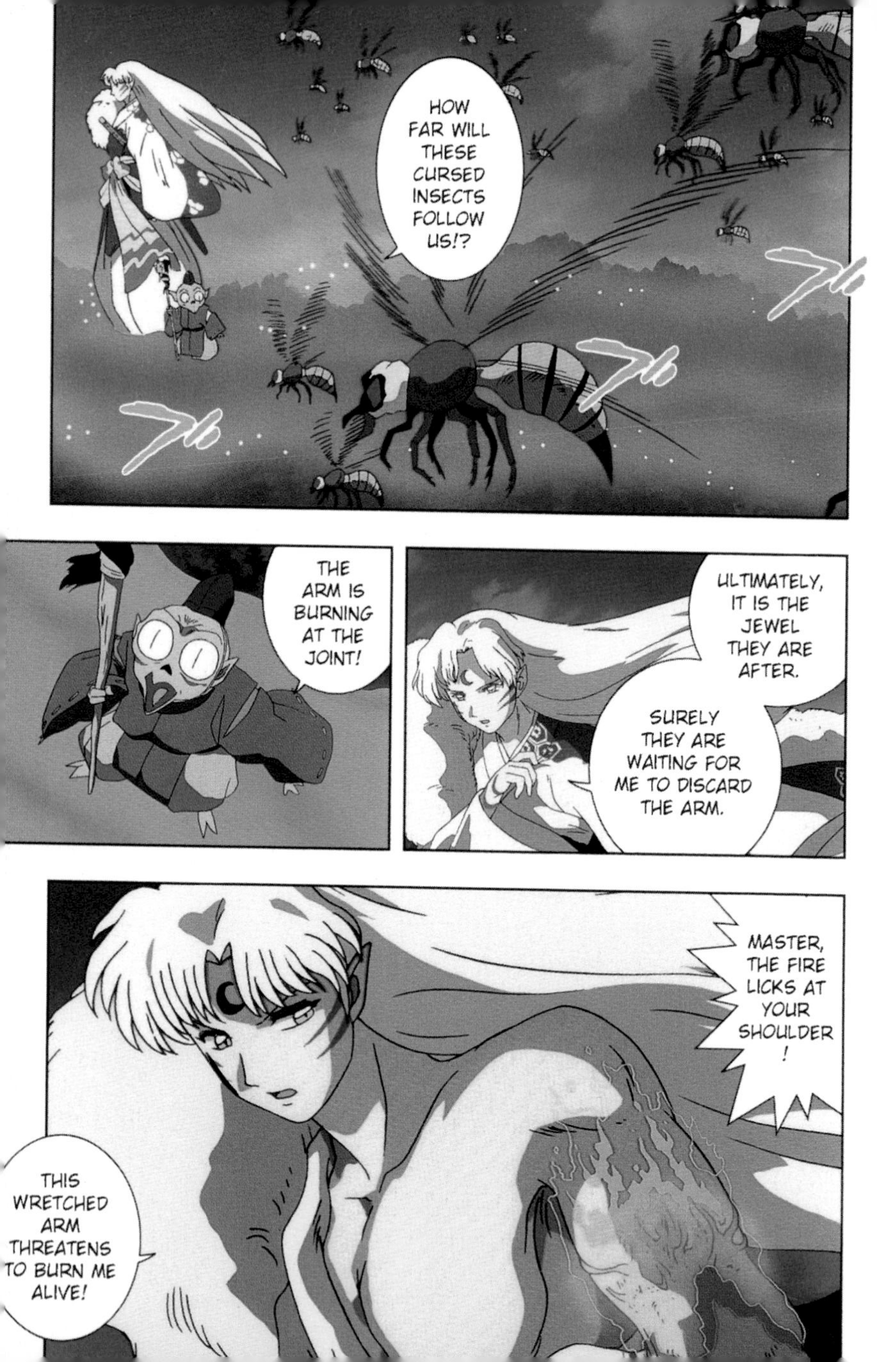
HOW FAR WILL THESE CURSED INSECTS FOLLOW US!?
ULTIMATELY, IT IS THE JEWEL THEY ARE AFTER.
SURELY THEY ARE WAITING FOR ME TO DISCARD THE ARM.
THE ARM IS BURNING AT THE JOINT!
MASTER, THE FIRE LICKS AT YOUR SHOULDER!
THIS WRETCHED ARM THREATENS TO BURN ME ALIVE!

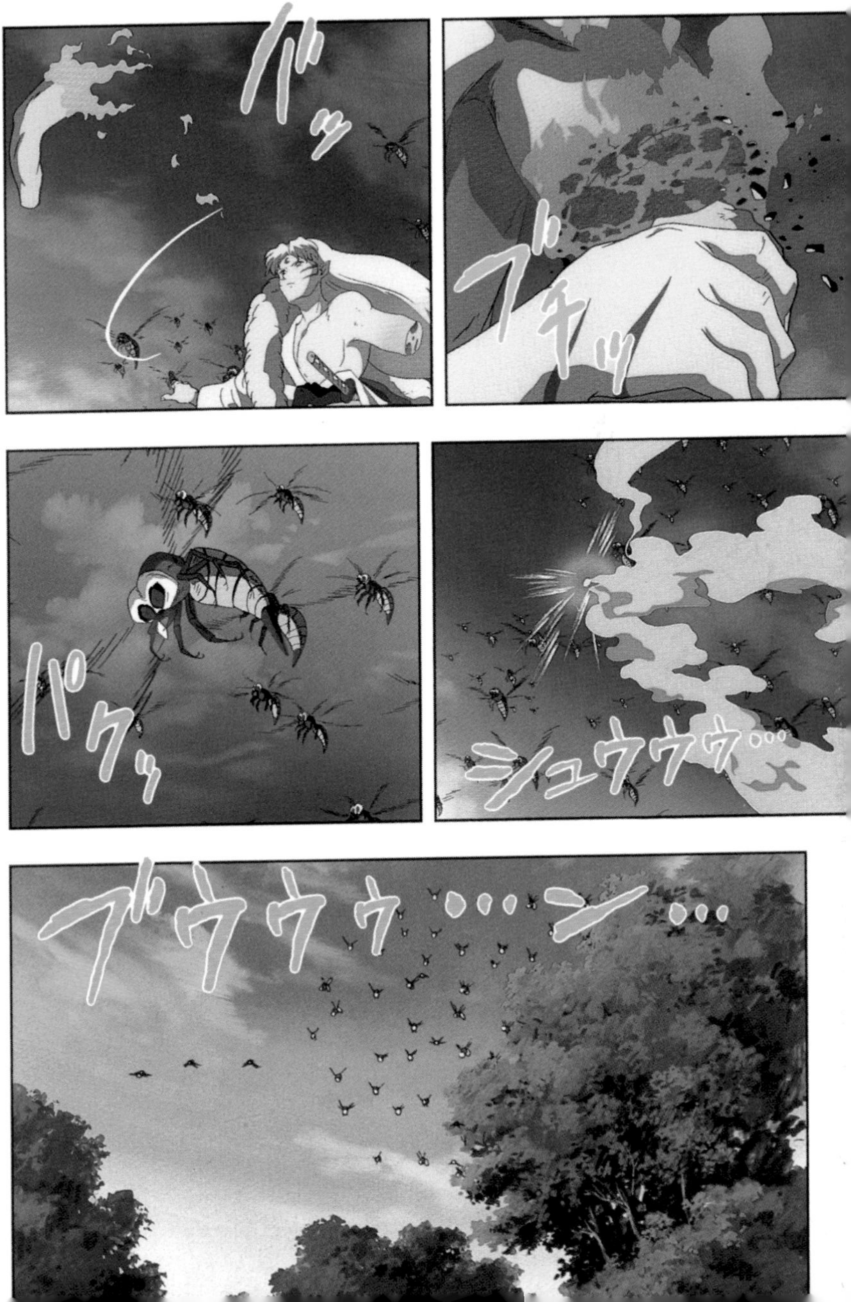
ブチッ
ブッ
シュウウウ‥
バクッ
ブウウウ…ン…

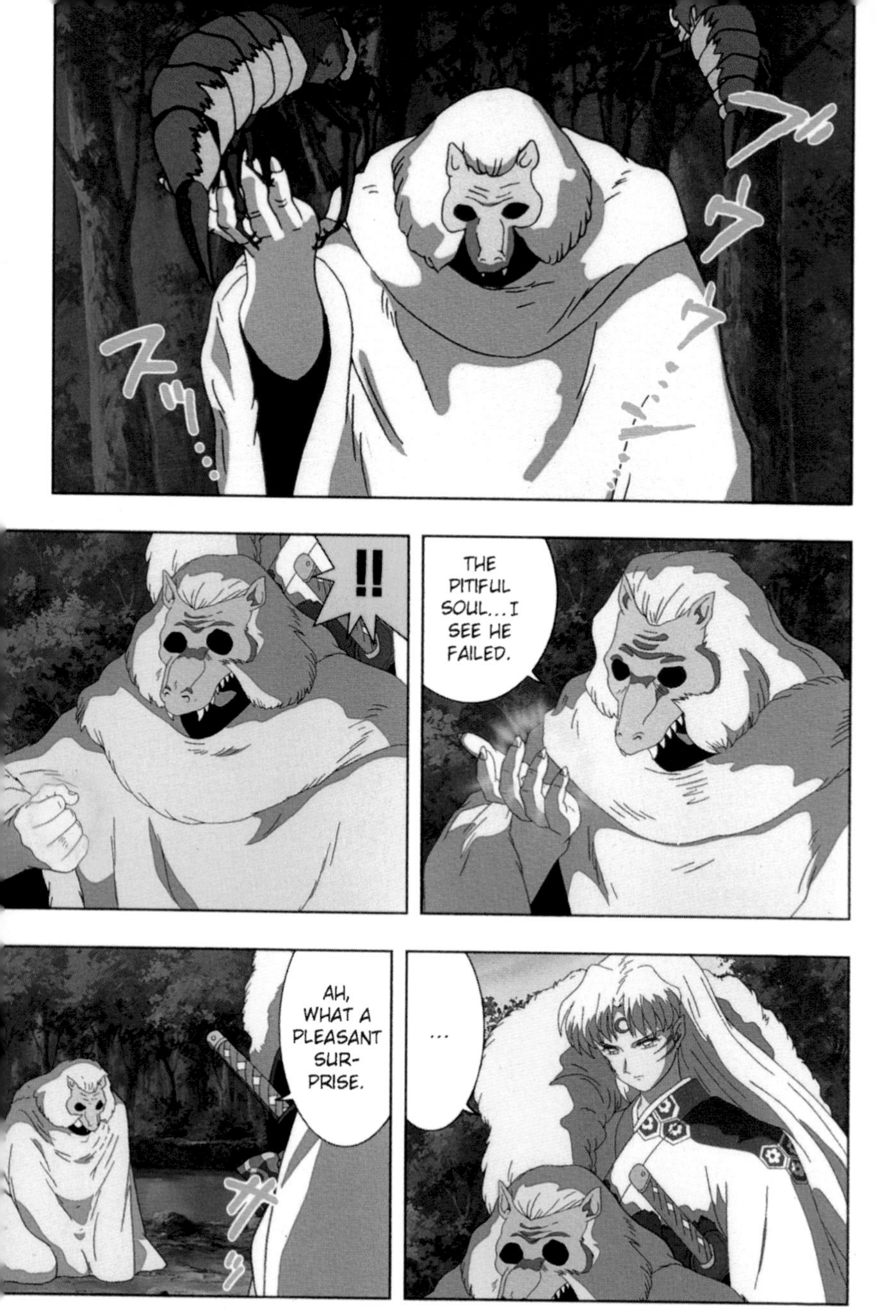
THE PITIFUL SOUL... I SEE HE FAILED.
!!
...
AH, WHAT A PLEASANT SUR-PRISE.

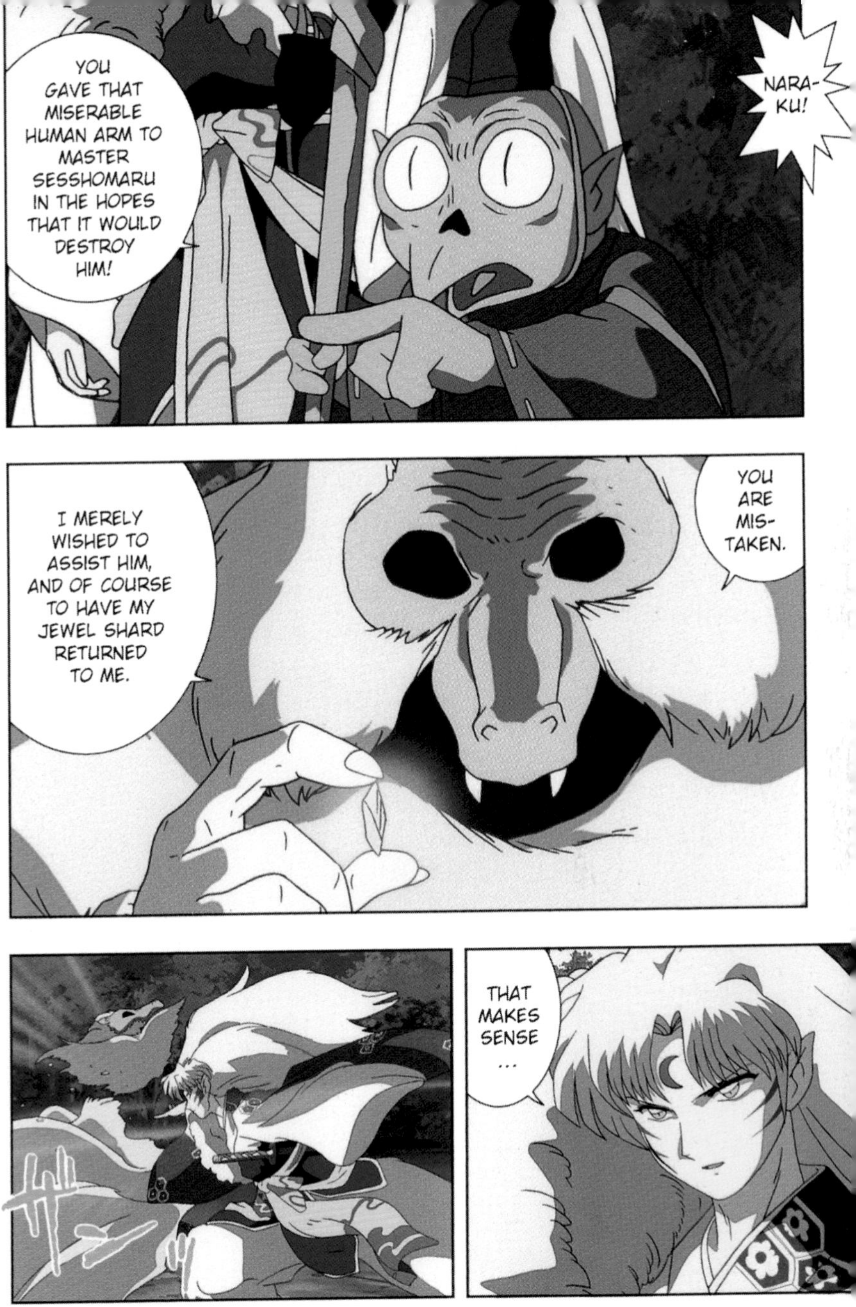
NARA-KU!
YOU GAVE THAT MISERABLE HUMAN ARM TO MASTER SESSHOMARU IN THE HOPES THAT IT WOULD DESTROY HIM!
YOU ARE MIS-TAKEN.
I MERELY WISHED TO ASSIST HIM, AND OF COURSE TO HAVE MY JEWEL SHARD RETURNED TO ME.
THAT MAKES SENSE ...

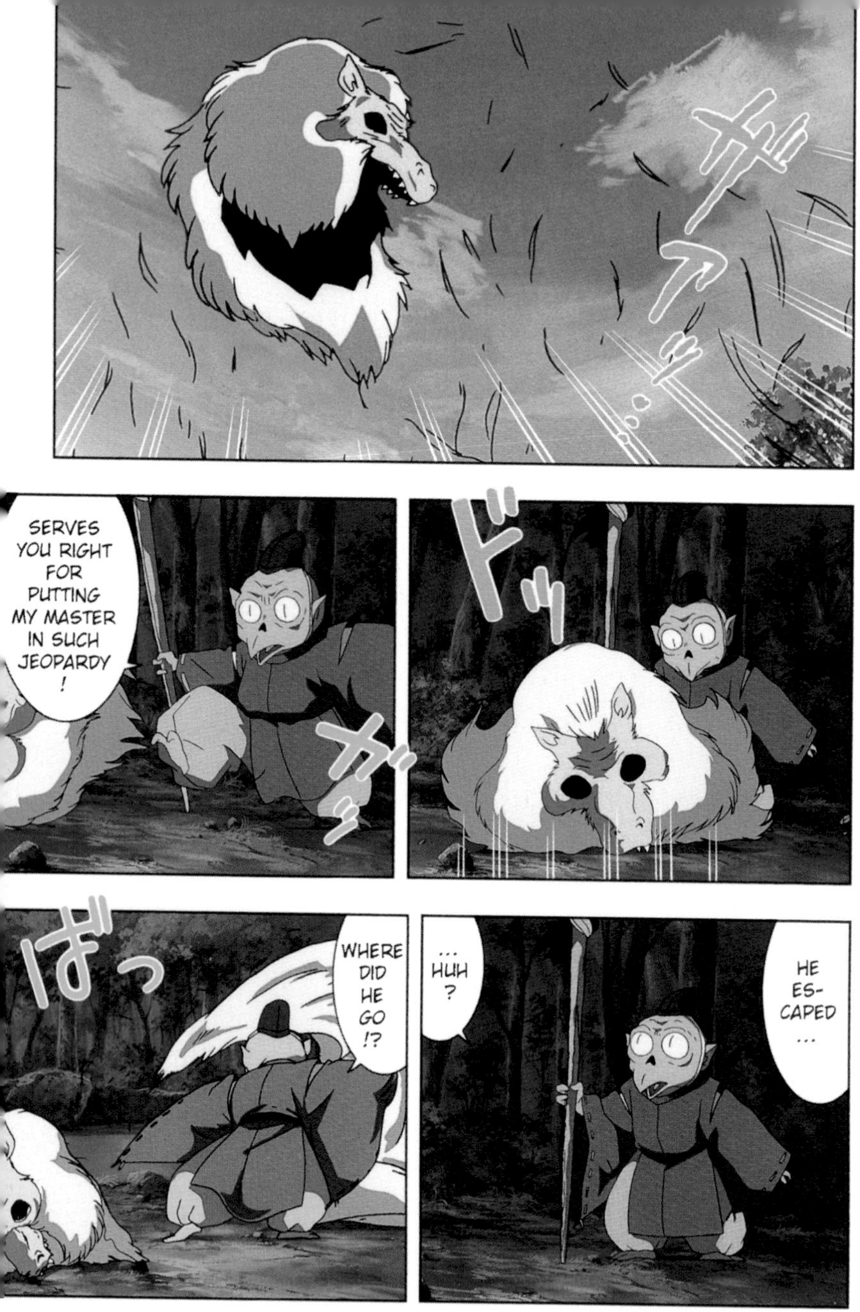
ドッ
SERVES YOU RIGHT FOR PUTTING MY MASTER IN SUCH JEOPARDY!
ガッ
HE ES-CAPED ...
... HUH?
WHERE DID HE GO!?
ぱっ

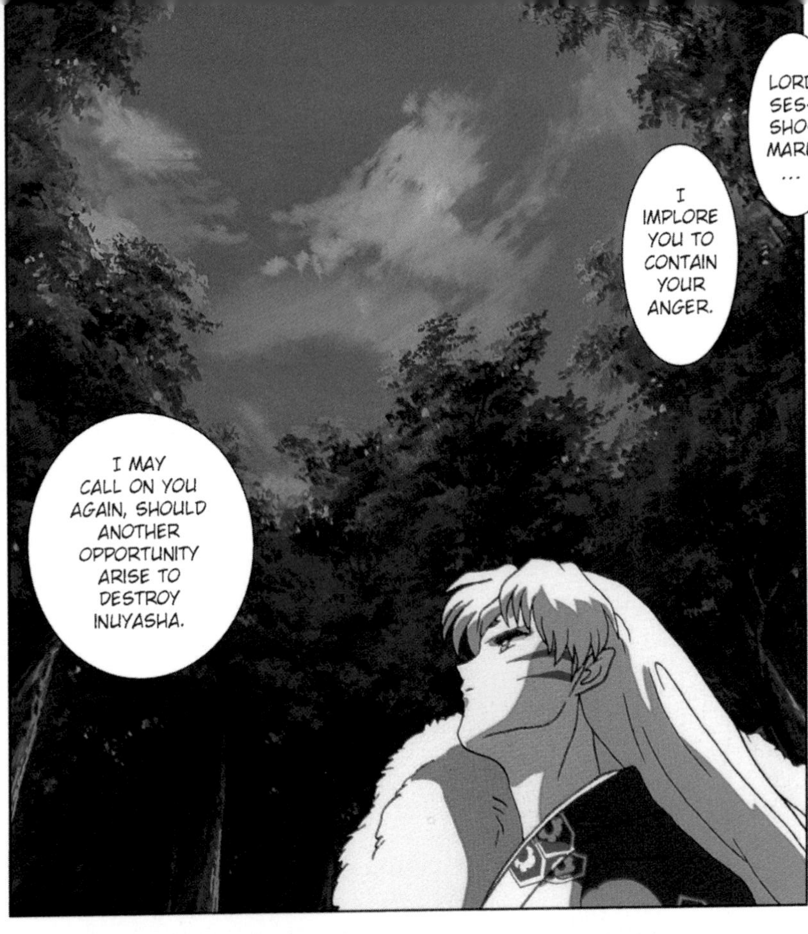
LORD SES-SHO-MARU ...
I IMPLORE YOU TO CONTAIN YOUR ANGER.
I MAY CALL ON YOU AGAIN, SHOULD ANOTHER OPPORTUNITY ARISE TO DESTROY INUYASHA.
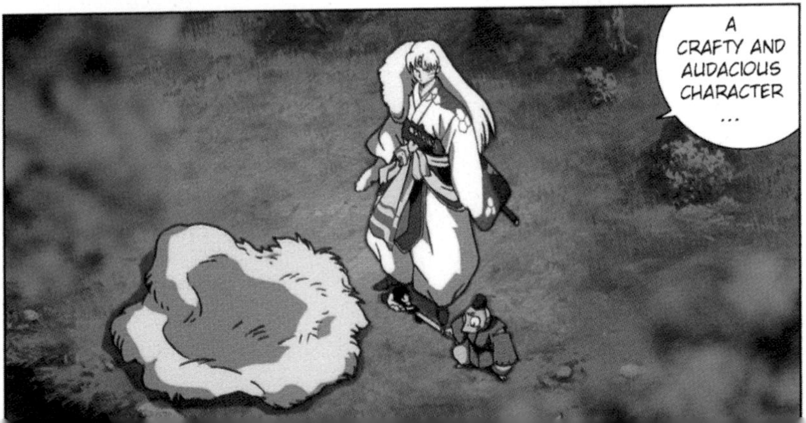
A CRAFTY AND AUDACIOUS CHARACTER ...

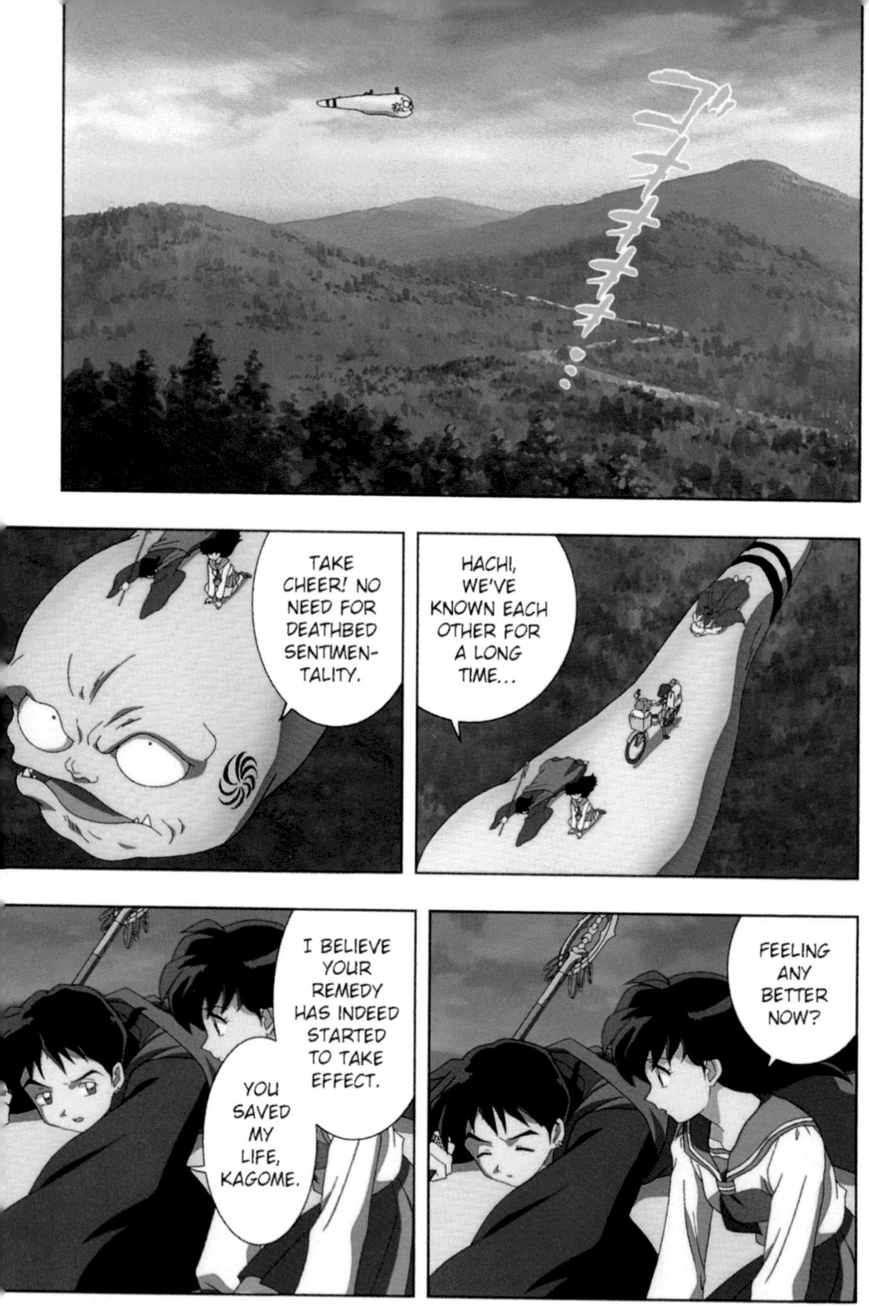
HACHI, WE'VE KNOWN EACH OTHER FOR A LONG TIME...
TAKE CHEER! NO NEED FOR DEATHBED SENTIMEN-TALITY.
FEELING ANY BETTER NOW?
I BELIEVE YOUR REMEDY HAS INDEED STARTED TO TAKE EFFECT.
YOU SAVED MY LIFE, KAGOME.

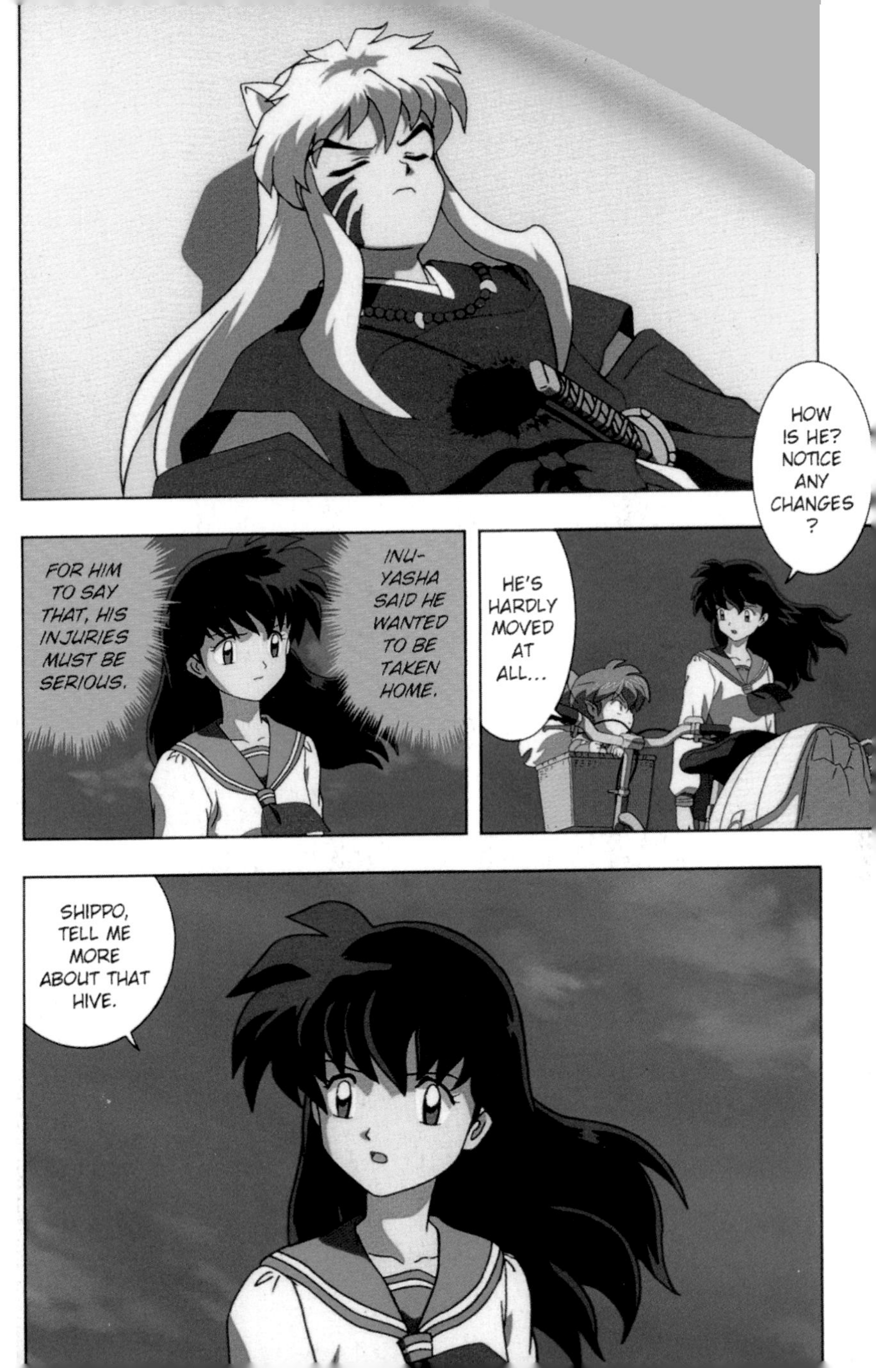
HOW IS HE? NOTICE ANY CHANGES?
HE'S HARDLY MOVED AT ALL...
INU-YASHA SAID HE WANTED TO BE TAKEN HOME.
FOR HIM TO SAY THAT, HIS INJURIES MUST BE SERIOUS.
SHIPPO, TELL ME MORE ABOUT THAT HIVE.

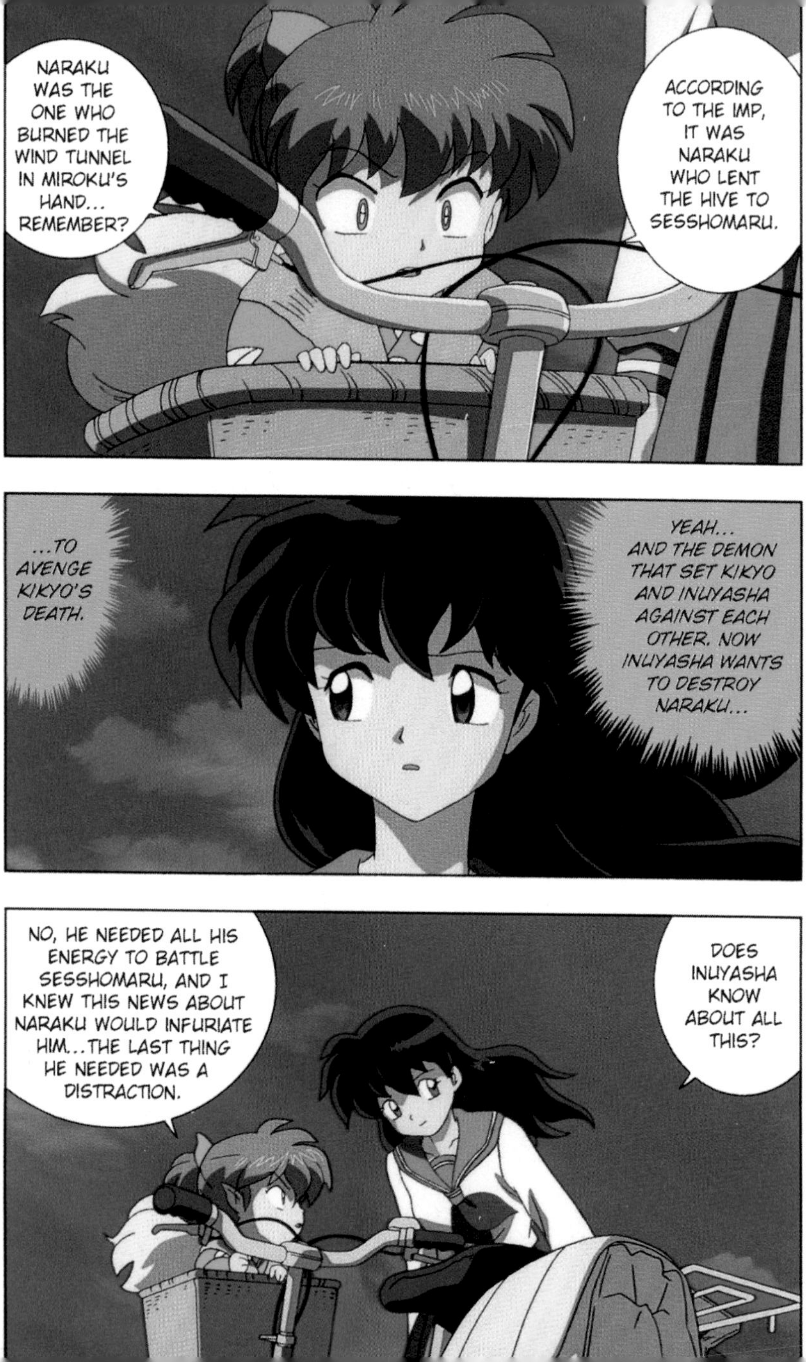
ACCORDING TO THE IMP, IT WAS NARAKU WHO LENT THE HIVE TO SESSHOMARU.
NARAKU WAS THE ONE WHO BURNED THE WIND TUNNEL IN MIROKU'S HAND... REMEMBER?
YEAH... AND THE DEMON THAT SET KIKYO AND INUYASHA AGAINST EACH OTHER. NOW INUYASHA WANTS TO DESTROY NARAKU...
...TO AVENGE KIKYO'S DEATH.
DOES INUYASHA KNOW ABOUT ALL THIS?
NO, HE NEEDED ALL HIS ENERGY TO BATTLE SESSHOMARU, AND I KNEW THIS NEWS ABOUT NARAKU WOULD INFURIATE HIM...THE LAST THING HE NEEDED WAS A DISTRACTION.

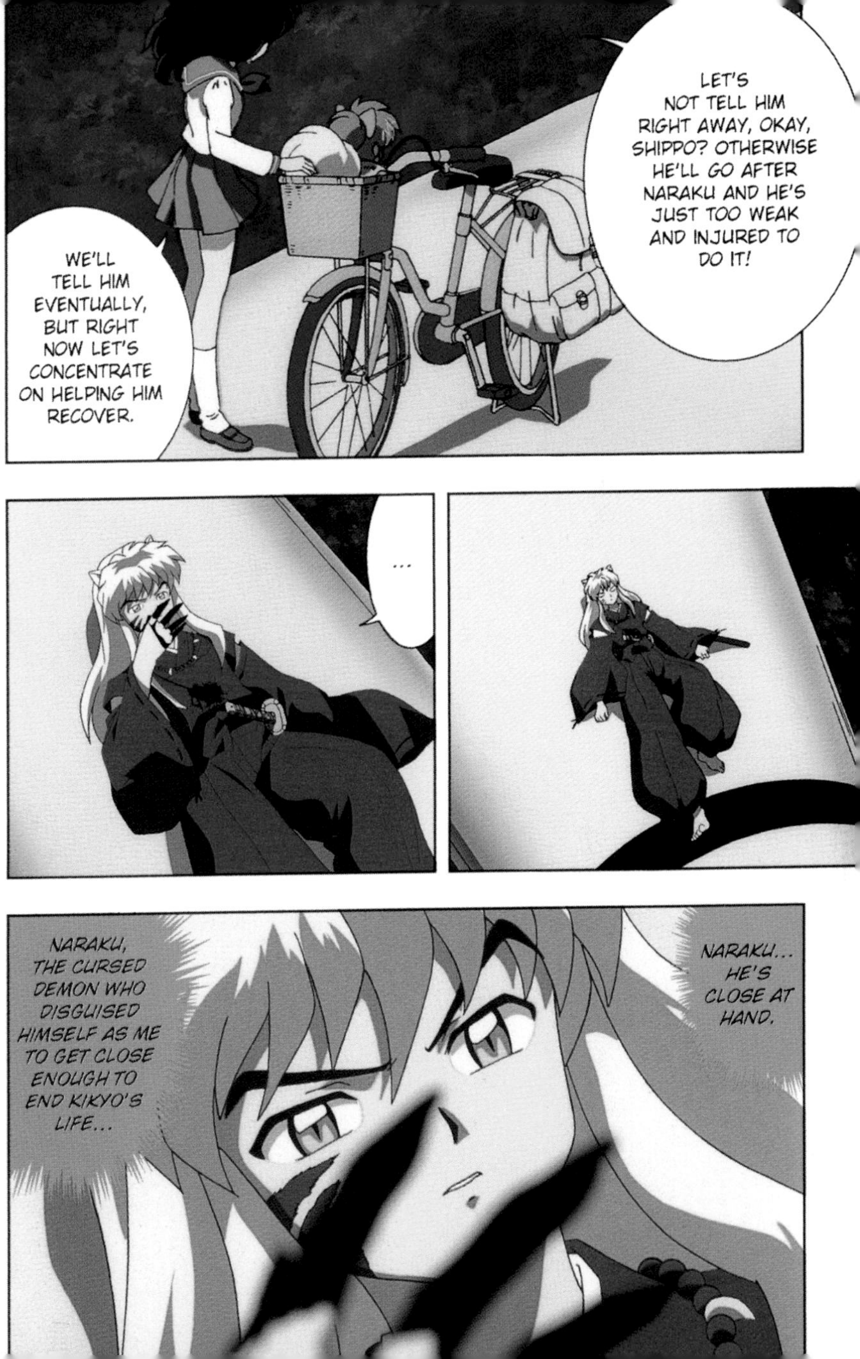
LET'S NOT TELL HIM RIGHT AWAY, OKAY, SHIPPO? OTHERWISE HE'LL GO AFTER NARAKU AND HE'S JUST TOO WEAK AND INJURED TO DO IT!
WE'LL TELL HIM EVENTUALLY, BUT RIGHT NOW LET'S CONCENTRATE ON HELPING HIM RECOVER.
...
NARAKU... HE'S CLOSE AT HAND.
NARAKU, THE CURSED DEMON WHO DISGUISED HIMSELF AS ME TO GET CLOSE ENOUGH TO END KIKYO'S LIFE...

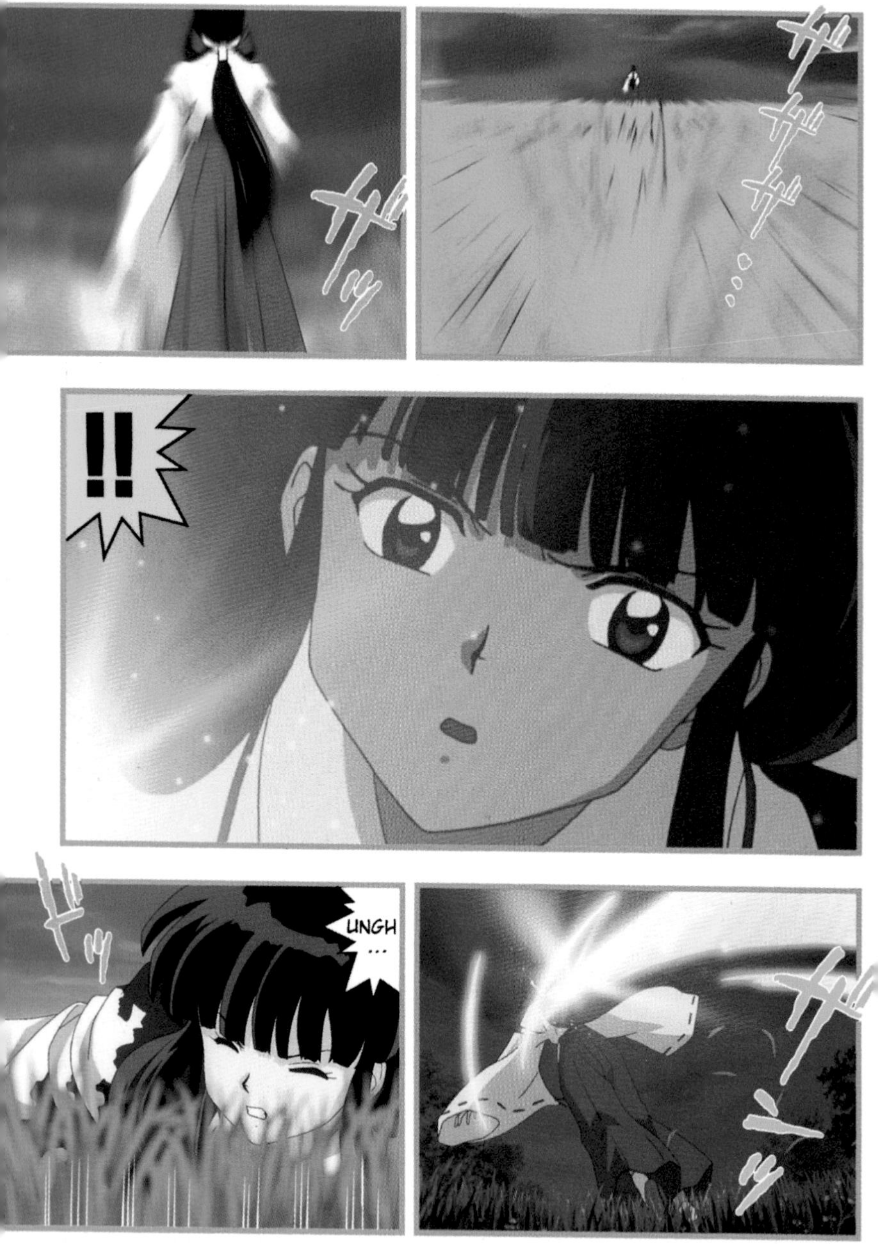
!!
UNGH ...

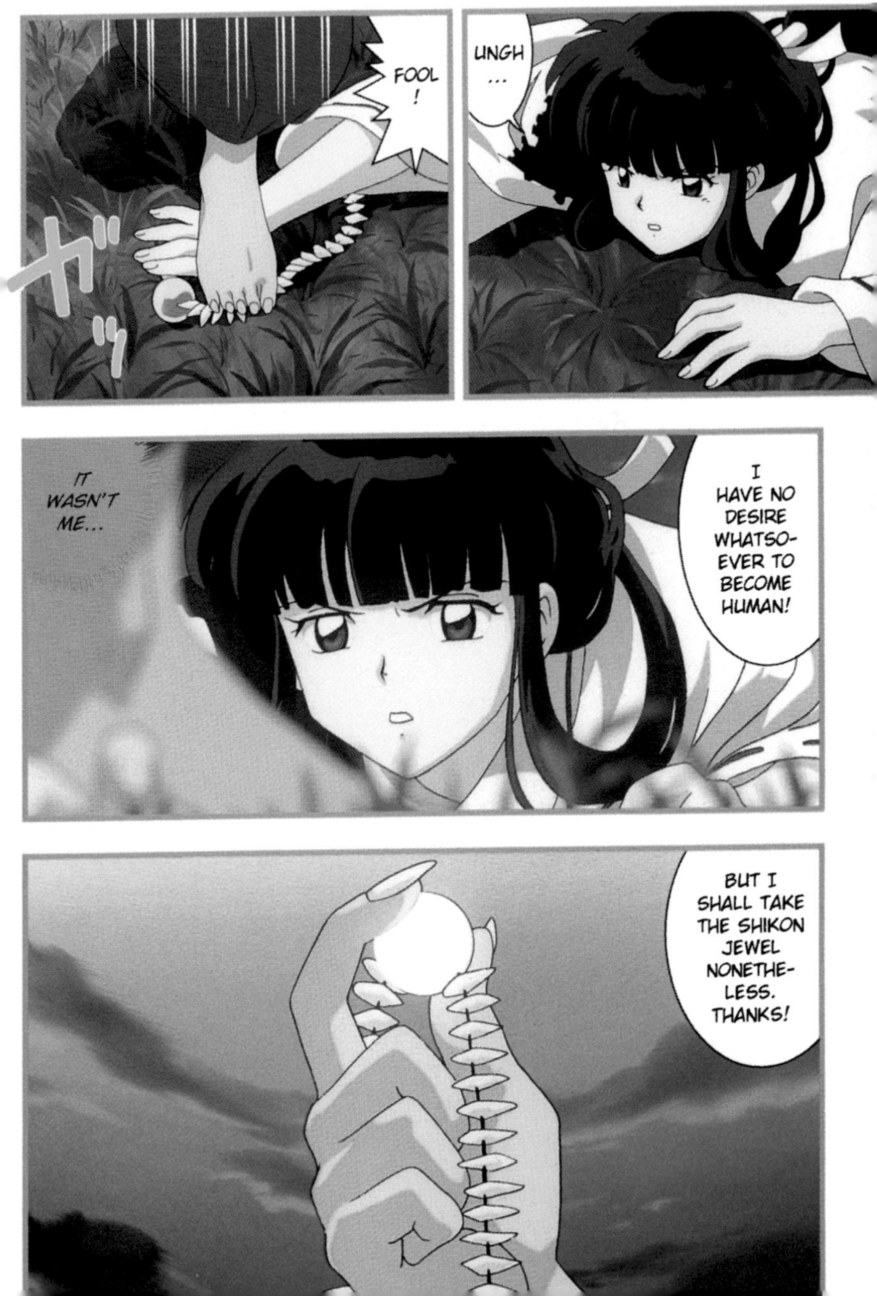
UNGH ...
FOOL !
ガッ
I HAVE NO DESIRE WHATSO-EVER TO BECOME HUMAN!
IT WASN'T ME...
BUT I SHALL TAKE THE SHIKON JEWEL NONETHE-LESS. THANKS!

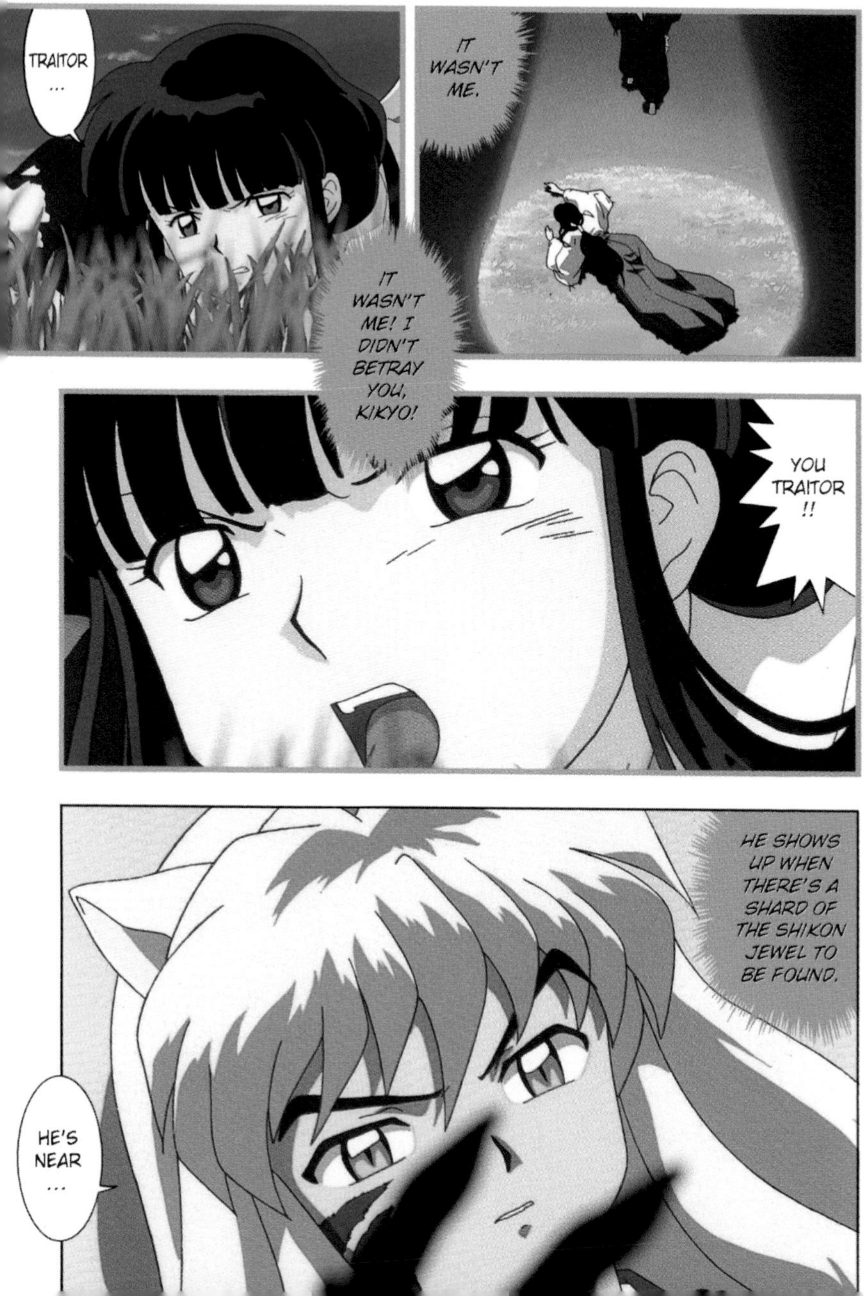
IT WASN'T ME.
TRAITOR ...
IT WASN'T ME! I DIDN'T BETRAY YOU, KIKYO!
YOU TRAITOR !!
HE SHOWS UP WHEN THERE'S A SHARD OF THE SHIKON JEWEL TO BE FOUND.
HE'S NEAR ...

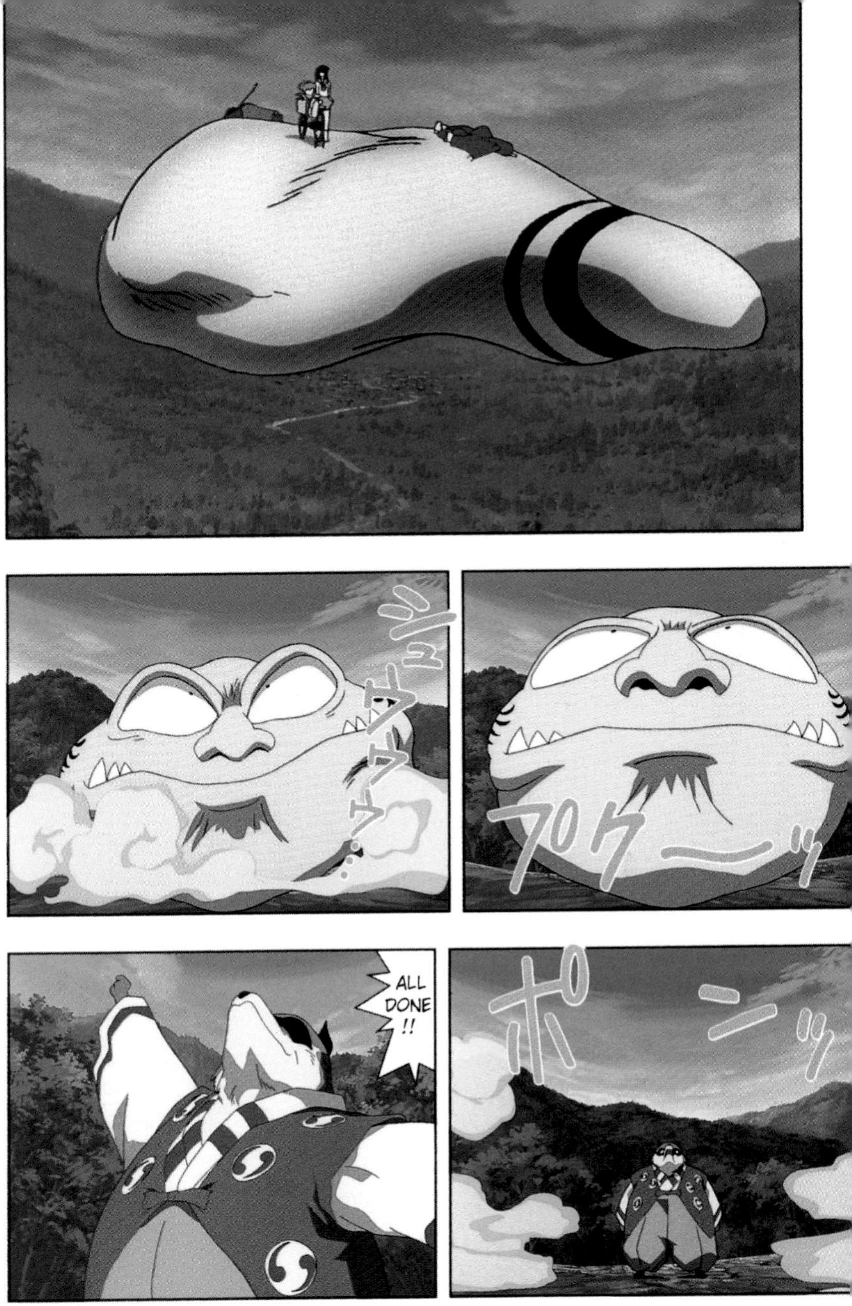
プクーッ
シュウウウ…
ポンッ
ALL DONE !!

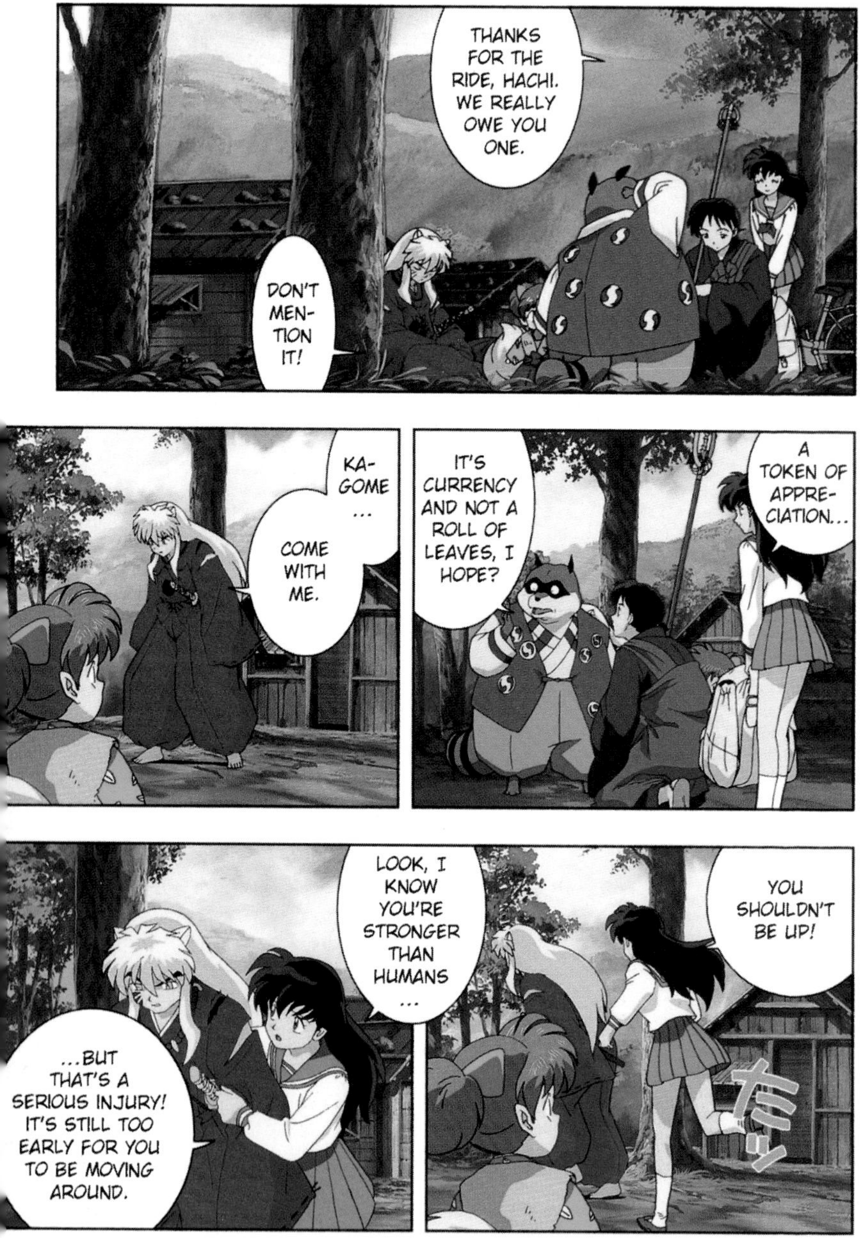
THANKS FOR THE RIDE, HACHI. WE REALLY OWE YOU ONE.
DON'T MEN-TION IT!
A TOKEN OF APPRE-CIATION...
IT'S CURRENCY AND NOT A ROLL OF LEAVES, I HOPE?
KA-GOME...
COME WITH ME.
YOU SHOULDN'T BE UP!
LOOK, I KNOW YOU'RE STRONGER THAN HUMANS...
...BUT THAT'S A SERIOUS INJURY! IT'S STILL TOO EARLY FOR YOU TO BE MOVING AROUND.

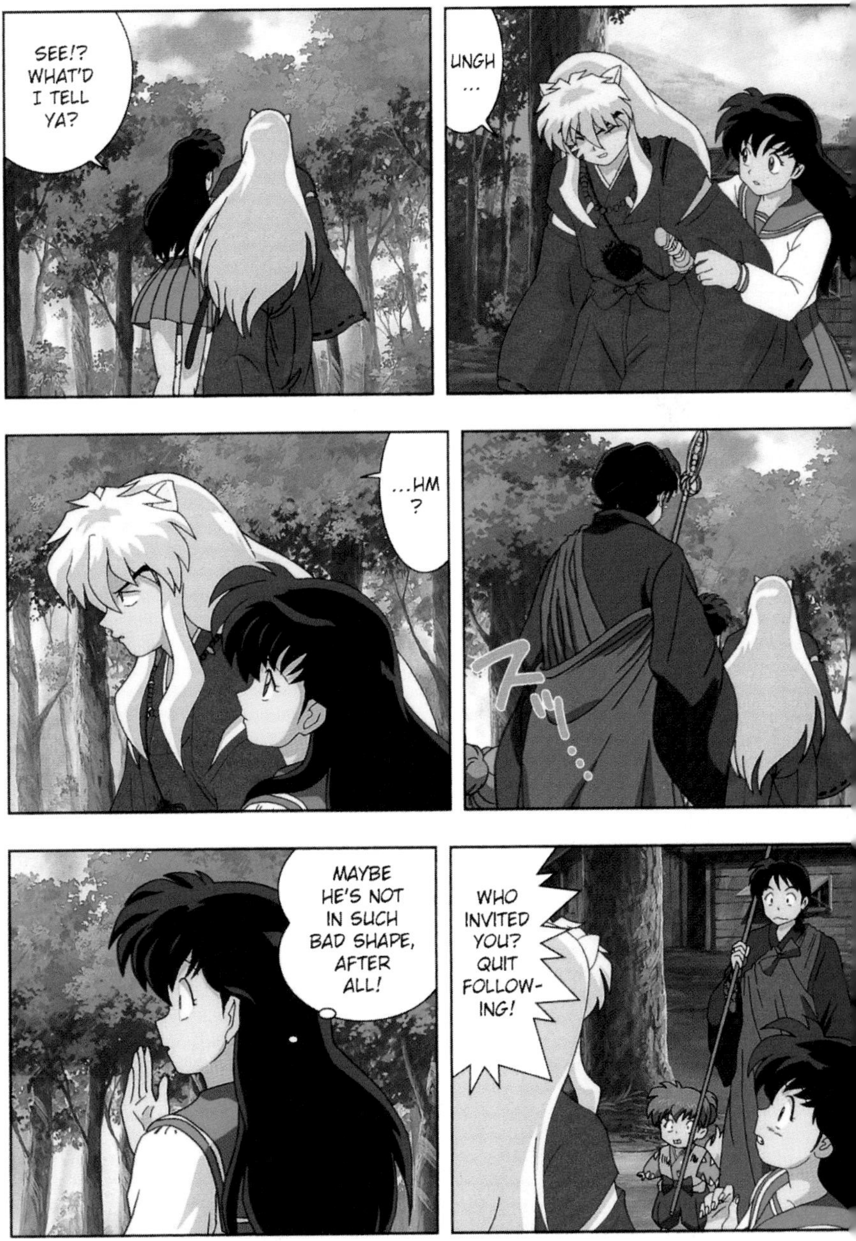
UNGH ...
SEE!? WHAT'D I TELL YA?
...HM ?
WHO INVITED YOU? QUIT FOLLOW-ING!
MAYBE HE'S NOT IN SUCH BAD SHAPE, AFTER ALL!

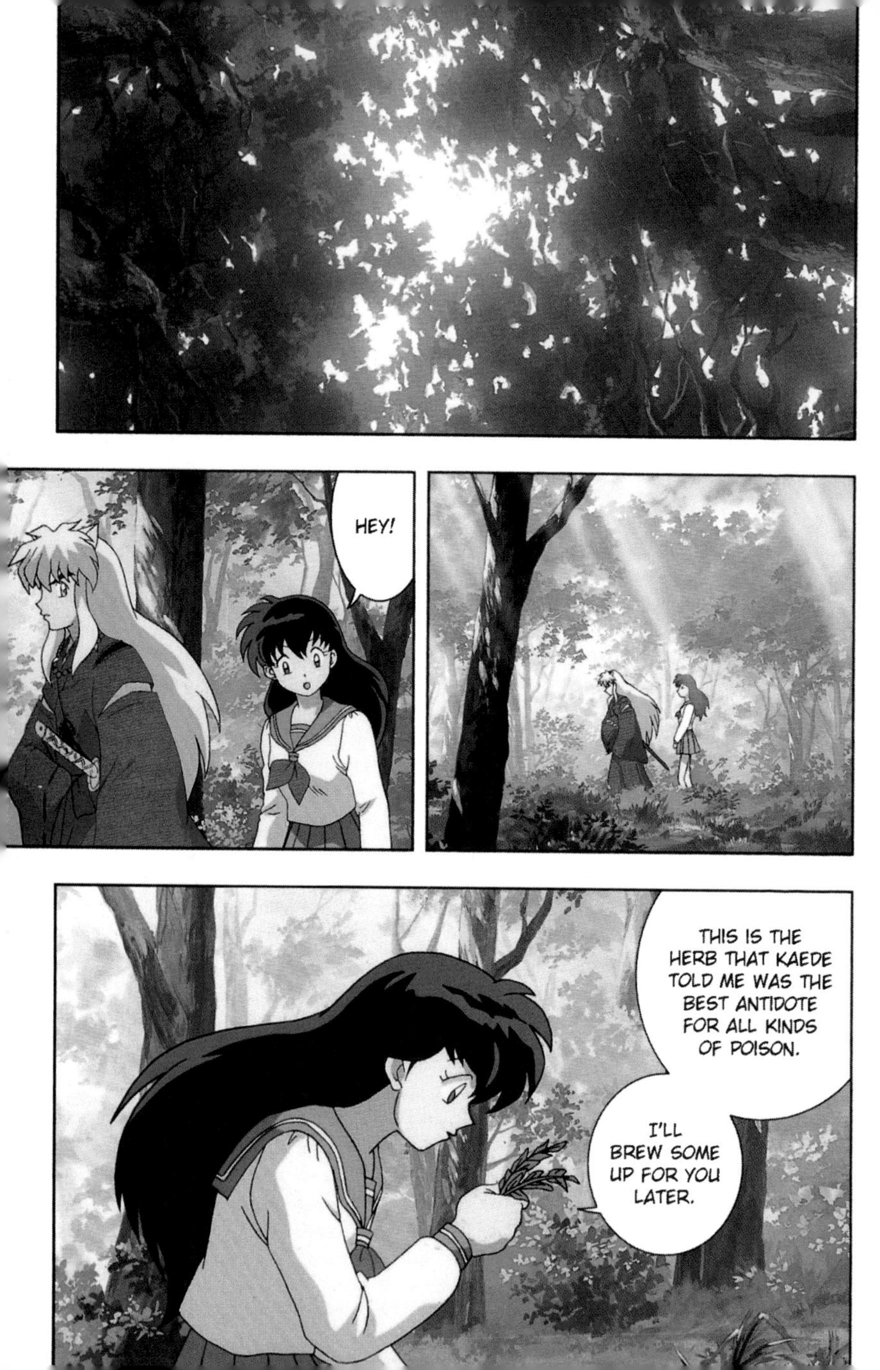
HEY!
THIS IS THE HERB THAT KAEDE TOLD ME WAS THE BEST ANTIDOTE FOR ALL KINDS OF POISON.
I'LL BREW SOME UP FOR YOU LATER.

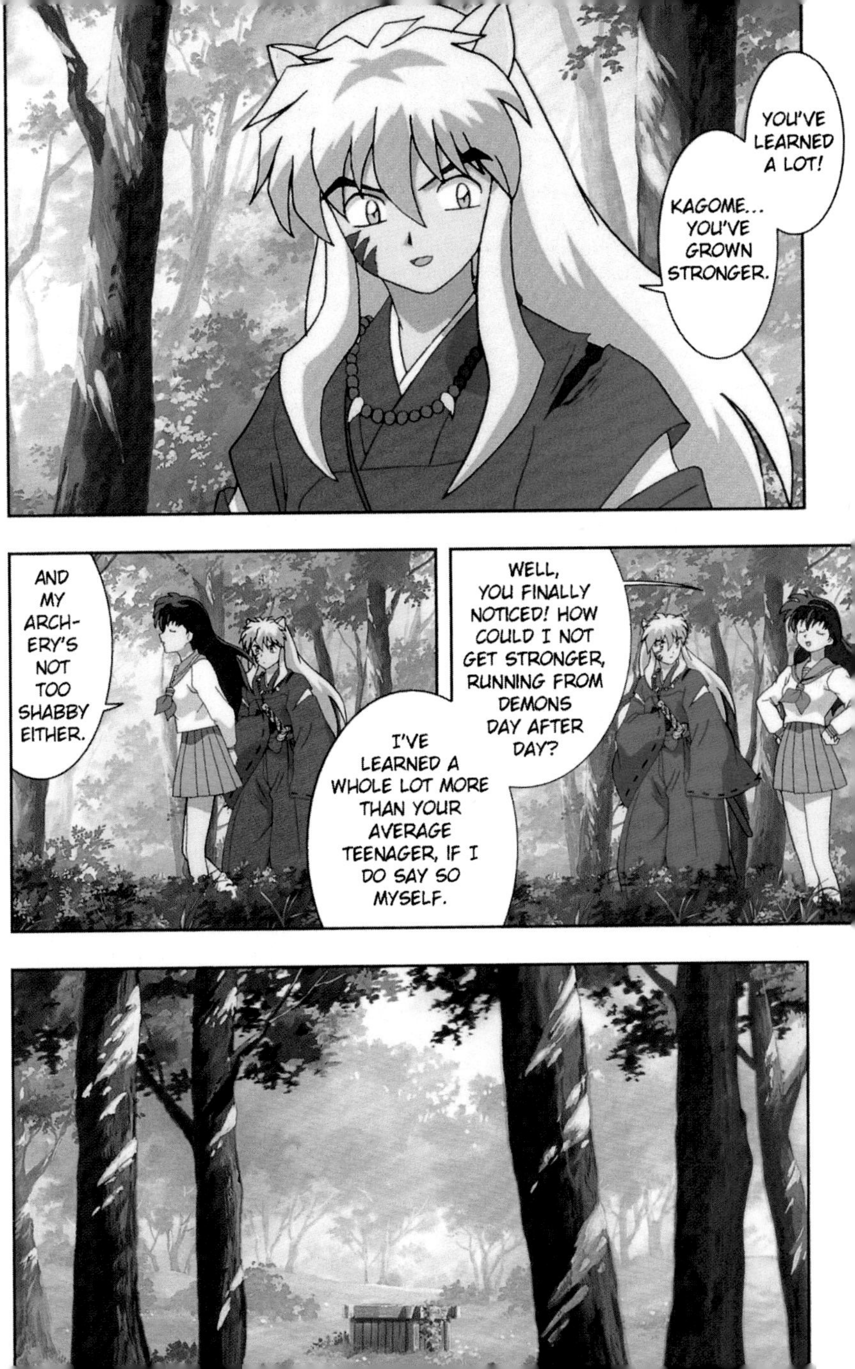
YOU'VE LEARNED A LOT!
KAGOME... YOU'VE GROWN STRONGER.
WELL, YOU FINALLY NOTICED! HOW COULD I NOT GET STRONGER, RUNNING FROM DEMONS DAY AFTER DAY?
I'VE LEARNED A WHOLE LOT MORE THAN YOUR AVERAGE TEENAGER, IF I DO SAY SO MYSELF.
AND MY ARCH-ERY'S NOT TOO SHABBY EITHER.

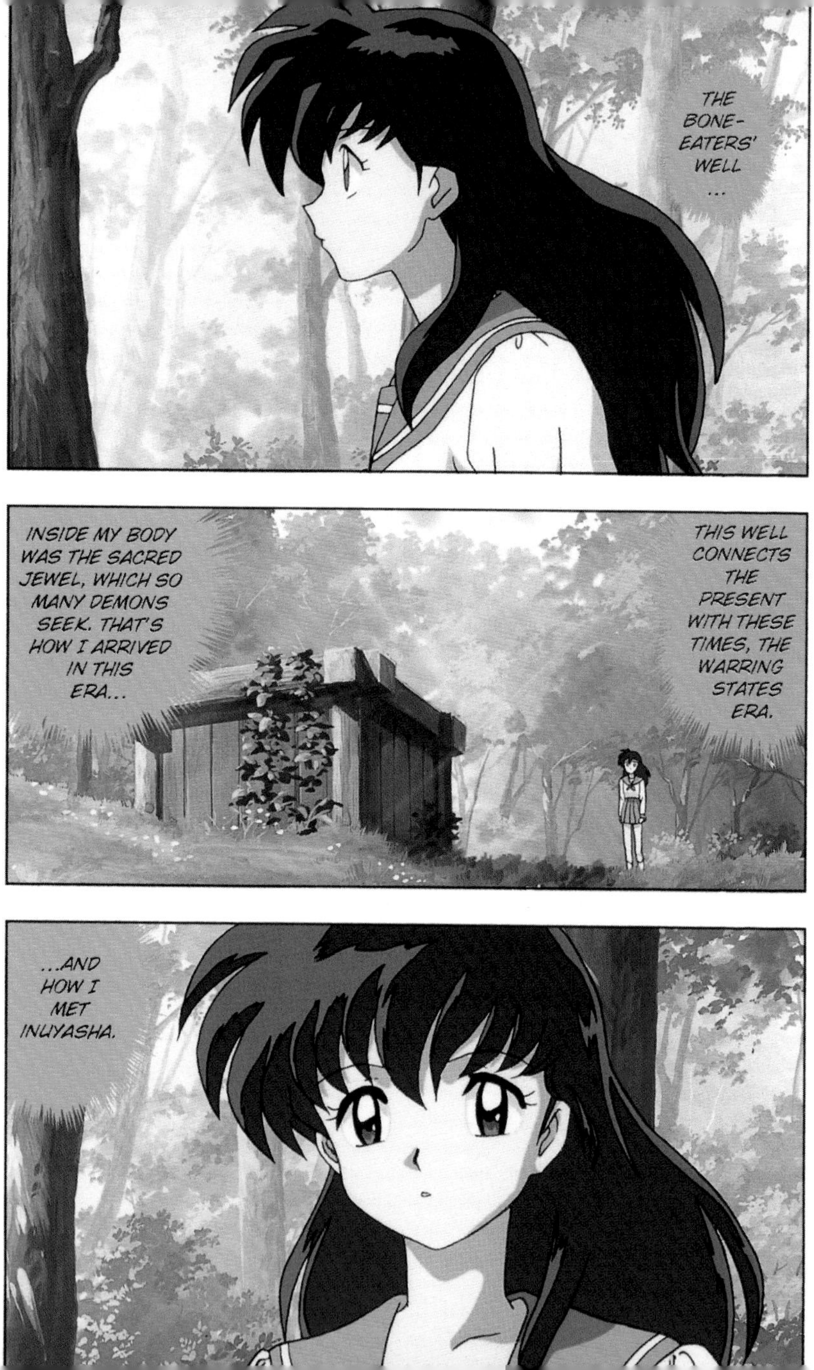
THE BONE-EATERS' WELL ...
THIS WELL CONNECTS THE PRESENT WITH THESE TIMES, THE WARRING STATES ERA.
INSIDE MY BODY WAS THE SACRED JEWEL, WHICH SO MANY DEMONS SEEK. THAT'S HOW I ARRIVED IN THIS ERA...
...AND HOW I MET INUYASHA.

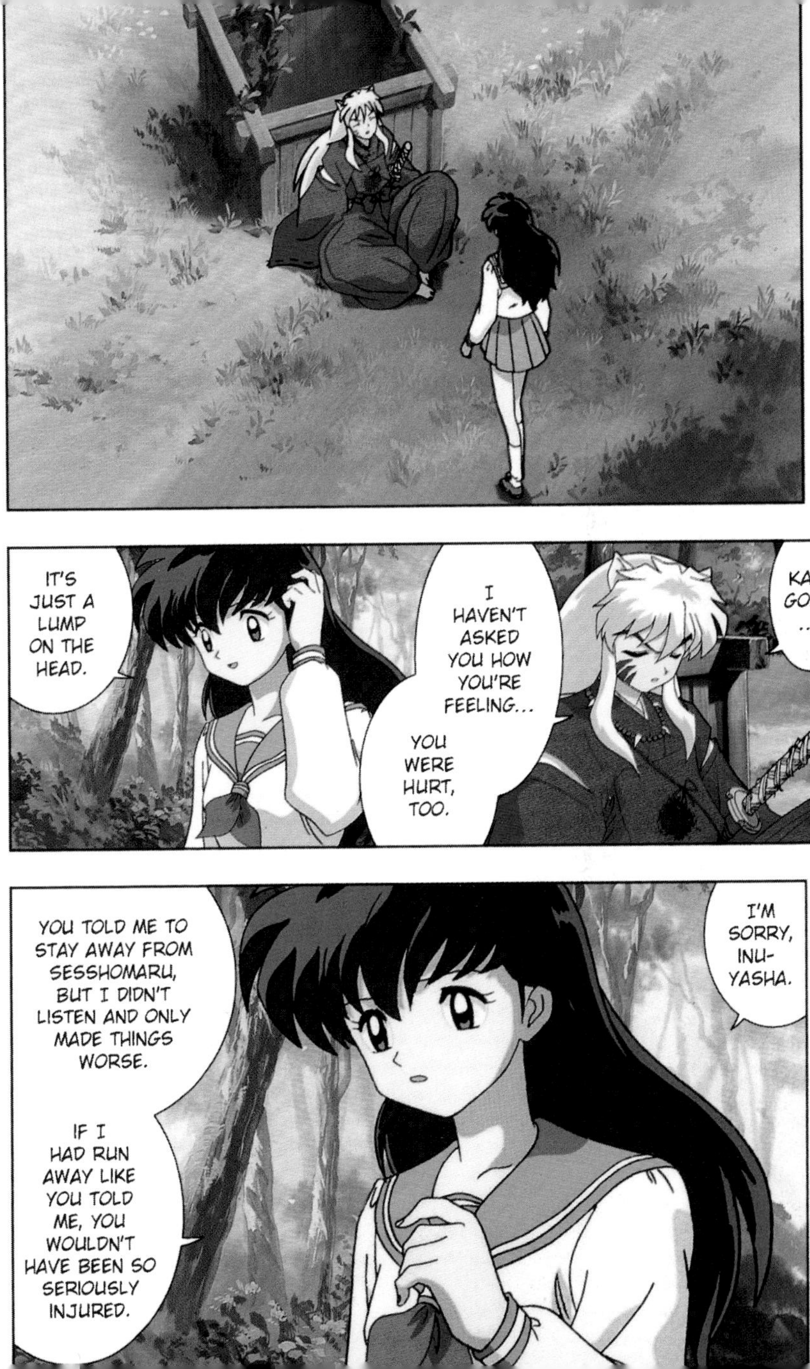
KA-GOME...
I HAVEN'T ASKED YOU HOW YOU'RE FEELING...
YOU WERE HURT, TOO.
IT'S JUST A LUMP ON THE HEAD.
I'M SORRY, INU-YASHA.
YOU TOLD ME TO STAY AWAY FROM SESSHOMARU, BUT I DIDN'T LISTEN AND ONLY MADE THINGS WORSE.
IF I HAD RUN AWAY LIKE YOU TOLD ME, YOU WOULDN'T HAVE BEEN SO SERIOUSLY INJURED.

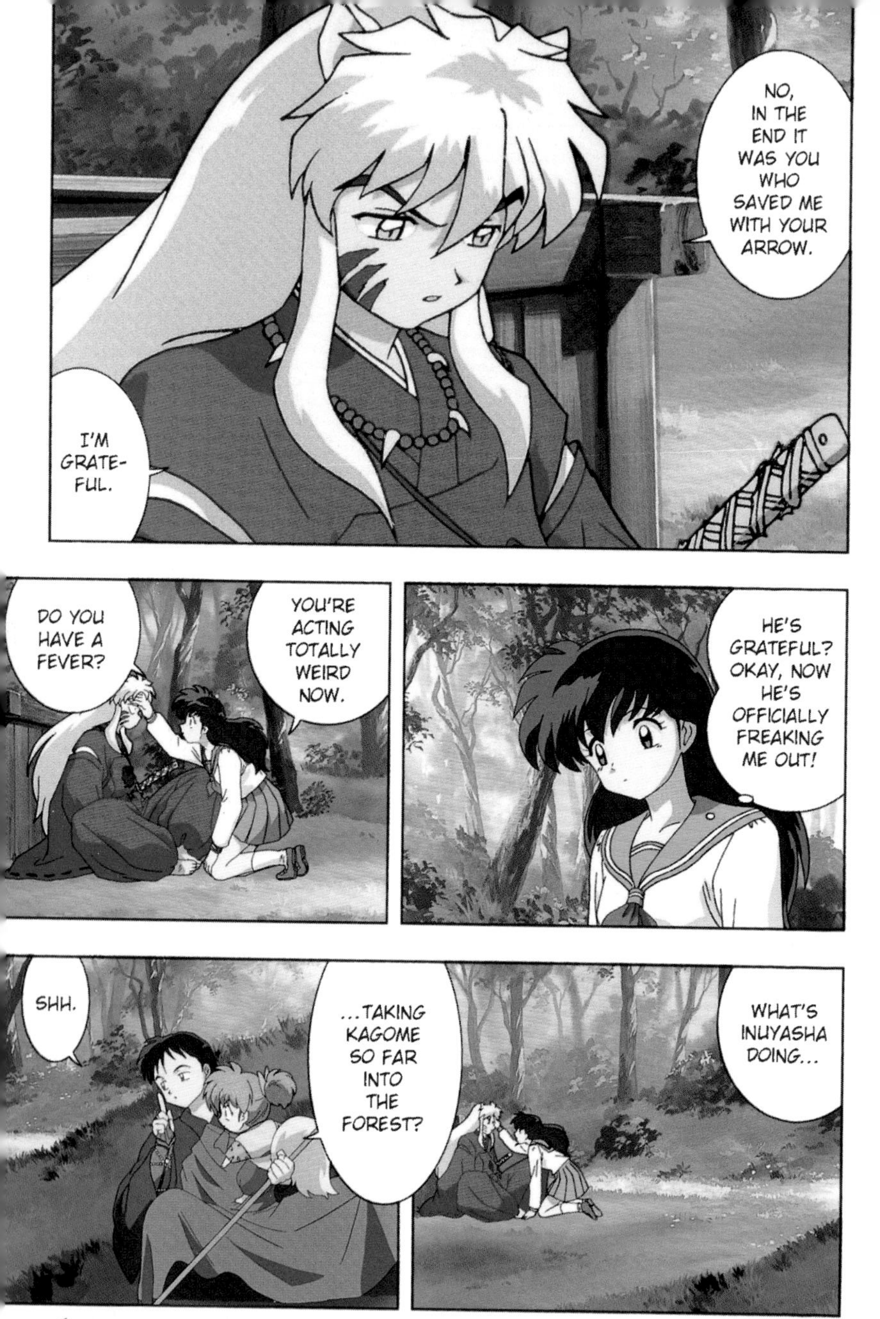
NO, IN THE END IT WAS YOU WHO SAVED ME WITH YOUR ARROW.
I'M GRATE-FUL.
HE'S GRATEFUL? OKAY, NOW HE'S OFFICIALLY FREAKING ME OUT!
YOU'RE ACTING TOTALLY WEIRD NOW.
DO YOU HAVE A FEVER?
WHAT'S INUYASHA DOING...
...TAKING KAGOME SO FAR INTO THE FOREST?
SHH.

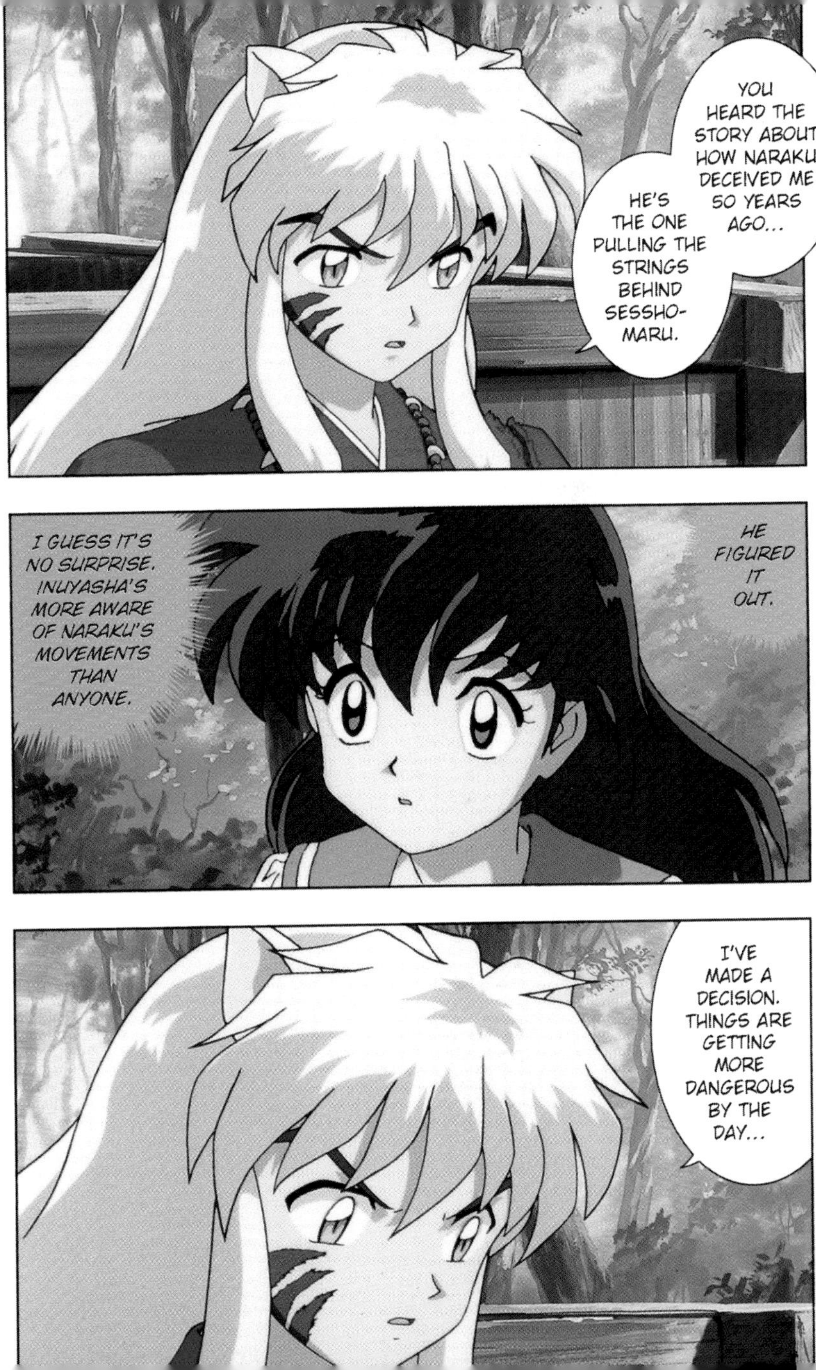
YOU HEARD THE STORY ABOUT HOW NARAKU DECEIVED ME 50 YEARS AGO...
HE'S THE ONE PULLING THE STRINGS BEHIND SESSHO-MARU.
HE FIGURED IT OUT.
I GUESS IT'S NO SURPRISE. INUYASHA'S MORE AWARE OF NARAKU'S MOVEMENTS THAN ANYONE.
I'VE MADE A DECISION. THINGS ARE GETTING MORE DANGEROUS BY THE DAY...

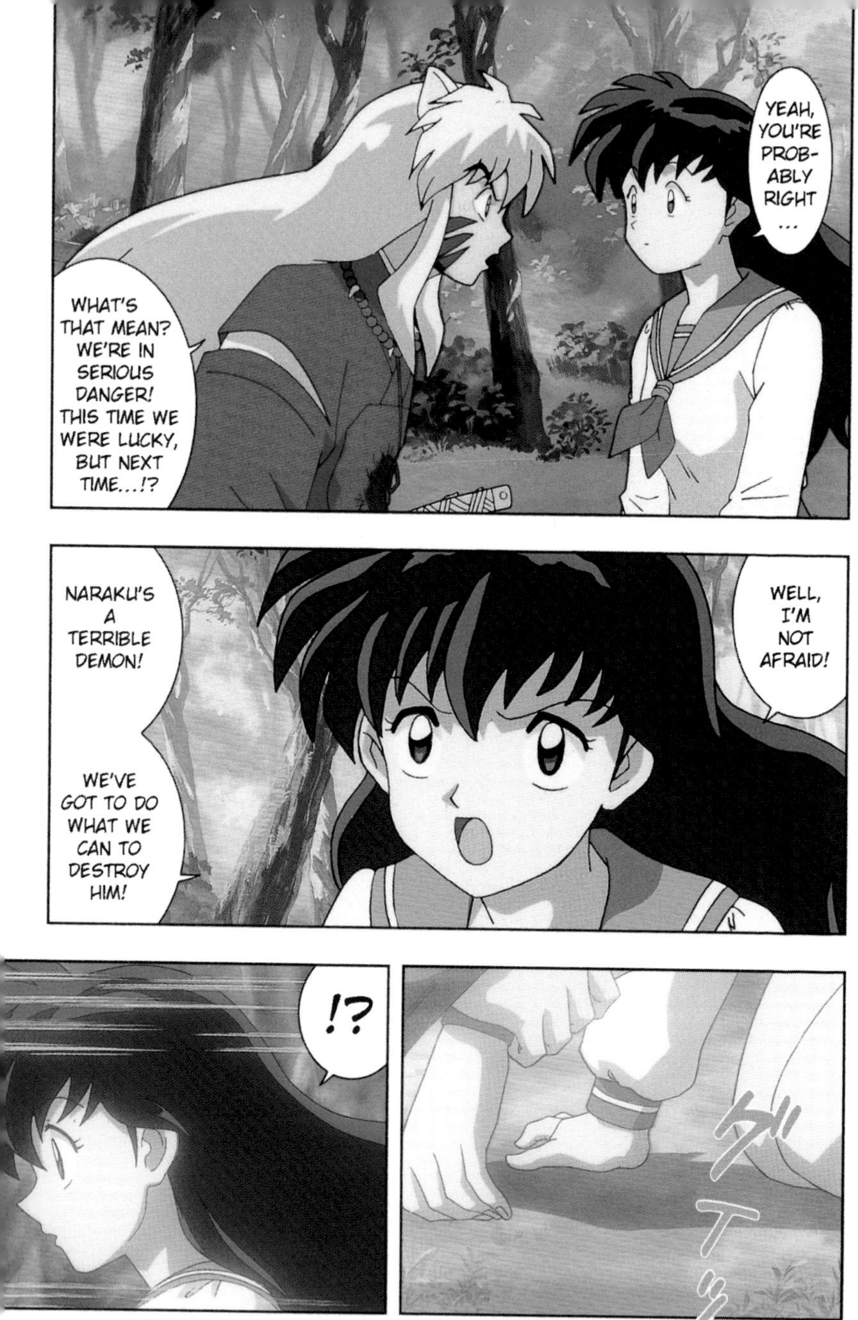
YEAH, YOU'RE PROB-ABLY RIGHT ...
WHAT'S THAT MEAN? WE'RE IN SERIOUS DANGER! THIS TIME WE WERE LUCKY, BUT NEXT TIME...!?
WELL, I'M NOT AFRAID!
NARAKU'S A TERRIBLE DEMON!
WE'VE GOT TO DO WHAT WE CAN TO DESTROY HIM!
!?

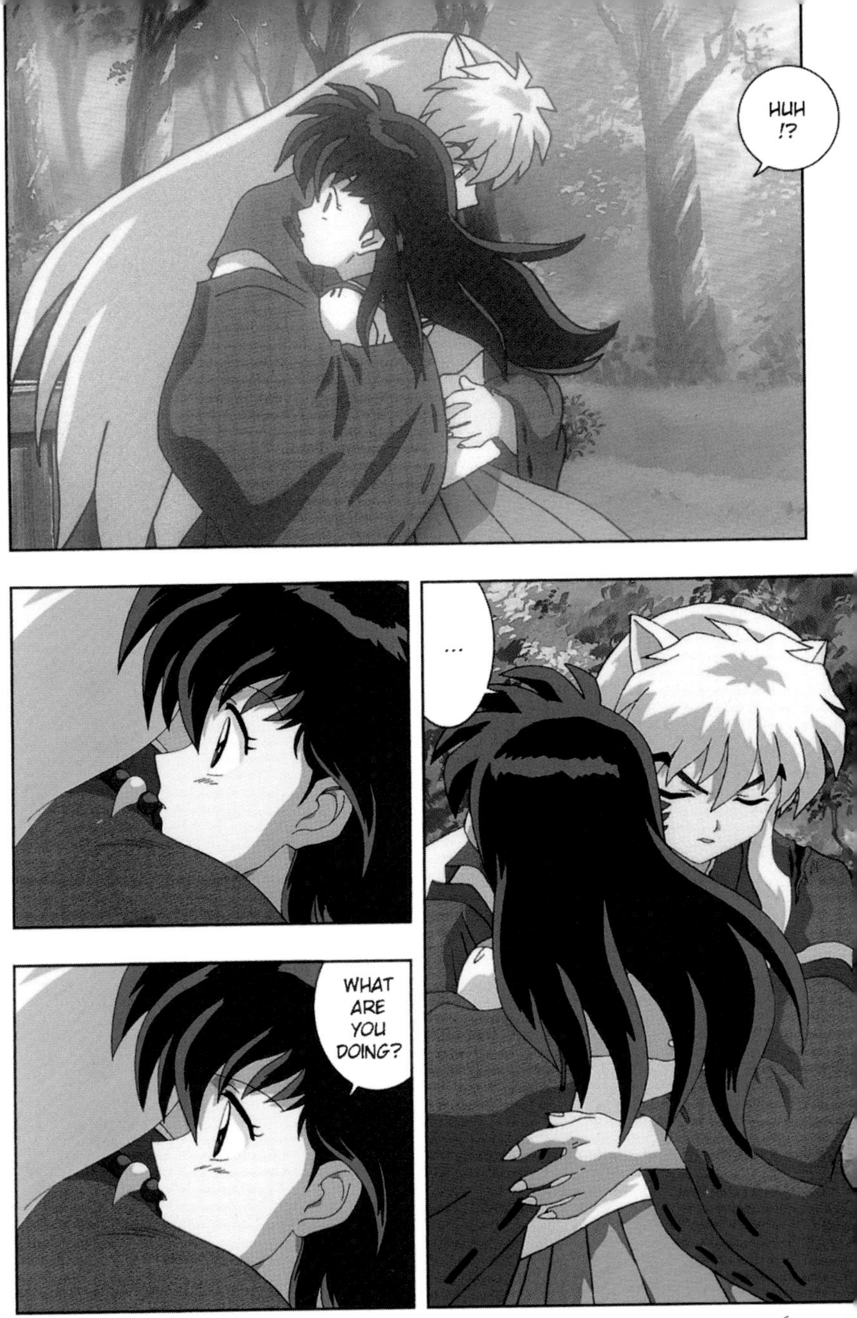
HUH !?
...
WHAT ARE YOU DOING?

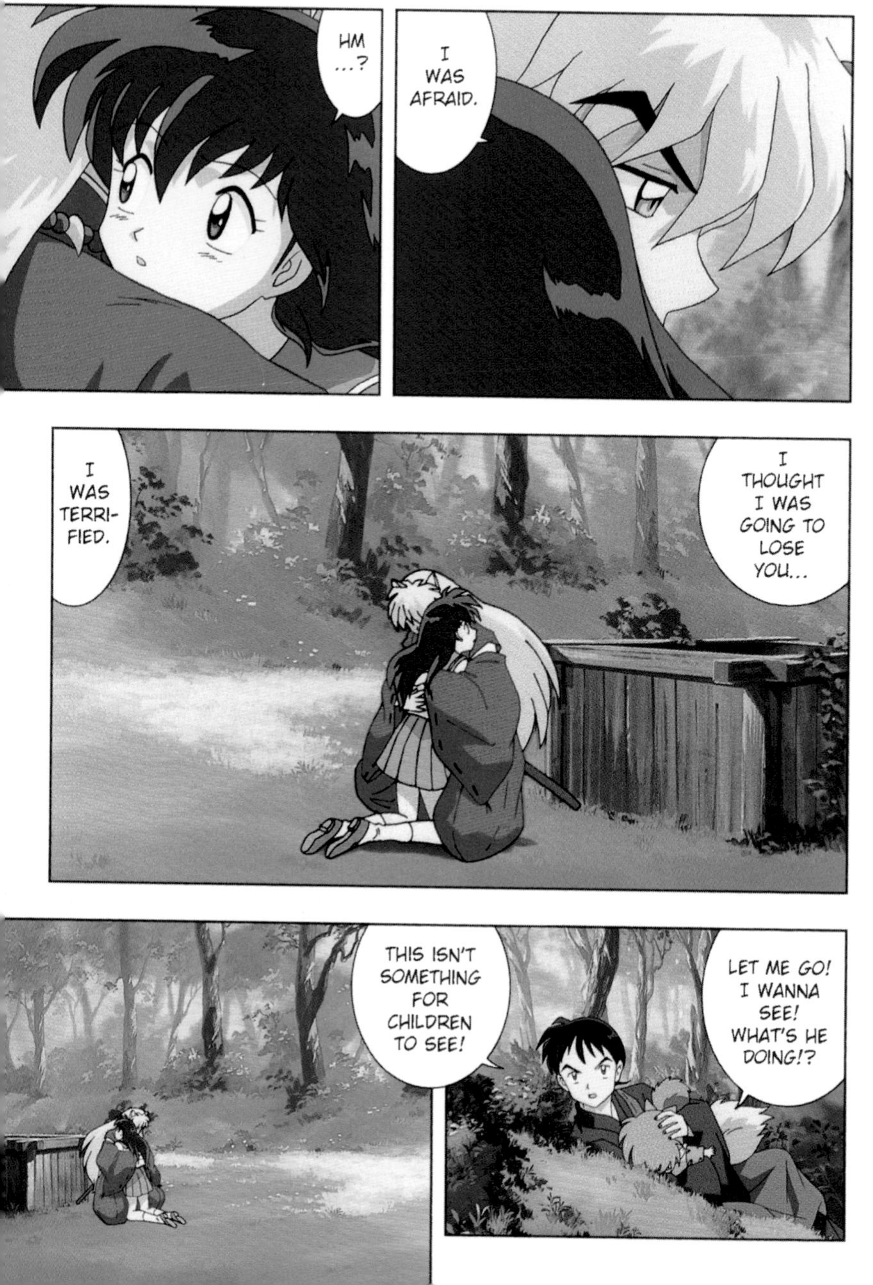
I WAS AFRAID.
HM ...?
I THOUGHT I WAS GOING TO LOSE YOU...
I WAS TERRI-FIED.
LET ME GO! I WANNA SEE! WHAT'S HE DOING!?
THIS ISN'T SOMETHING FOR CHILDREN TO SEE!

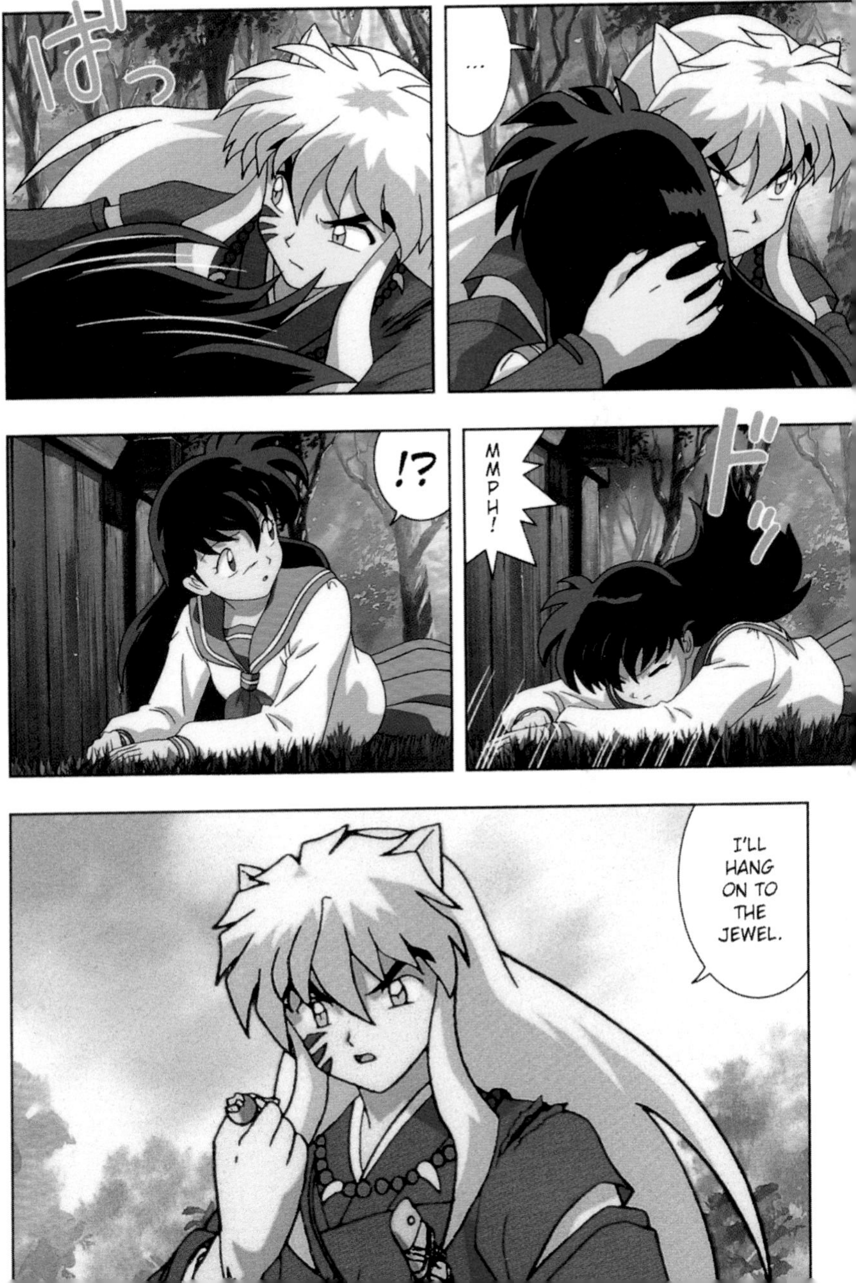
...
ぱっ
MMPH!
ドッ
!?
I'LL HANG ON TO THE JEWEL.

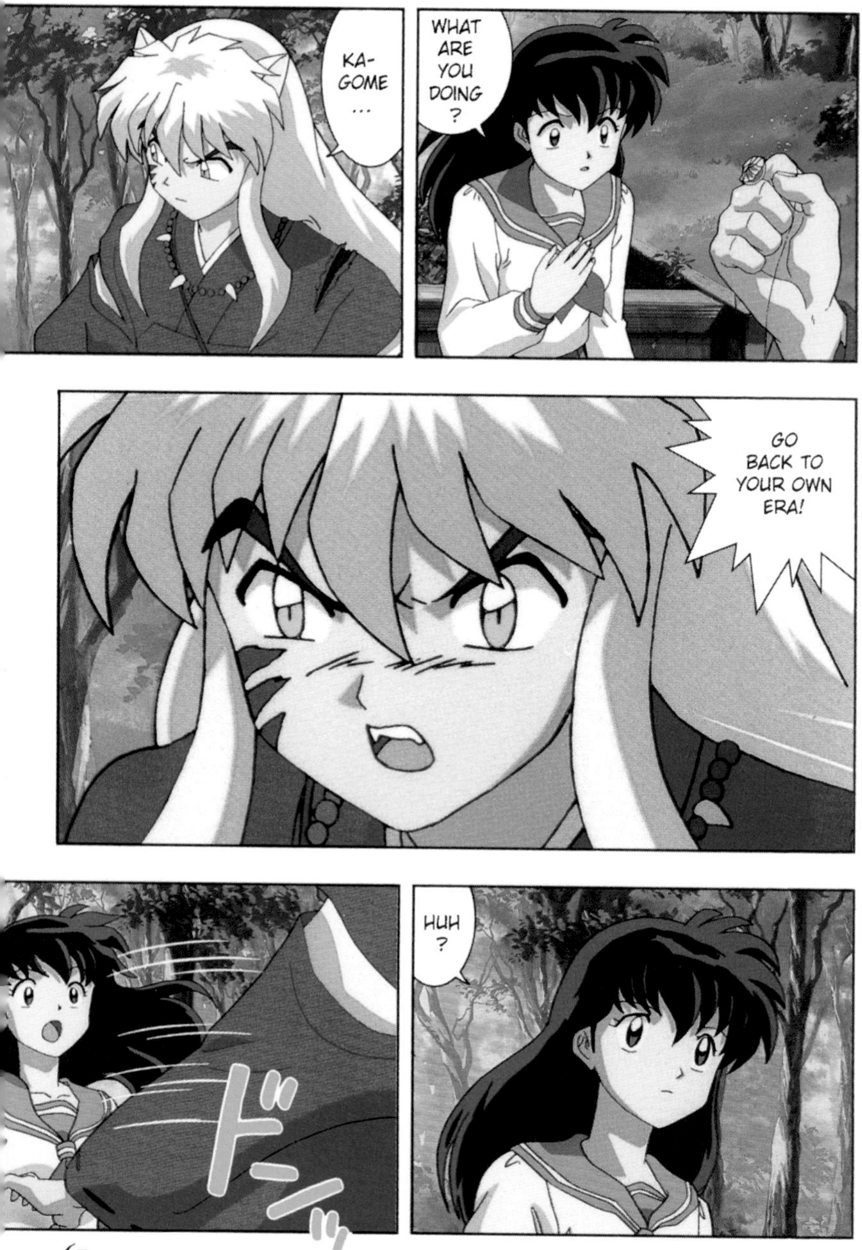
WHAT ARE YOU DOING ?
KA-GOME ...
GO BACK TO YOUR OWN ERA!
HUH ?
ドンッ

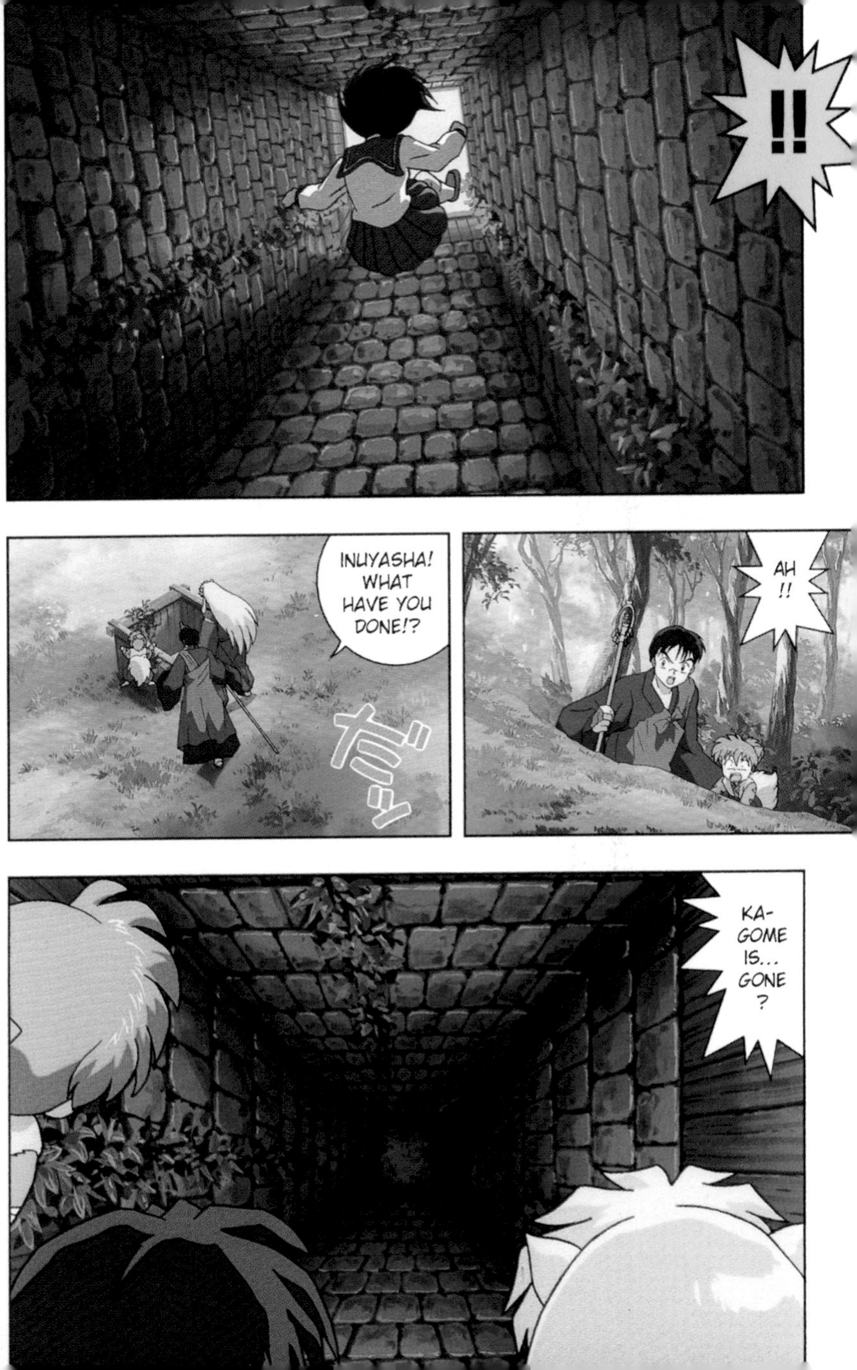
!!
AH !!
INUYASHA! WHAT HAVE YOU DONE!?
だッ
KA-GOME IS... GONE ?

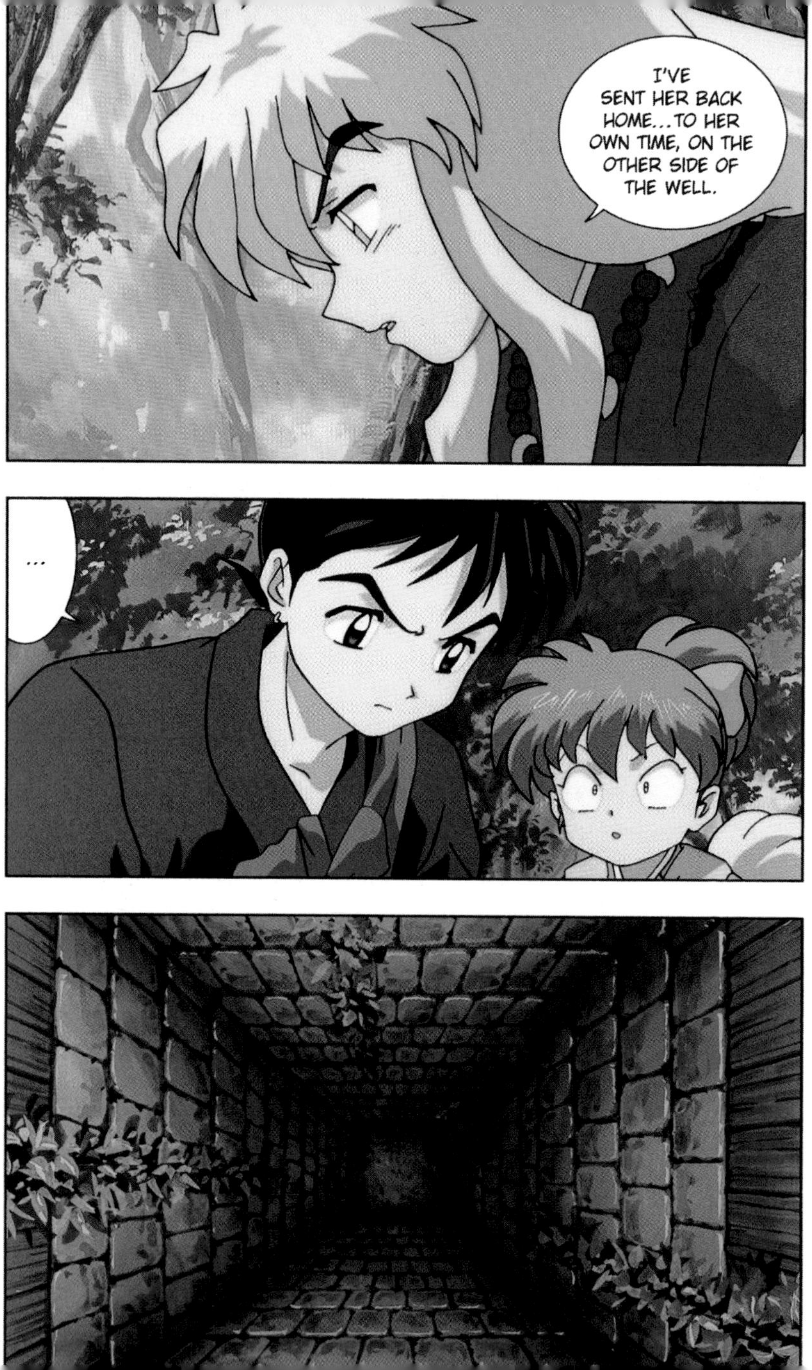
I'VE SENT HER BACK HOME...TO HER OWN TIME, ON THE OTHER SIDE OF THE WELL.
...

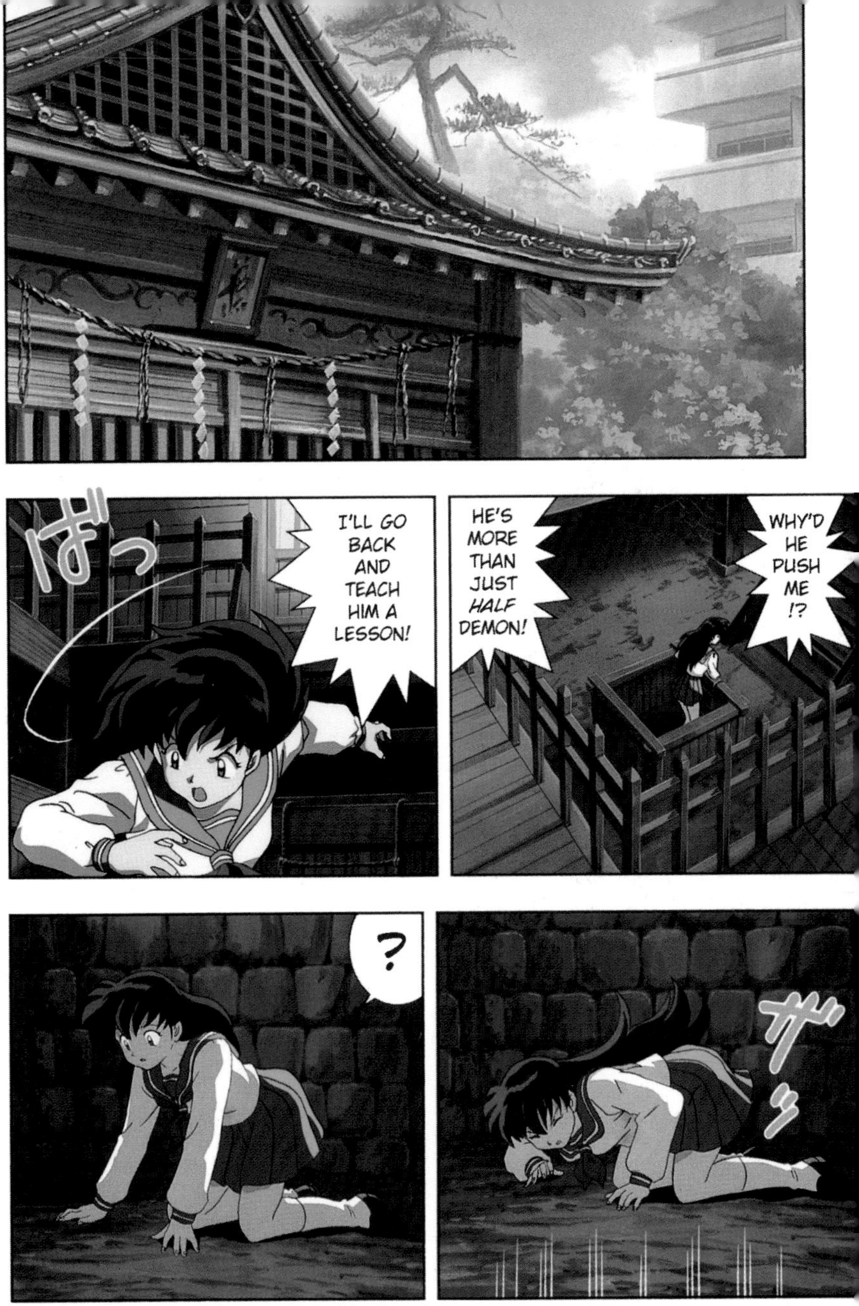
WHY'D HE PUSH ME !?
HE'S MORE THAN JUST *HALF* DEMON!
ぱっ
I'LL GO BACK AND TEACH HIM A LESSON!
ザッ
?

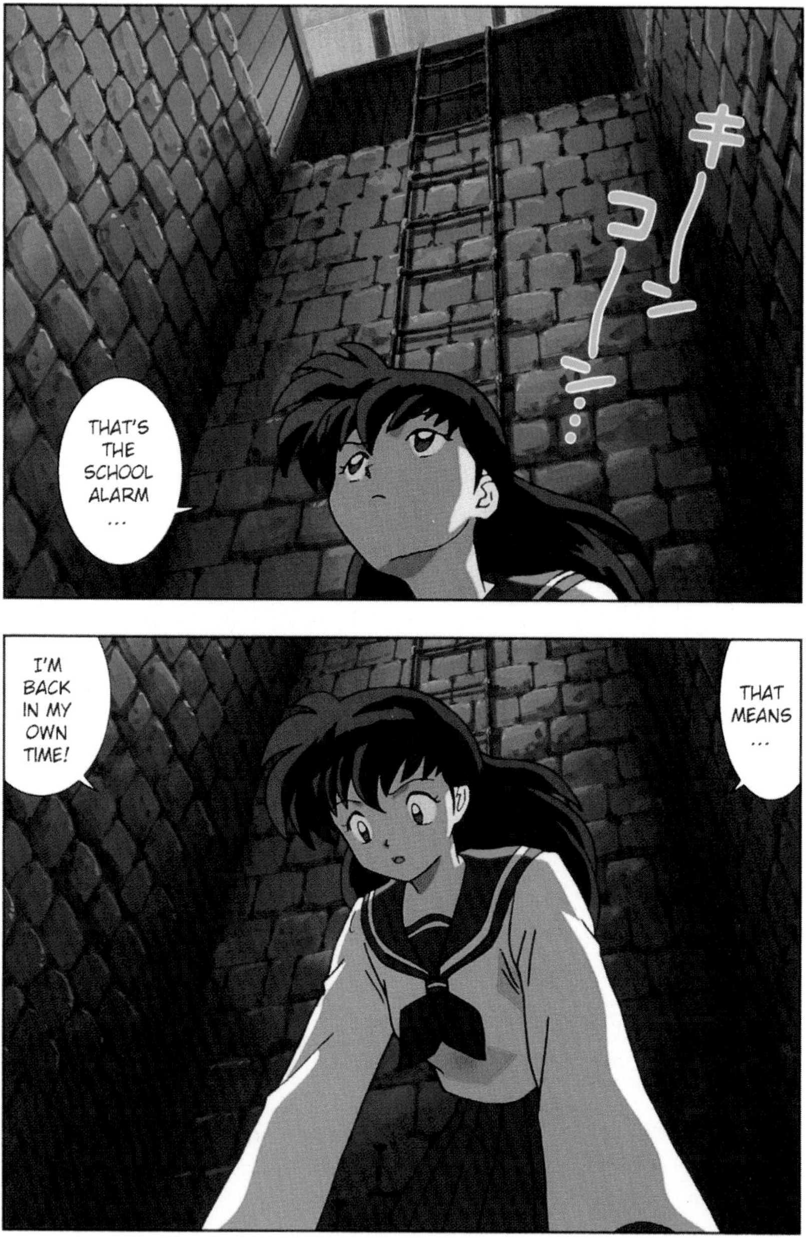
キーンコーン…
THAT'S THE SCHOOL ALARM ...
THAT MEANS ...
I'M BACK IN MY OWN TIME!

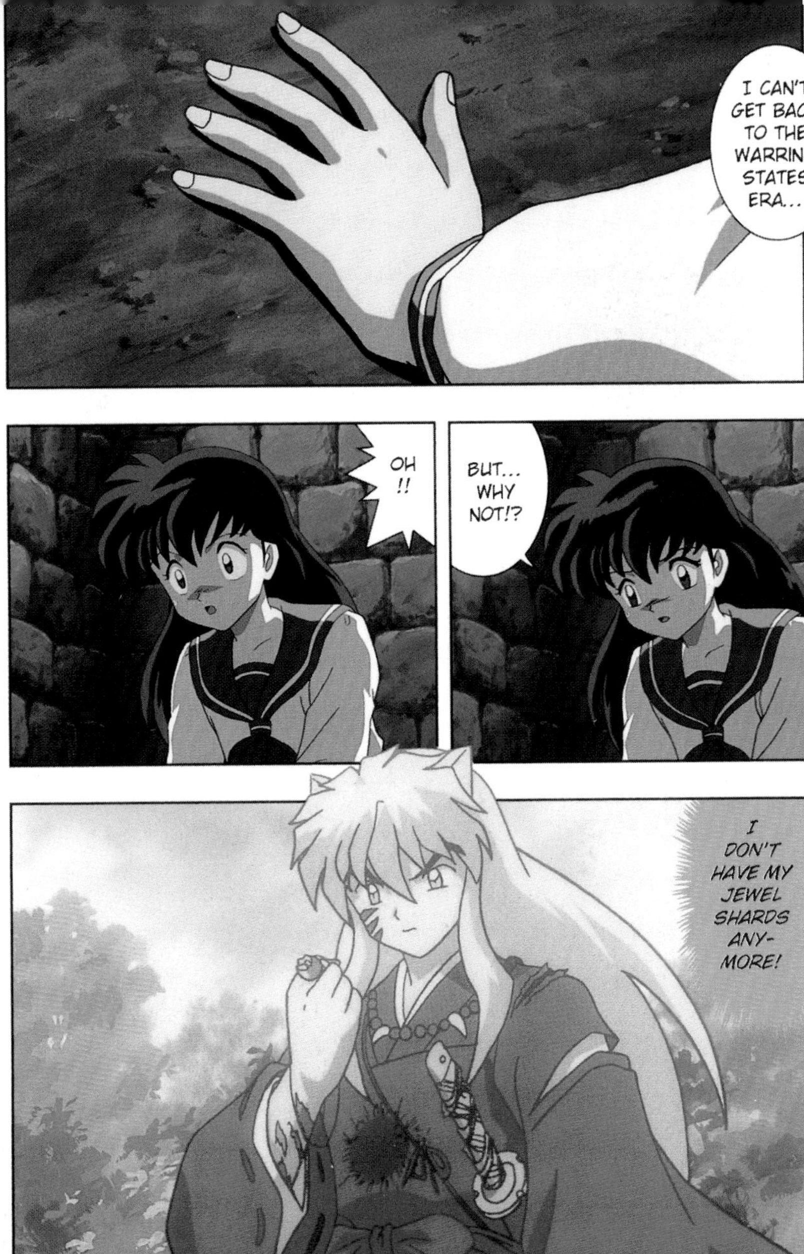
I CAN'T GET BACK TO THE WARRING STATES ERA...
OH !!
BUT... WHY NOT!?
I DON'T HAVE MY JEWEL SHARDS ANY-MORE!

20
Despicable Villain! The Mystery of Onigumo

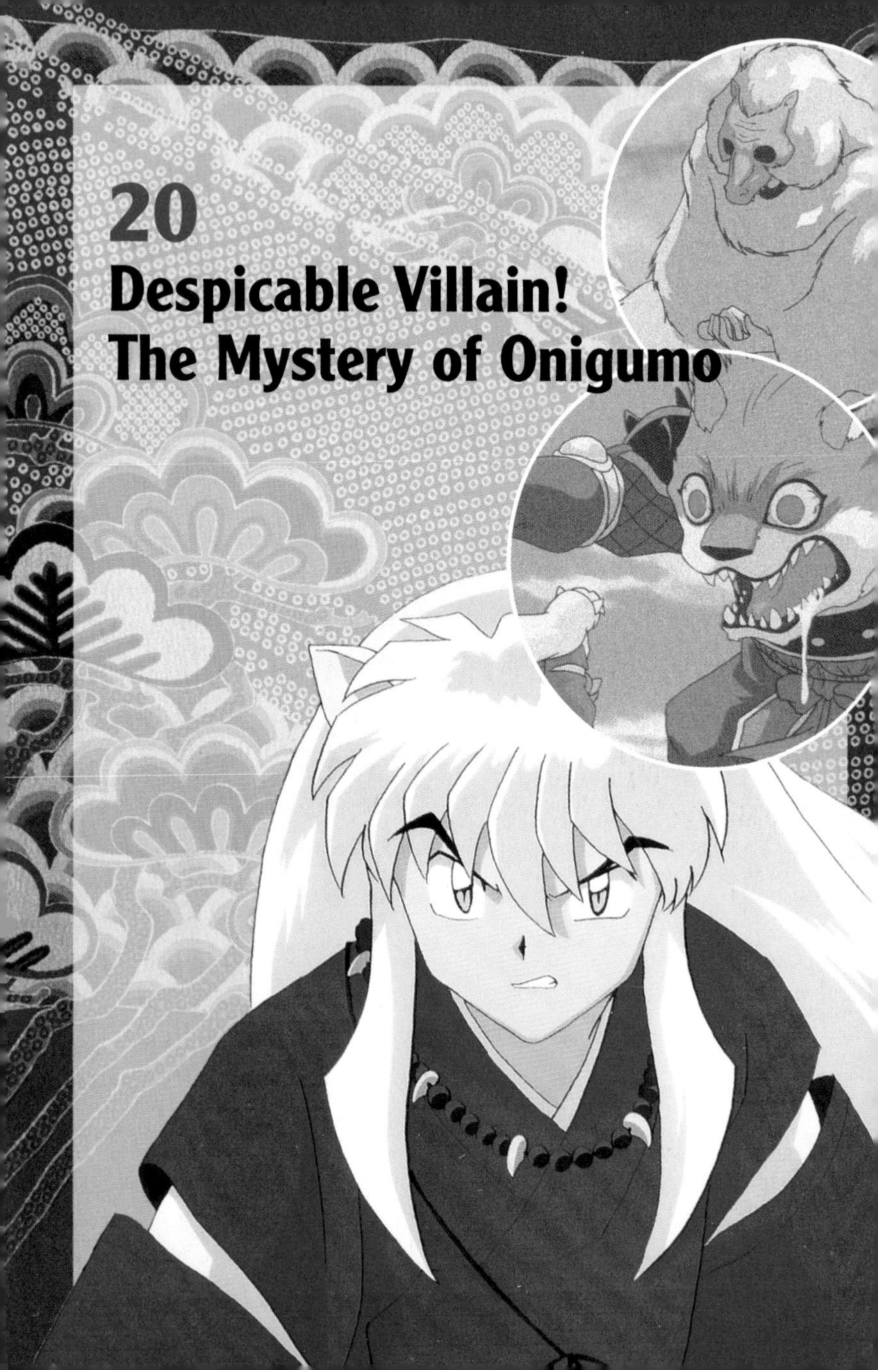

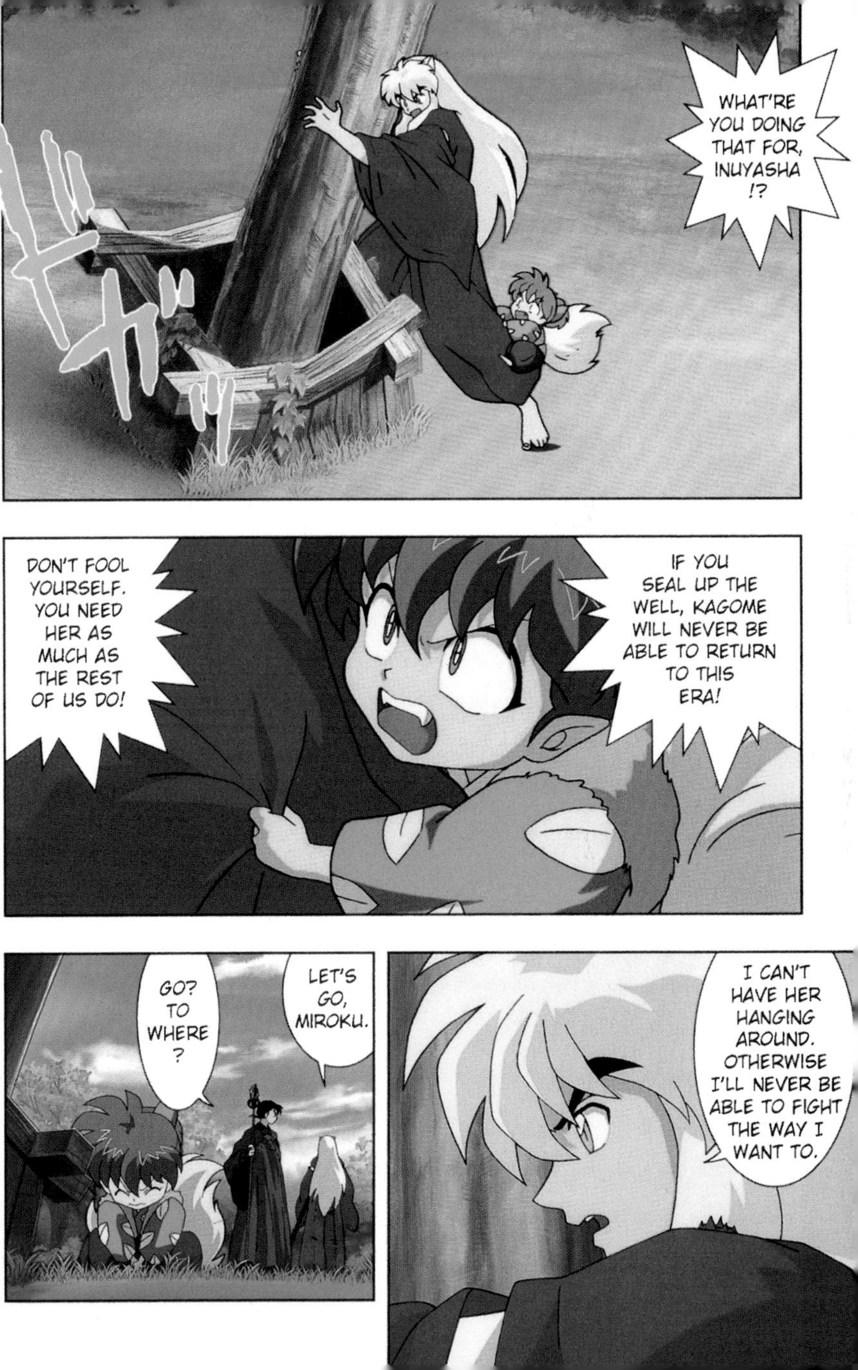
WHAT'RE YOU DOING THAT FOR, INUYASHA!?
IF YOU SEAL UP THE WELL, KAGOME WILL NEVER BE ABLE TO RETURN TO THIS ERA!
DON'T FOOL YOURSELF. YOU NEED HER AS MUCH AS THE REST OF US DO!
I CAN'T HAVE HER HANGING AROUND. OTHERWISE I'LL NEVER BE ABLE TO FIGHT THE WAY I WANT TO.
LET'S GO, MIROKU.
GO? TO WHERE?

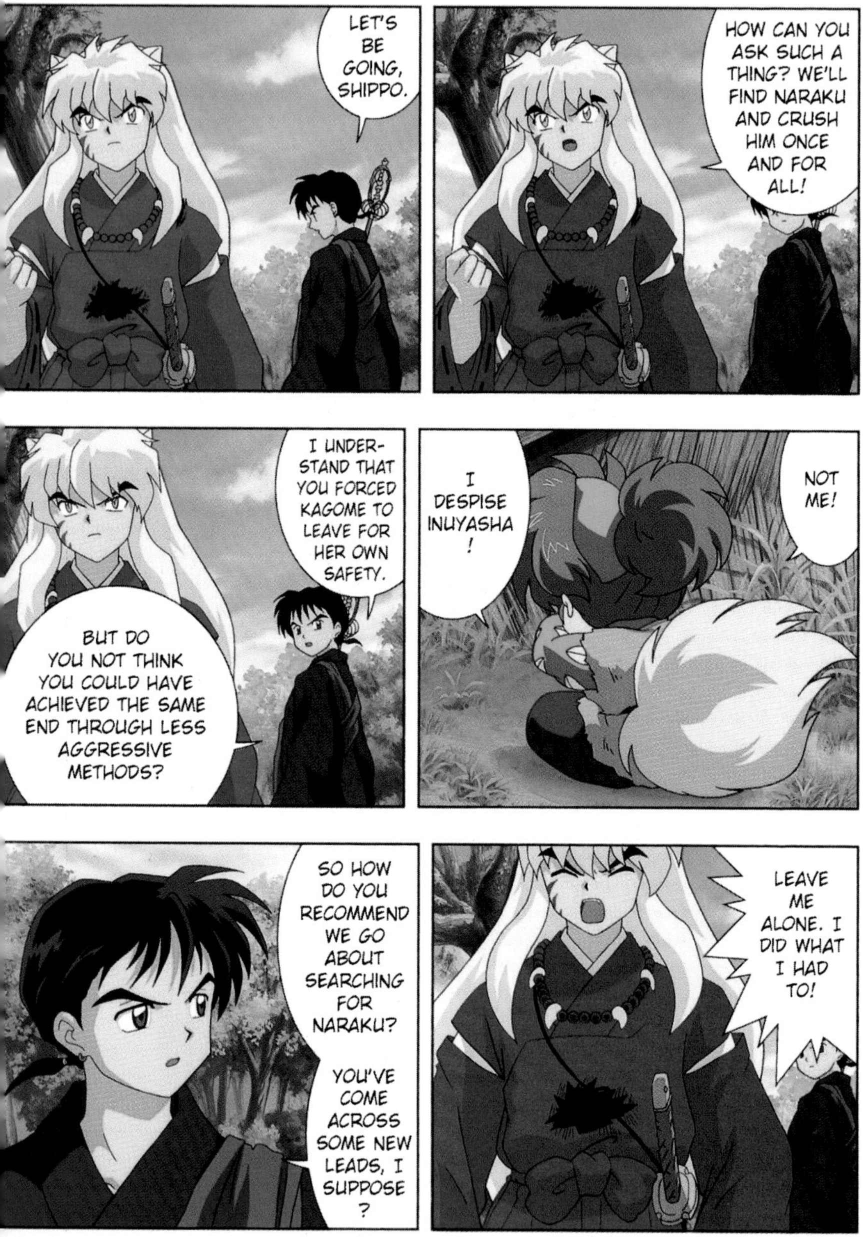
HOW CAN YOU ASK SUCH A THING? WE'LL FIND NARAKU AND CRUSH HIM ONCE AND FOR ALL!
LET'S BE GOING, SHIPPO.
NOT ME!
I DESPISE INUYASHA!
I UNDER-STAND THAT YOU FORCED KAGOME TO LEAVE FOR HER OWN SAFETY.
BUT DO YOU NOT THINK YOU COULD HAVE ACHIEVED THE SAME END THROUGH LESS AGGRESSIVE METHODS?
LEAVE ME ALONE. I DID WHAT I HAD TO!
SO HOW DO YOU RECOMMEND WE GO ABOUT SEARCHING FOR NARAKU?
YOU'VE COME ACROSS SOME NEW LEADS, I SUPPOSE?

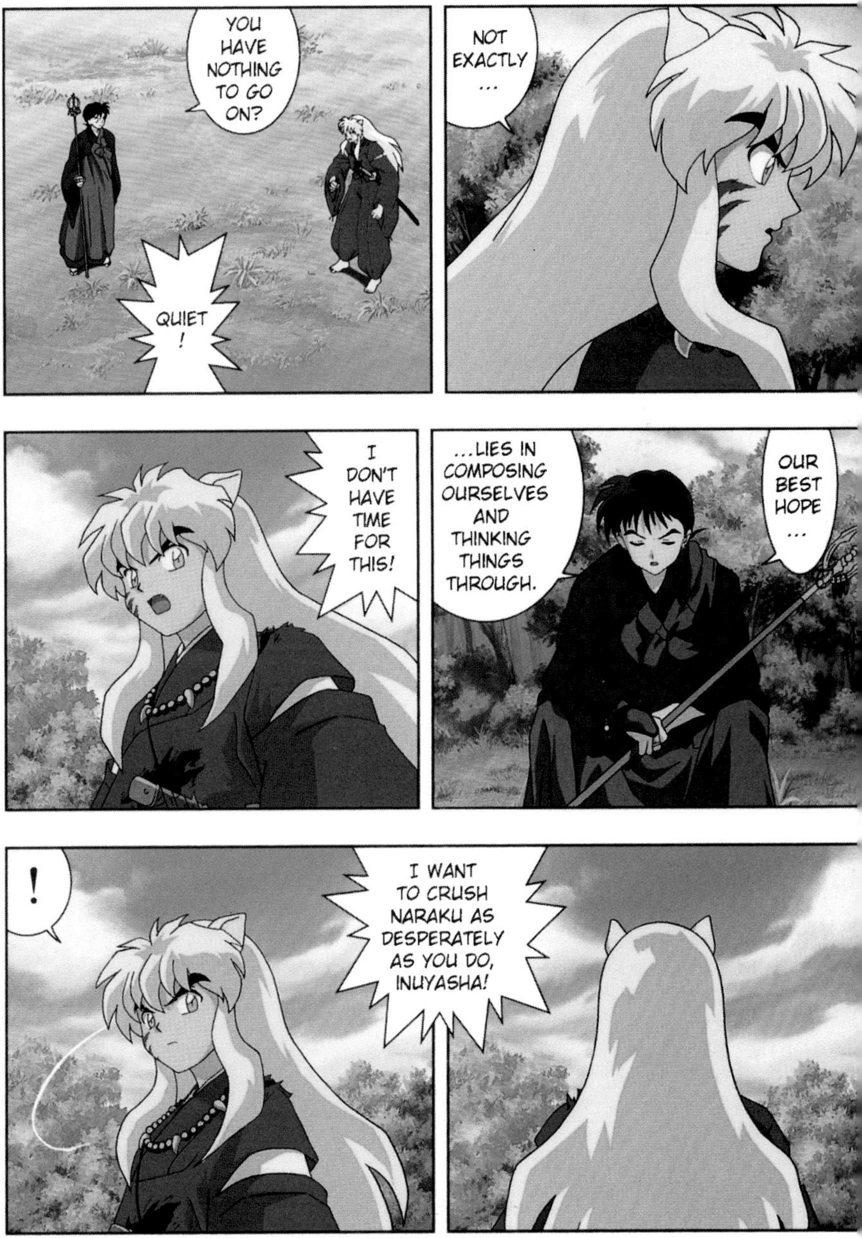
NOT EXACTLY ...
YOU HAVE NOTHING TO GO ON?
QUIET!
OUR BEST HOPE ...
...LIES IN COMPOSING OURSELVES AND THINKING THINGS THROUGH.
I DON'T HAVE TIME FOR THIS!
I WANT TO CRUSH NARAKU AS DESPERATELY AS YOU DO, INUYASHA!
!

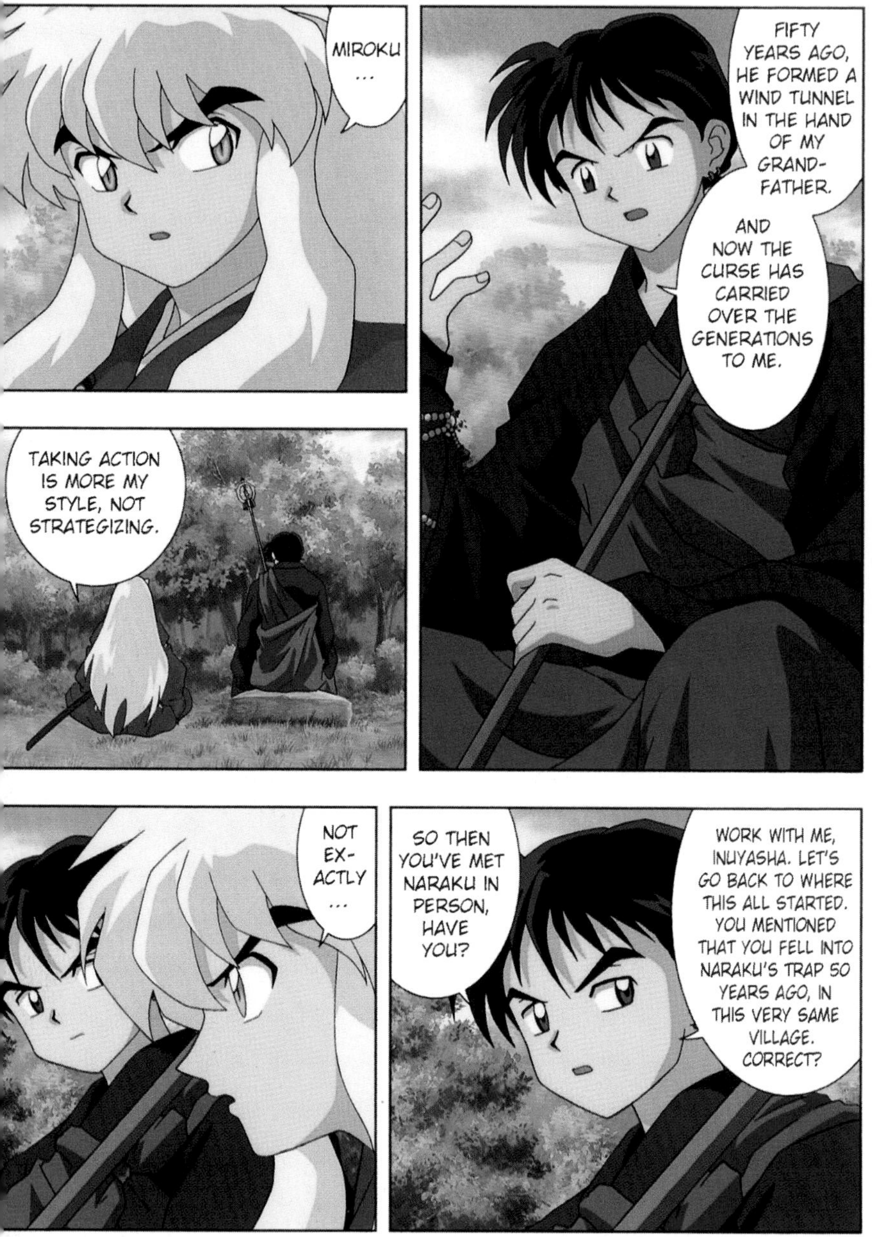
FIFTY YEARS AGO, HE FORMED A WIND TUNNEL IN THE HAND OF MY GRAND-FATHER.
AND NOW THE CURSE HAS CARRIED OVER THE GENERATIONS TO ME.
MIROKU ...
TAKING ACTION IS MORE MY STYLE, NOT STRATEGIZING.
WORK WITH ME, INUYASHA. LET'S GO BACK TO WHERE THIS ALL STARTED. YOU MENTIONED THAT YOU FELL INTO NARAKU'S TRAP 50 YEARS AGO, IN THIS VERY SAME VILLAGE. CORRECT?
SO THEN YOU'VE MET NARAKU IN PERSON, HAVE YOU?
NOT EX-ACTLY ...

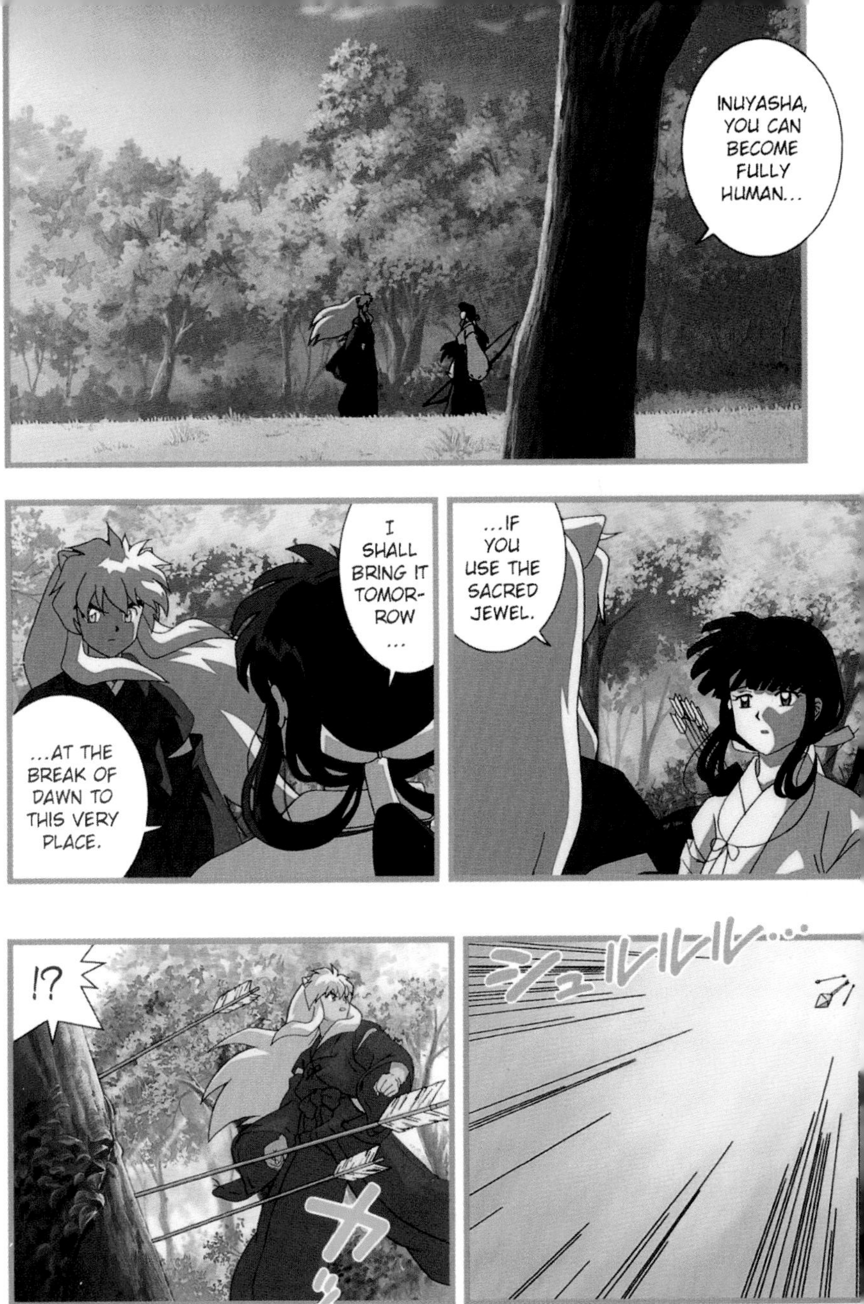
INUYASHA, YOU CAN BECOME FULLY HUMAN...
...IF YOU USE THE SACRED JEWEL.
I SHALL BRING IT TOMORROW...
...AT THE BREAK OF DAWN TO THIS VERY PLACE.
シュルルルル…
!?
カッ

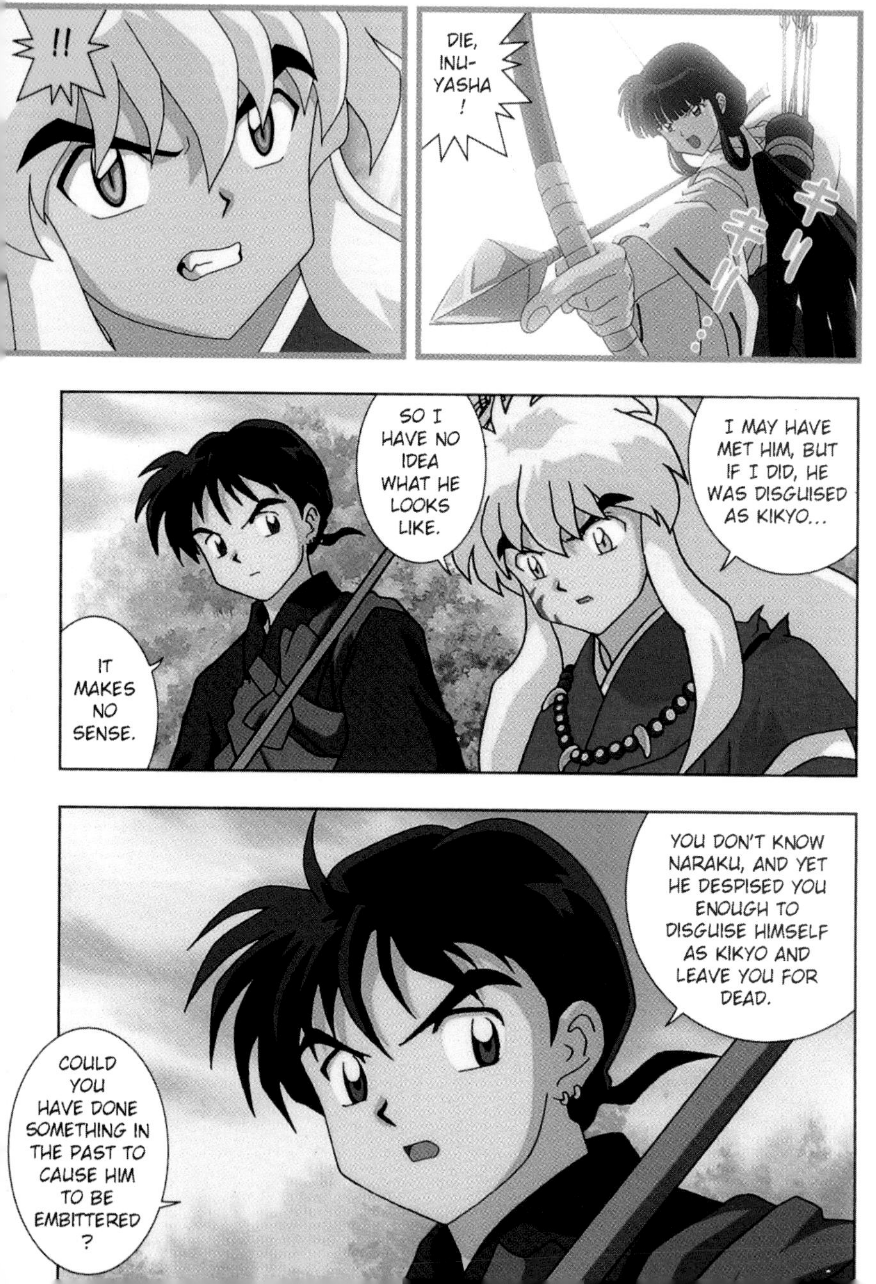
DIE, INU-YASHA!
キリキリ
!!
I MAY HAVE MET HIM, BUT IF I DID, HE WAS DISGUISED AS KIKYO...
SO I HAVE NO IDEA WHAT HE LOOKS LIKE.
IT MAKES NO SENSE.
YOU DON'T KNOW NARAKU, AND YET HE DESPISED YOU ENOUGH TO DISGUISE HIMSELF AS KIKYO AND LEAVE YOU FOR DEAD.
COULD YOU HAVE DONE SOMETHING IN THE PAST TO CAUSE HIM TO BE EMBITTERED?

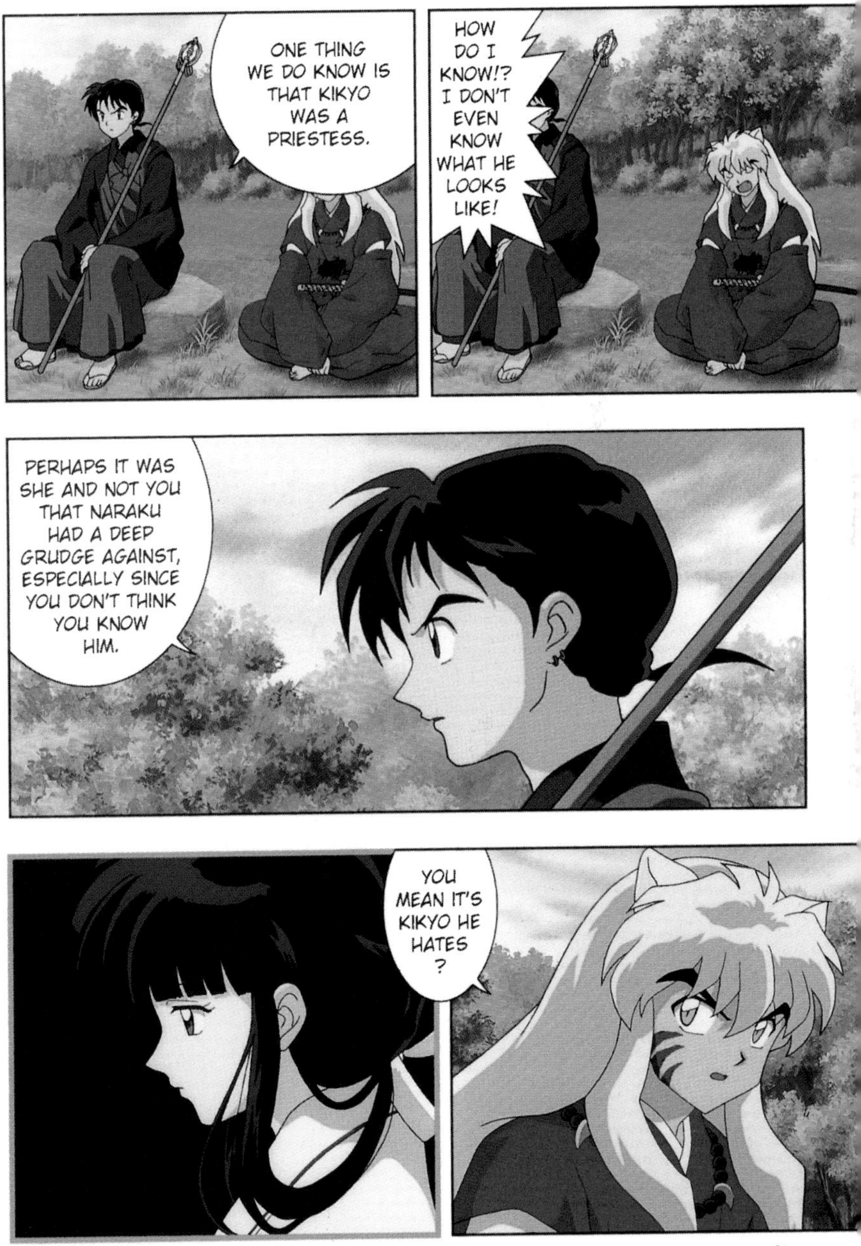
HOW DO I KNOW!? I DON'T EVEN KNOW WHAT HE LOOKS LIKE!
ONE THING WE DO KNOW IS THAT KIKYO WAS A PRIESTESS.
PERHAPS IT WAS SHE AND NOT YOU THAT NARAKU HAD A DEEP GRUDGE AGAINST, ESPECIALLY SINCE YOU DON'T THINK YOU KNOW HIM.
YOU MEAN IT'S KIKYO HE HATES ?

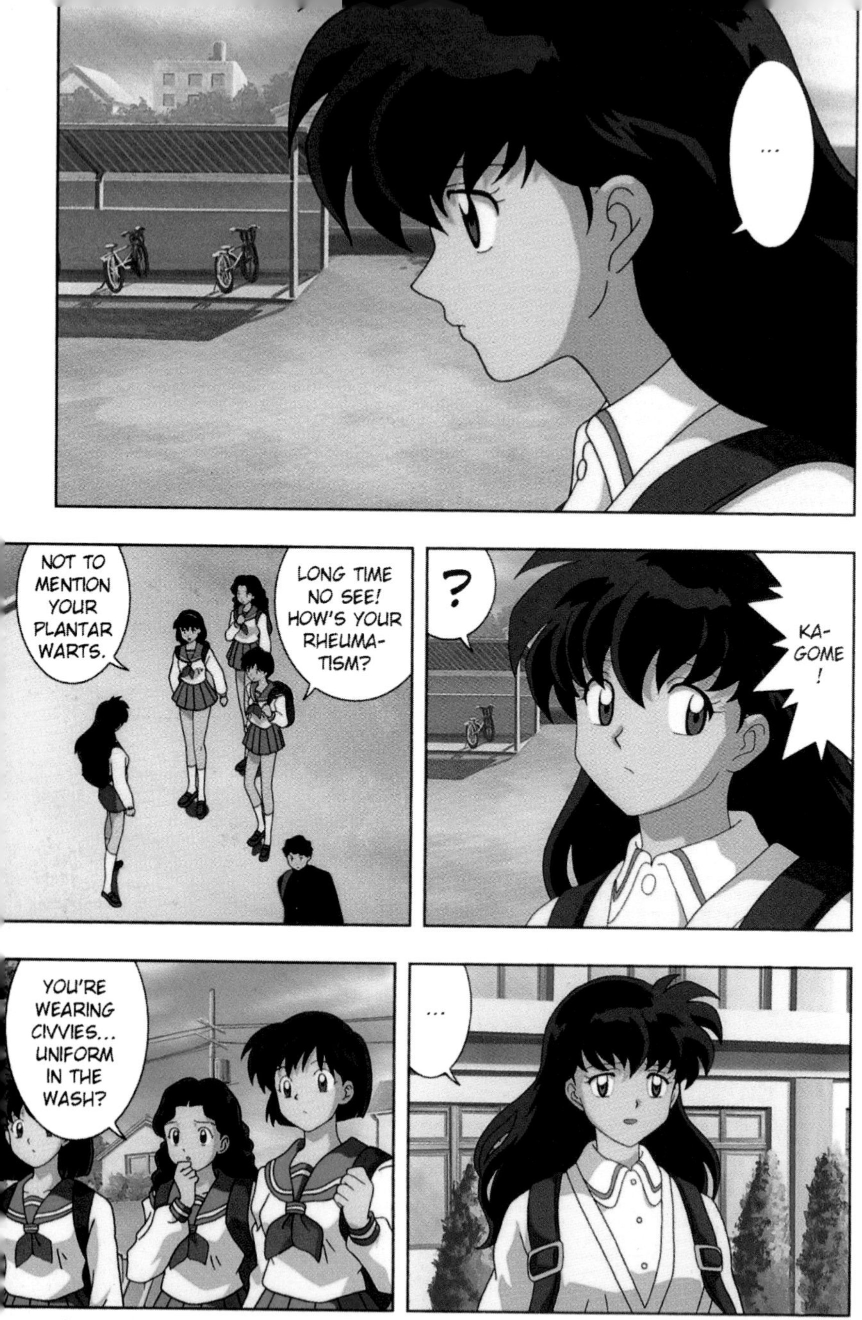
...
KA-GOME!
?
LONG TIME NO SEE! HOW'S YOUR RHEUMA-TISM?
NOT TO MENTION YOUR PLANTAR WARTS.
...
YOU'RE WEARING CIVVIES... UNIFORM IN THE WASH?

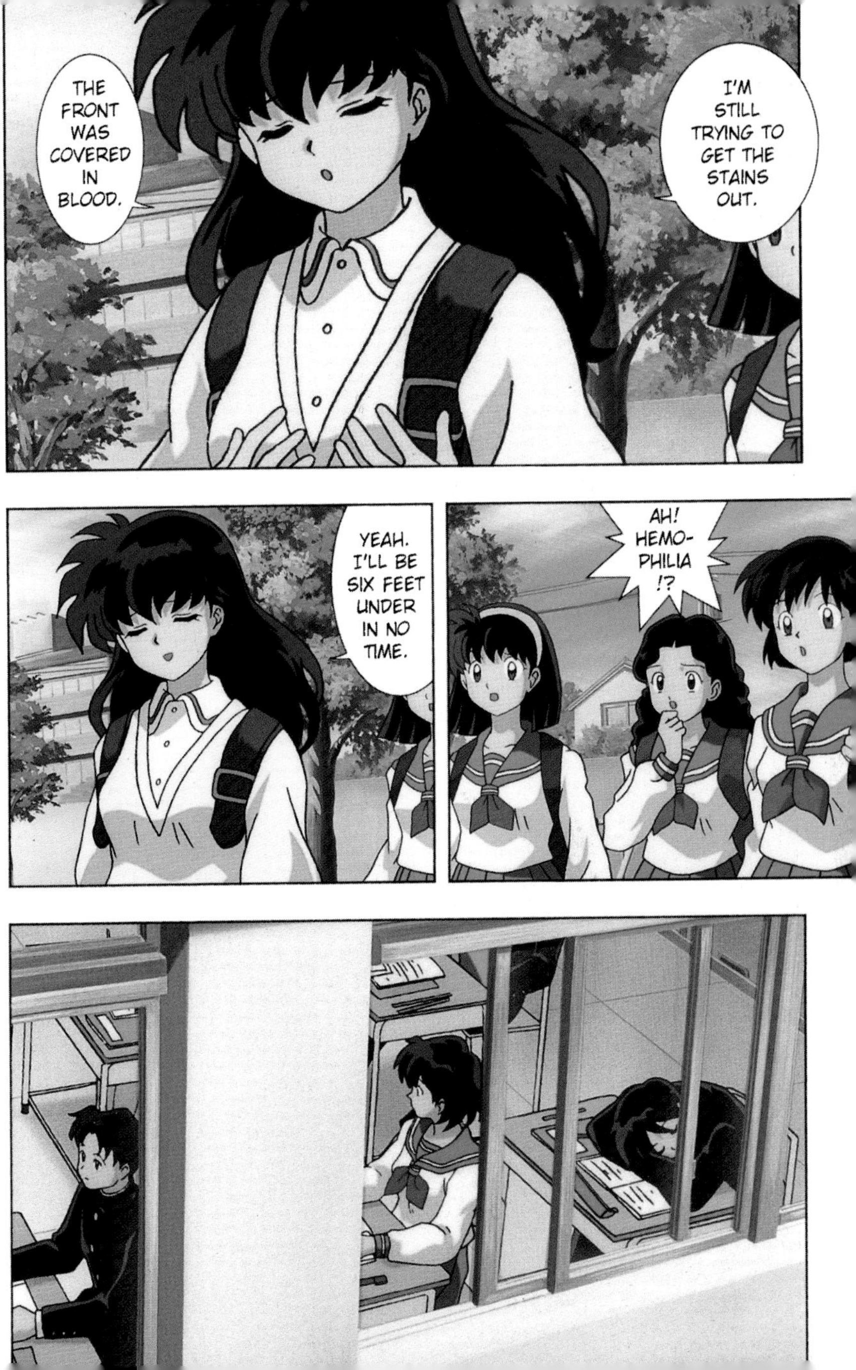
I'M STILL TRYING TO GET THE STAINS OUT.
THE FRONT WAS COVERED IN BLOOD.
AH! HEMO-PHILIA!?
YEAH. I'LL BE SIX FEET UNDER IN NO TIME.

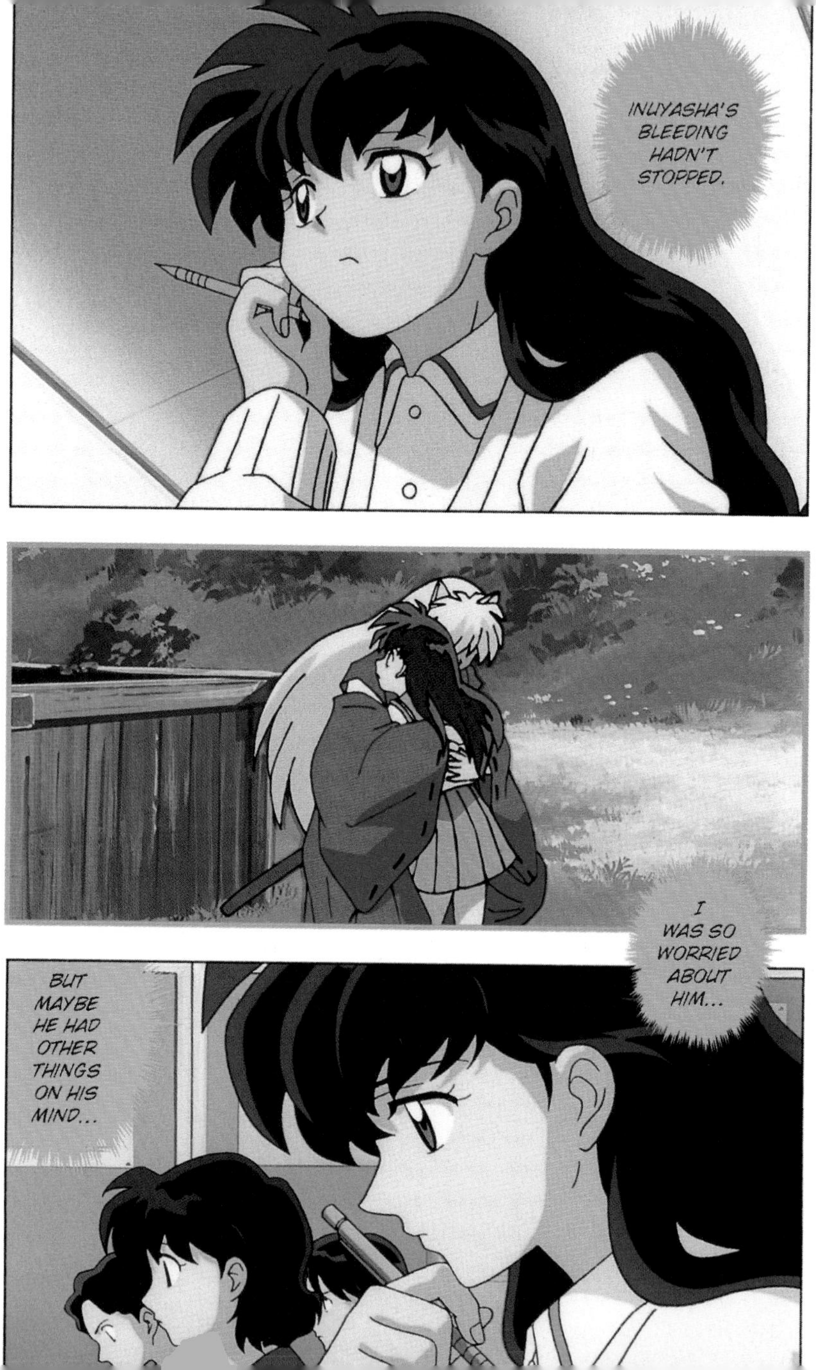
INUYASHA'S BLEEDING HADN'T STOPPED.
I WAS SO WORRIED ABOUT HIM...
BUT MAYBE HE HAD OTHER THINGS ON HIS MIND...

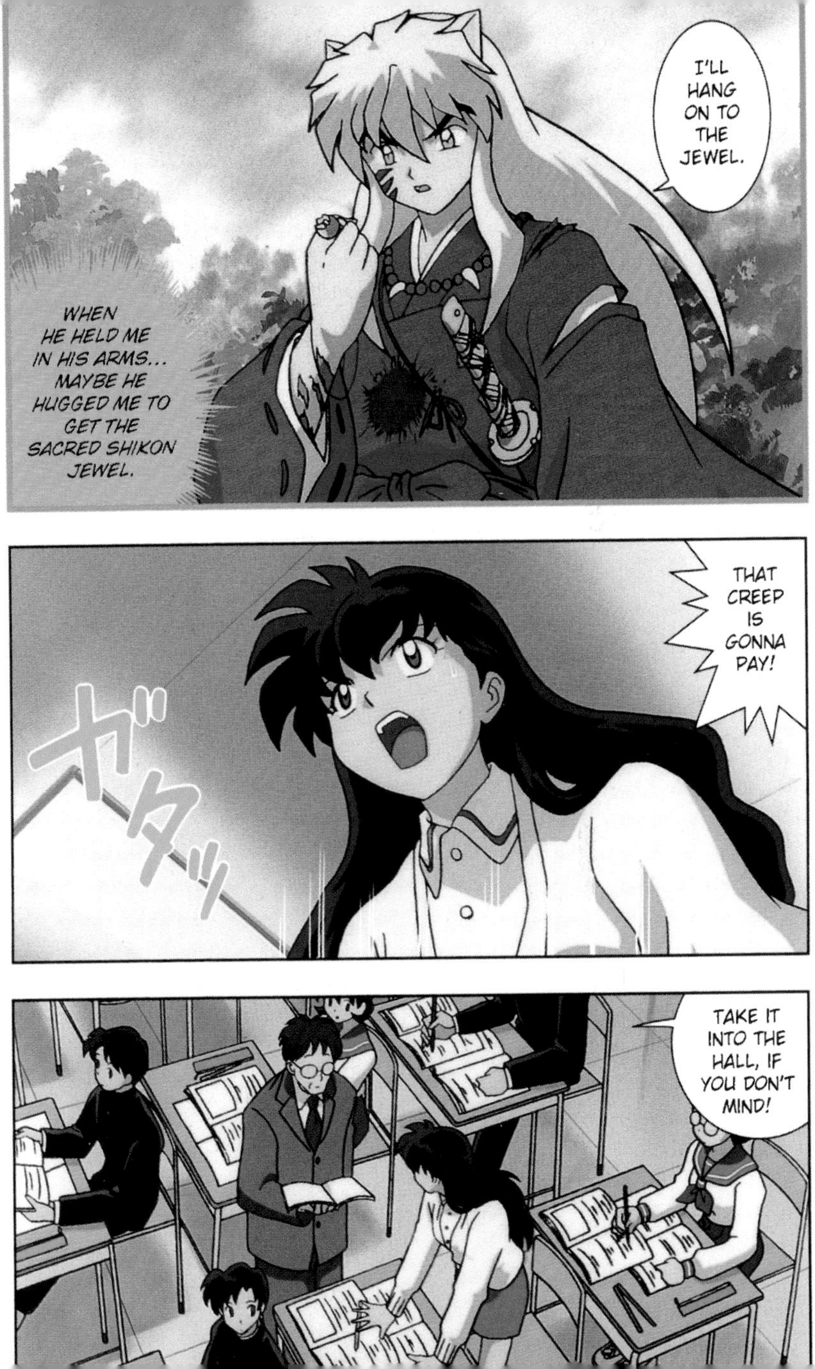
I'LL HANG ON TO THE JEWEL.
WHEN HE HELD ME IN HIS ARMS... MAYBE HE HUGGED ME TO GET THE SACRED SHIKON JEWEL.
THAT CREEP IS GONNA PAY!
ガタッ
TAKE IT INTO THE HALL, IF YOU DON'T MIND!

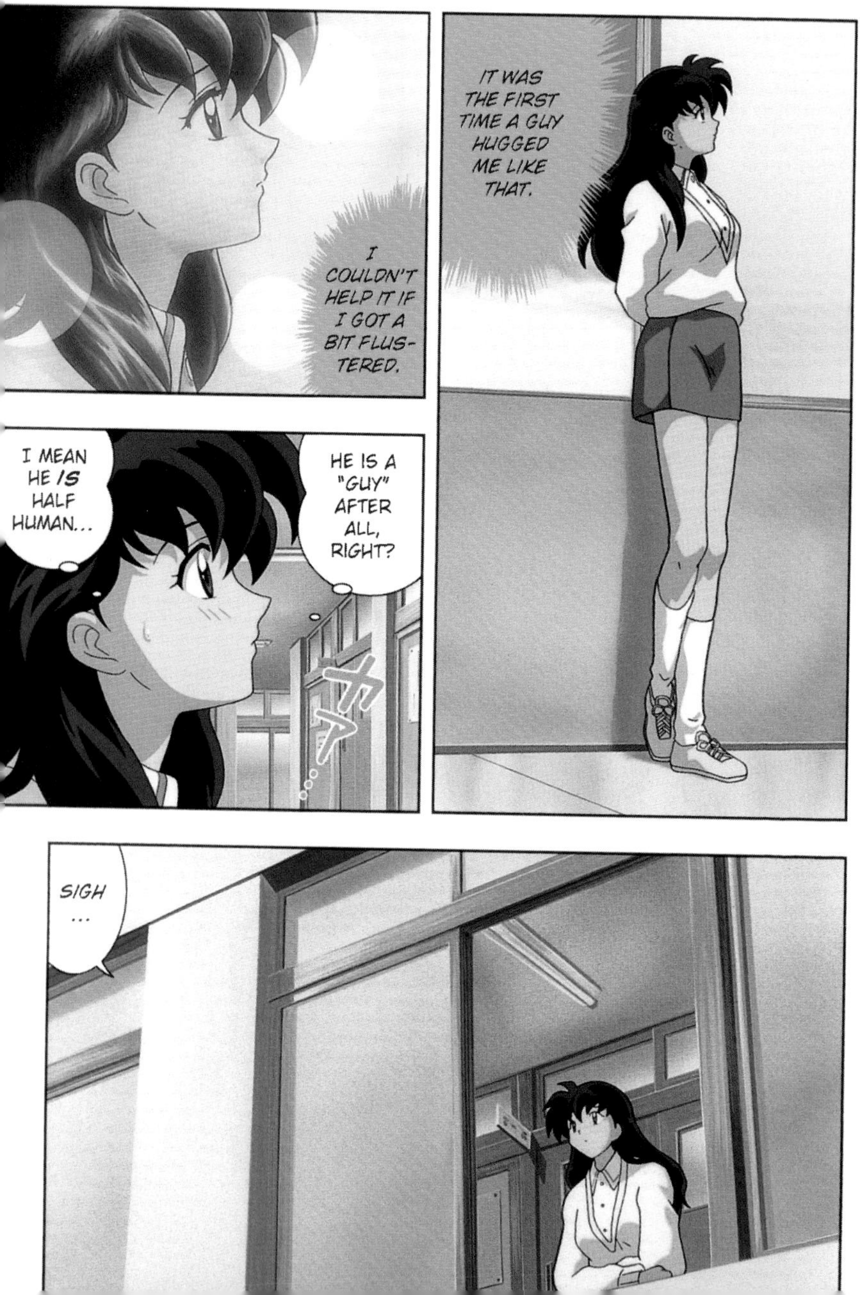
IT WAS THE FIRST TIME A GUY HUGGED ME LIKE THAT.
I COULDN'T HELP IT IF I GOT A BIT FLUS-TERED.
HE IS A "GUY" AFTER ALL, RIGHT?
I MEAN HE *IS* HALF HUMAN...
SIGH ...

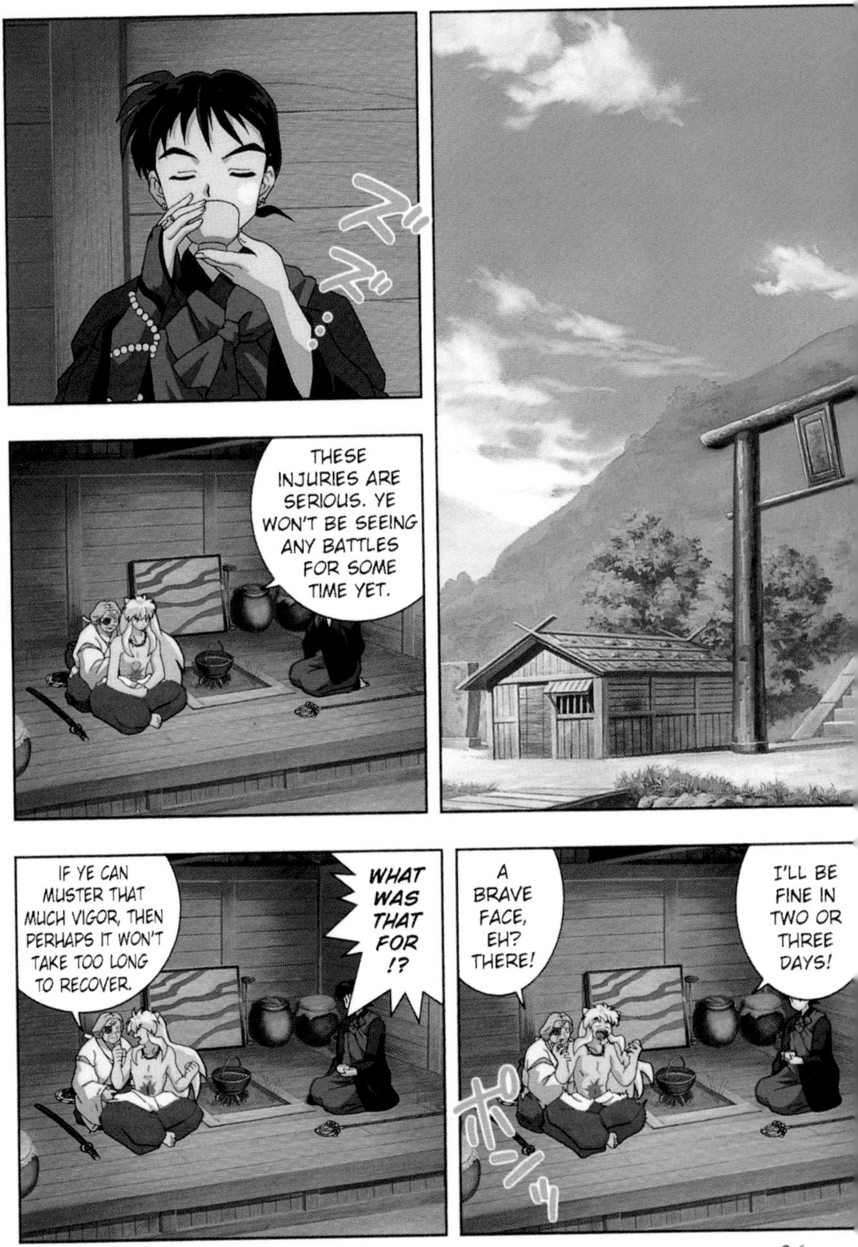
THESE INJURIES ARE SERIOUS. YE WON'T BE SEEING ANY BATTLES FOR SOME TIME YET.
I'LL BE FINE IN TWO OR THREE DAYS!
A BRAVE FACE, EH? THERE!
WHAT WAS THAT FOR!?
IF YE CAN MUSTER THAT MUCH VIGOR, THEN PERHAPS IT WON'T TAKE TOO LONG TO RECOVER.

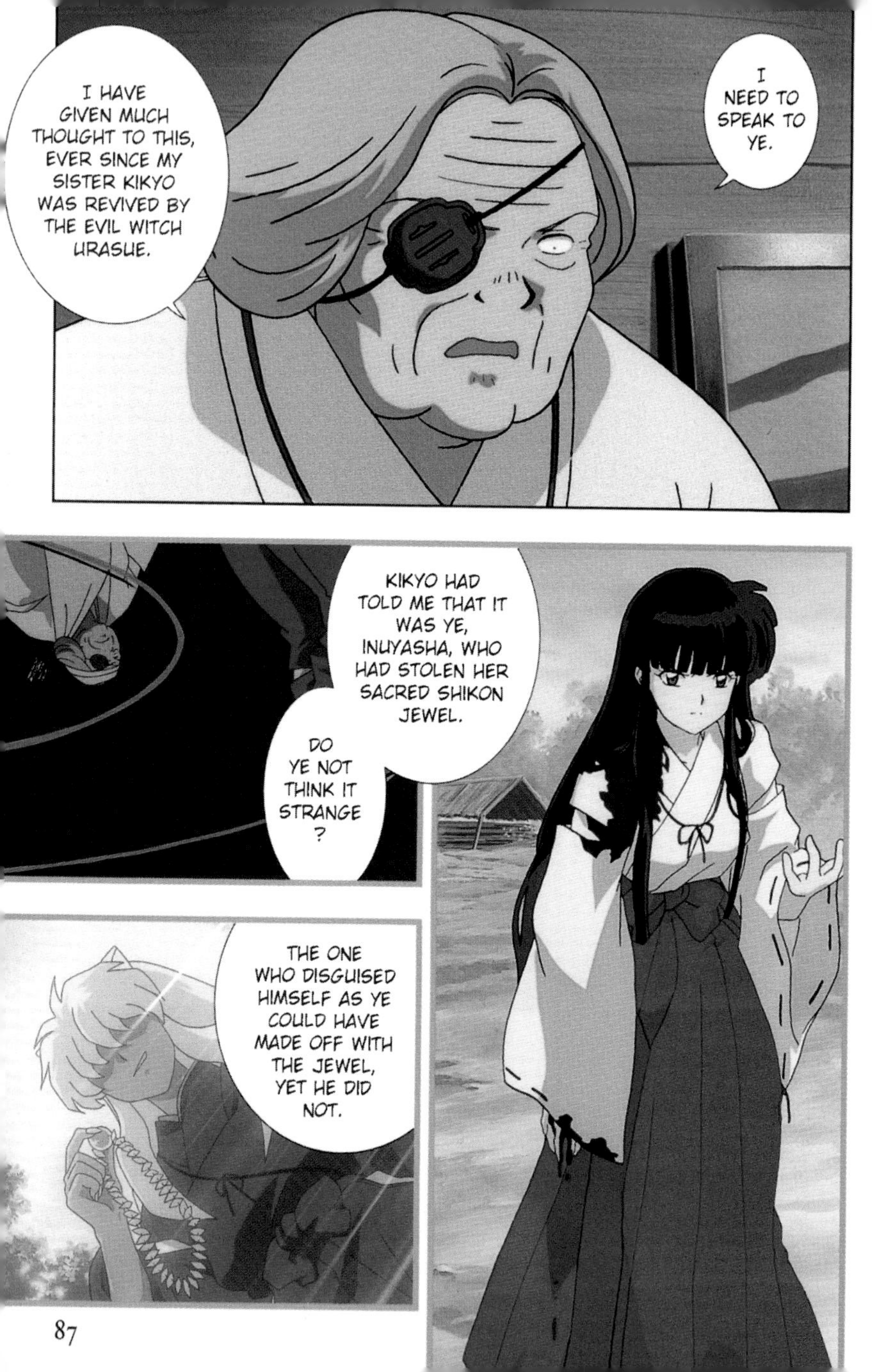
I NEED TO SPEAK TO YE.
I HAVE GIVEN MUCH THOUGHT TO THIS, EVER SINCE MY SISTER KIKYO WAS REVIVED BY THE EVIL WITCH URASUE.
KIKYO HAD TOLD ME THAT IT WAS YE, INUYASHA, WHO HAD STOLEN HER SACRED SHIKON JEWEL.
DO YE NOT THINK IT STRANGE ?
THE ONE WHO DISGUISED HIMSELF AS YE COULD HAVE MADE OFF WITH THE JEWEL, YET HE DID NOT.

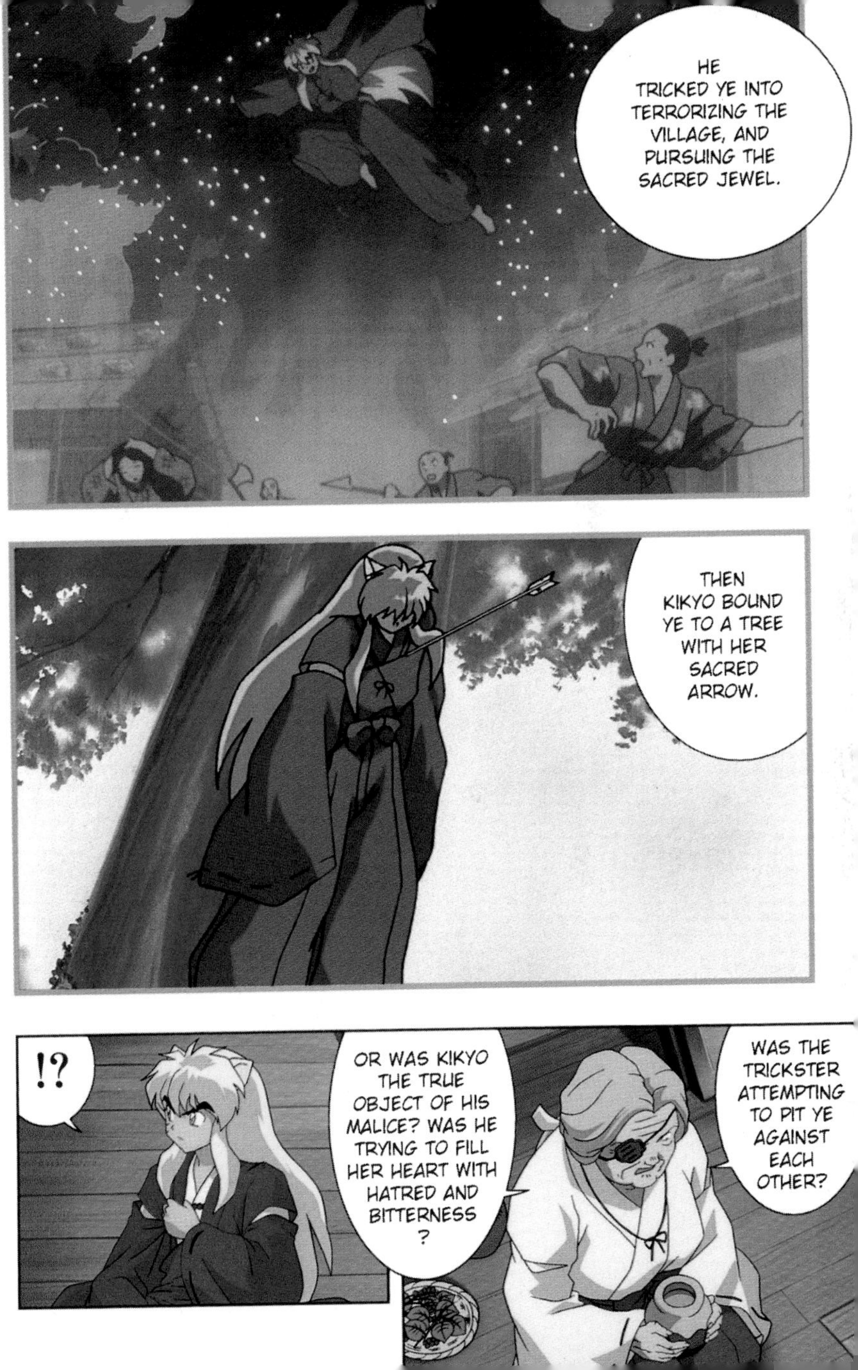
HE TRICKED YE INTO TERRORIZING THE VILLAGE, AND PURSUING THE SACRED JEWEL.
THEN KIKYO BOUND YE TO A TREE WITH HER SACRED ARROW.
WAS THE TRICKSTER ATTEMPTING TO PIT YE AGAINST EACH OTHER?
OR WAS KIKYO THE TRUE OBJECT OF HIS MALICE? WAS HE TRYING TO FILL HER HEART WITH HATRED AND BITTERNESS?
!?

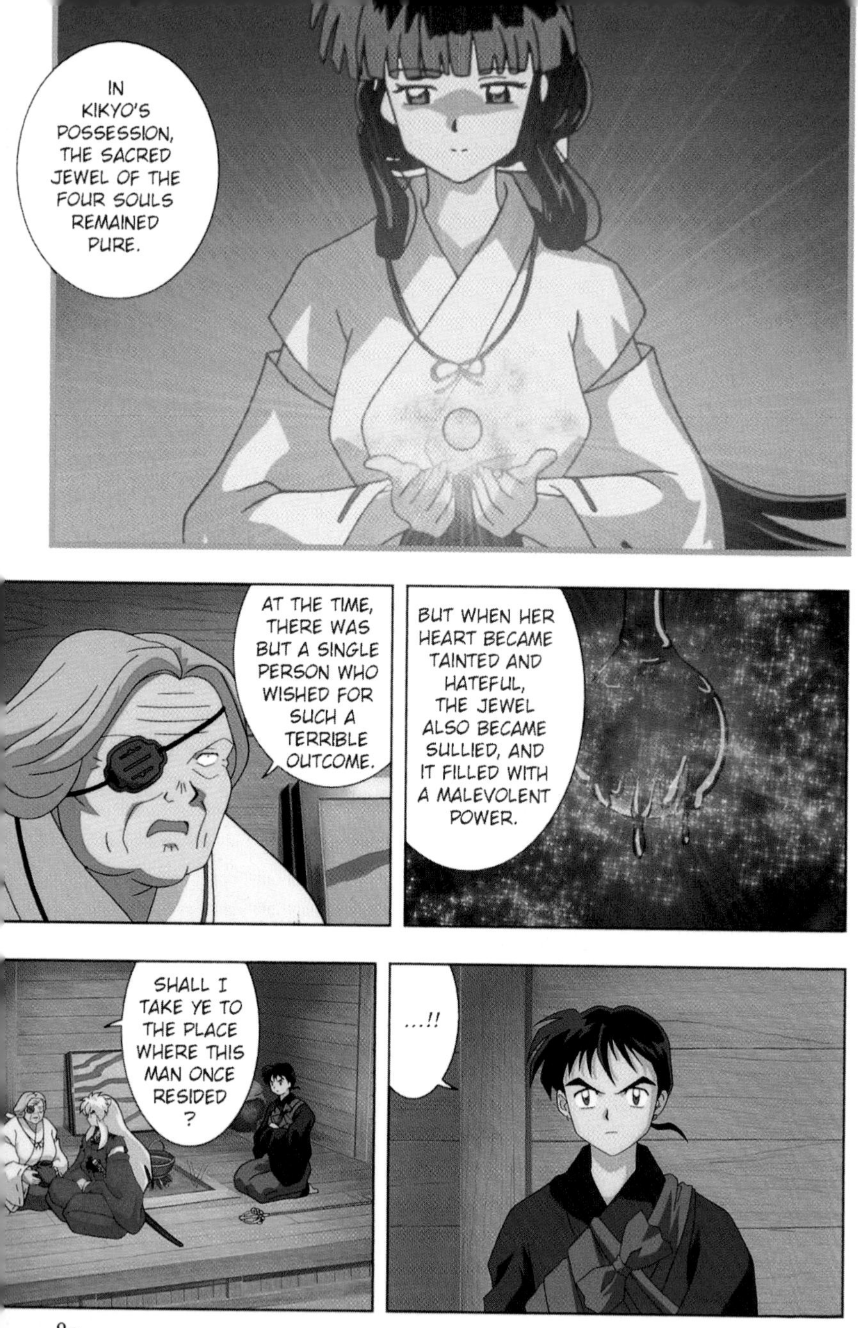
IN KIKYO'S POSSESSION, THE SACRED JEWEL OF THE FOUR SOULS REMAINED PURE.
BUT WHEN HER HEART BECAME TAINTED AND HATEFUL, THE JEWEL ALSO BECAME SULLIED, AND IT FILLED WITH A MALEVOLENT POWER.
AT THE TIME, THERE WAS BUT A SINGLE PERSON WHO WISHED FOR SUCH A TERRIBLE OUTCOME.
...!!
SHALL I TAKE YE TO THE PLACE WHERE THIS MAN ONCE RESIDED ?

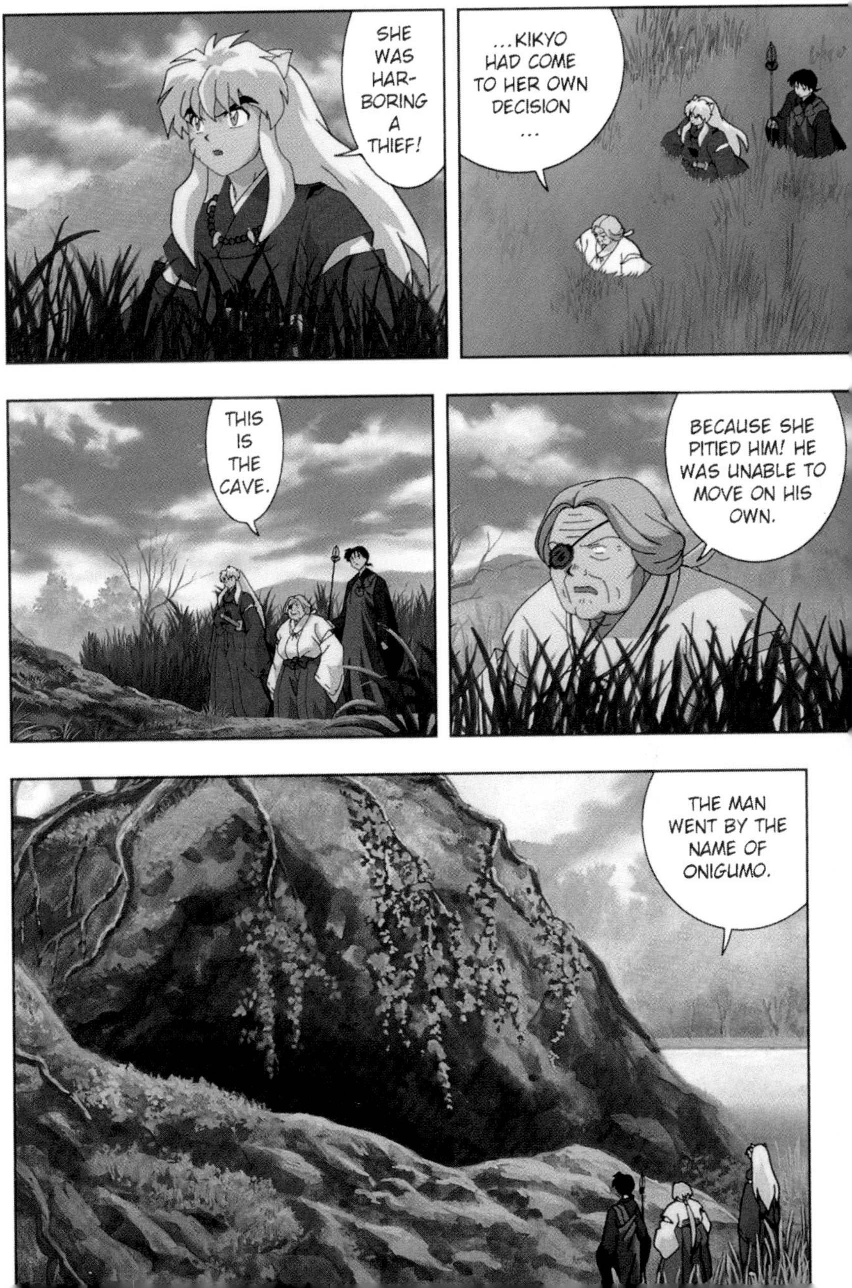
...KIKYO HAD COME TO HER OWN DECISION ...
SHE WAS HAR-BORING A THIEF!
BECAUSE SHE PITIED HIM! HE WAS UNABLE TO MOVE ON HIS OWN.
THIS IS THE CAVE.
THE MAN WENT BY THE NAME OF ONIGUMO.

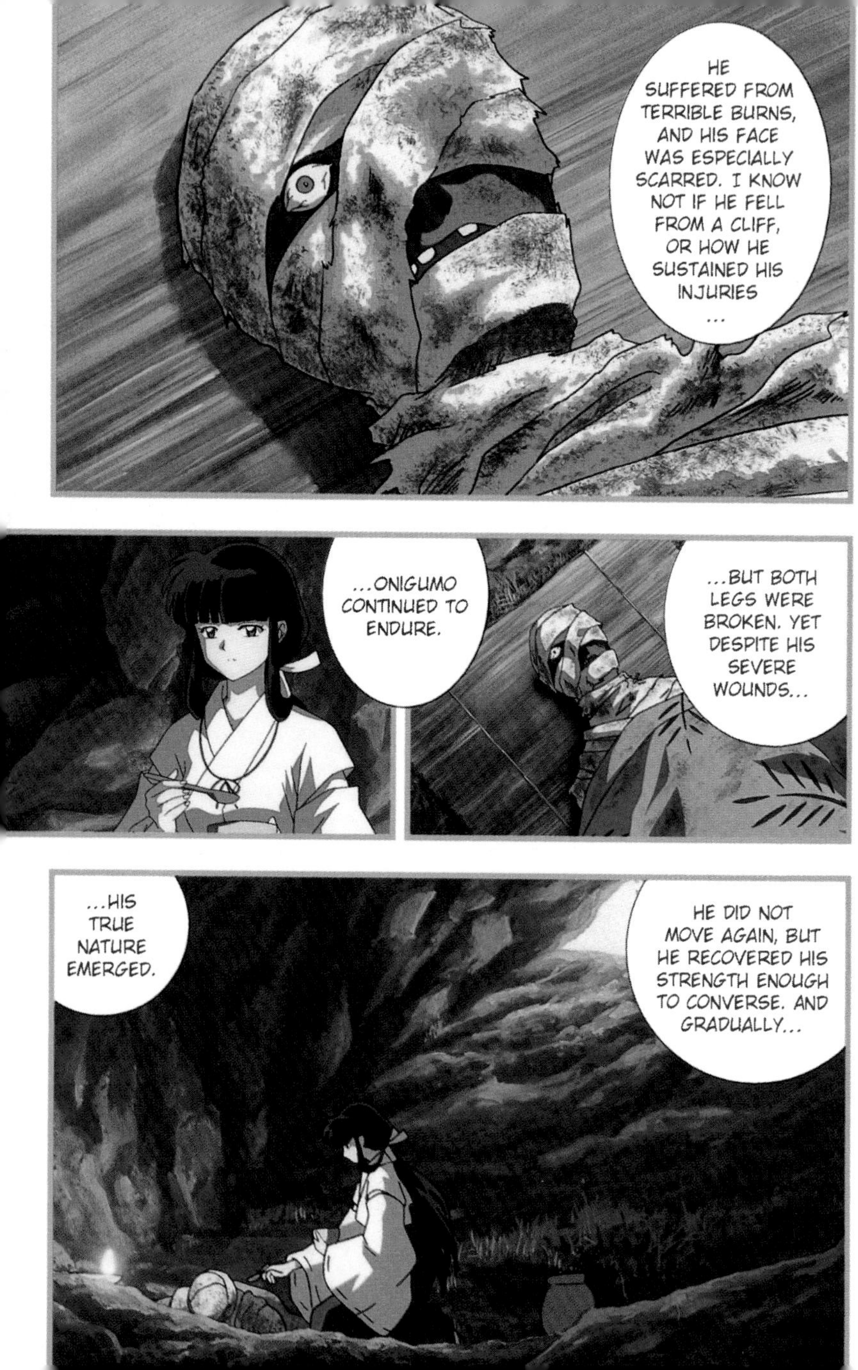
HE SUFFERED FROM TERRIBLE BURNS, AND HIS FACE WAS ESPECIALLY SCARRED. I KNOW NOT IF HE FELL FROM A CLIFF, OR HOW HE SUSTAINED HIS INJURIES ...
...BUT BOTH LEGS WERE BROKEN. YET DESPITE HIS SEVERE WOUNDS...
...ONIGUMO CONTINUED TO ENDURE.
HE DID NOT MOVE AGAIN, BUT HE RECOVERED HIS STRENGTH ENOUGH TO CONVERSE. AND GRADUALLY...
...HIS TRUE NATURE EMERGED.

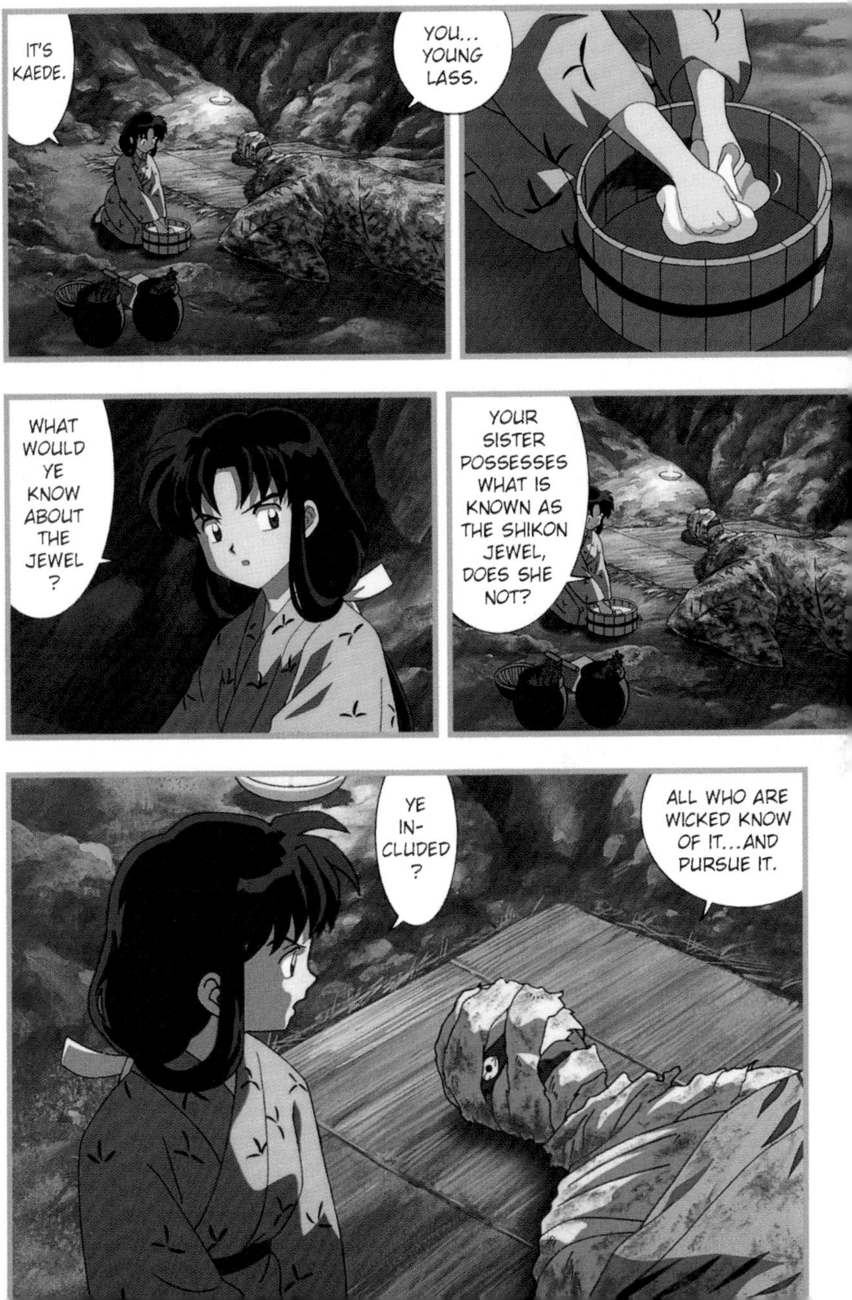
YOU... YOUNG LASS.
IT'S KAEDE.
YOUR SISTER POSSESSES WHAT IS KNOWN AS THE SHIKON JEWEL, DOES SHE NOT?
WHAT WOULD YE KNOW ABOUT THE JEWEL?
ALL WHO ARE WICKED KNOW OF IT...AND PURSUE IT.
YE IN-CLUDED?

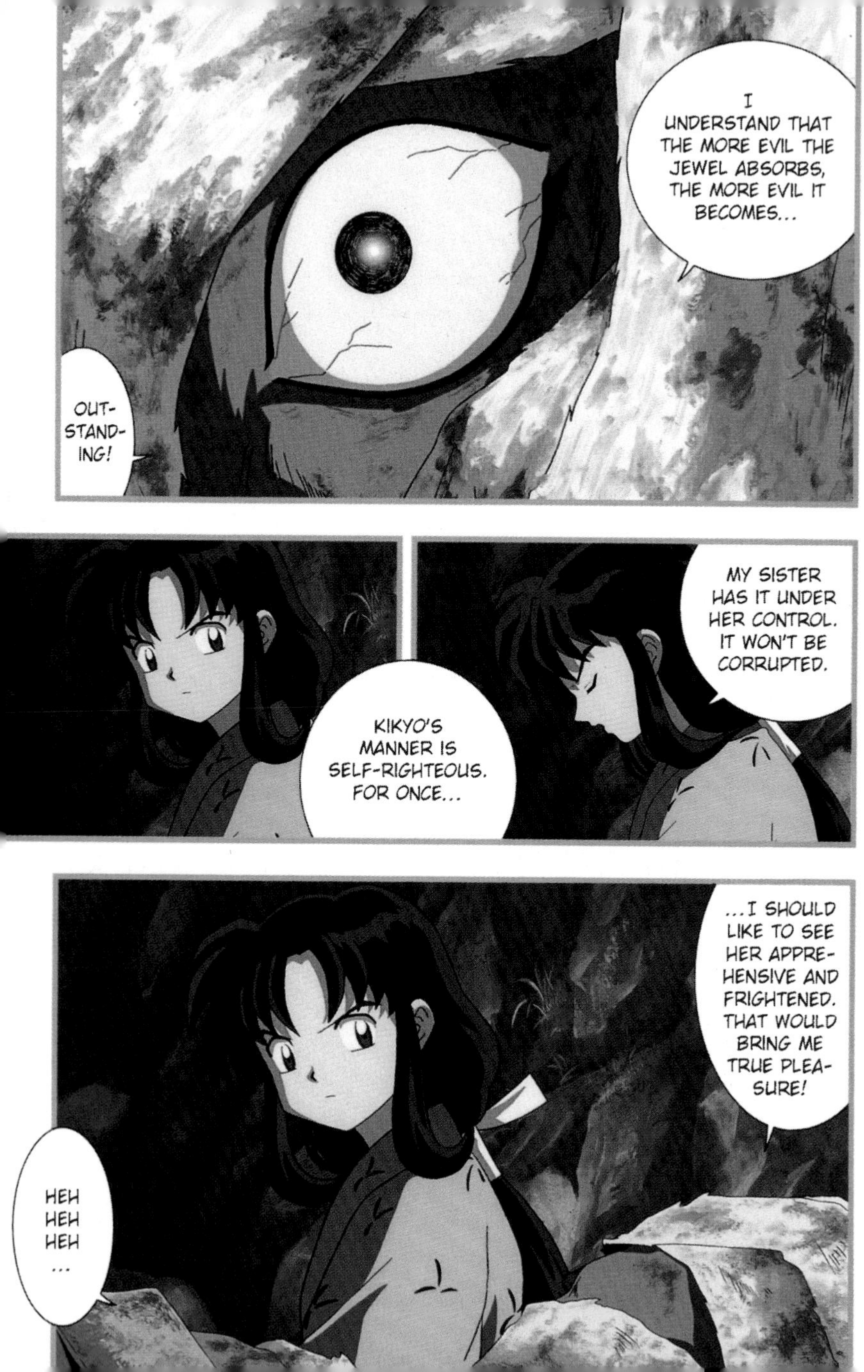
I UNDERSTAND THAT THE MORE EVIL THE JEWEL ABSORBS, THE MORE EVIL IT BECOMES...
OUT-STANDING!
MY SISTER HAS IT UNDER HER CONTROL. IT WON'T BE CORRUPTED.
KIKYO'S MANNER IS SELF-RIGHTEOUS. FOR ONCE...
...I SHOULD LIKE TO SEE HER APPRE-HENSIVE AND FRIGHTENED. THAT WOULD BRING ME TRUE PLEA-SURE!
HEH HEH HEH ...

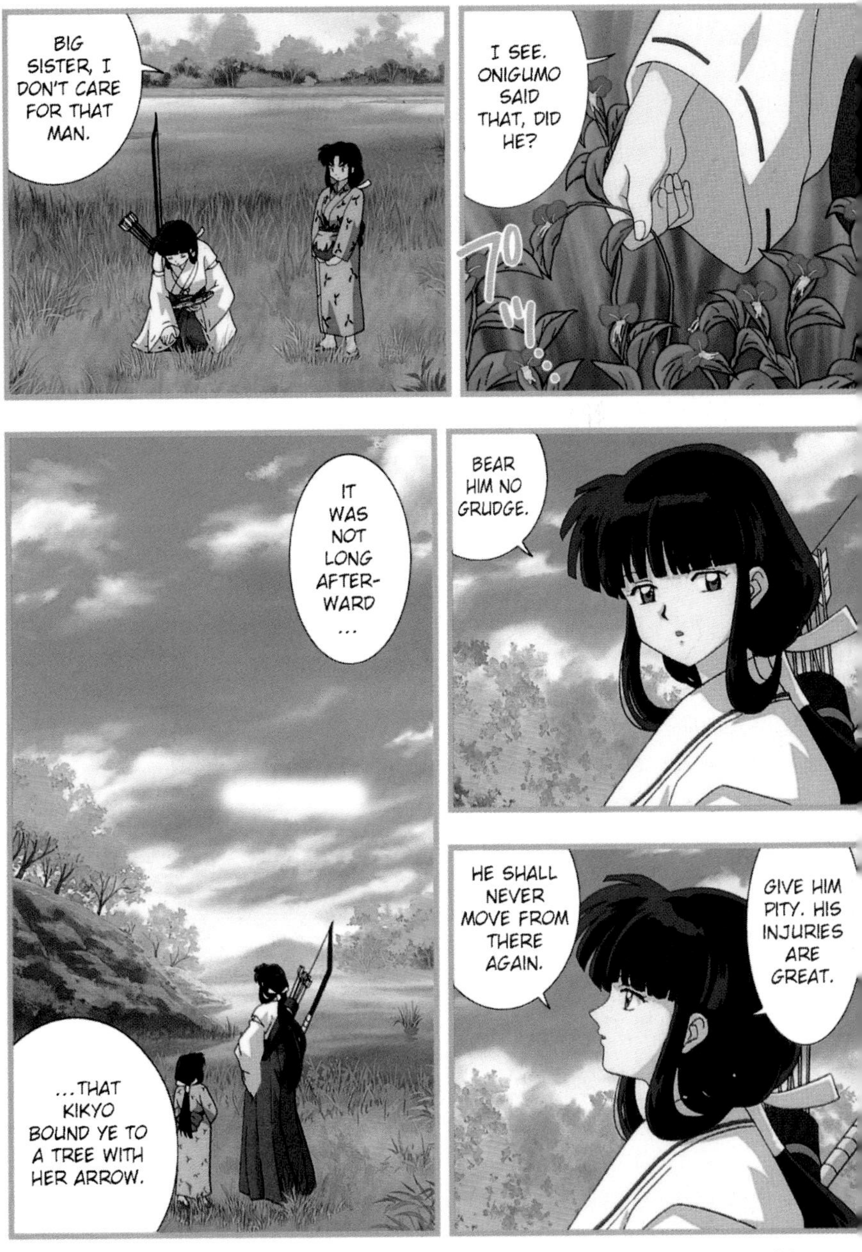
I SEE. ONIGUMO SAID THAT, DID HE?
BIG SISTER, I DON'T CARE FOR THAT MAN.
BEAR HIM NO GRUDGE.
GIVE HIM PITY. HIS INJURIES ARE GREAT.
HE SHALL NEVER MOVE FROM THERE AGAIN.
IT WAS NOT LONG AFTER-WARD ...
...THAT KIKYO BOUND YE TO A TREE WITH HER ARROW.

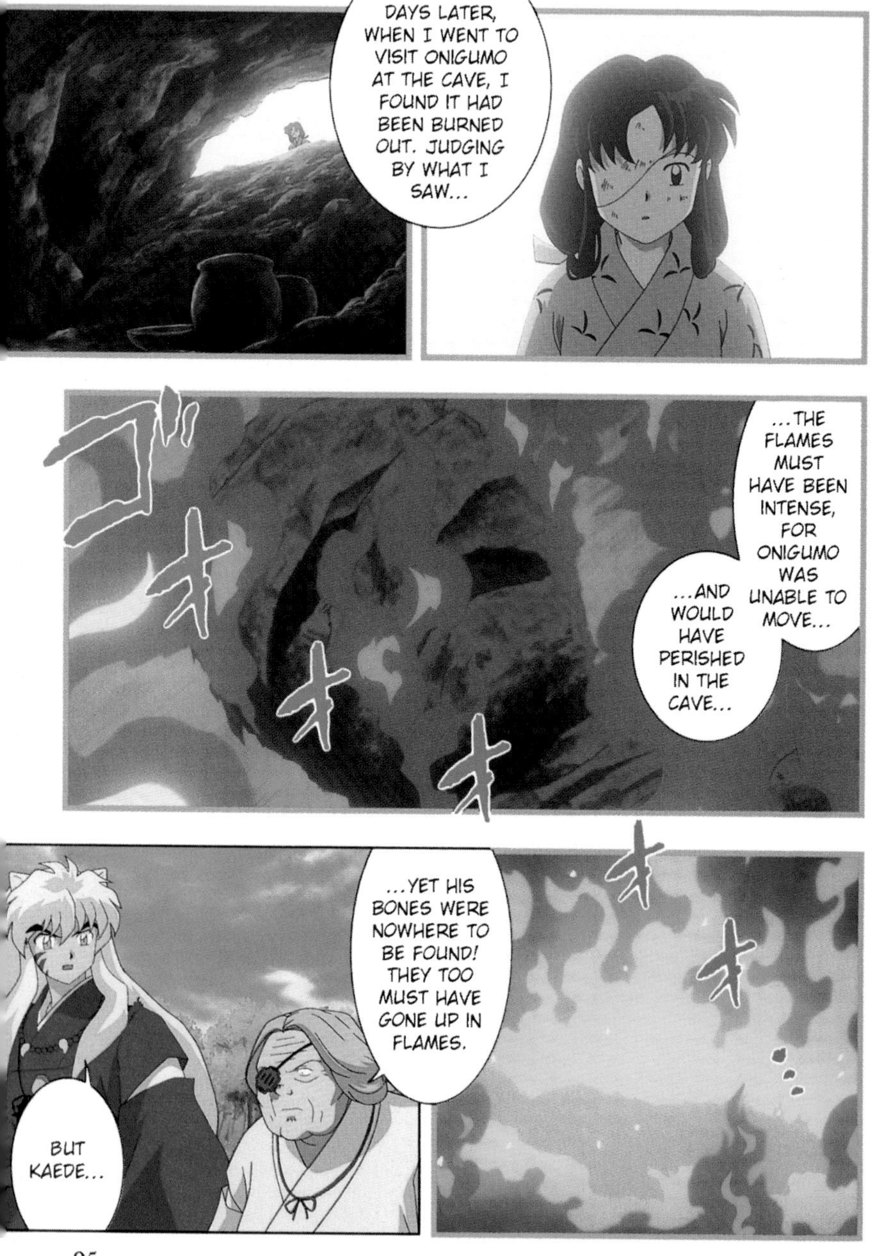
SEVERAL DAYS LATER, WHEN I WENT TO VISIT ONIGUMO AT THE CAVE, I FOUND IT HAD BEEN BURNED OUT. JUDGING BY WHAT I SAW...
ゴオオオ
...THE FLAMES MUST HAVE BEEN INTENSE, FOR ONIGUMO WAS UNABLE TO MOVE...
...AND WOULD HAVE PERISHED IN THE CAVE...
オオ
...YET HIS BONES WERE NOWHERE TO BE FOUND! THEY TOO MUST HAVE GONE UP IN FLAMES.
BUT KAEDE...

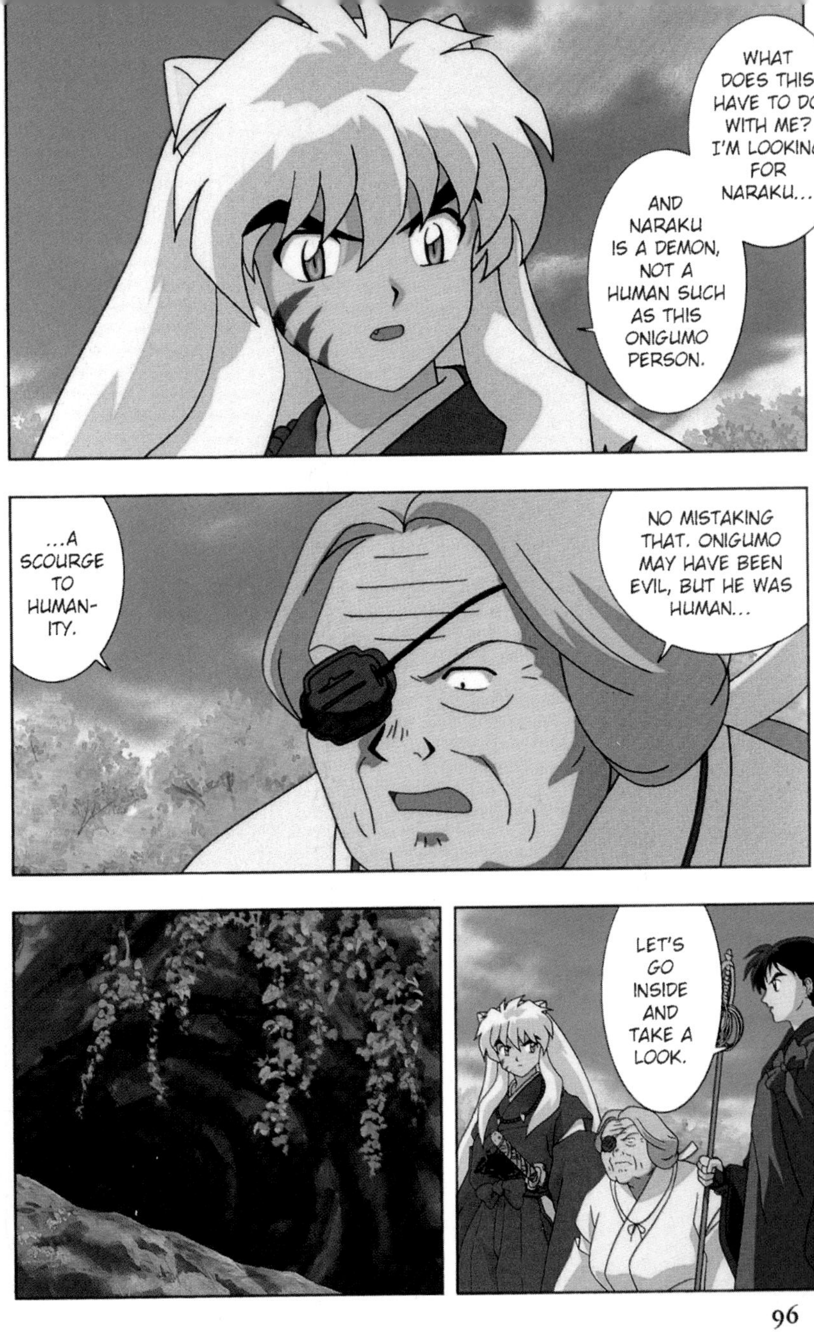
WHAT DOES THIS HAVE TO DO WITH ME? I'M LOOKING FOR NARAKU...
AND NARAKU IS A DEMON, NOT A HUMAN SUCH AS THIS ONIGUMO PERSON.
NO MISTAKING THAT. ONIGUMO MAY HAVE BEEN EVIL, BUT HE WAS HUMAN...
...A SCOURGE TO HUMAN-ITY.
LET'S GO INSIDE AND TAKE A LOOK.

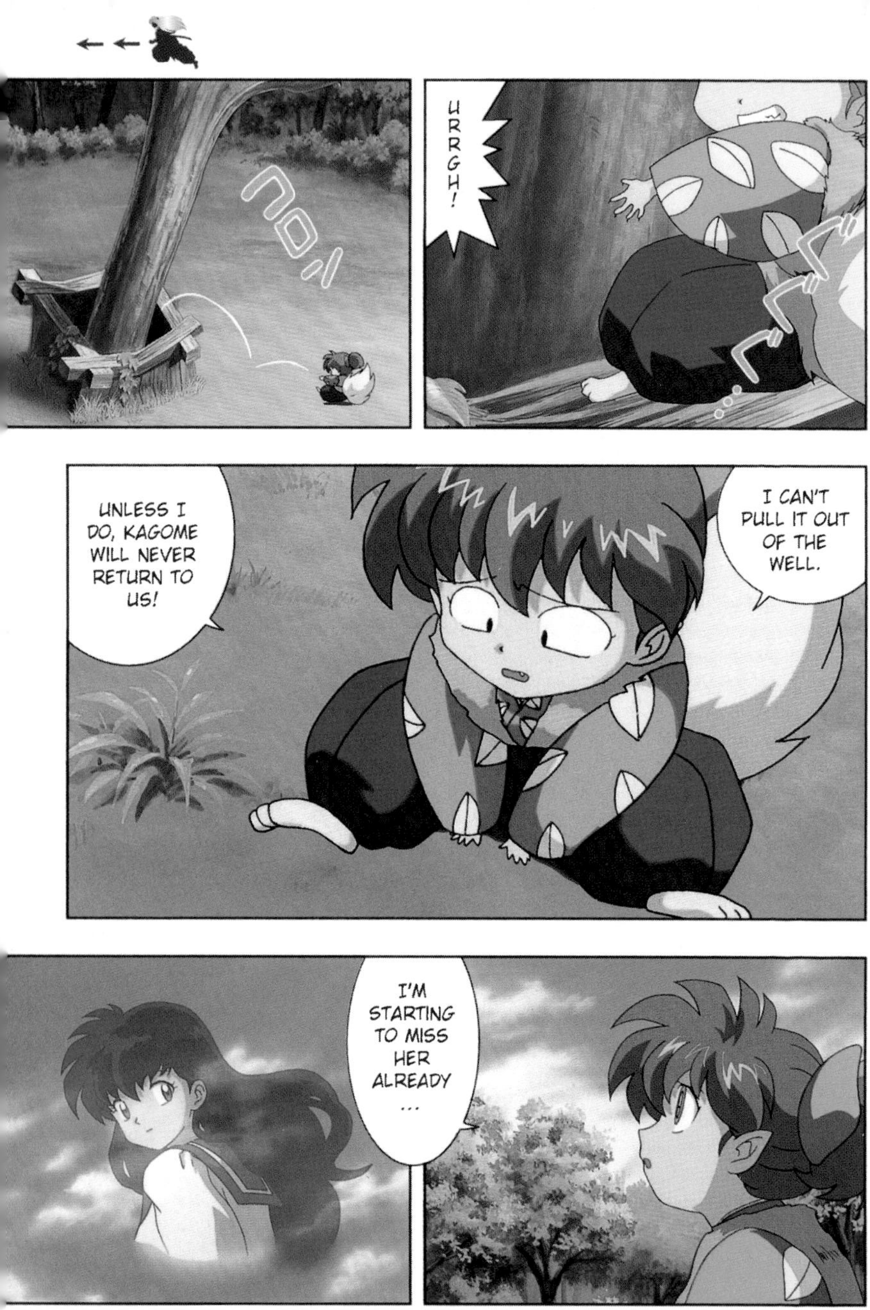
URRGH!
I CAN'T PULL IT OUT OF THE WELL.
UNLESS I DO, KAGOME WILL NEVER RETURN TO US!
I'M STARTING TO MISS HER ALREADY ...

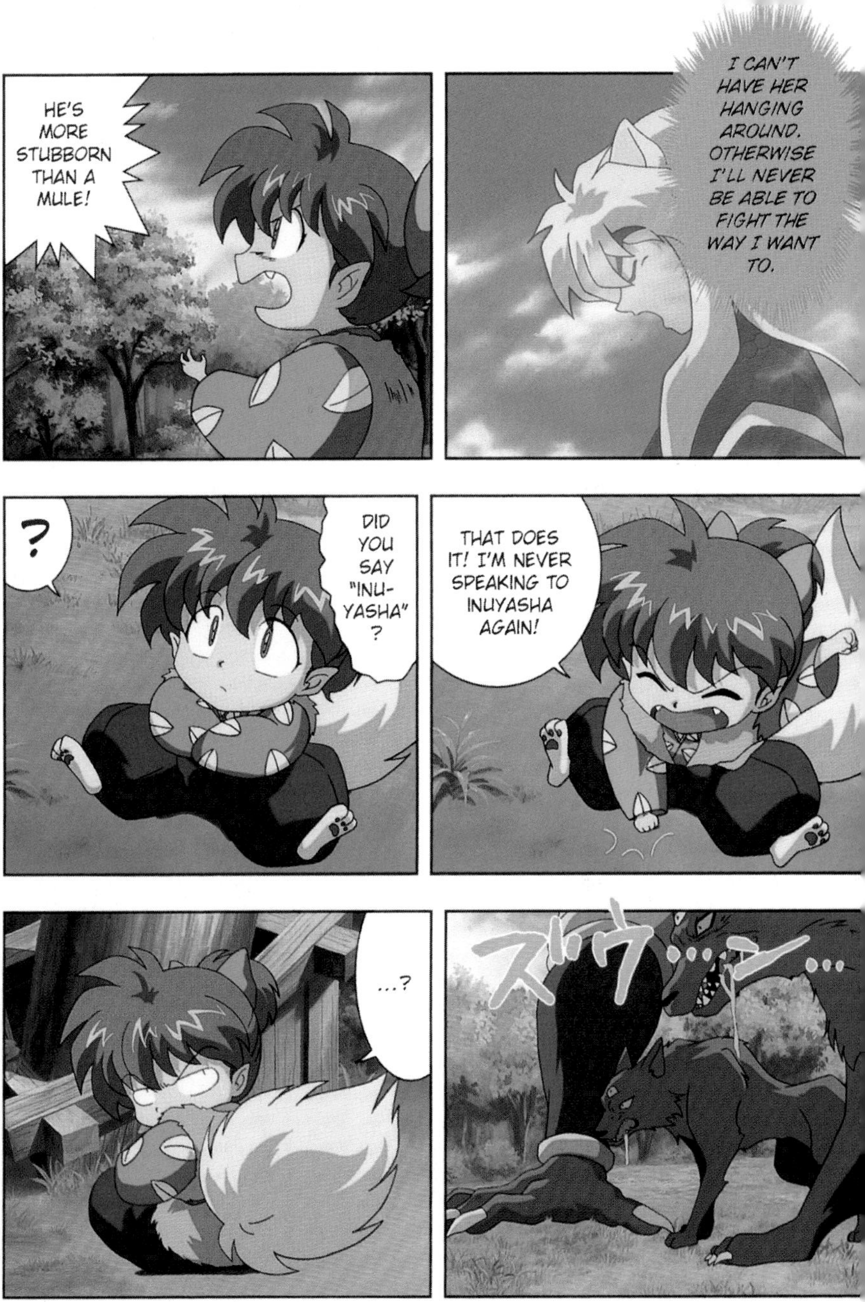
I CAN'T HAVE HER HANGING AROUND. OTHERWISE I'LL NEVER BE ABLE TO FIGHT THE WAY I WANT TO.
HE'S MORE STUBBORN THAN A MULE!
THAT DOES IT! I'M NEVER SPEAKING TO INUYASHA AGAIN!
DID YOU SAY "INU-YASHA"?
?
...?

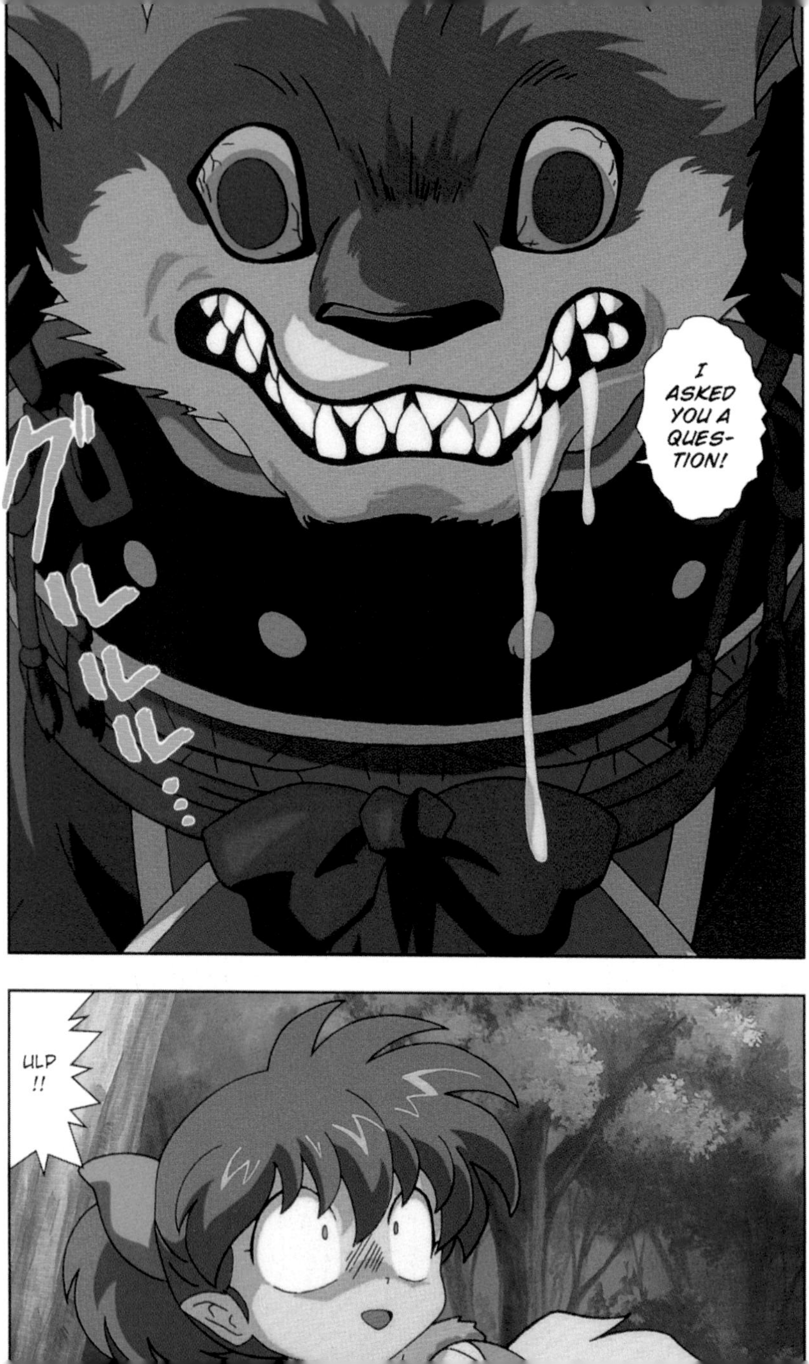

I ASKED YOU A QUES-TION!
グルルル…
ULP !!

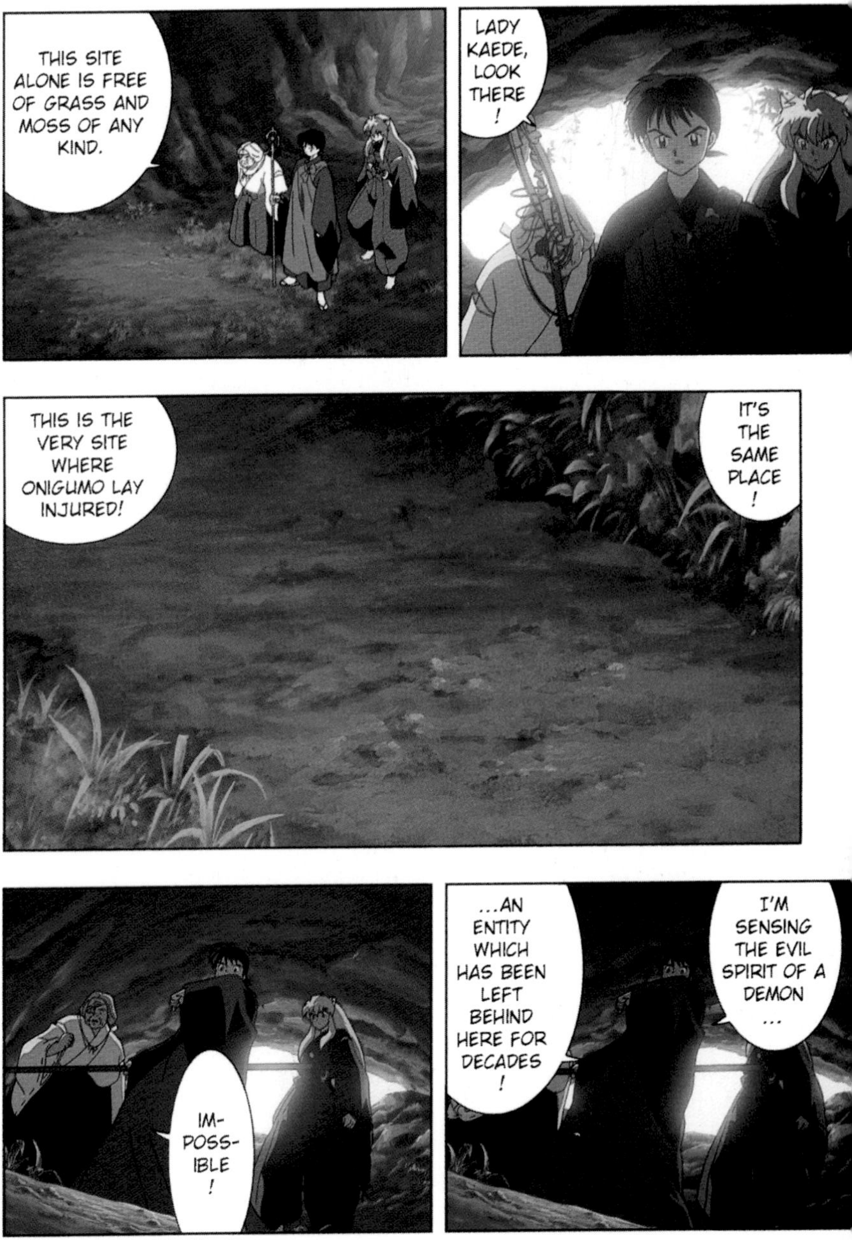
LADY KAEDE, LOOK THERE!
THIS SITE ALONE IS FREE OF GRASS AND MOSS OF ANY KIND.
IT'S THE SAME PLACE!
THIS IS THE VERY SITE WHERE ONIGUMO LAY INJURED!
I'M SENSING THE EVIL SPIRIT OF A DEMON...
...AN ENTITY WHICH HAS BEEN LEFT BEHIND HERE FOR DECADES!
IM-POSS-IBLE!

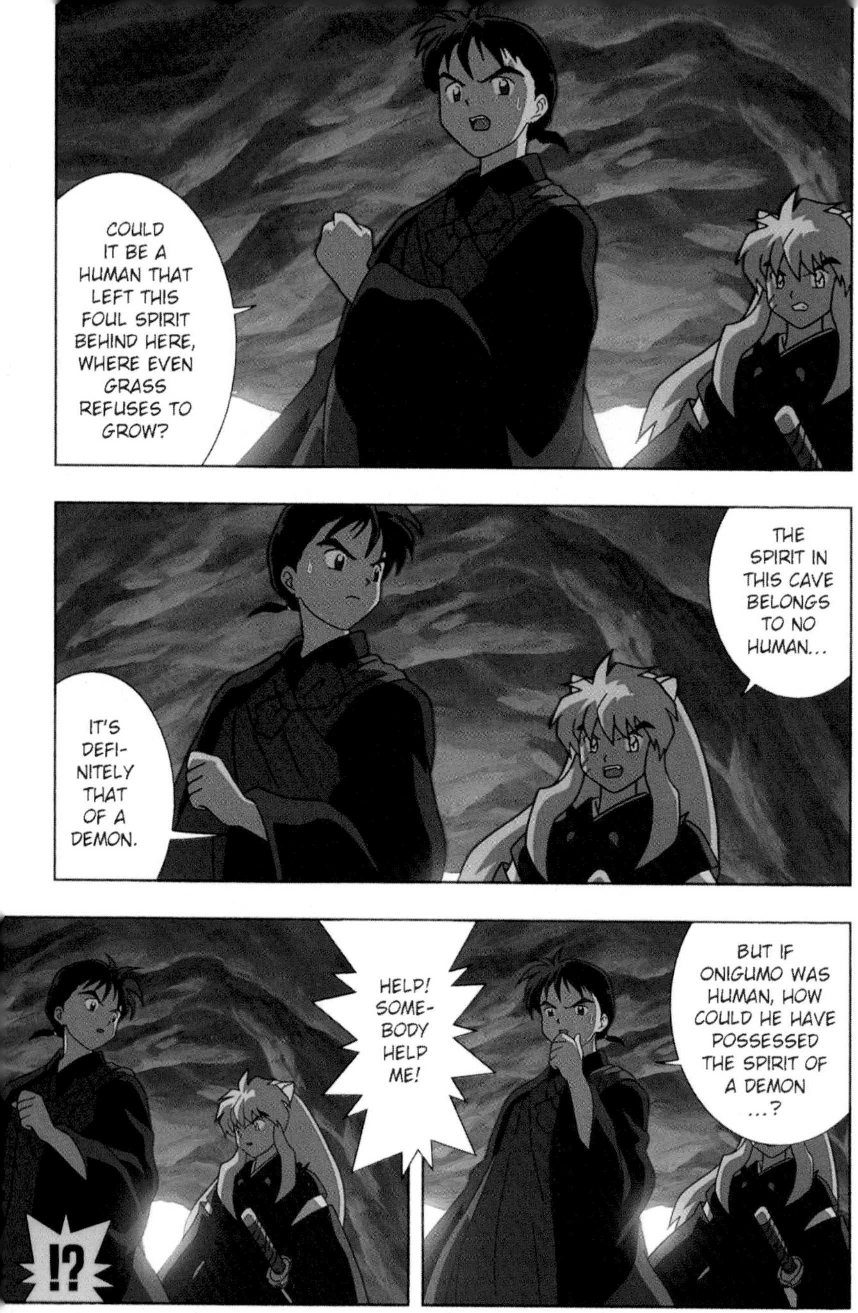
COULD IT BE A HUMAN THAT LEFT THIS FOUL SPIRIT BEHIND HERE, WHERE EVEN GRASS REFUSES TO GROW?
THE SPIRIT IN THIS CAVE BELONGS TO NO HUMAN...
IT'S DEFI-NITELY THAT OF A DEMON.
BUT IF ONIGUMO WAS HUMAN, HOW COULD HE HAVE POSSESSED THE SPIRIT OF A DEMON ...?
HELP! SOME-BODY HELP ME!
!?

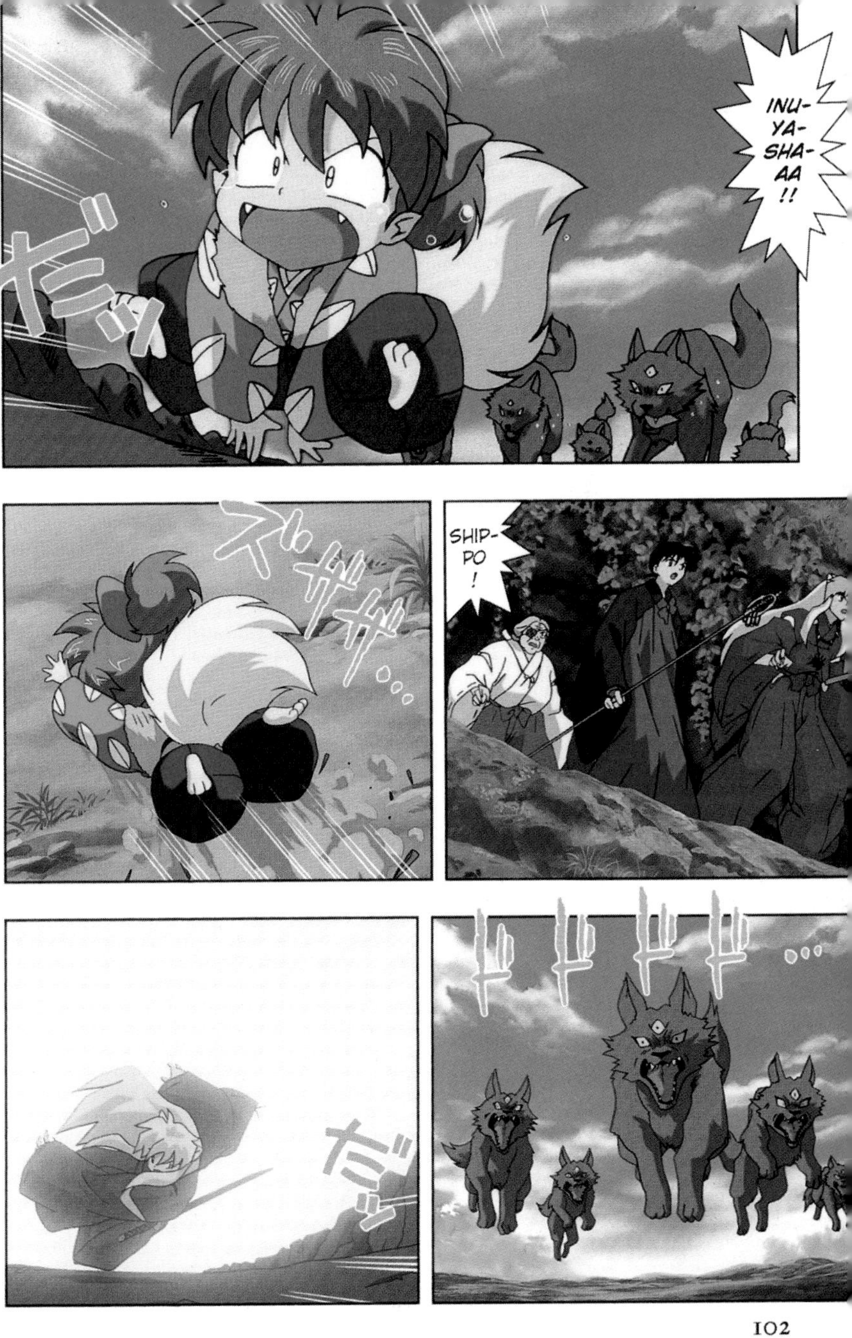
INU-YA-SHA-AA!!
ダッ
SHIP-PO!
ズザザ…
ドドドド…
だっ

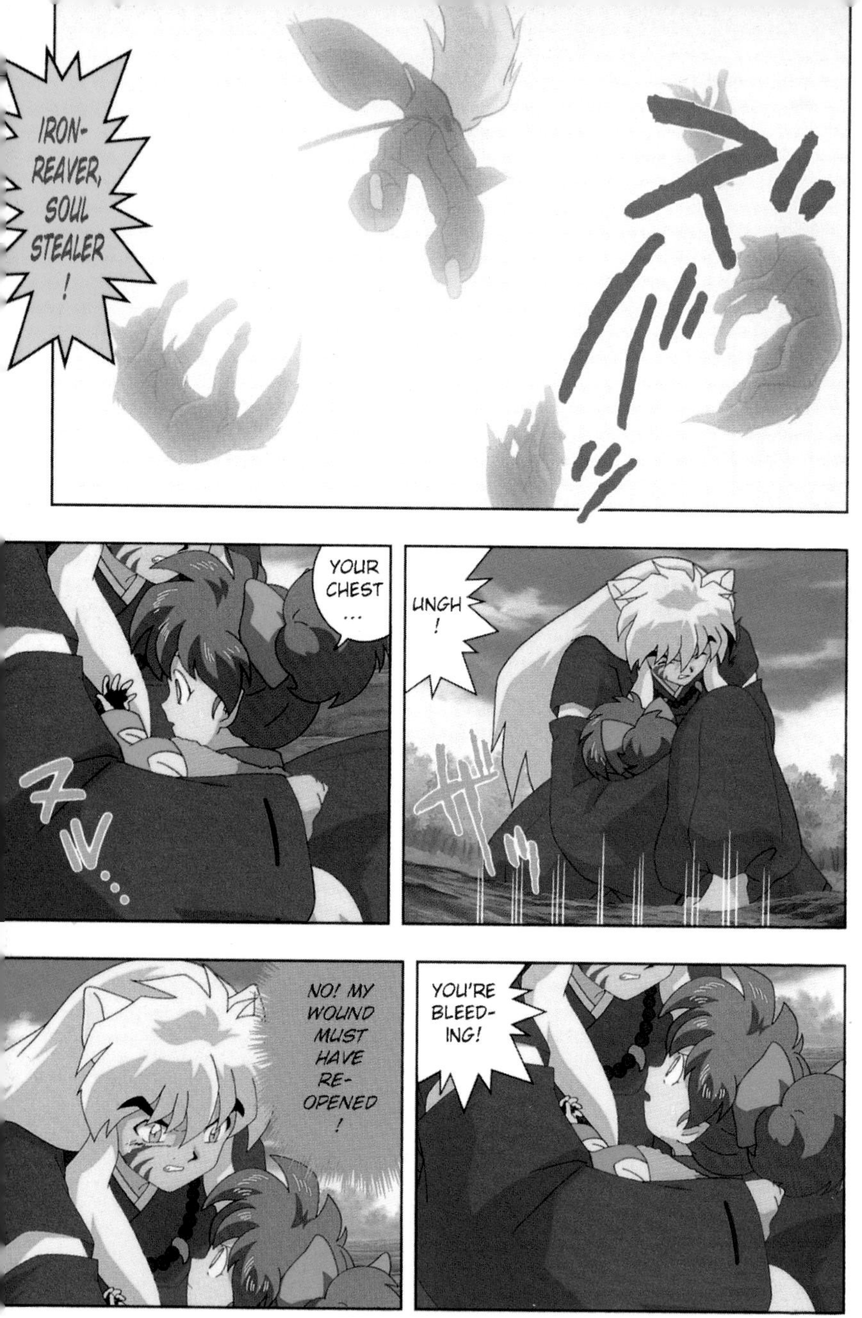
IRON-REAVER, SOUL STEALER!
UNGH!
YOUR CHEST...
YOU'RE BLEED-ING!
NO! MY WOUND MUST HAVE RE-OPENED!

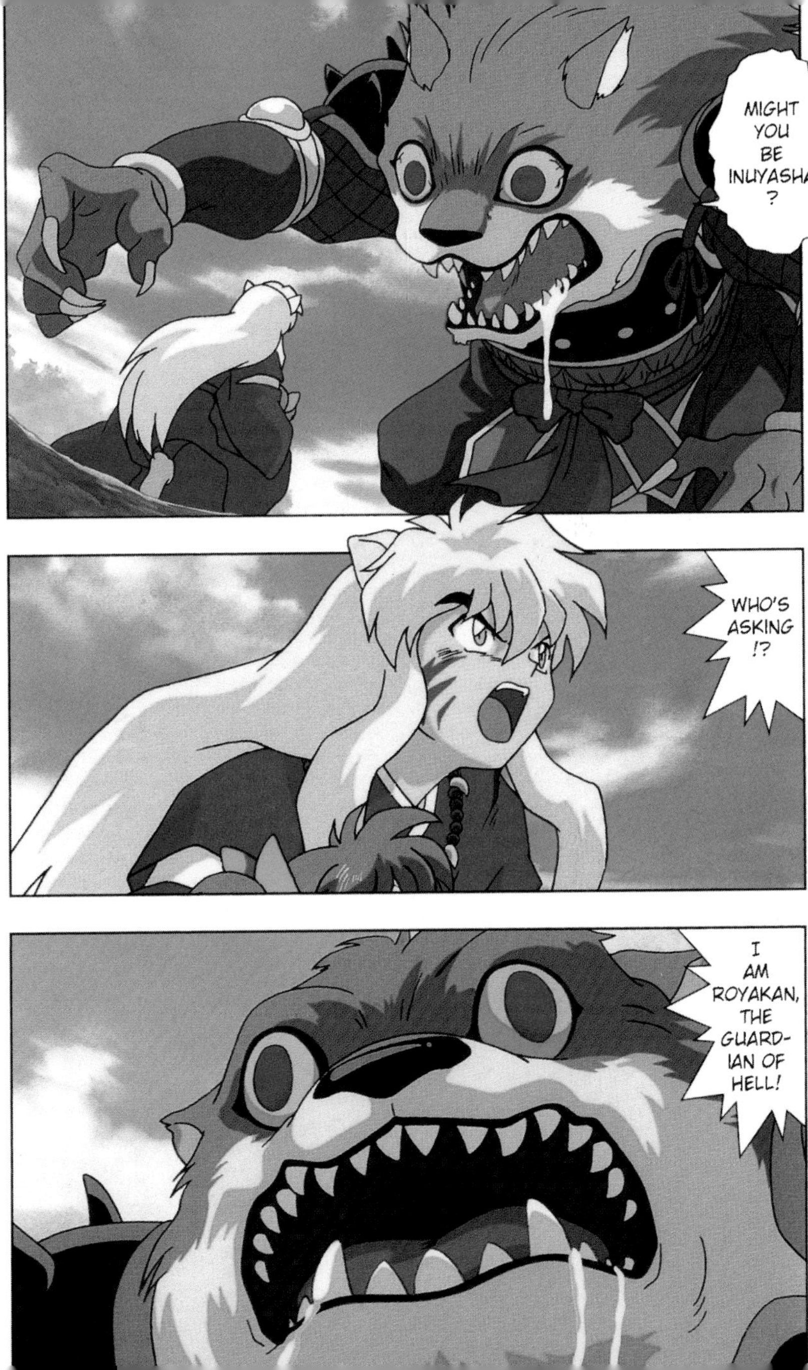
MIGHT YOU BE INUYASHA ?
WHO'S ASKING !?
I AM ROYAKAN, THE GUARD-IAN OF HELL!

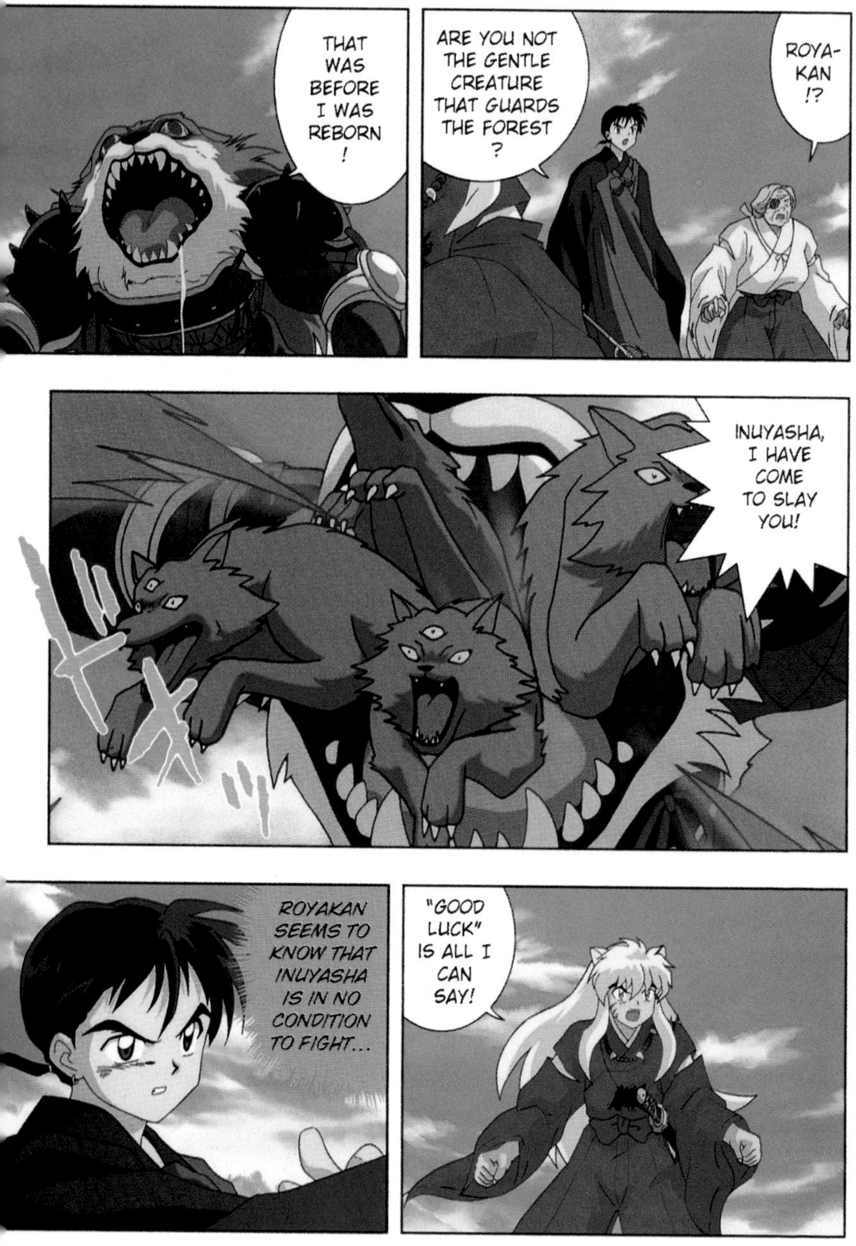
ROYA-KAN!?
ARE YOU NOT THE GENTLE CREATURE THAT GUARDS THE FOREST?
THAT WAS BEFORE I WAS REBORN!
INUYASHA, I HAVE COME TO SLAY YOU!
"GOOD LUCK" IS ALL I CAN SAY!
ROYAKAN SEEMS TO KNOW THAT INUYASHA IS IN NO CONDITION TO FIGHT...

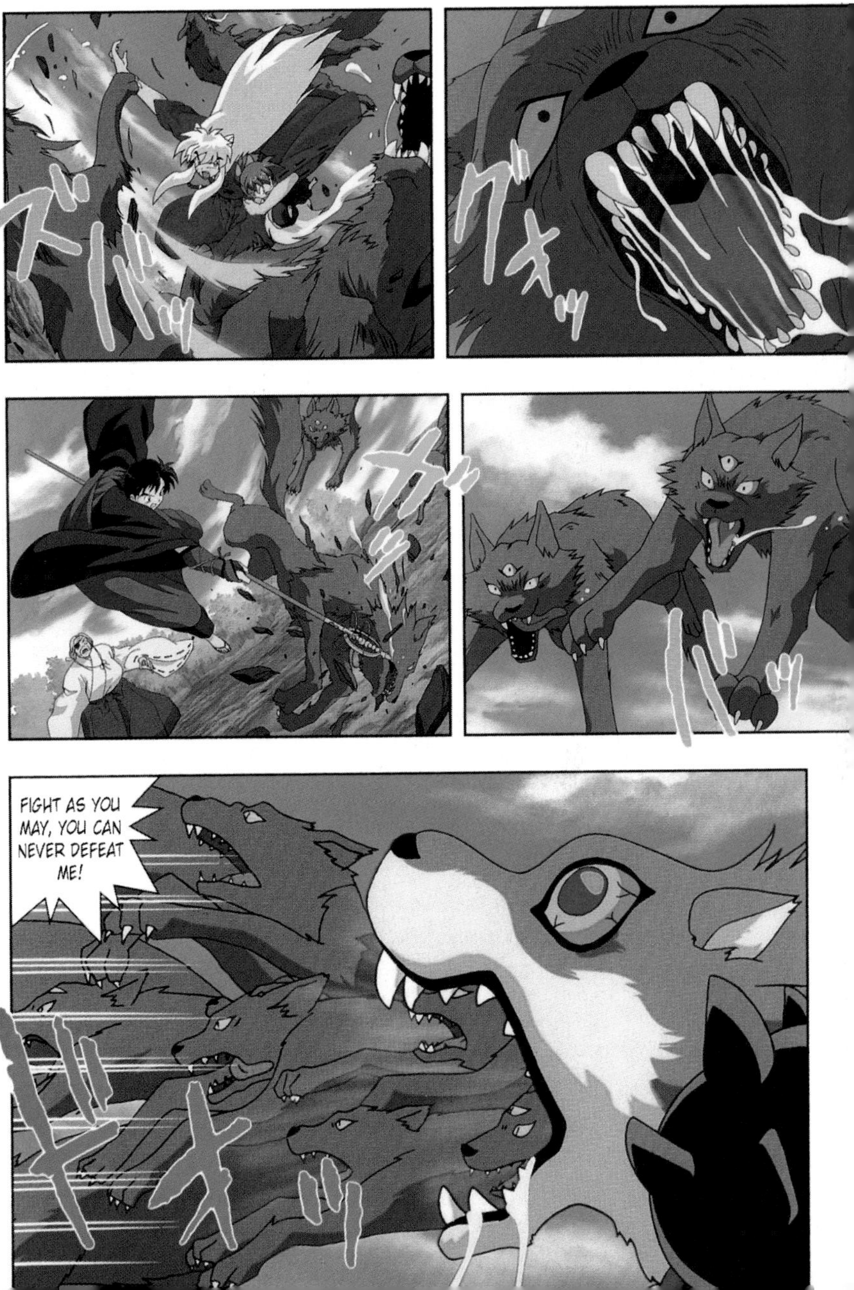
FIGHT AS YOU MAY, YOU CAN NEVER DEFEAT ME!

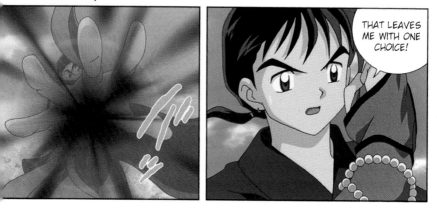

THAT LEAVES ME WITH ONE CHOICE!

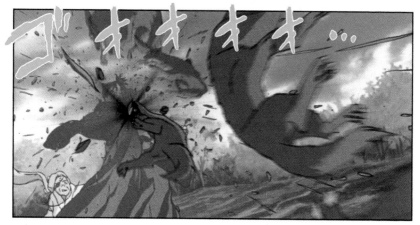

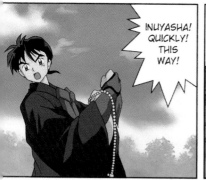

INUYASHA! QUICKLY! THIS WAY!

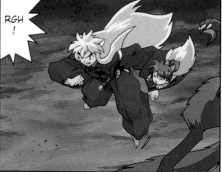

RGH!

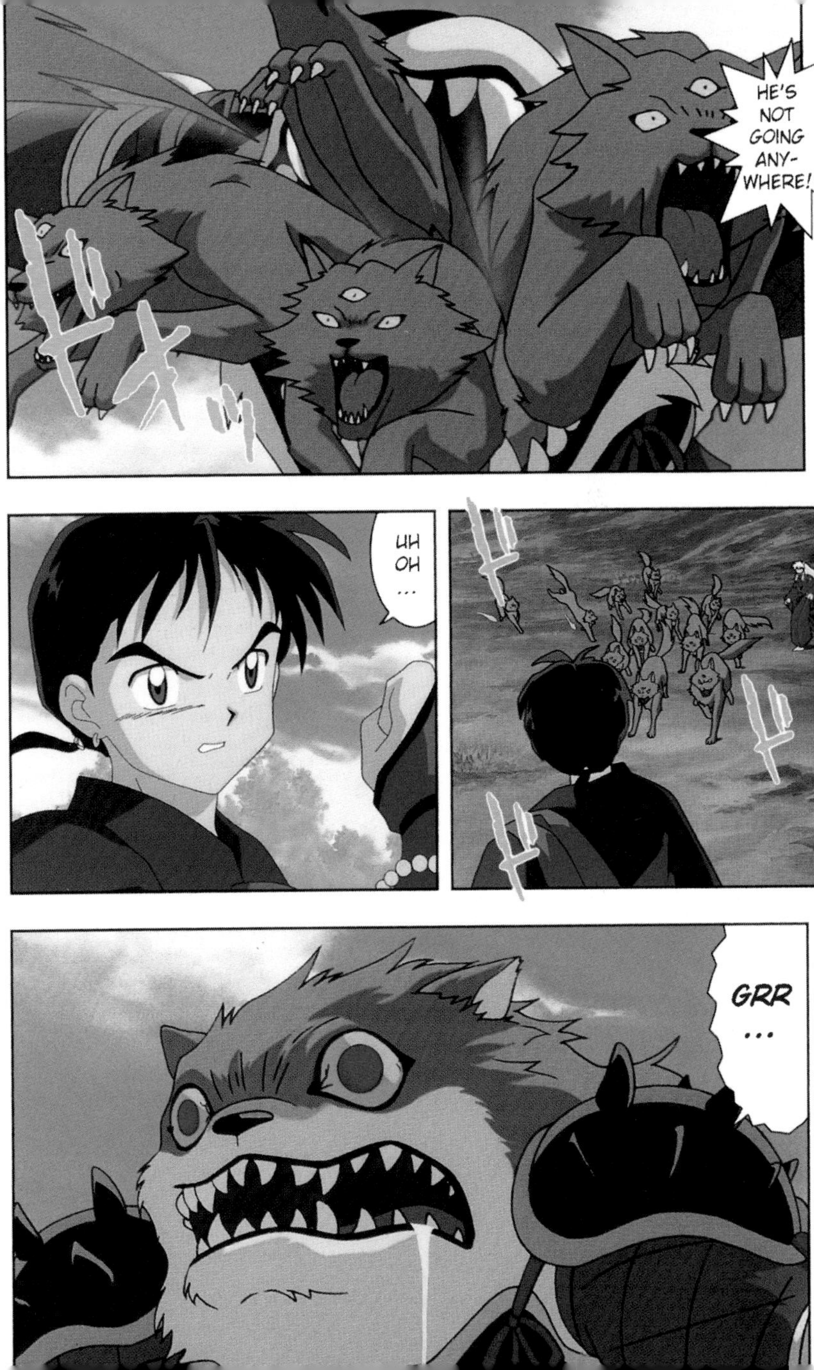
HE'S NOT GOING ANYWHERE!
UH OH ...
GRR ...

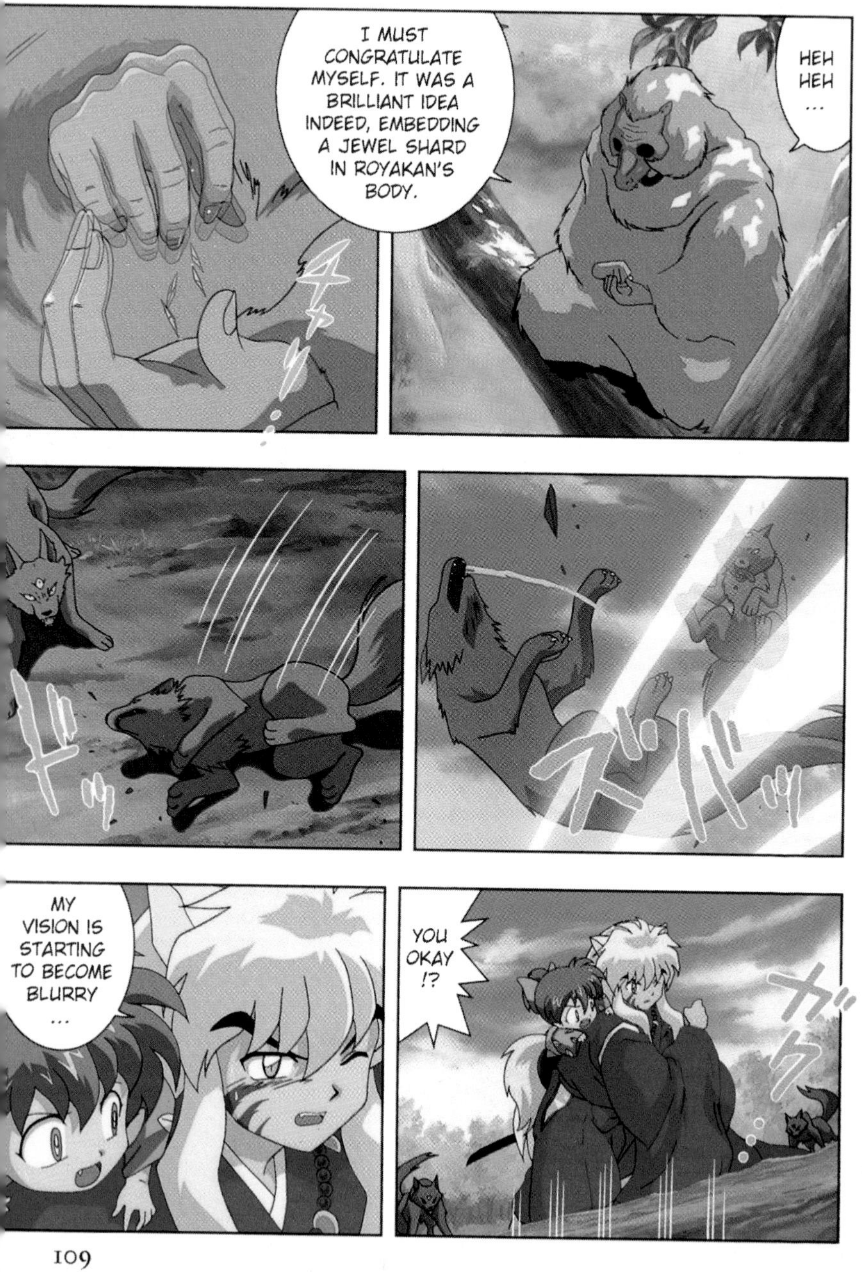
HEH HEH ...
I MUST CONGRATULATE MYSELF. IT WAS A BRILLIANT IDEA INDEED, EMBEDDING A JEWEL SHARD IN ROYAKAN'S BODY.
ズバッ
ドッ
YOU OKAY !?
MY VISION IS STARTING TO BECOME BLURRY ...

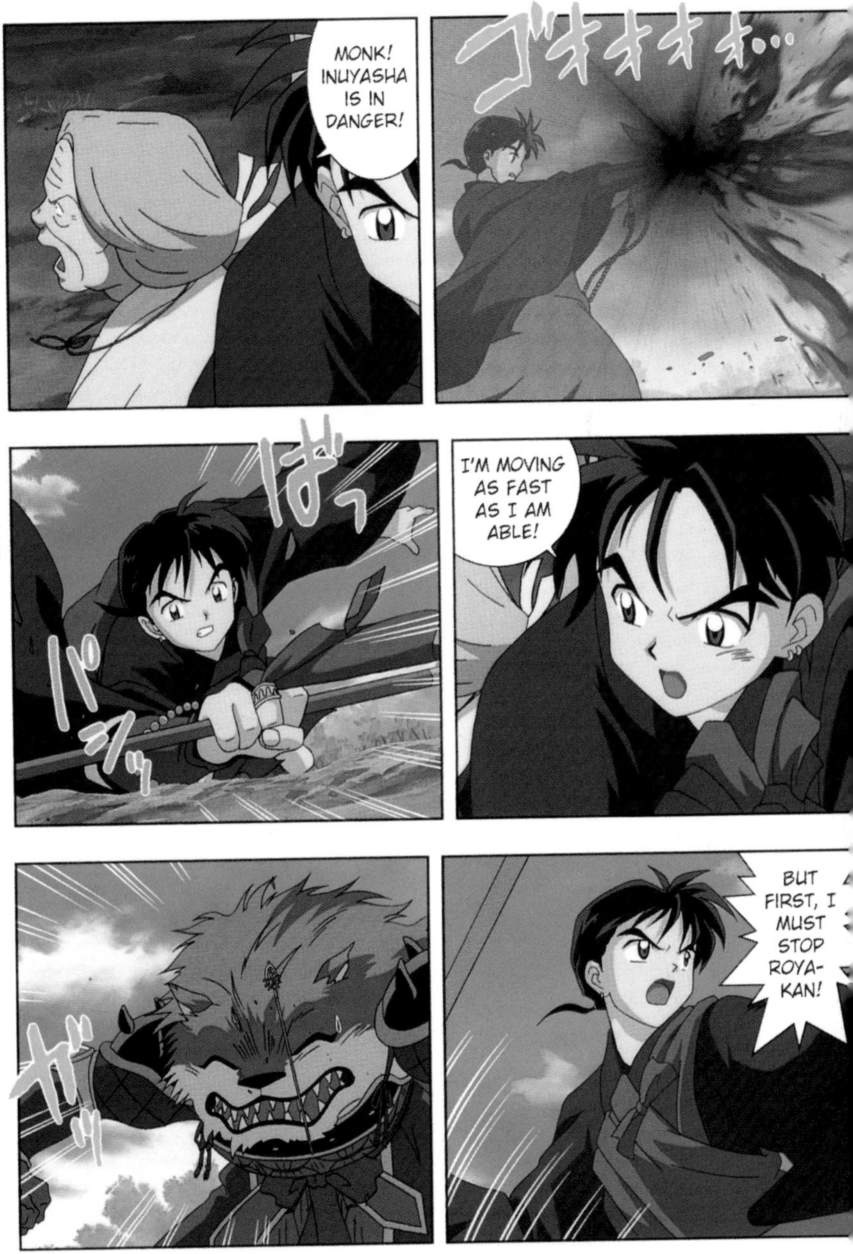
ゴオオオオ…
MONK! INUYASHA IS IN DANGER!
I'M MOVING AS FAST AS I AM ABLE!
ばっ
パシッ
BUT FIRST, I MUST STOP ROYA-KAN!
ガッ

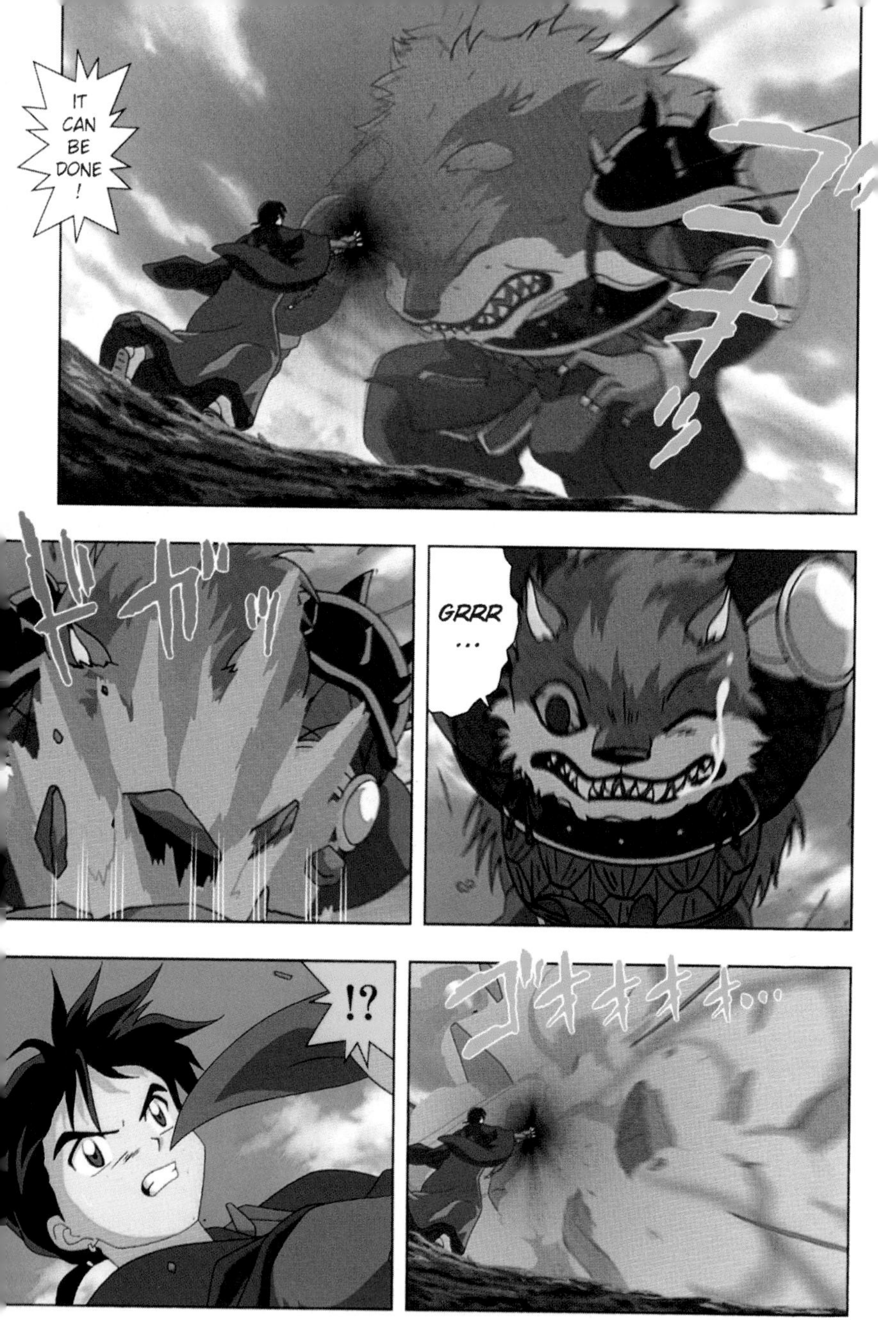
IT CAN BE DONE!
GRRR...
!?

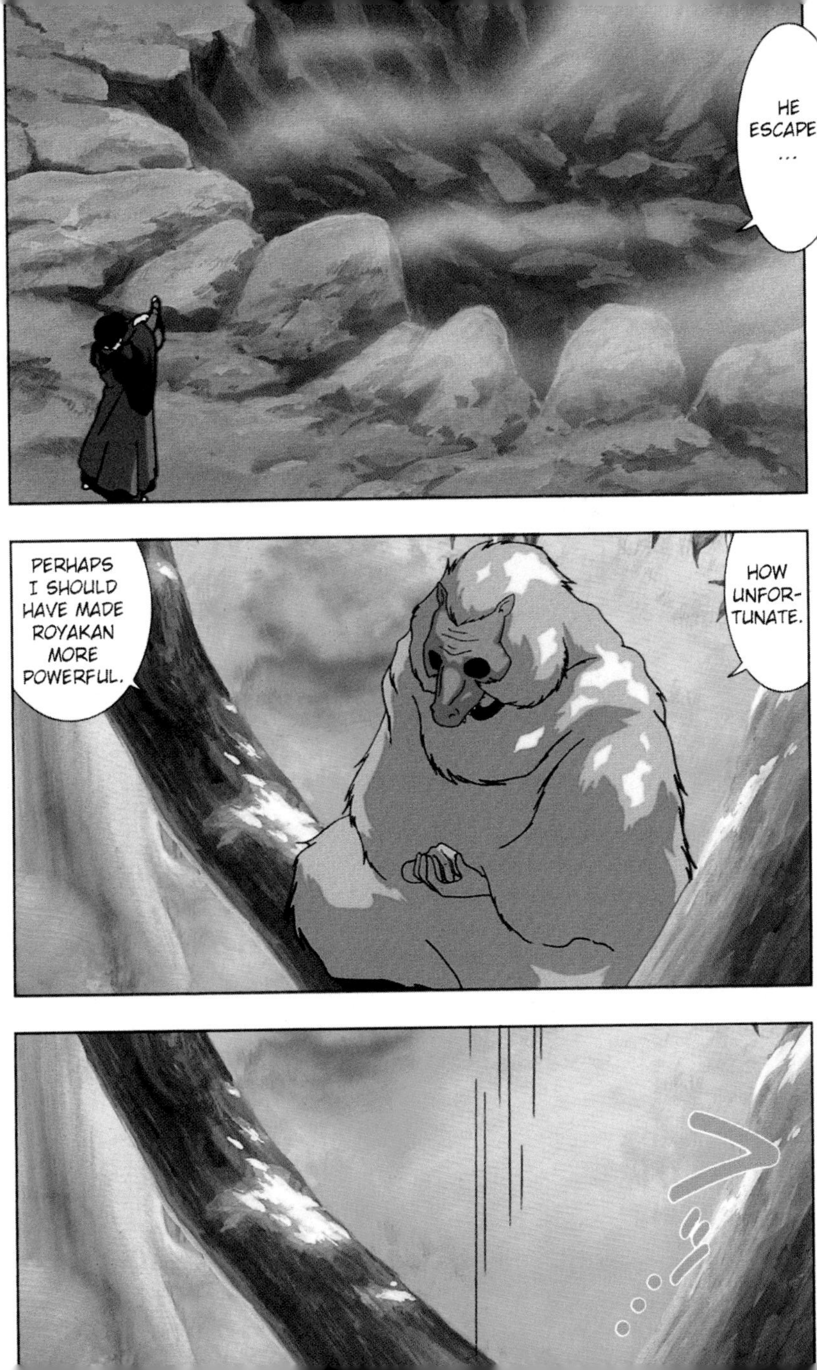
HE ESCAPED ...
HOW UNFOR-TUNATE.
PERHAPS I SHOULD HAVE MADE ROYAKAN MORE POWERFUL.

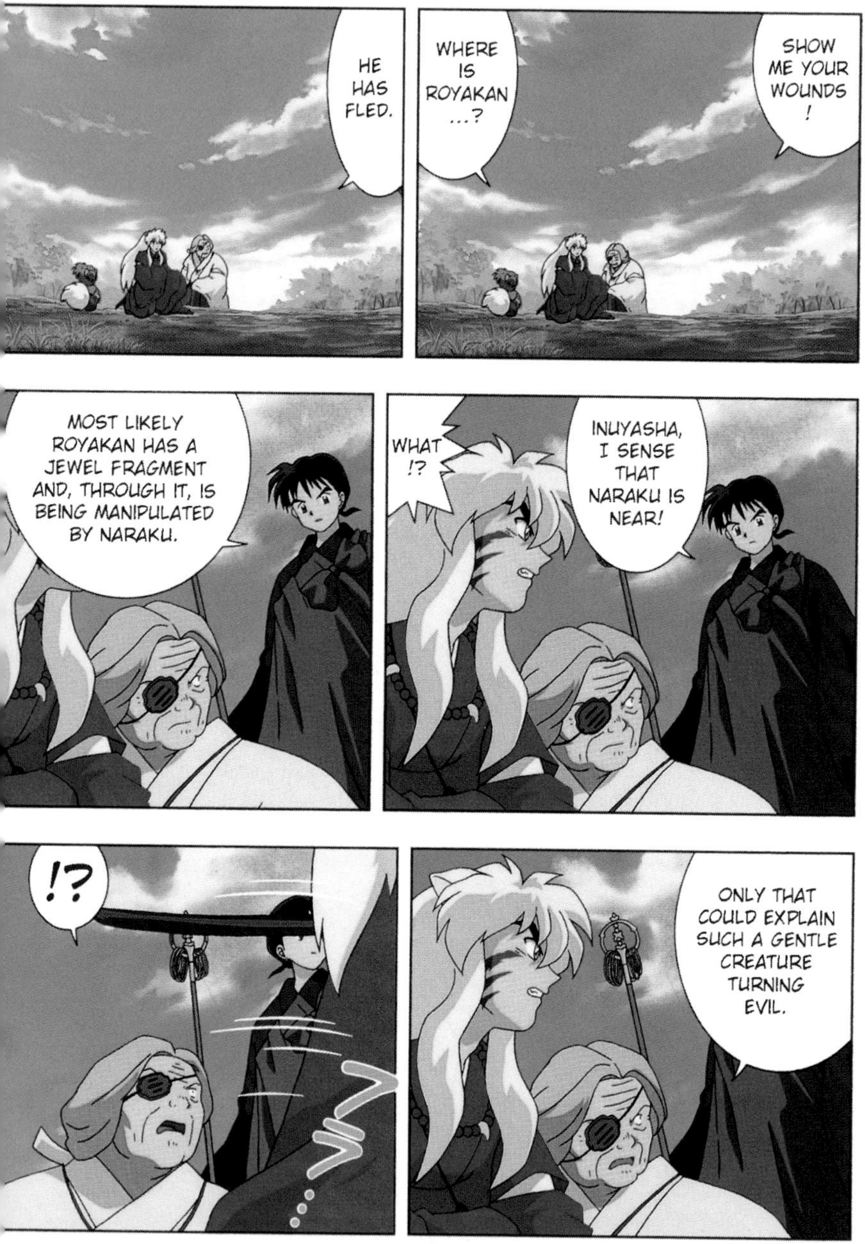
SHOW ME YOUR WOUNDS!
WHERE IS ROYAKAN ...?
HE HAS FLED.
INUYASHA, I SENSE THAT NARAKU IS NEAR!
WHAT!?
MOST LIKELY ROYAKAN HAS A JEWEL FRAGMENT AND, THROUGH IT, IS BEING MANIPULATED BY NARAKU.
ONLY THAT COULD EXPLAIN SUCH A GENTLE CREATURE TURNING EVIL.
!?

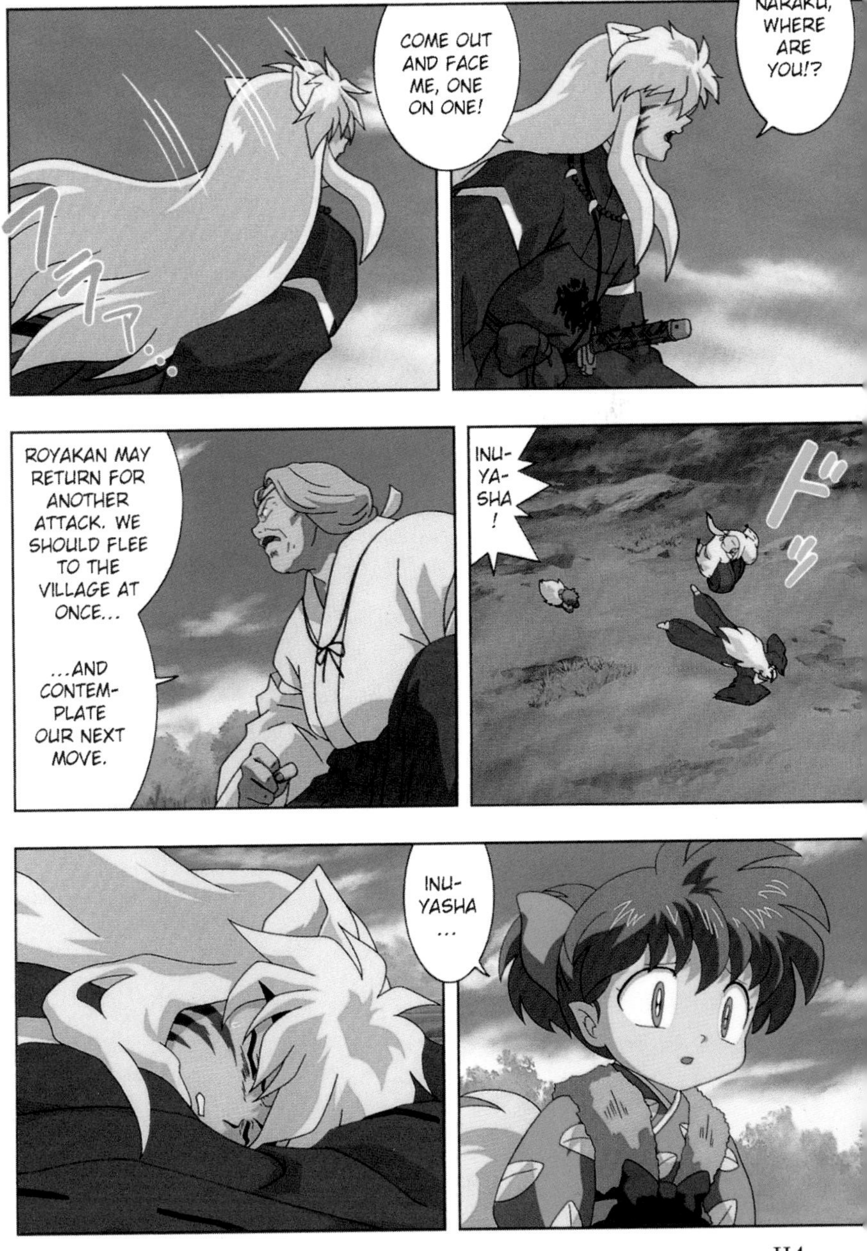
NARAKU, WHERE ARE YOU!?
COME OUT AND FACE ME, ONE ON ONE!
ドッ
INU-YASHA!
ROYAKAN MAY RETURN FOR ANOTHER ATTACK. WE SHOULD FLEE TO THE VILLAGE AT ONCE...
...AND CONTEMPLATE OUR NEXT MOVE.
INU-YASHA...

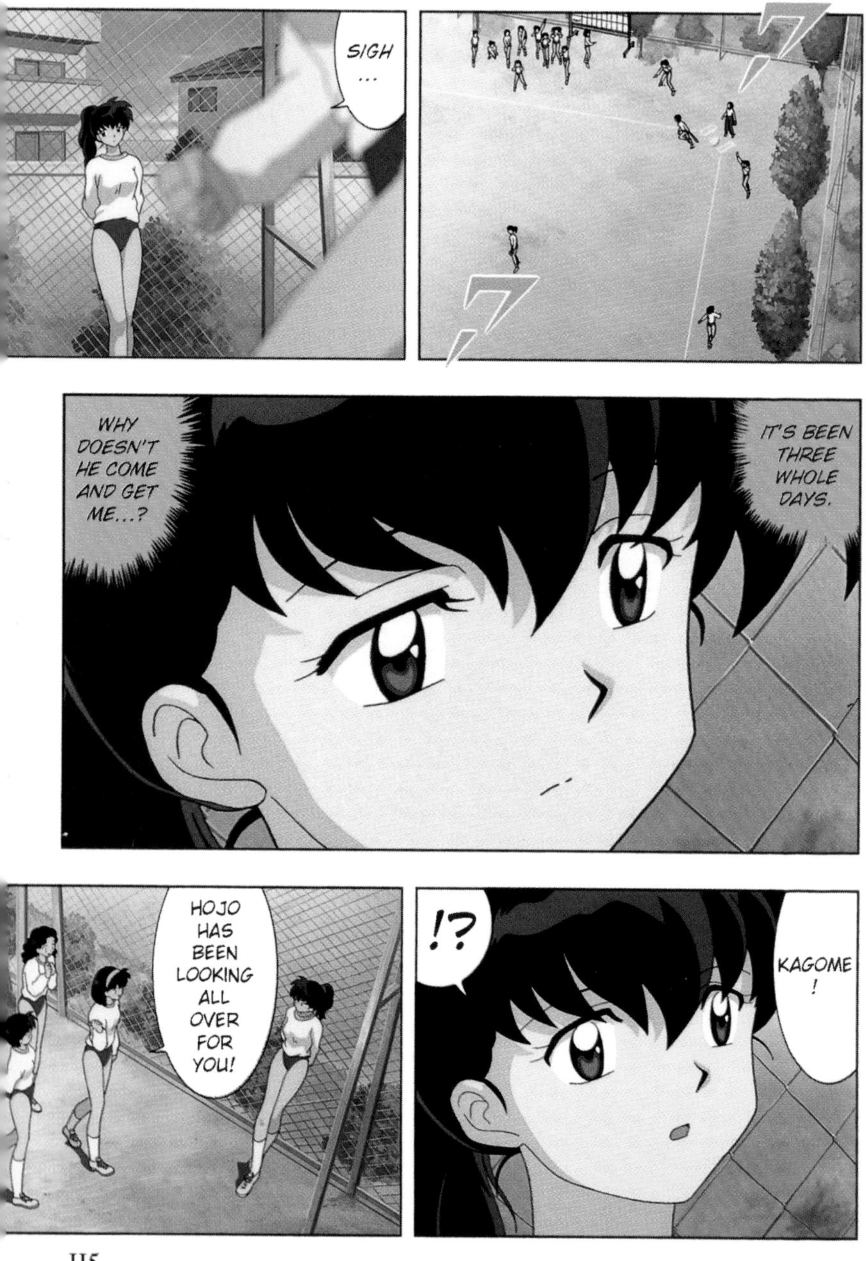
SIGH ...
IT'S BEEN THREE WHOLE DAYS.
WHY DOESN'T HE COME AND GET ME...?
KAGOME!
!?
HOJO HAS BEEN LOOKING ALL OVER FOR YOU!

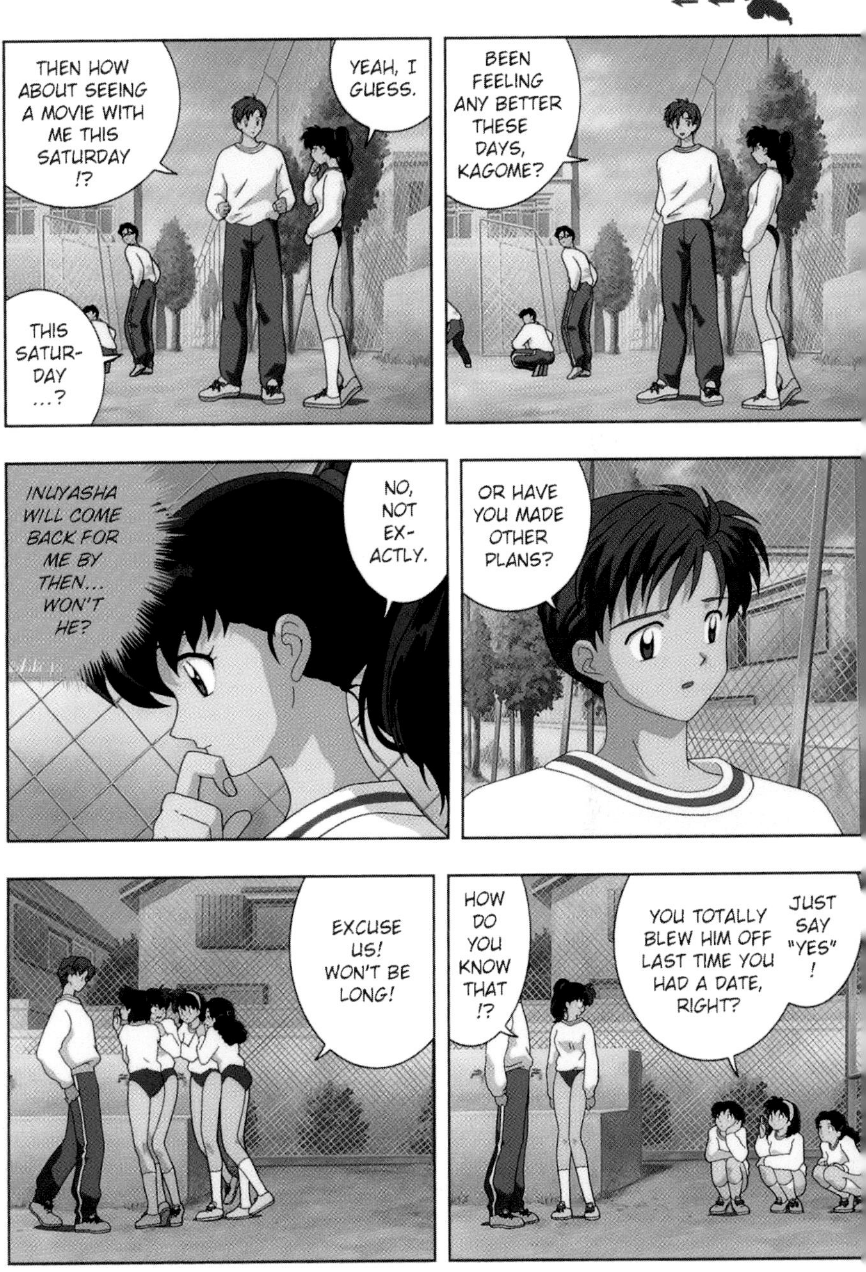
BEEN FEELING ANY BETTER THESE DAYS, KAGOME?
YEAH, I GUESS.
THEN HOW ABOUT SEEING A MOVIE WITH ME THIS SATURDAY !?
THIS SATUR-DAY ...?
OR HAVE YOU MADE OTHER PLANS?
NO, NOT EX-ACTLY.
INUYASHA WILL COME BACK FOR ME BY THEN... WON'T HE?
JUST SAY "YES" !
YOU TOTALLY BLEW HIM OFF LAST TIME YOU HAD A DATE, RIGHT?
HOW DO YOU KNOW THAT !?
EXCUSE US! WON'T BE LONG!

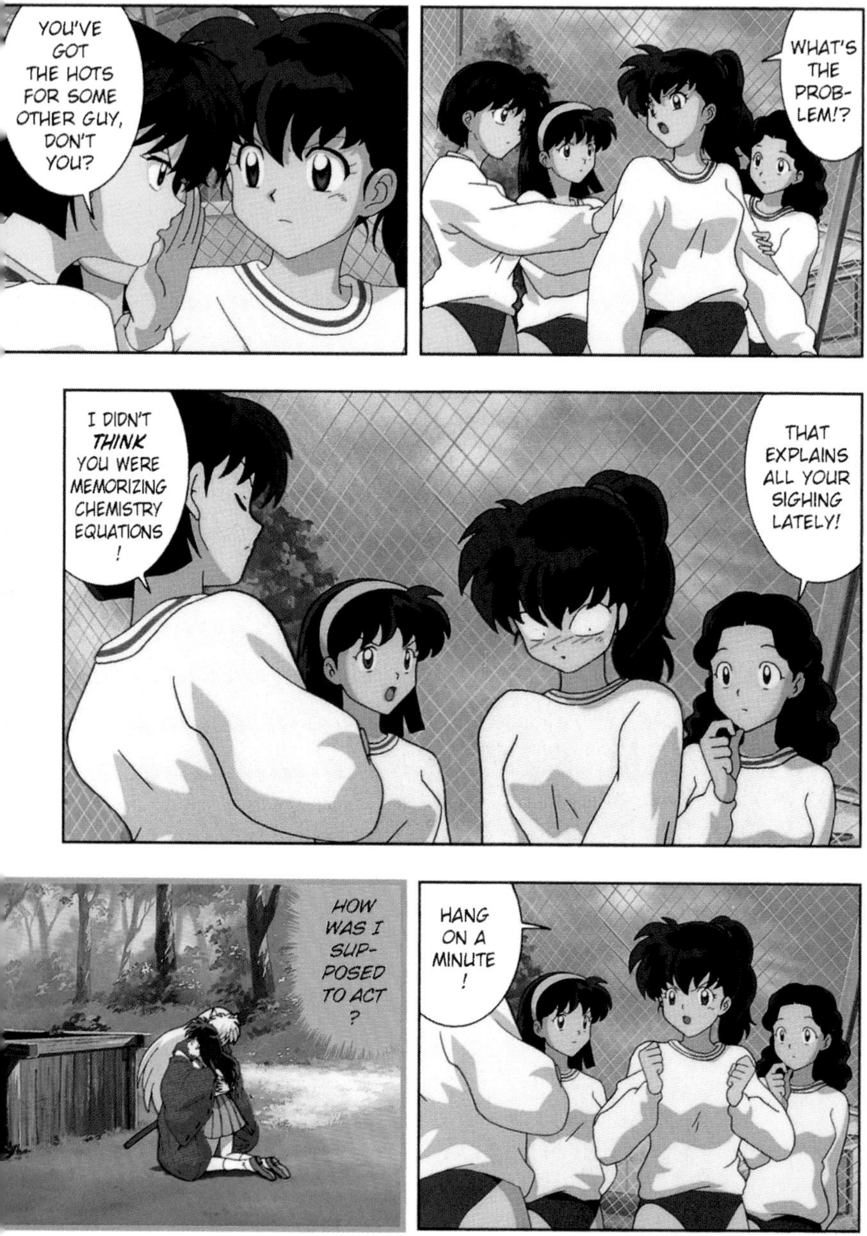
WHAT'S THE PROB-LEM!?
YOU'VE GOT THE HOTS FOR SOME OTHER GUY, DON'T YOU?
THAT EXPLAINS ALL YOUR SIGHING LATELY!
I DIDN'T *THINK* YOU WERE MEMORIZING CHEMISTRY EQUATIONS!
HANG ON A MINUTE!
HOW WAS I SUP-POSED TO ACT?

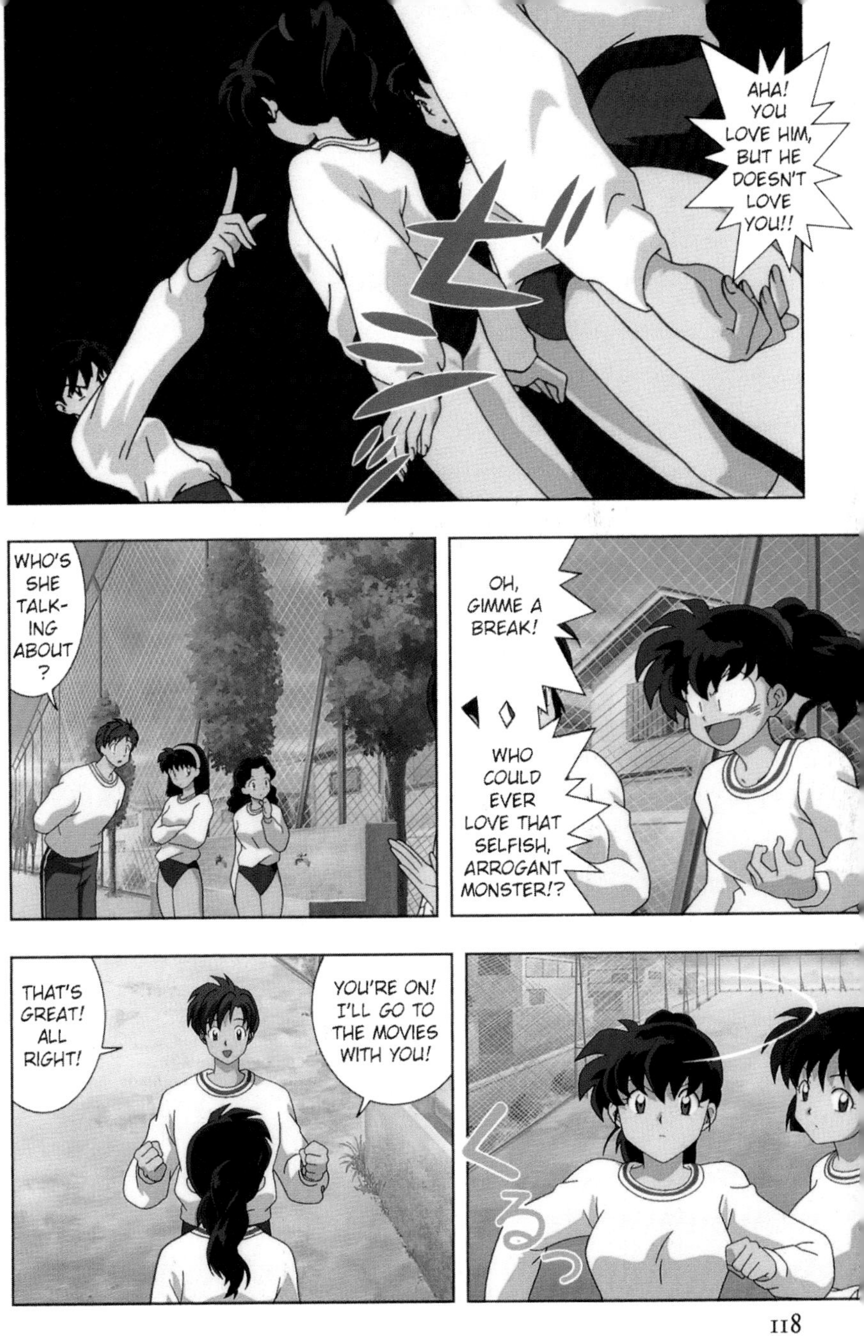
AHA! YOU LOVE HIM, BUT HE DOESN'T LOVE YOU!!
OH, GIMME A BREAK!
WHO COULD EVER LOVE THAT SELFISH, ARROGANT MONSTER!?
WHO'S SHE TALKING ABOUT?
YOU'RE ON! I'LL GO TO THE MOVIES WITH YOU!
THAT'S GREAT! ALL RIGHT!

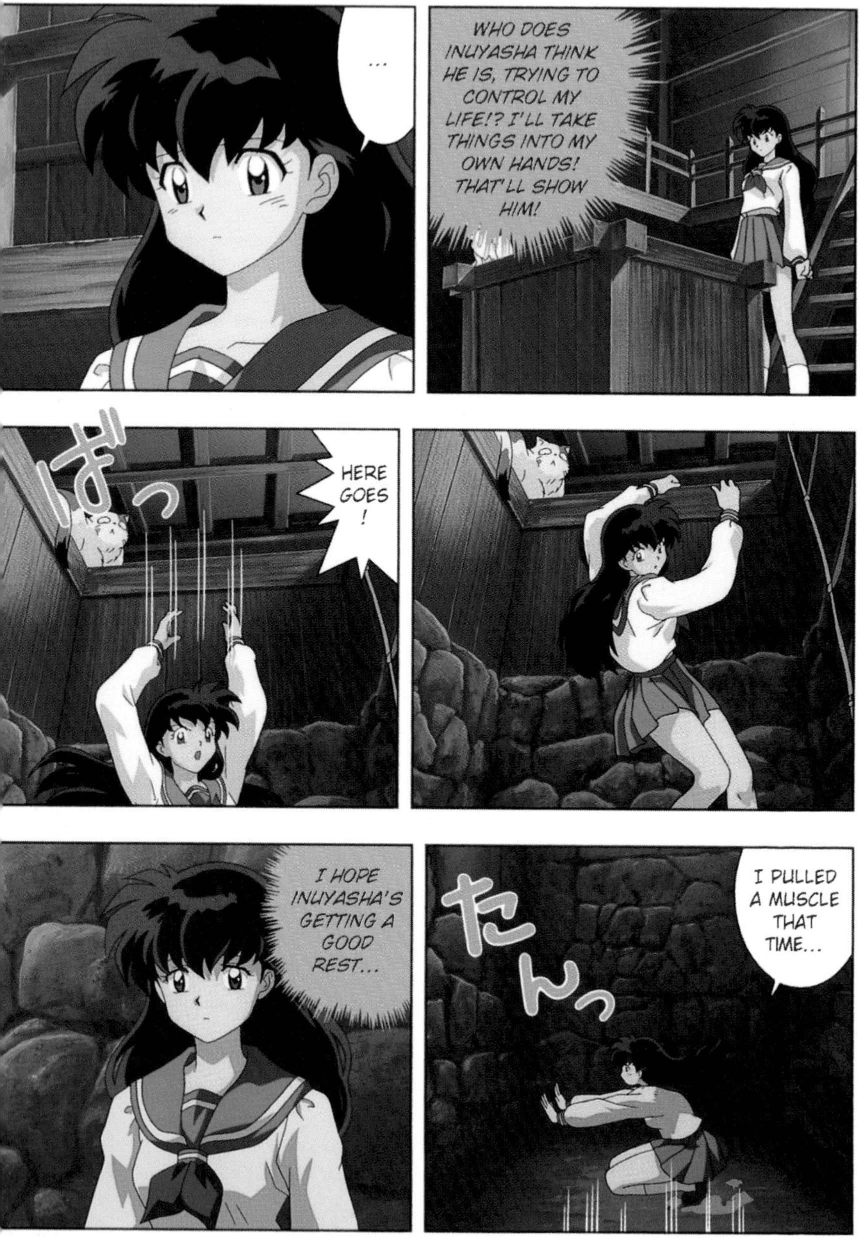
WHO DOES INUYASHA THINK HE IS, TRYING TO CONTROL MY LIFE!? I'LL TAKE THINGS INTO MY OWN HANDS! THAT'LL SHOW HIM!
...
ぱっ
HERE GOES!
たんっ
I PULLED A MUSCLE THAT TIME...
I HOPE INUYASHA'S GETTING A GOOD REST...

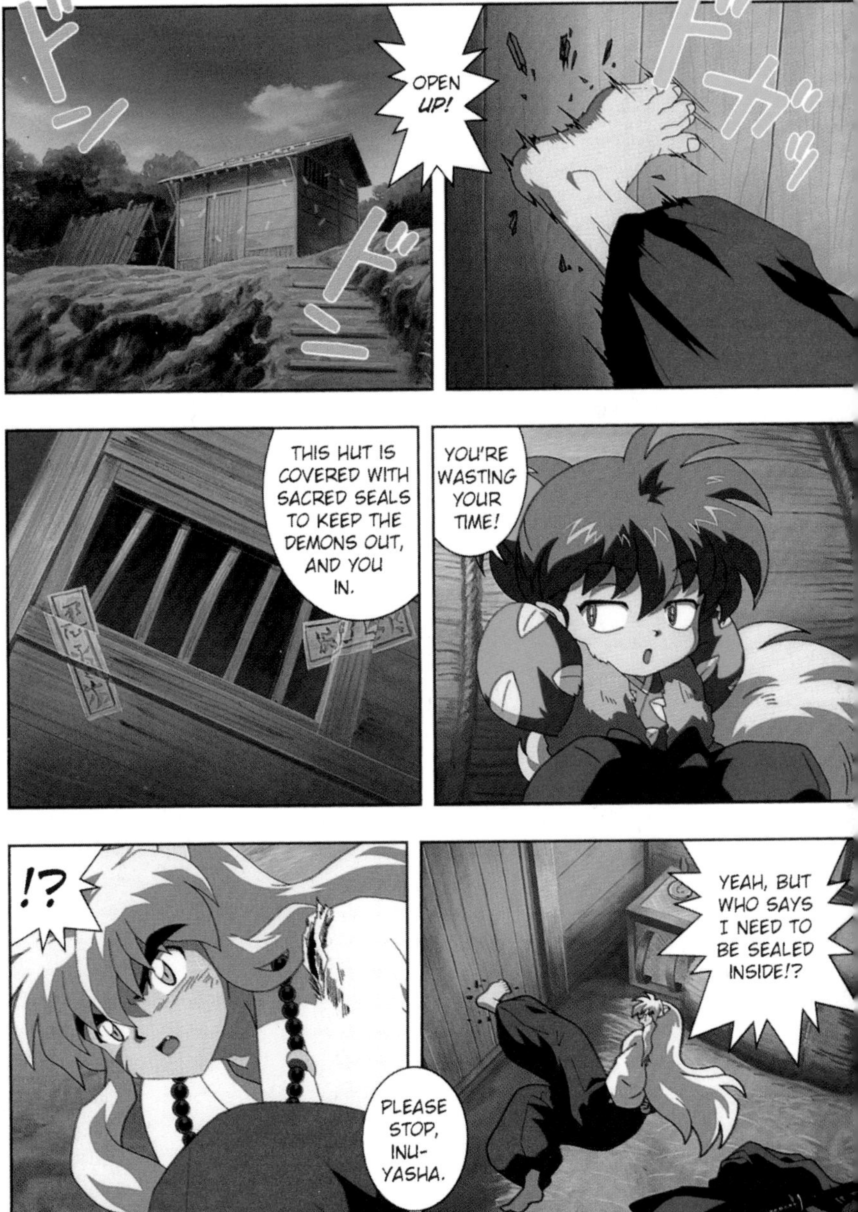
ドガッ
OPEN UP!
YOU'RE WASTING YOUR TIME!
THIS HUT IS COVERED WITH SACRED SEALS TO KEEP THE DEMONS OUT, AND YOU IN.
YEAH, BUT WHO SAYS I NEED TO BE SEALED INSIDE!?
!?
PLEASE STOP, INU-YASHA.

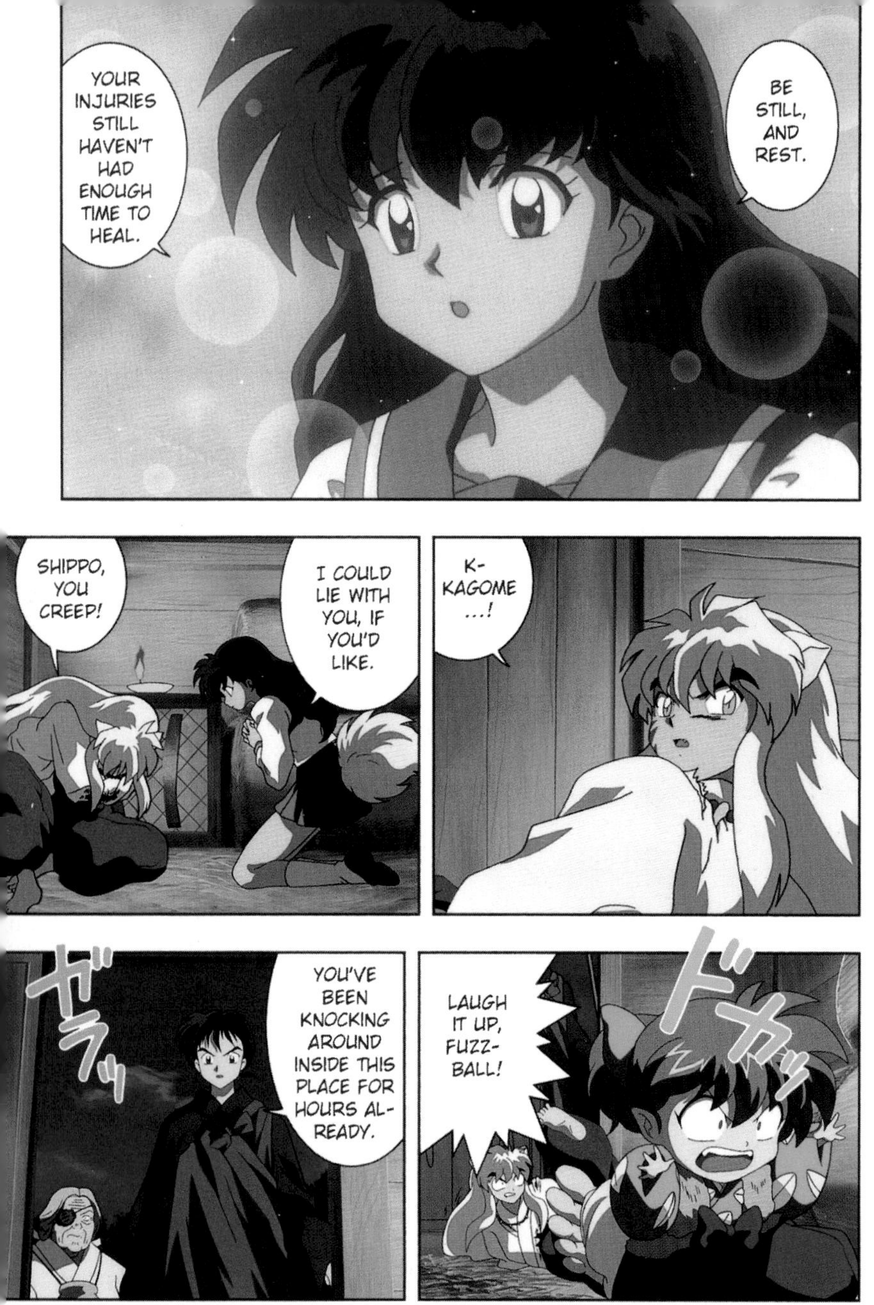
BE STILL, AND REST.
YOUR INJURIES STILL HAVEN'T HAD ENOUGH TIME TO HEAL.
K-KAGOME ...!
I COULD LIE WITH YOU, IF YOU'D LIKE.
SHIPPO, YOU CREEP!
ドカッ
LAUGH IT UP, FUZZ-BALL!
YOU'VE BEEN KNOCKING AROUND INSIDE THIS PLACE FOR HOURS AL-READY.
ガラッ

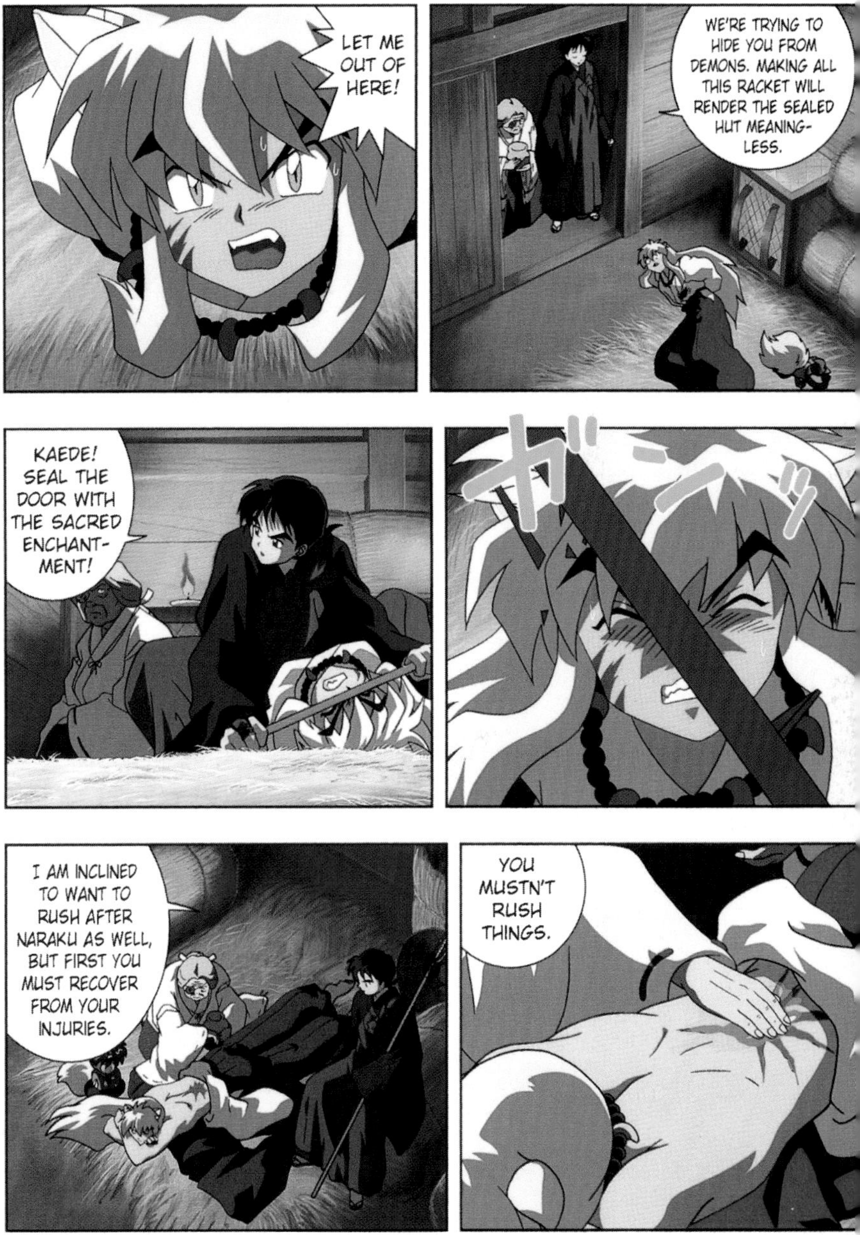
WE'RE TRYING TO HIDE YOU FROM DEMONS. MAKING ALL THIS RACKET WILL RENDER THE SEALED HUT MEANING-LESS.
LET ME OUT OF HERE!
ガーンッ
KAEDE! SEAL THE DOOR WITH THE SACRED ENCHANT-MENT!
YOU MUSTN'T RUSH THINGS.
I AM INCLINED TO WANT TO RUSH AFTER NARAKU AS WELL, BUT FIRST YOU MUST RECOVER FROM YOUR INJURIES.

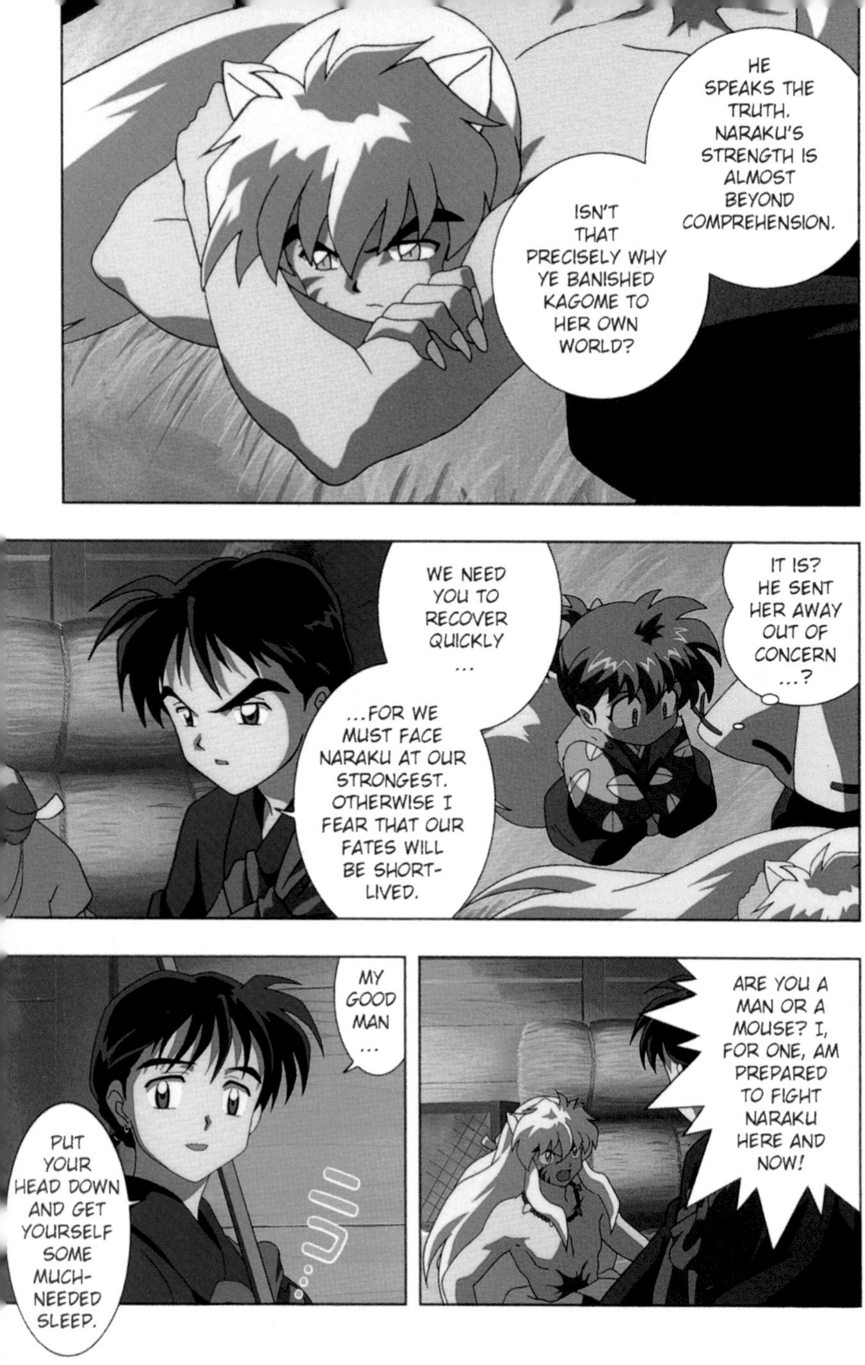
HE SPEAKS THE TRUTH. NARAKU'S STRENGTH IS ALMOST BEYOND COMPREHENSION.
ISN'T THAT PRECISELY WHY YE BANISHED KAGOME TO HER OWN WORLD?
IT IS? HE SENT HER AWAY OUT OF CONCERN ...?
WE NEED YOU TO RECOVER QUICKLY ...
...FOR WE MUST FACE NARAKU AT OUR STRONGEST. OTHERWISE I FEAR THAT OUR FATES WILL BE SHORT-LIVED.
ARE YOU A MAN OR A MOUSE? I, FOR ONE, AM PREPARED TO FIGHT NARAKU HERE AND NOW!
MY GOOD MAN ...
PUT YOUR HEAD DOWN AND GET YOURSELF SOME MUCH-NEEDED SLEEP.

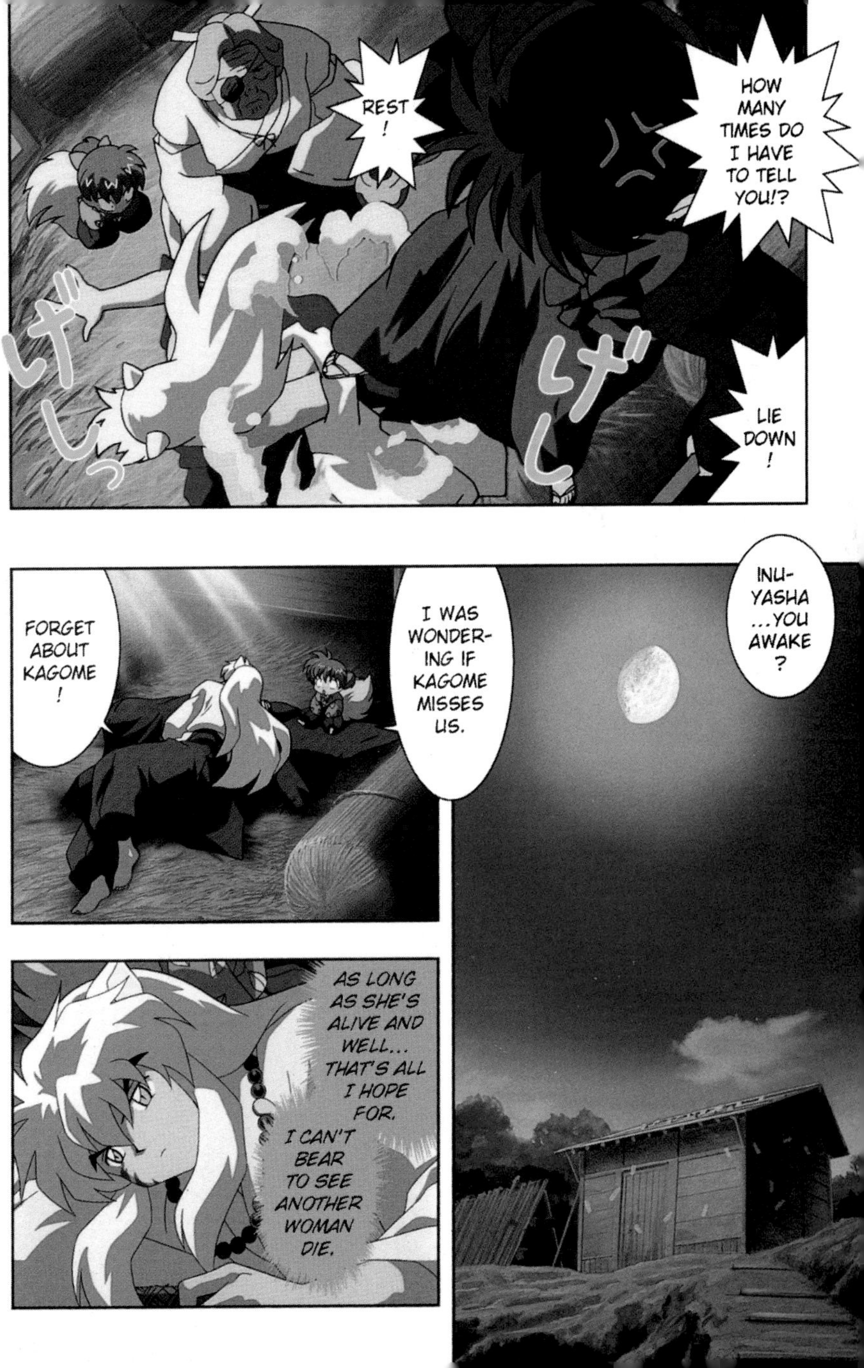
HOW MANY TIMES DO I HAVE TO TELL YOU!?
REST!
LIE DOWN!
げし
げしっ
INU-YASHA ...YOU AWAKE?
I WAS WONDERING IF KAGOME MISSES US.
FORGET ABOUT KAGOME!
AS LONG AS SHE'S ALIVE AND WELL... THAT'S ALL I HOPE FOR.
I CAN'T BEAR TO SEE ANOTHER WOMAN DIE.

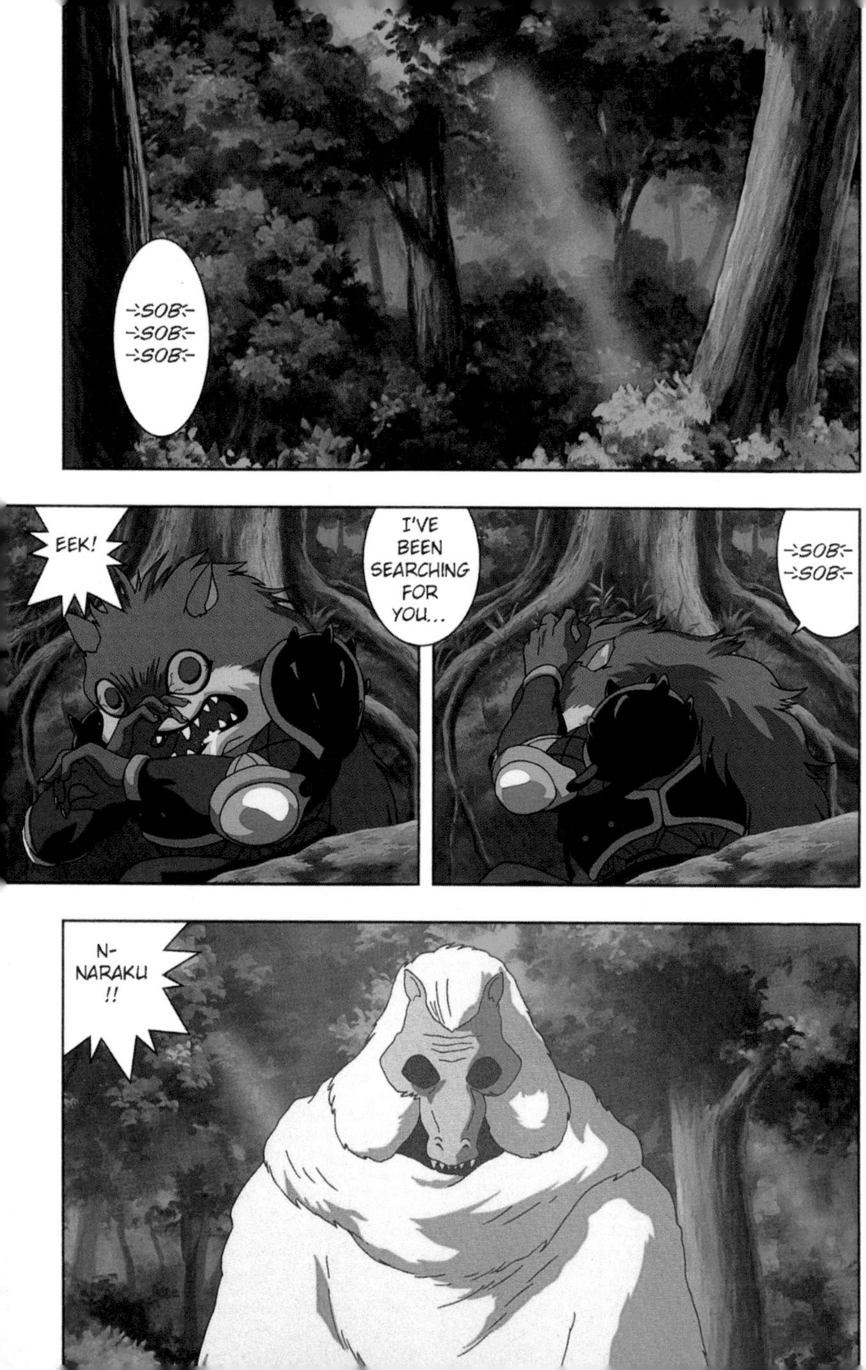
-SOB- -SOB- -SOB-
-SOB- -SOB-
I'VE BEEN SEARCHING FOR YOU...
EEK!
N-NARAKU !!

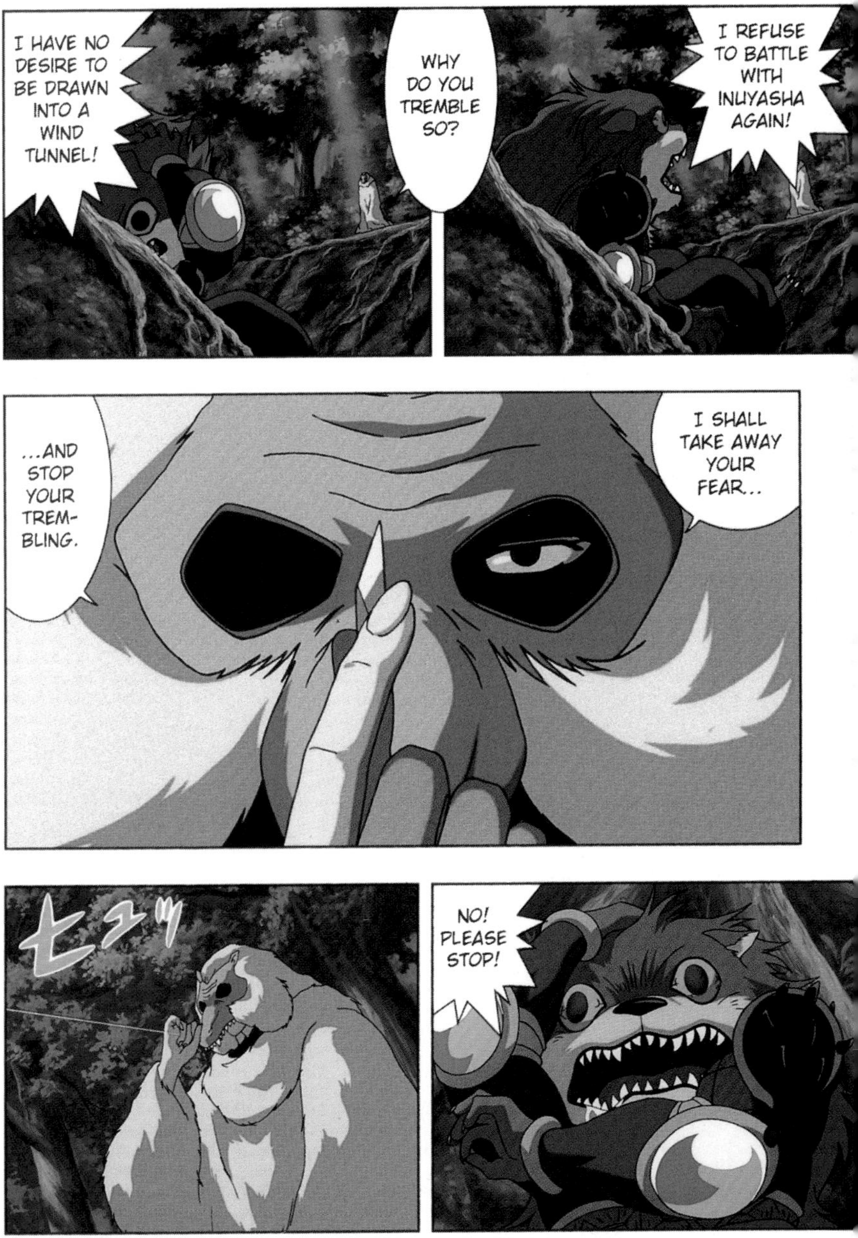
I REFUSE TO BATTLE WITH INUYASHA AGAIN!
WHY DO YOU TREMBLE SO?
I HAVE NO DESIRE TO BE DRAWN INTO A WIND TUNNEL!
I SHALL TAKE AWAY YOUR FEAR...
...AND STOP YOUR TREM-BLING.
NO! PLEASE STOP!
ヒュッ

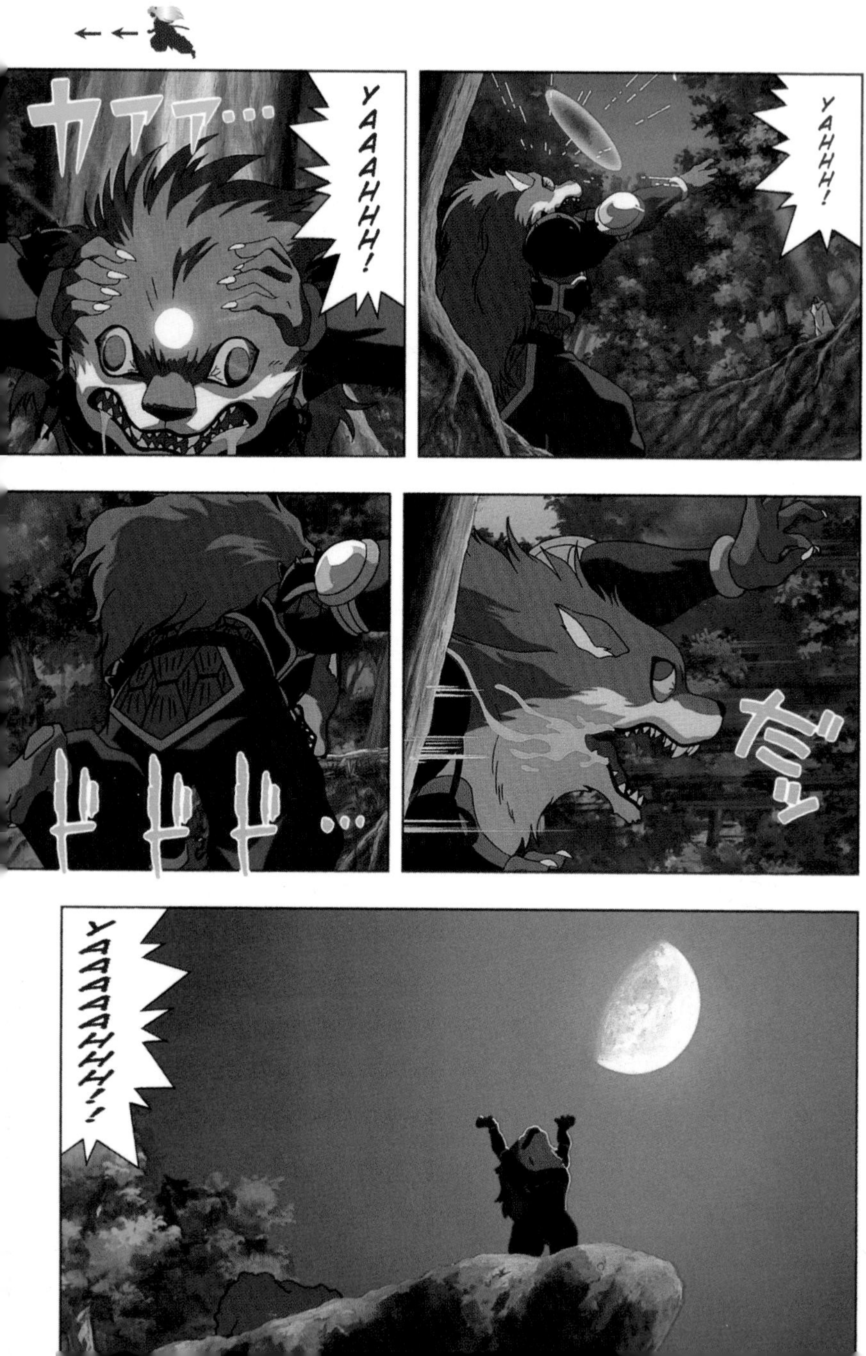
YAHHH!
YAAAAHHH!
カァァ...
だッ
ドドド...
YAAAAAHHH!!

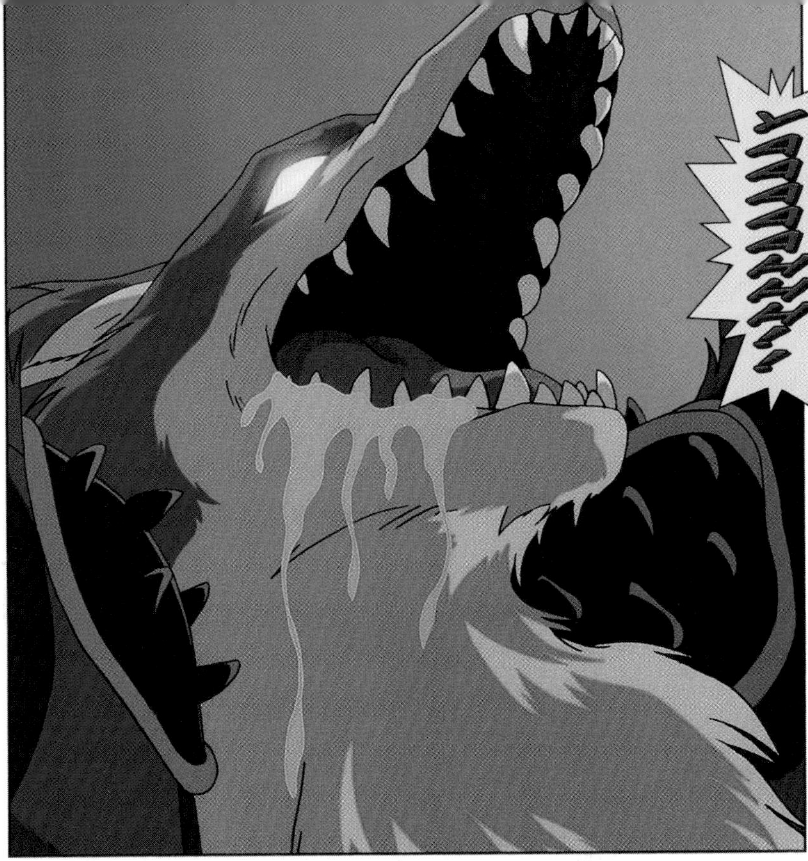

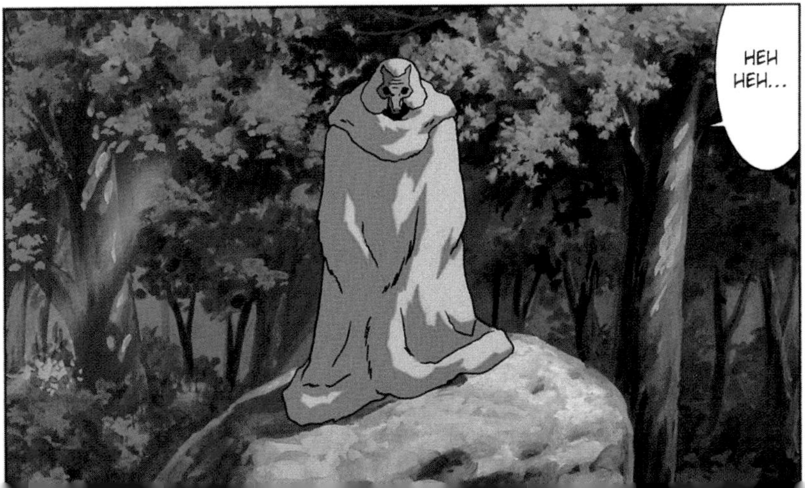
HEH
HEH...

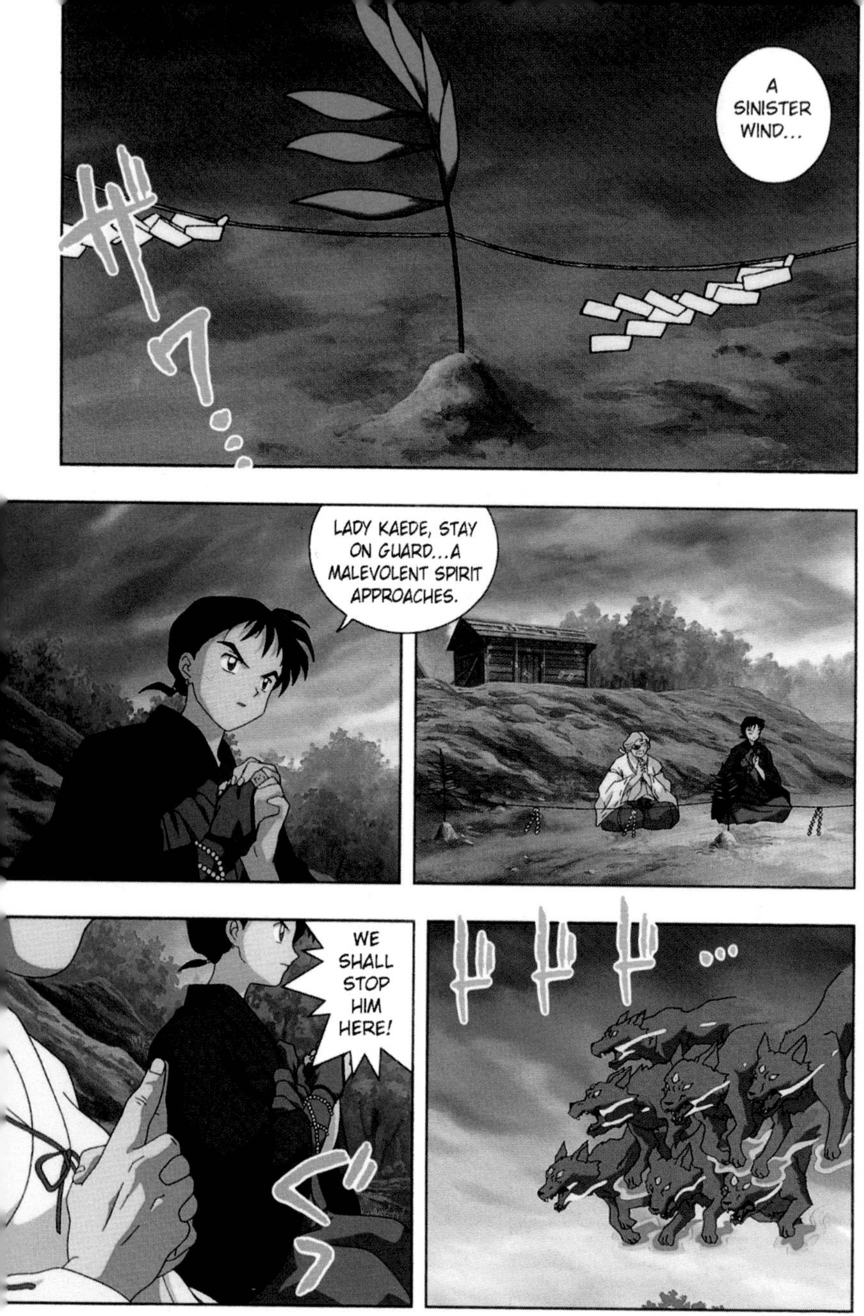
A SINISTER WIND...
ザワ...
LADY KAEDE, STAY ON GUARD...A MALEVOLENT SPIRIT APPROACHES.
WE SHALL STOP HIM HERE!

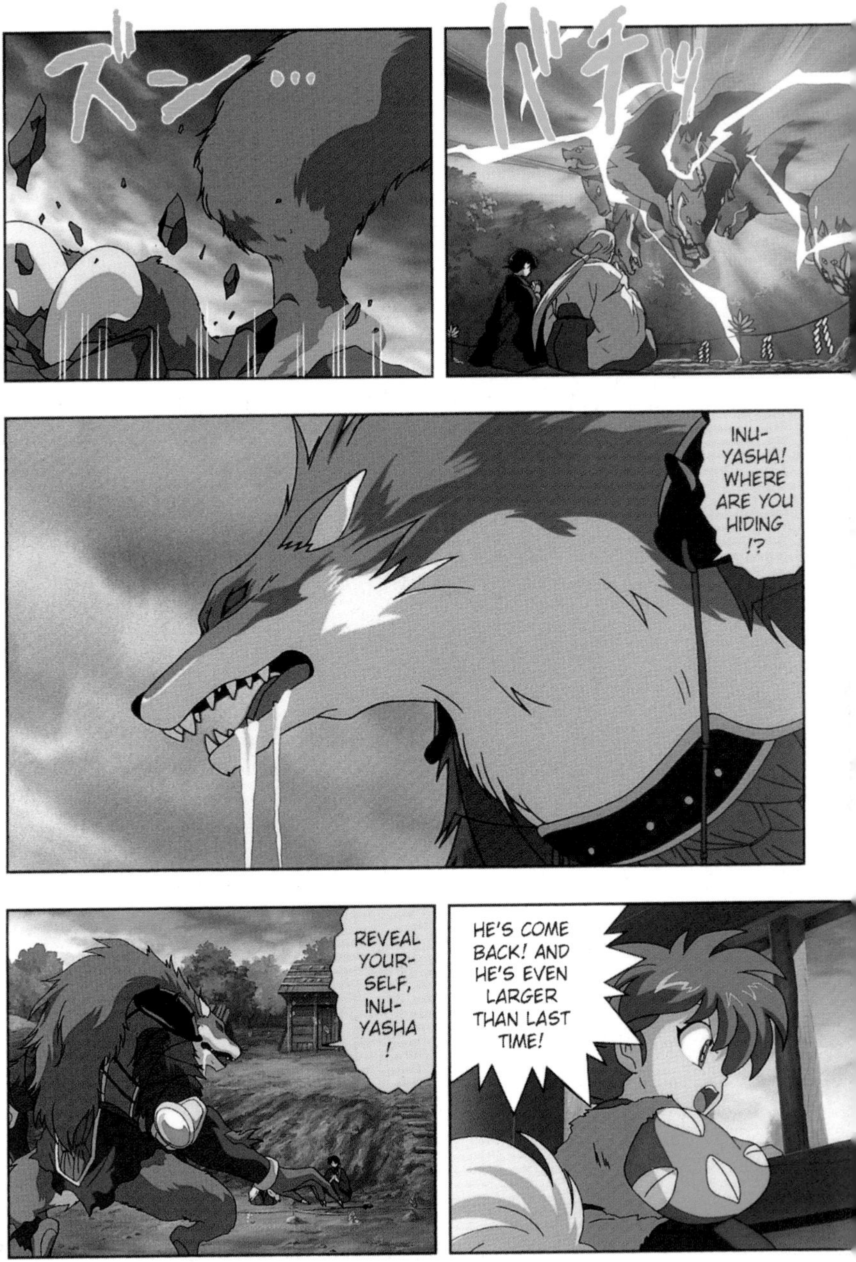

バチッ
ズーン…
INU-YASHA! WHERE ARE YOU HIDING !?
HE'S COME BACK! AND HE'S EVEN LARGER THAN LAST TIME!
REVEAL YOUR-SELF, INU-YASHA !

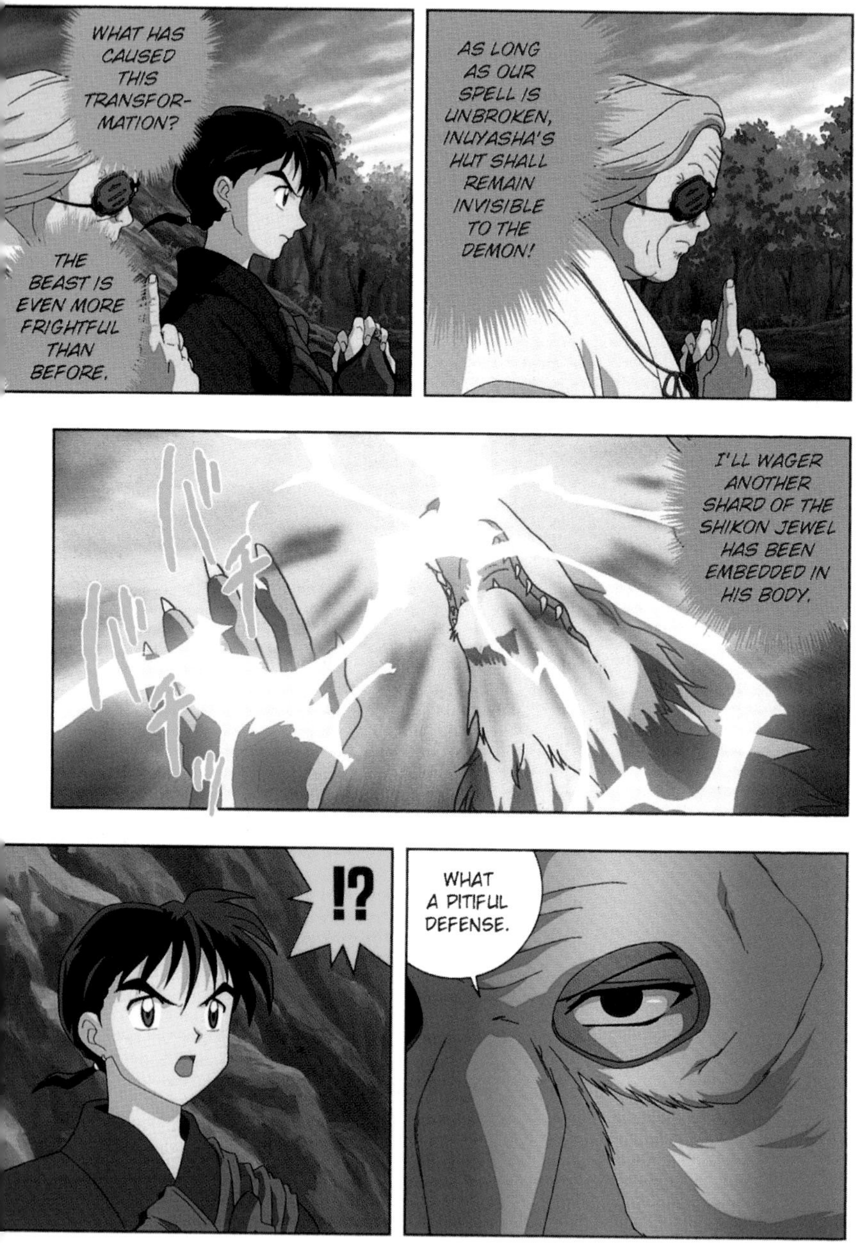

AS LONG AS OUR SPELL IS UNBROKEN, INUYASHA'S HUT SHALL REMAIN INVISIBLE TO THE DEMON!
WHAT HAS CAUSED THIS TRANSFORMATION?
THE BEAST IS EVEN MORE FRIGHTFUL THAN BEFORE.
I'LL WAGER ANOTHER SHARD OF THE SHIKON JEWEL HAS BEEN EMBEDDED IN HIS BODY.
バチ
バチッ
WHAT A PITIFUL DEFENSE.
!?

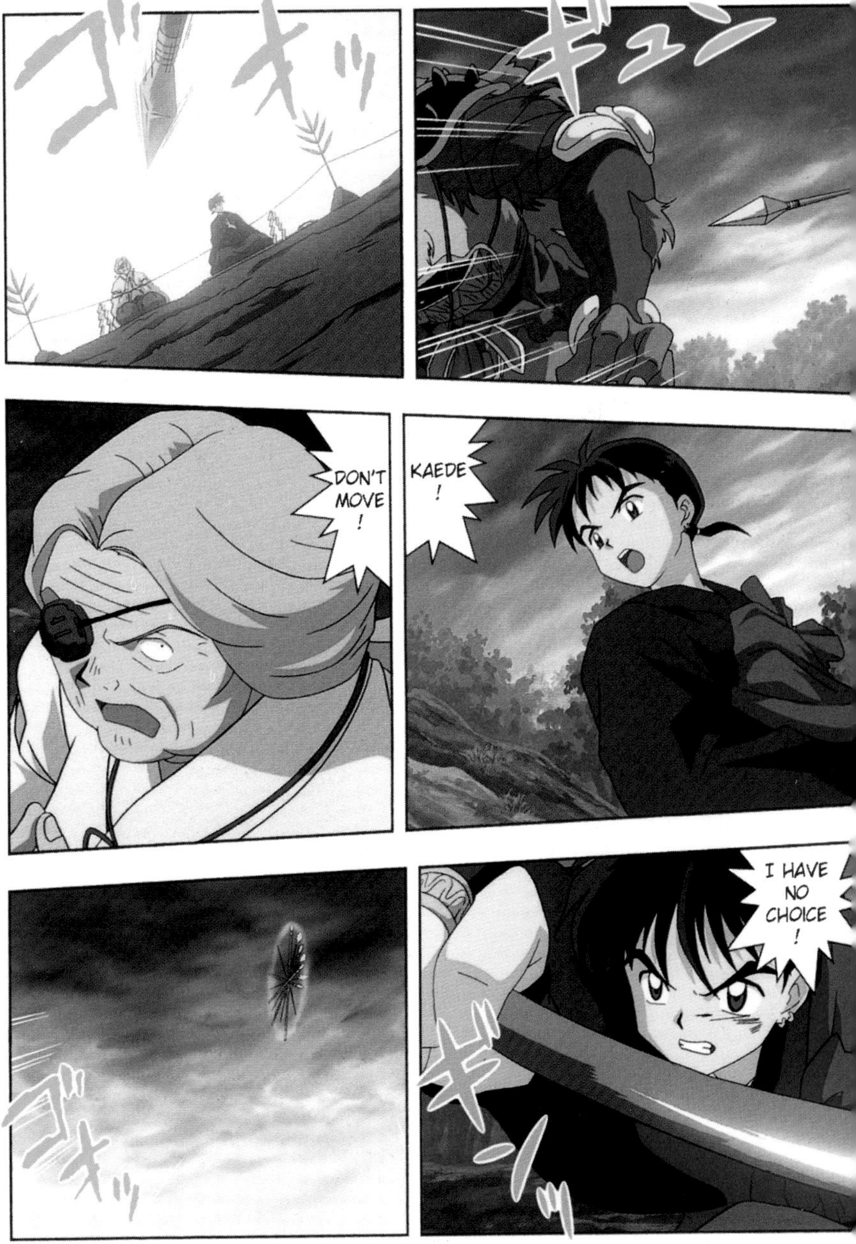
KAEDE!
DON'T MOVE!
I HAVE NO CHOICE!

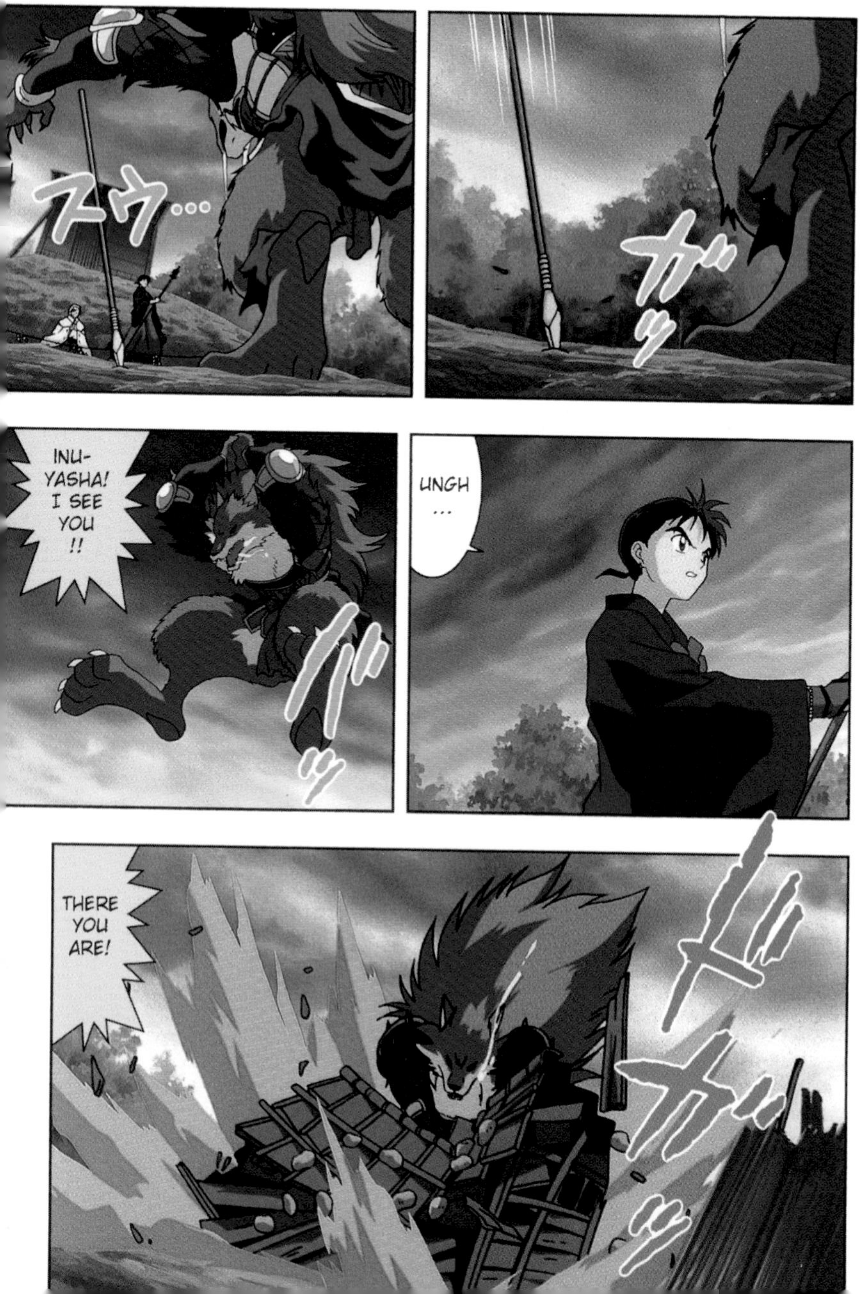
ガッ
スゥ…
UNGH …
INU-YASHA! I SEE YOU!!
ドッ
ドガッ
THERE YOU ARE!

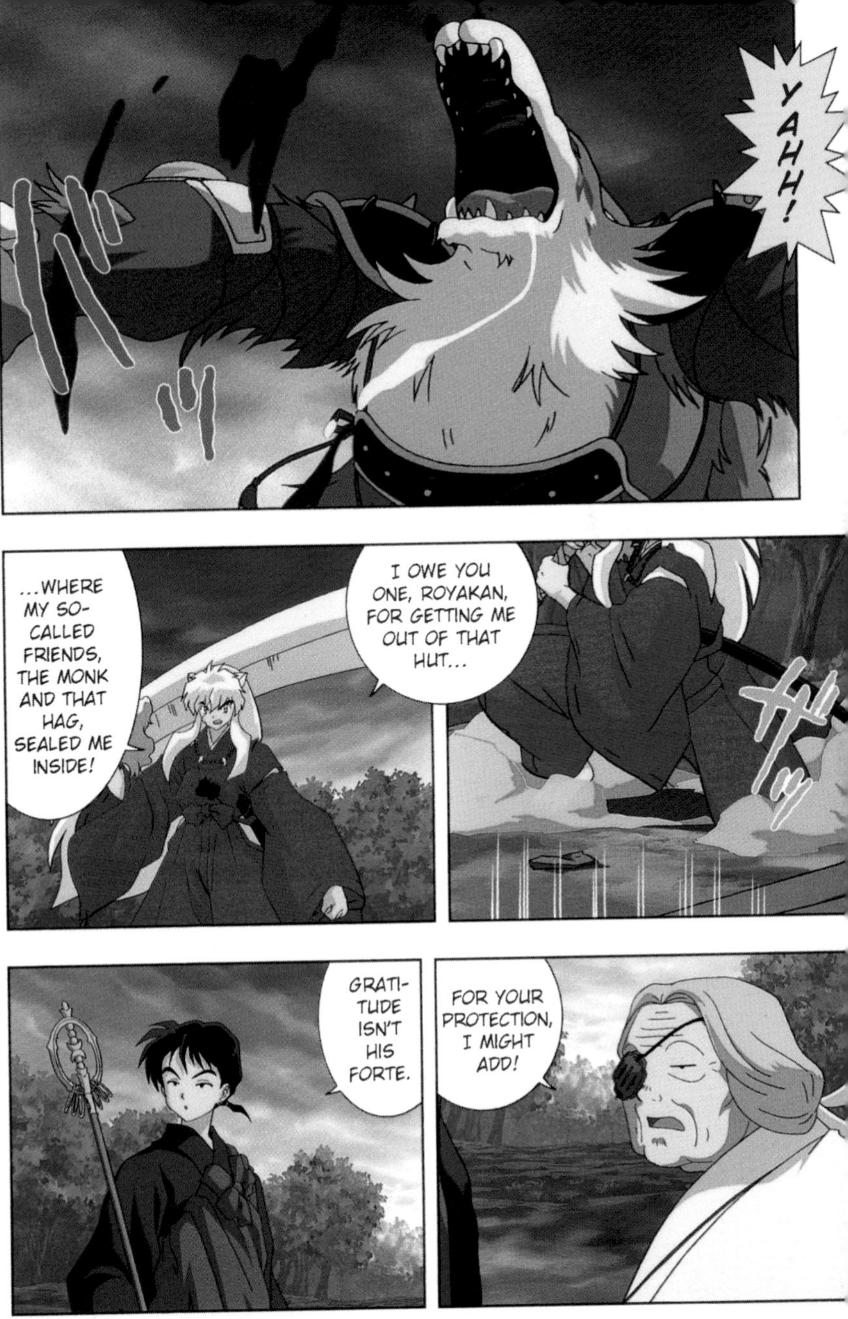
YAHH!
I OWE YOU ONE, ROYAKAN, FOR GETTING ME OUT OF THAT HUT...
...WHERE MY SO-CALLED FRIENDS, THE MONK AND THAT HAG, SEALED ME INSIDE!
FOR YOUR PROTECTION, I MIGHT ADD!
GRATI-TUDE ISN'T HIS FORTE.

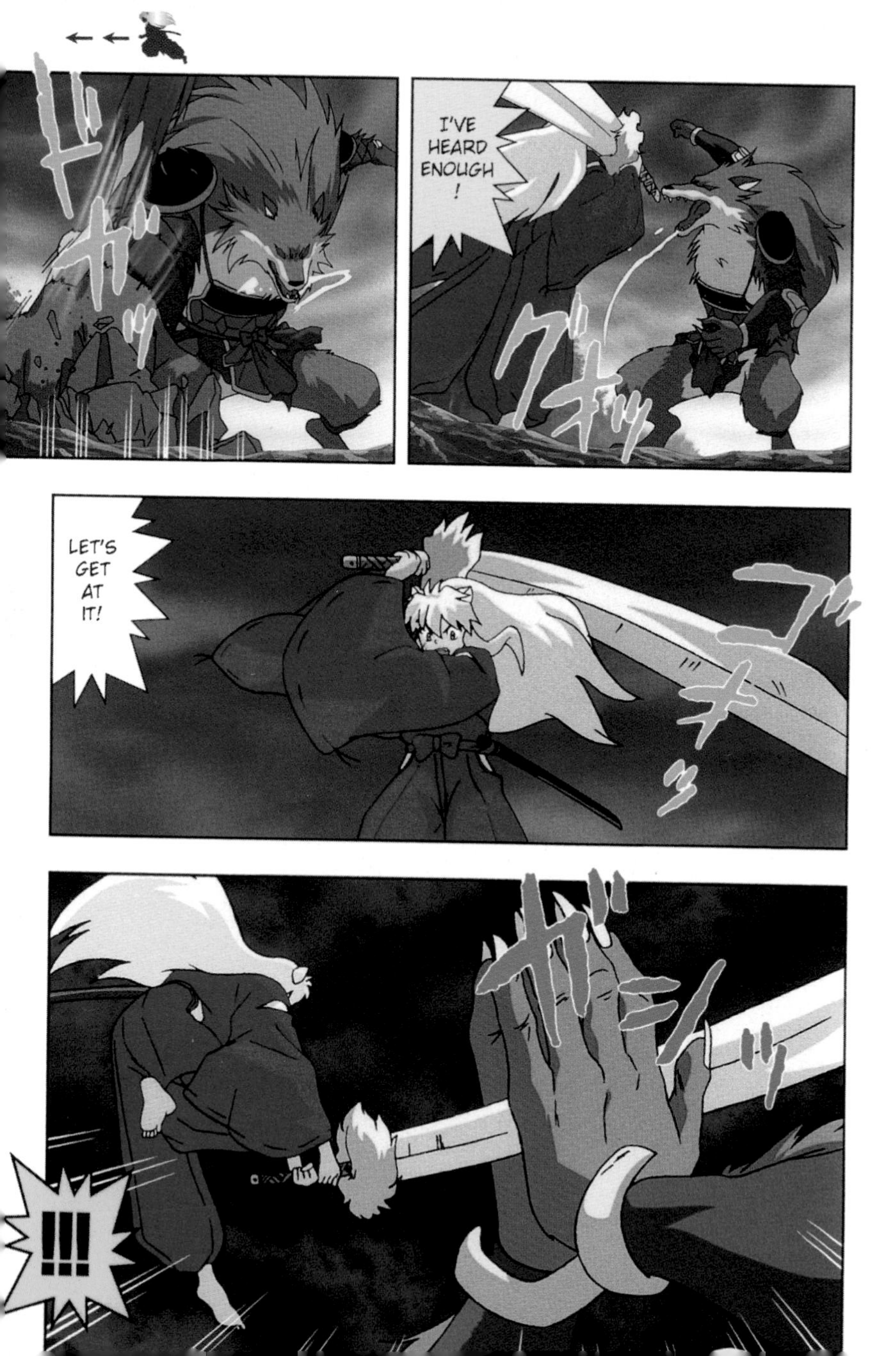
I'VE HEARD ENOUGH!
LET'S GET AT IT!
!!!

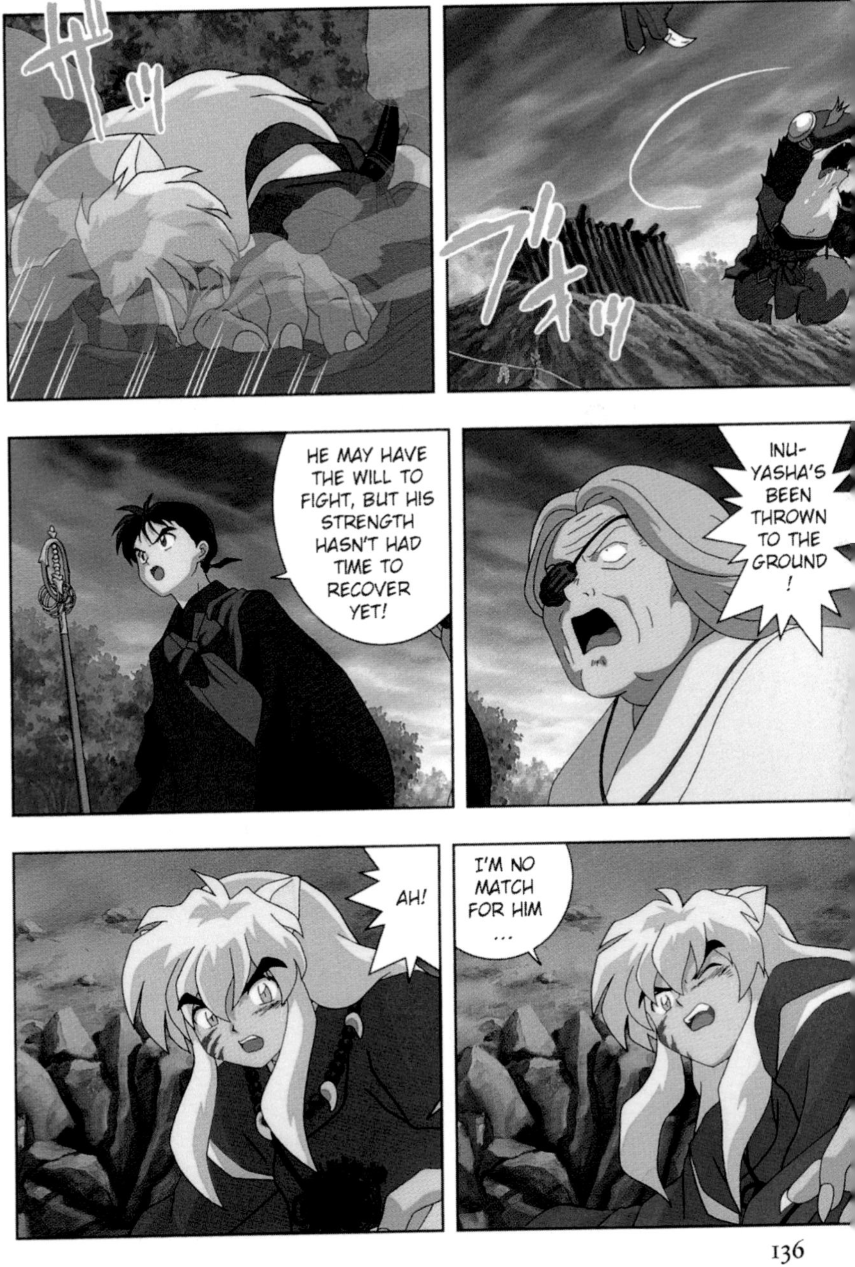
INU-YASHA'S BEEN THROWN TO THE GROUND!
HE MAY HAVE THE WILL TO FIGHT, BUT HIS STRENGTH HASN'T HAD TIME TO RECOVER YET!
I'M NO MATCH FOR HIM...
AH!

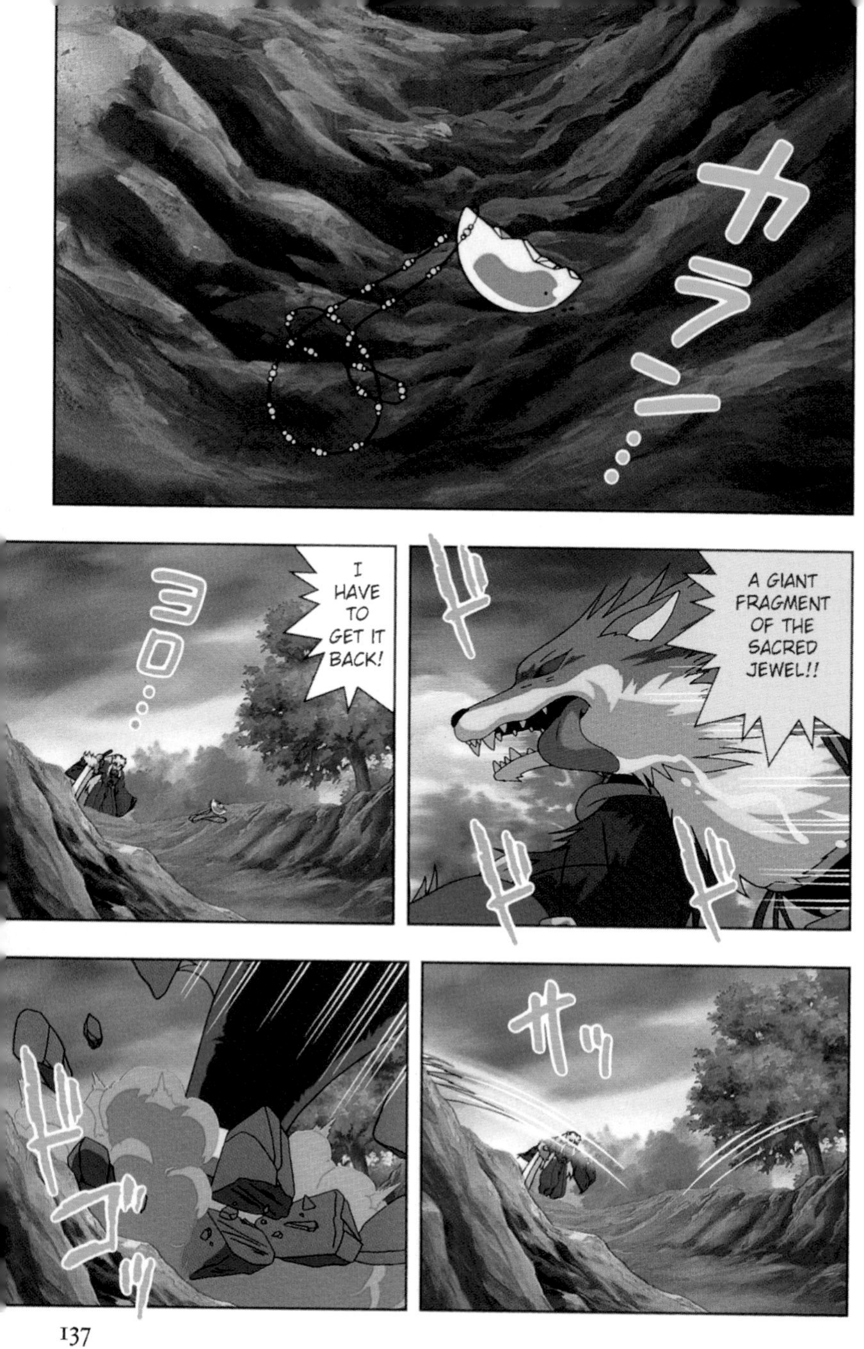
カラン…
ドドド
A GIANT FRAGMENT OF THE SACRED JEWEL!!
I HAVE TO GET IT BACK!
ヨロ…
サッ
ドゴッ

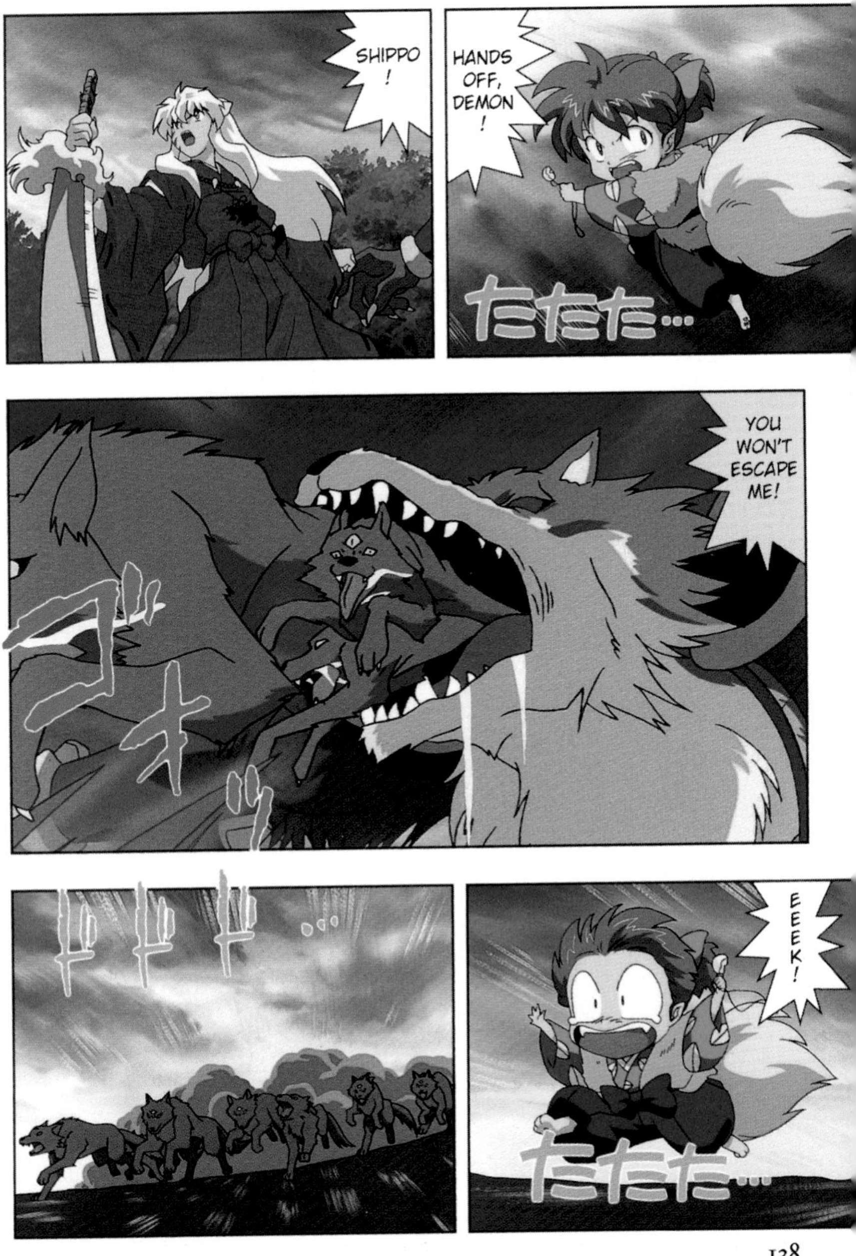
HANDS OFF, DEMON!
たたた...
SHIPPO!
YOU WON'T ESCAPE ME!
ゴォッ
EEEK!
たたた...
ドドド...

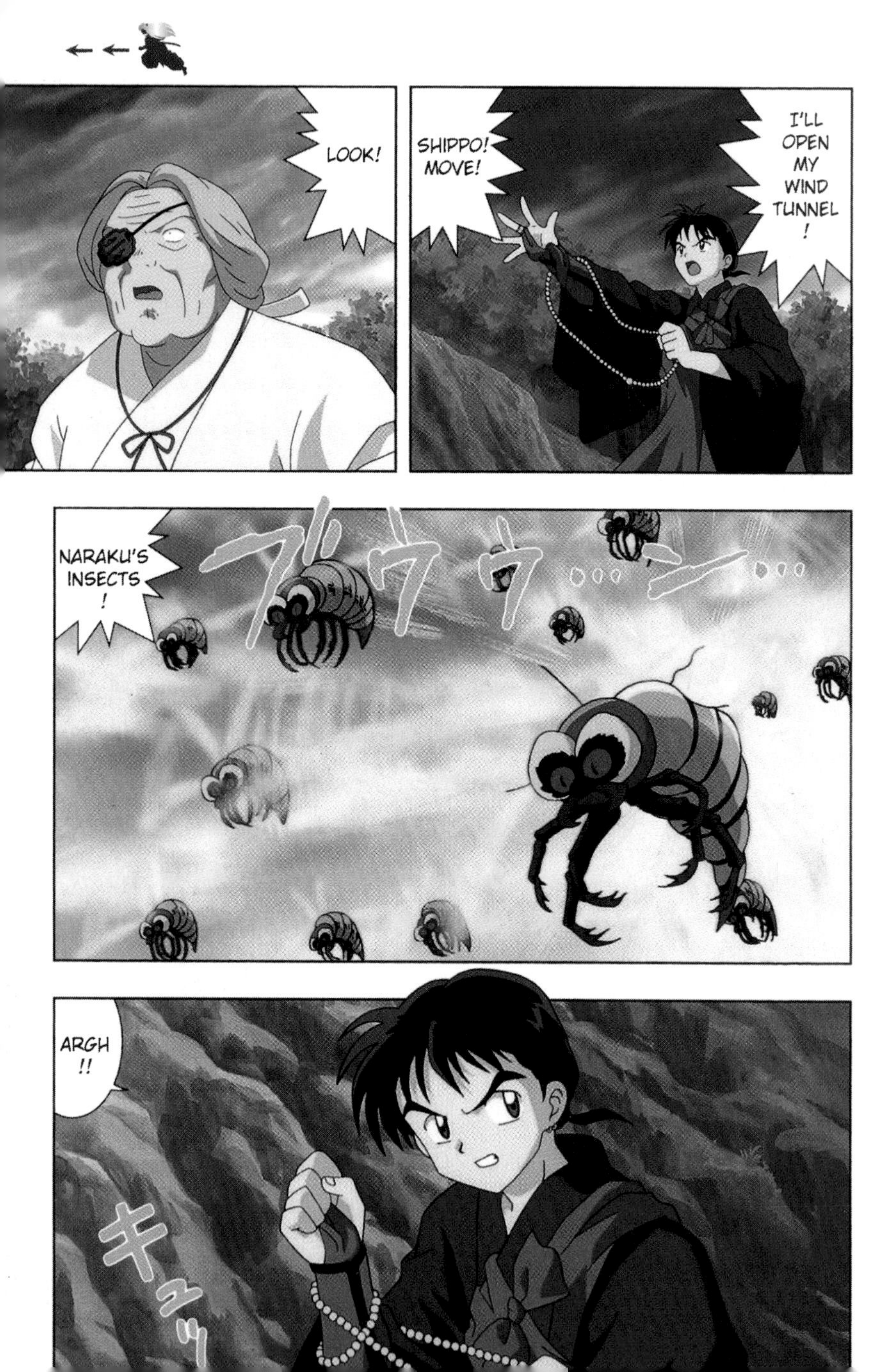
I'LL OPEN MY WIND TUNNEL!
SHIPPO! MOVE!
LOOK!
ブウウ…ン…
NARAKU'S INSECTS!
ARGH!!
キュッ

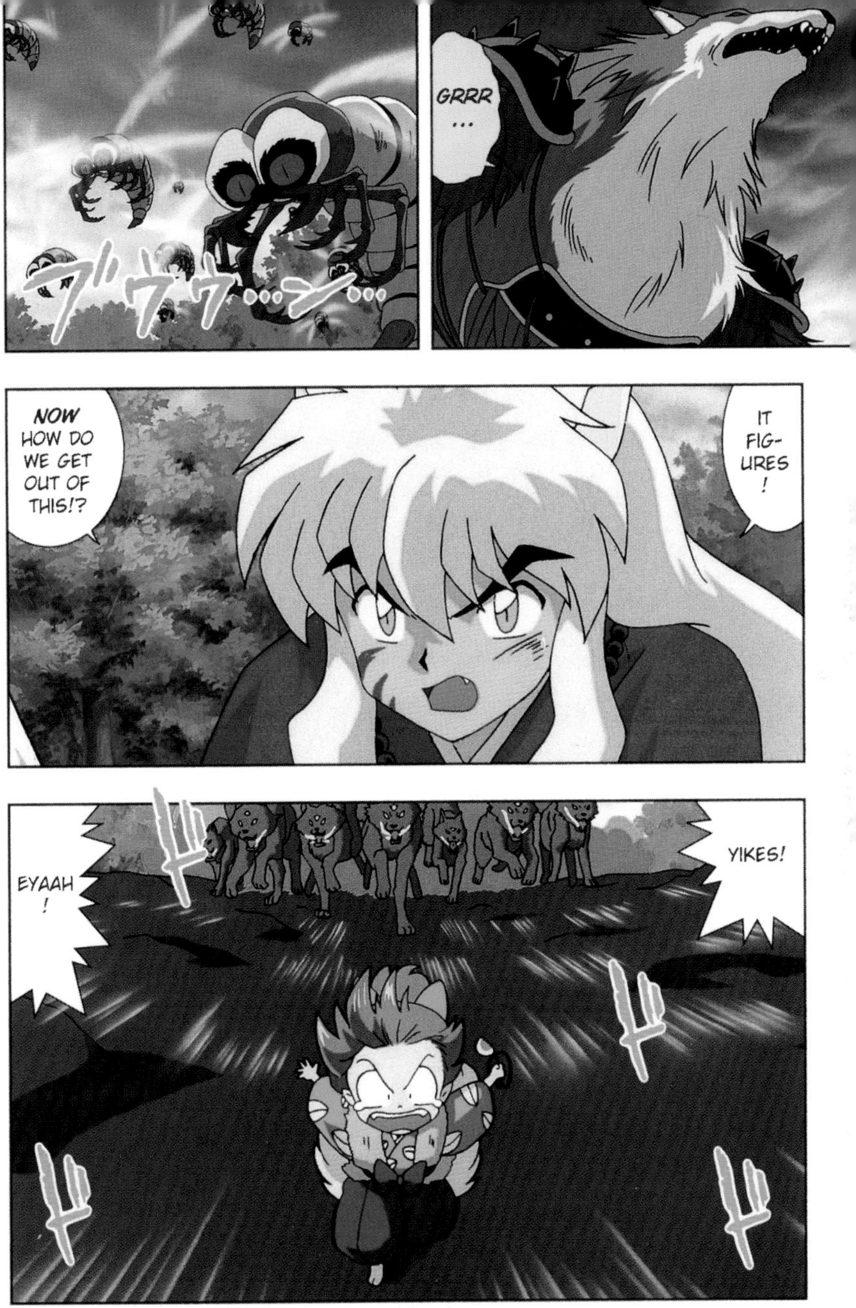
GRRR ...
ヴヴウ…ン…
IT FIGURES!
NOW HOW DO WE GET OUT OF THIS!?
YIKES!
EYAAH!

21 Naraku's True Identity Unveiled

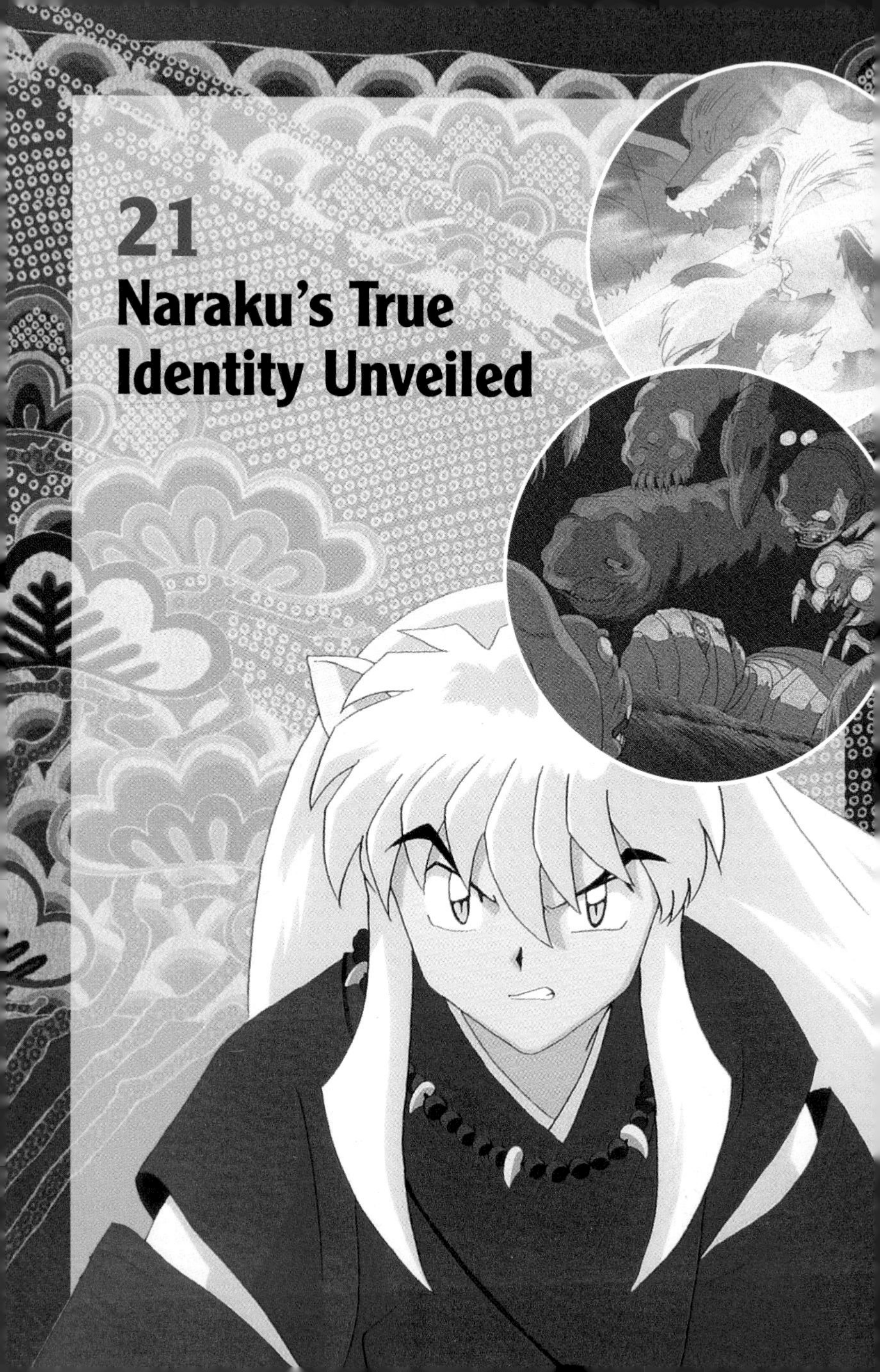

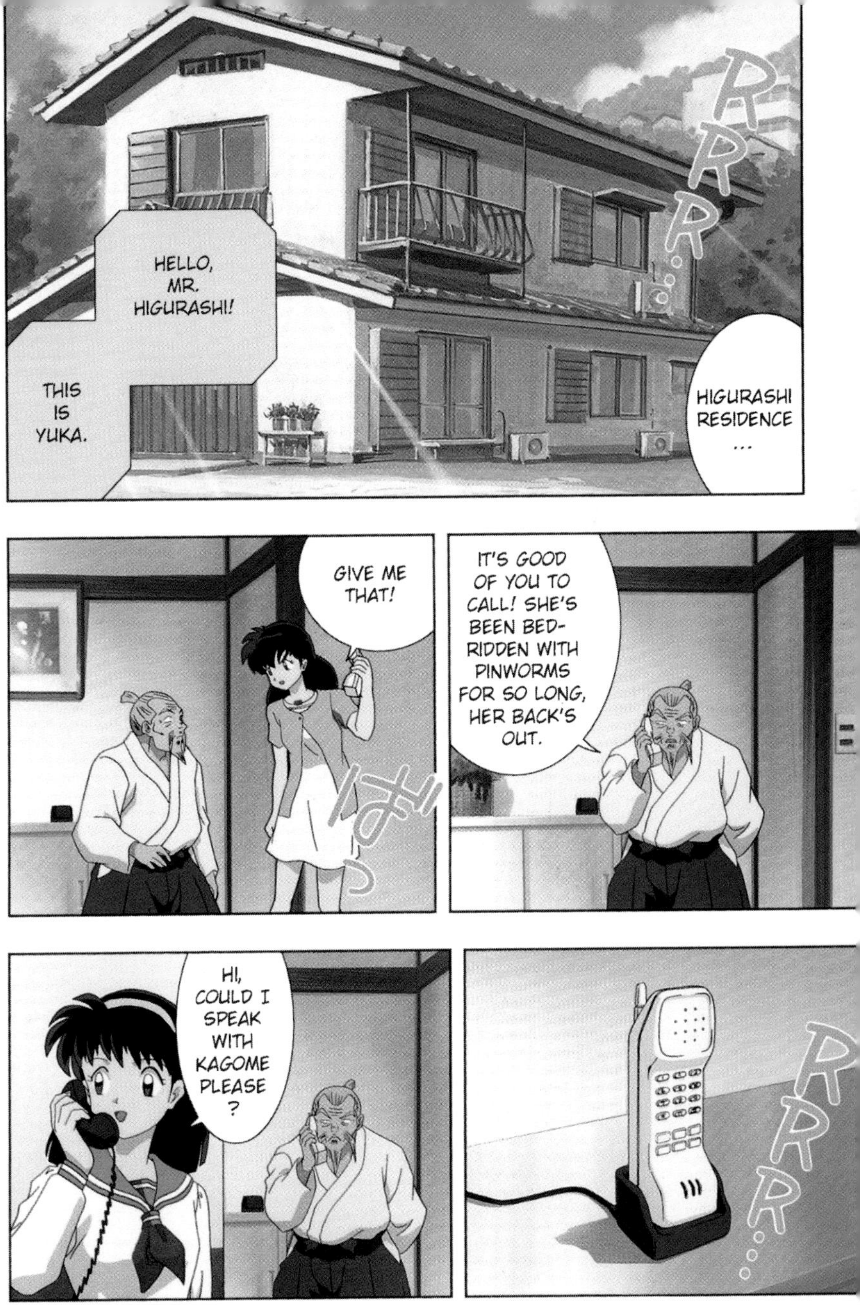
RRR...
HIGURASHI RESIDENCE ...
HELLO, MR. HIGURASHI!
THIS IS YUKA.
IT'S GOOD OF YOU TO CALL! SHE'S BEEN BED-RIDDEN WITH PINWORMS FOR SO LONG, HER BACK'S OUT.
GIVE ME THAT!
はっ
RRR...
HI, COULD I SPEAK WITH KAGOME PLEASE?

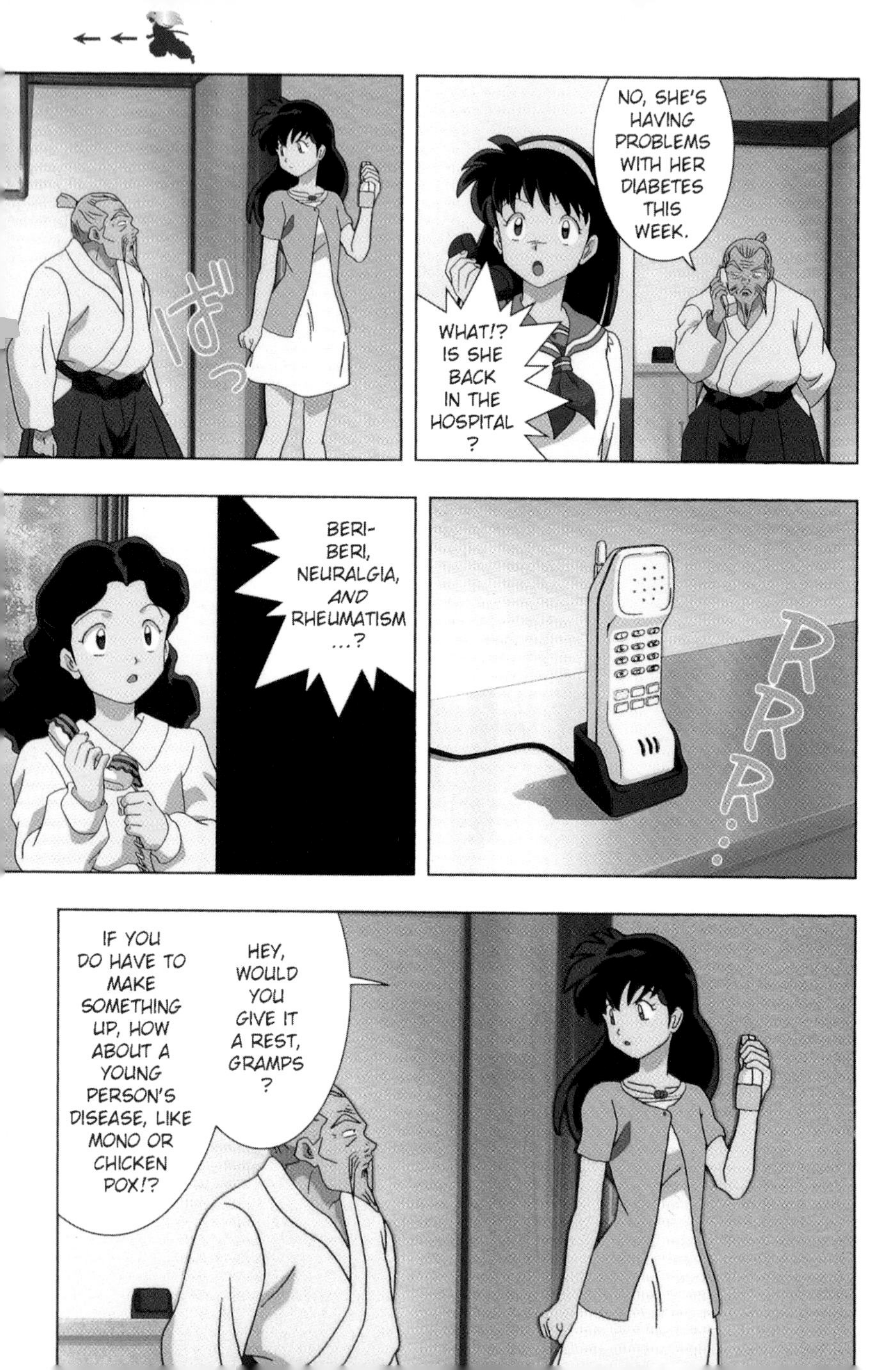
NO, SHE'S HAVING PROBLEMS WITH HER DIABETES THIS WEEK.
WHAT!? IS SHE BACK IN THE HOSPITAL?
ばっ
RRR...
BERI-BERI, NEURALGIA, *AND* RHEUMATISM...?
HEY, WOULD YOU GIVE IT A REST, GRAMPS?
IF YOU DO HAVE TO MAKE SOMETHING UP, HOW ABOUT A YOUNG PERSON'S DISEASE, LIKE MONO OR CHICKEN POX!?

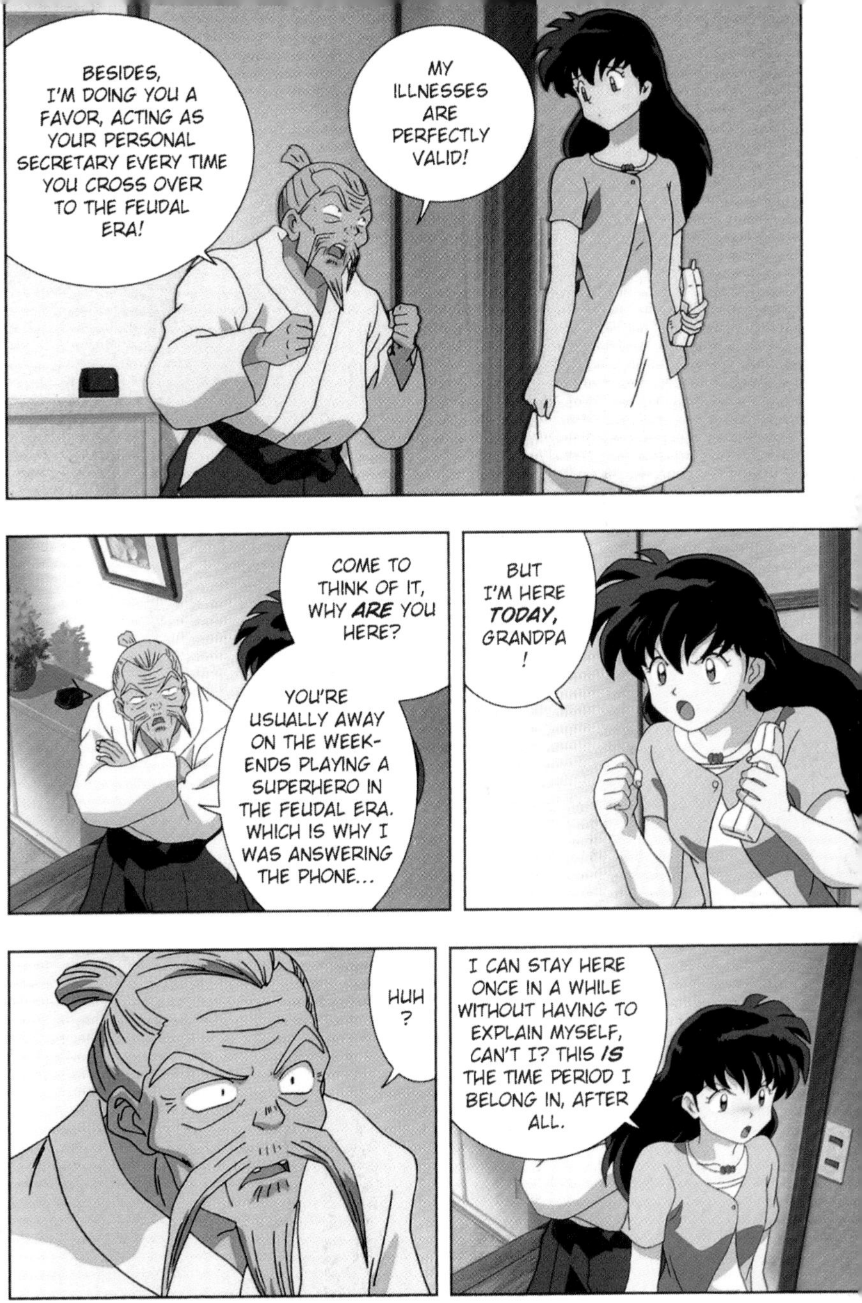
BESIDES, I'M DOING YOU A FAVOR, ACTING AS YOUR PERSONAL SECRETARY EVERY TIME YOU CROSS OVER TO THE FEUDAL ERA!
MY ILLNESSES ARE PERFECTLY VALID!
COME TO THINK OF IT, WHY ***ARE*** YOU HERE?
YOU'RE USUALLY AWAY ON THE WEEK-ENDS PLAYING A SUPERHERO IN THE FEUDAL ERA. WHICH IS WHY I WAS ANSWERING THE PHONE...
BUT I'M HERE ***TODAY,*** GRANDPA!
HUH?
I CAN STAY HERE ONCE IN A WHILE WITHOUT HAVING TO EXPLAIN MYSELF, CAN'T I? THIS ***IS*** THE TIME PERIOD I BELONG IN, AFTER ALL.

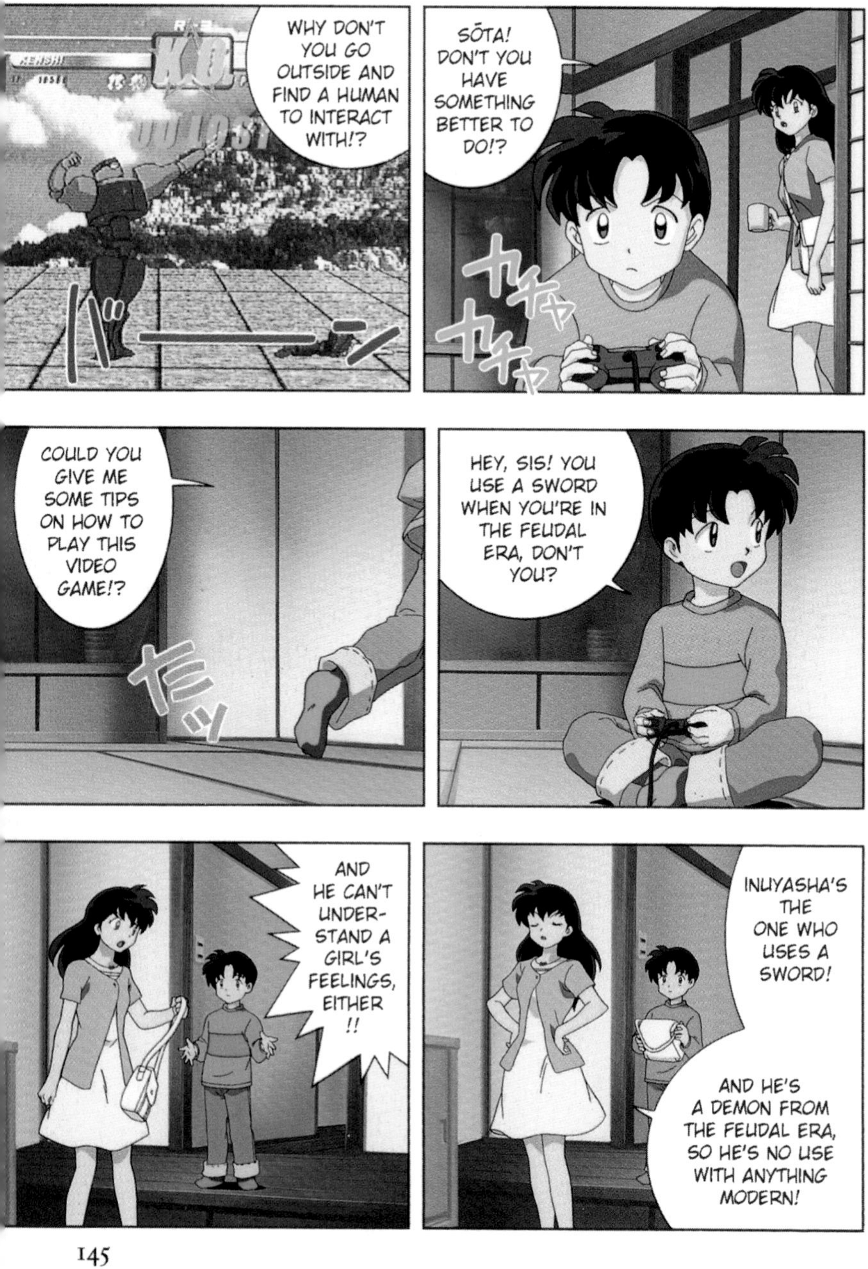

SŌTA! DON'T YOU HAVE SOMETHING BETTER TO DO!?
カチャ カチャ
WHY DON'T YOU GO OUTSIDE AND FIND A HUMAN TO INTERACT WITH!?
HEY, SIS! YOU USE A SWORD WHEN YOU'RE IN THE FEUDAL ERA, DON'T YOU?
COULD YOU GIVE ME SOME TIPS ON HOW TO PLAY THIS VIDEO GAME!?
INUYASHA'S THE ONE WHO USES A SWORD!
AND HE'S A DEMON FROM THE FEUDAL ERA, SO HE'S NO USE WITH ANYTHING MODERN!
AND HE CAN'T UNDER-STAND A GIRL'S FEELINGS, EITHER !!

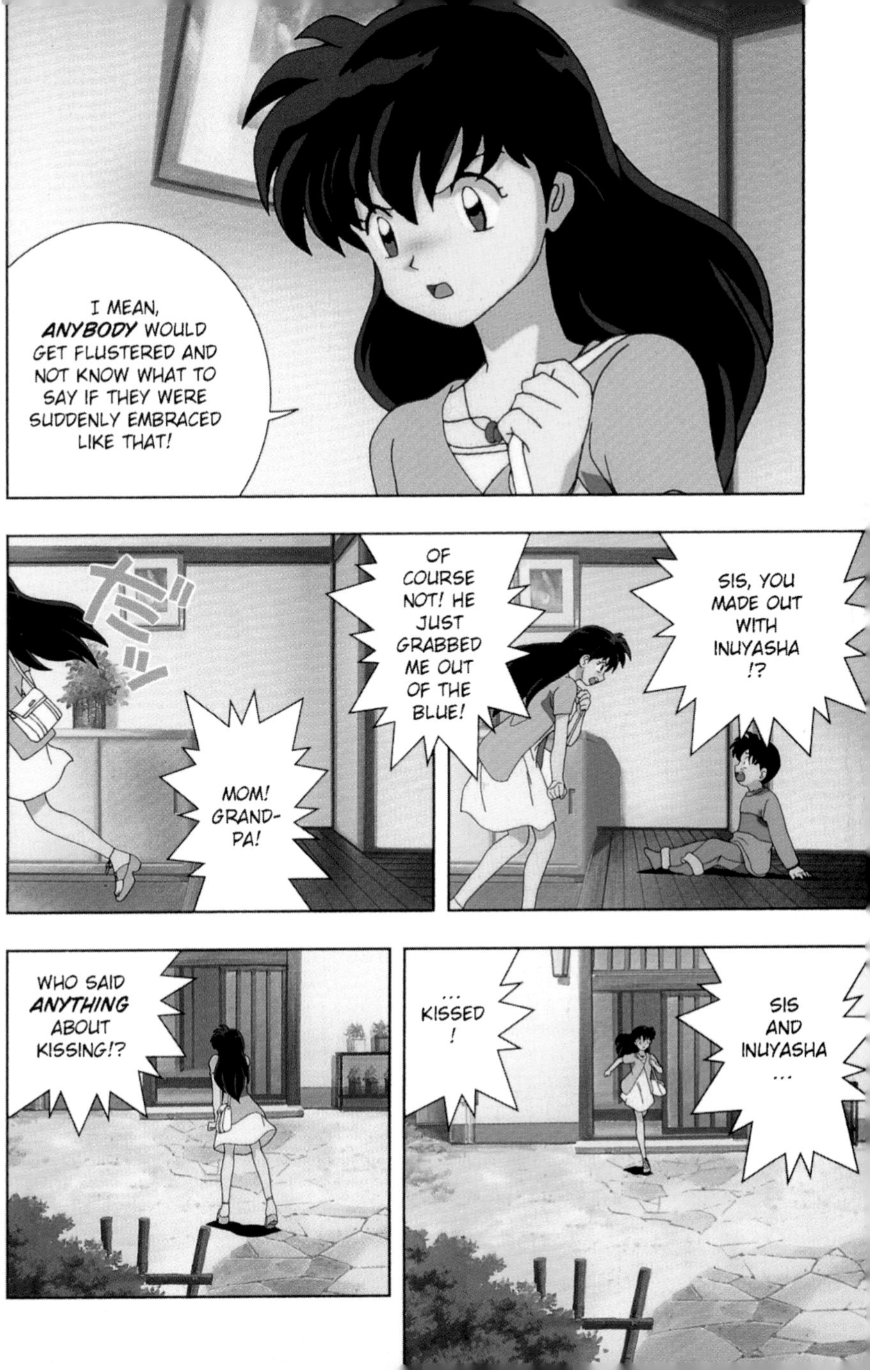
I MEAN, **ANYBODY** WOULD GET FLUSTERED AND NOT KNOW WHAT TO SAY IF THEY WERE SUDDENLY EMBRACED LIKE THAT!
SIS, YOU MADE OUT WITH INUYASHA !?
OF COURSE NOT! HE JUST GRABBED ME OUT OF THE BLUE!
だッ
MOM! GRAND-PA!
SIS AND INUYASHA ...
... KISSED !
WHO SAID **ANYTHING** ABOUT KISSING!?

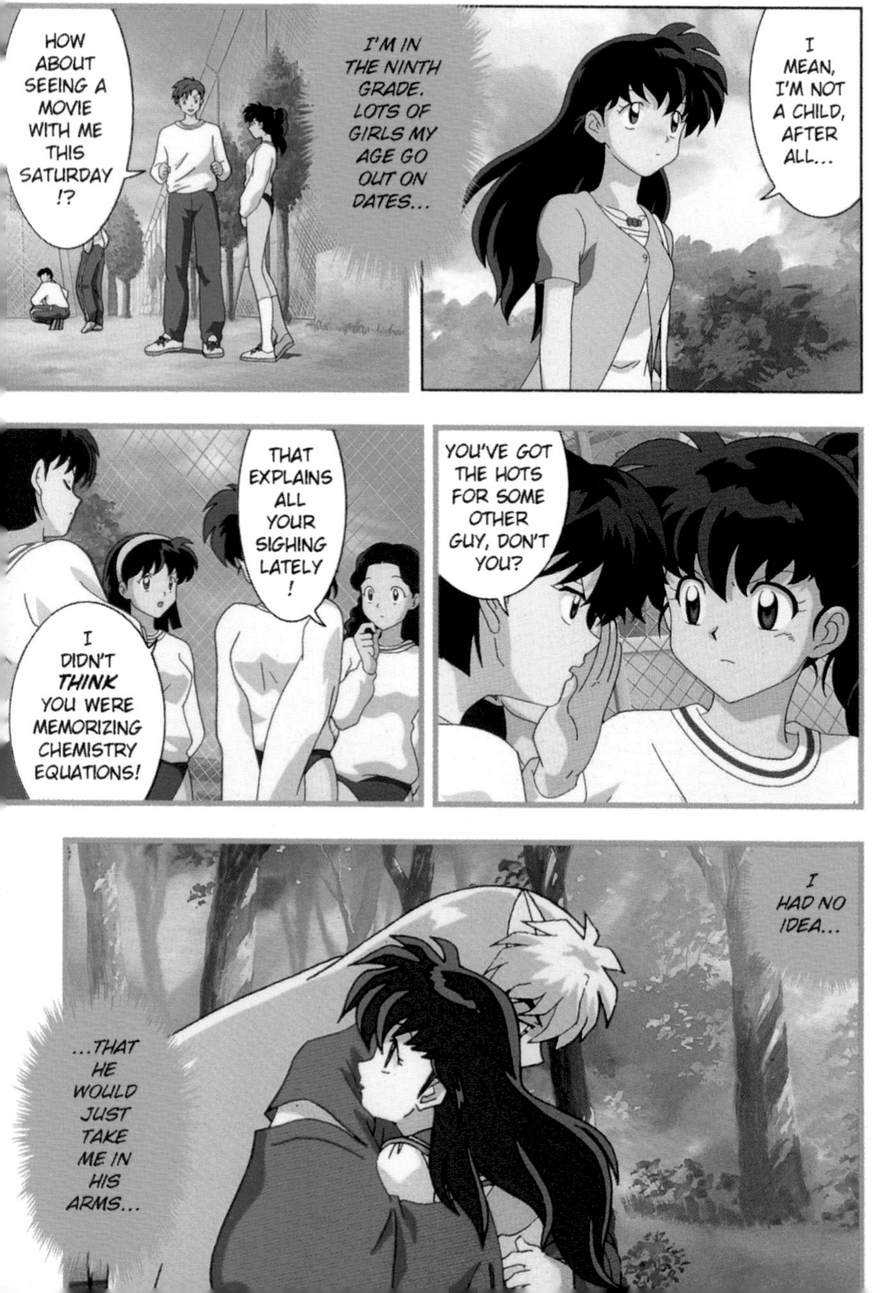
I MEAN, I'M NOT A CHILD, AFTER ALL...
I'M IN THE NINTH GRADE. LOTS OF GIRLS MY AGE GO OUT ON DATES...
HOW ABOUT SEEING A MOVIE WITH ME THIS SATURDAY !?
YOU'VE GOT THE HOTS FOR SOME OTHER GUY, DON'T YOU?
THAT EXPLAINS ALL YOUR SIGHING LATELY !
I DIDN'T *THINK* YOU WERE MEMORIZING CHEMISTRY EQUATIONS!
I HAD NO IDEA...
...THAT HE WOULD JUST TAKE ME IN HIS ARMS...

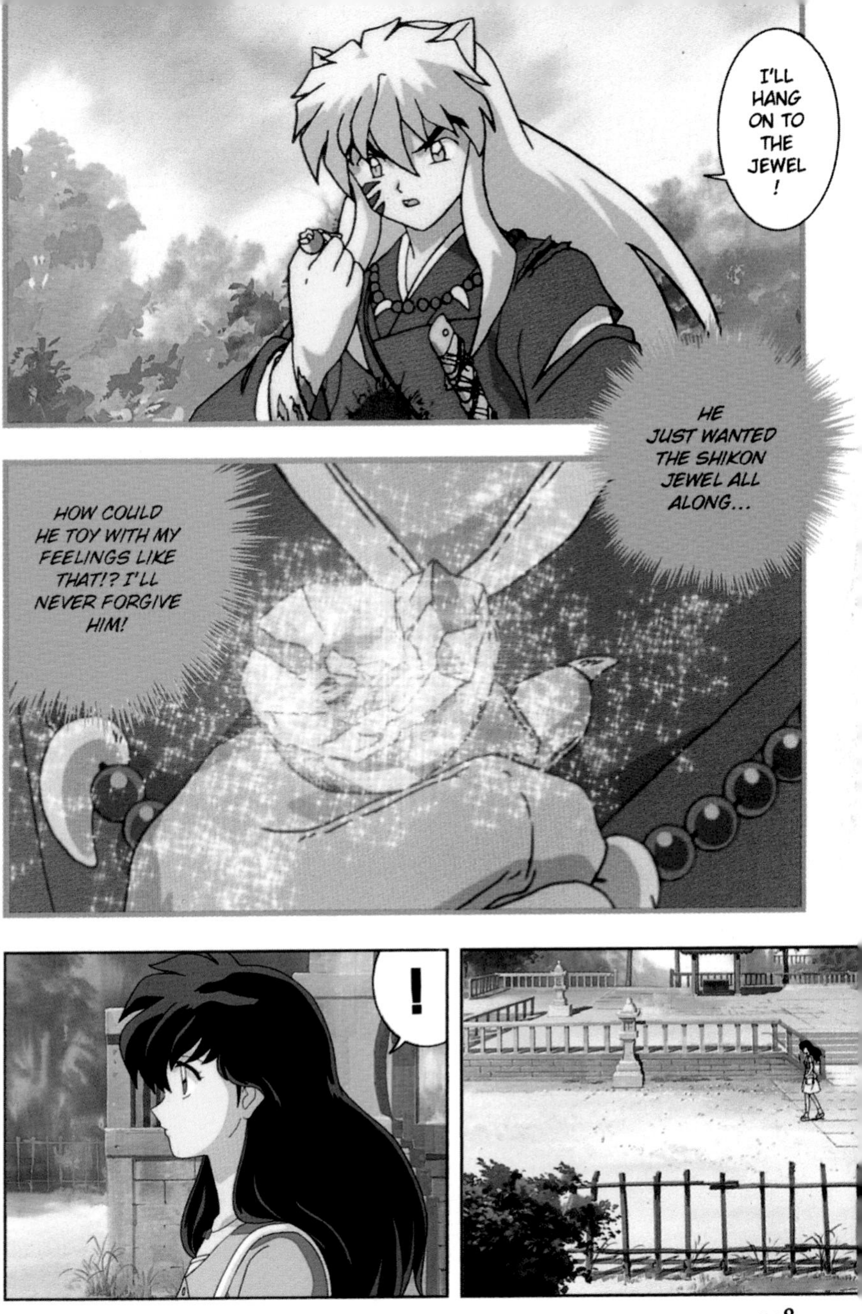
I'LL HANG ON TO THE JEWEL!
HE JUST WANTED THE SHIKON JEWEL ALL ALONG...
HOW COULD HE TOY WITH MY FEELINGS LIKE THAT!? I'LL NEVER FORGIVE HIM!
!

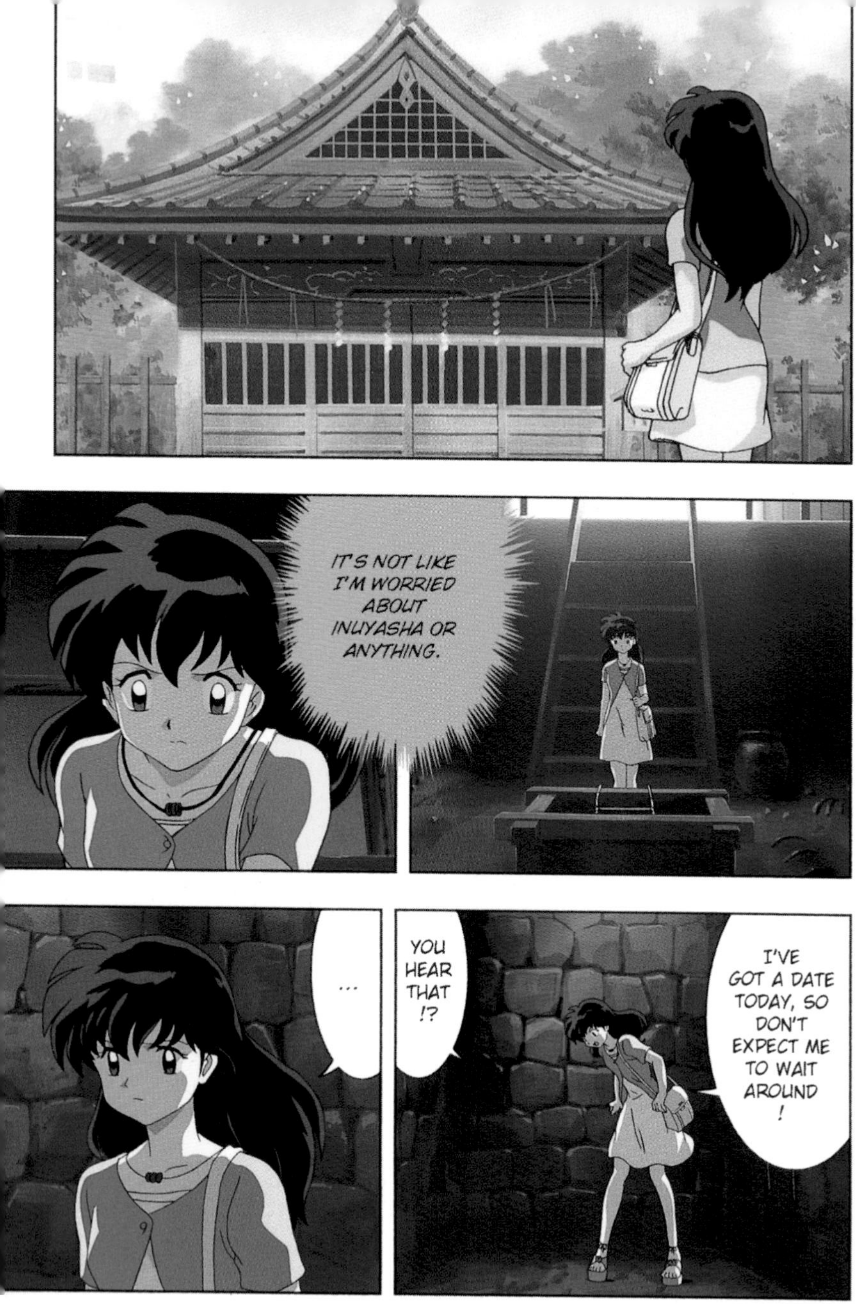
IT'S NOT LIKE I'M WORRIED ABOUT INUYASHA OR ANYTHING.
I'VE GOT A DATE TODAY, SO DON'T EXPECT ME TO WAIT AROUND!
YOU HEAR THAT!?
...

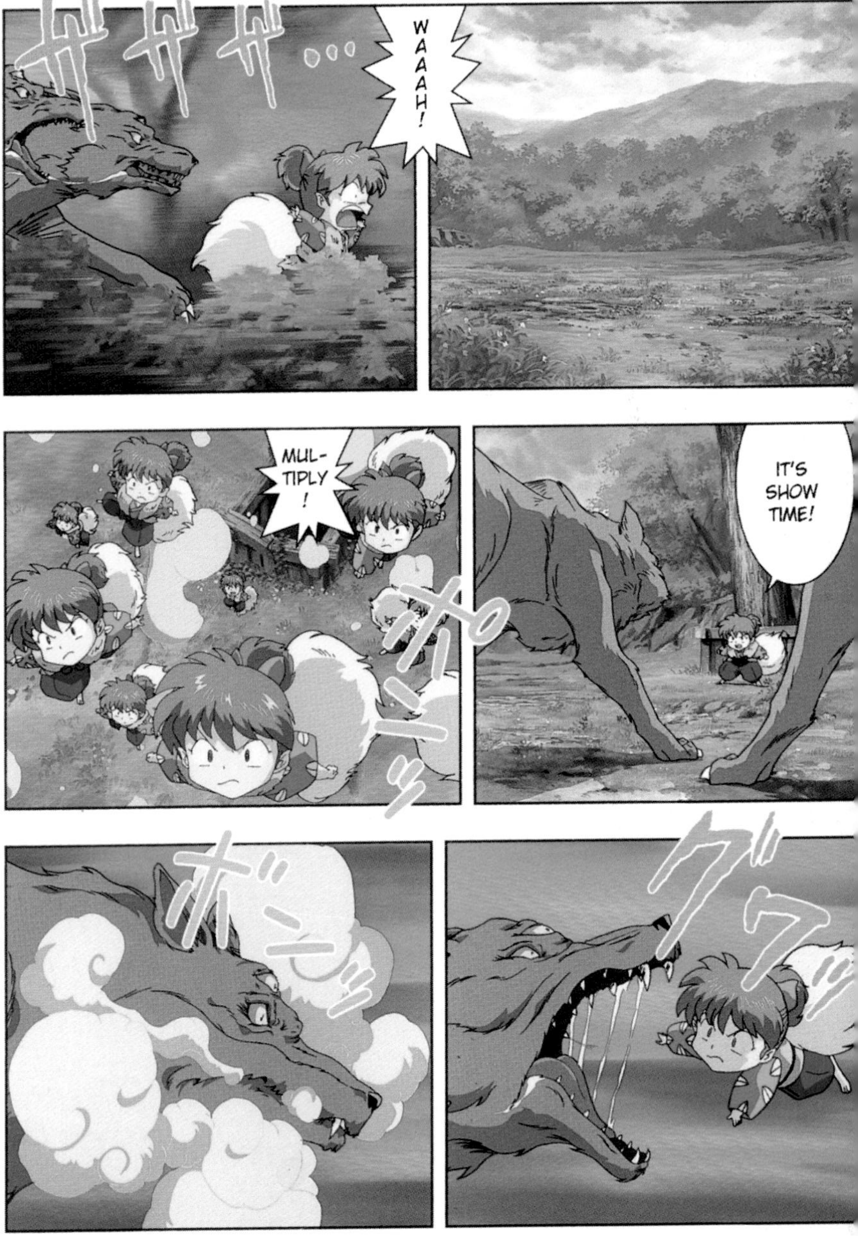
WAAAAH!
ザザザ…
IT'S SHOW TIME!
MUL-TIPLY!
ポンッ
グワッ
ボンッ

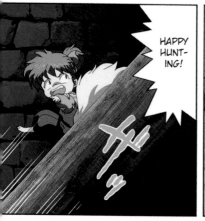

HAPPY HUNT-ING!

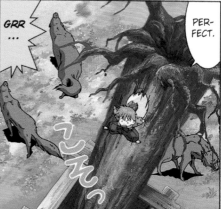

GRR...

PER-FECT.

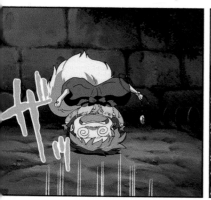

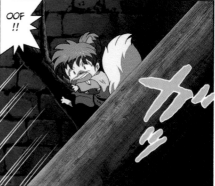

OOF!!

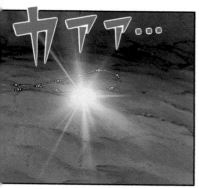

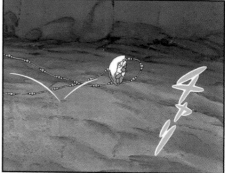

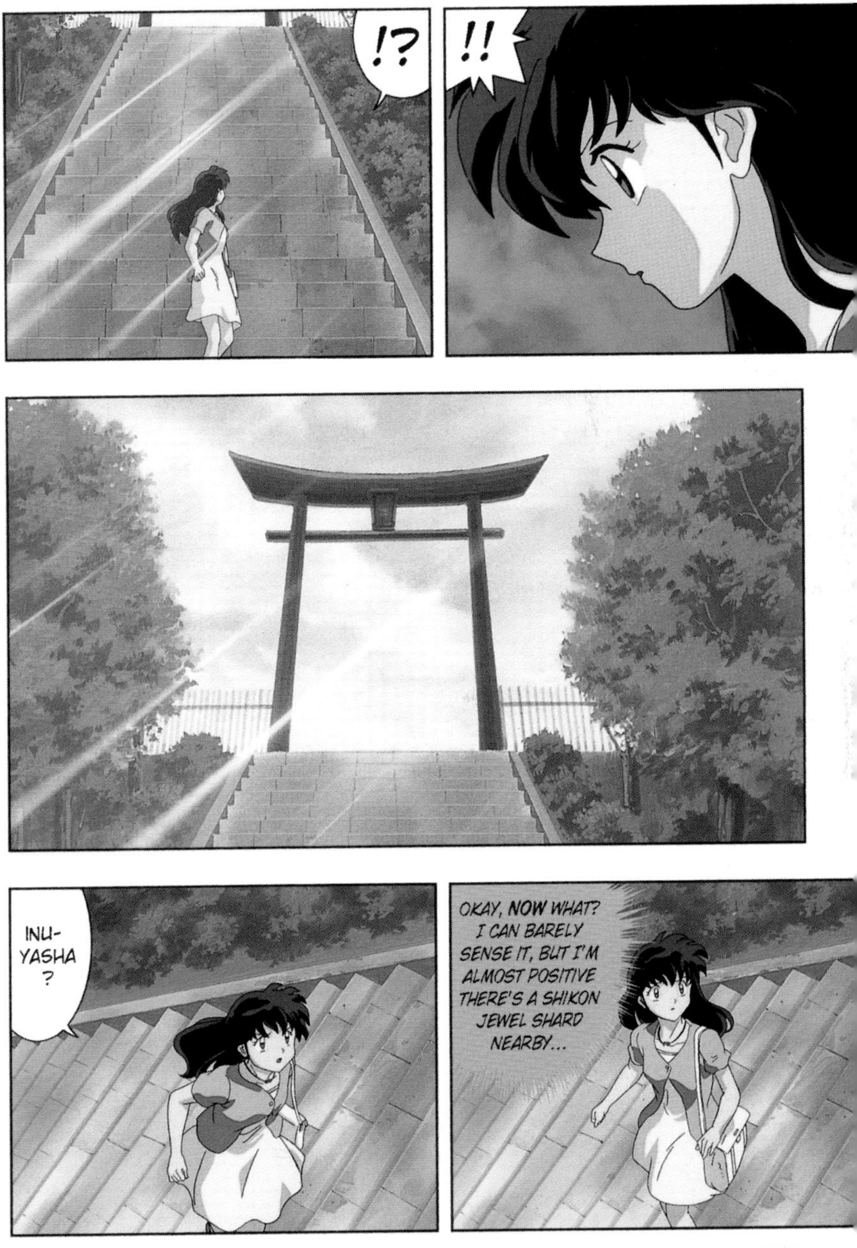
!!
!?
OKAY, NOW WHAT? I CAN BARELY SENSE IT, BUT I'M ALMOST POSITIVE THERE'S A SHIKON JEWEL SHARD NEARBY...
INU-YASHA?

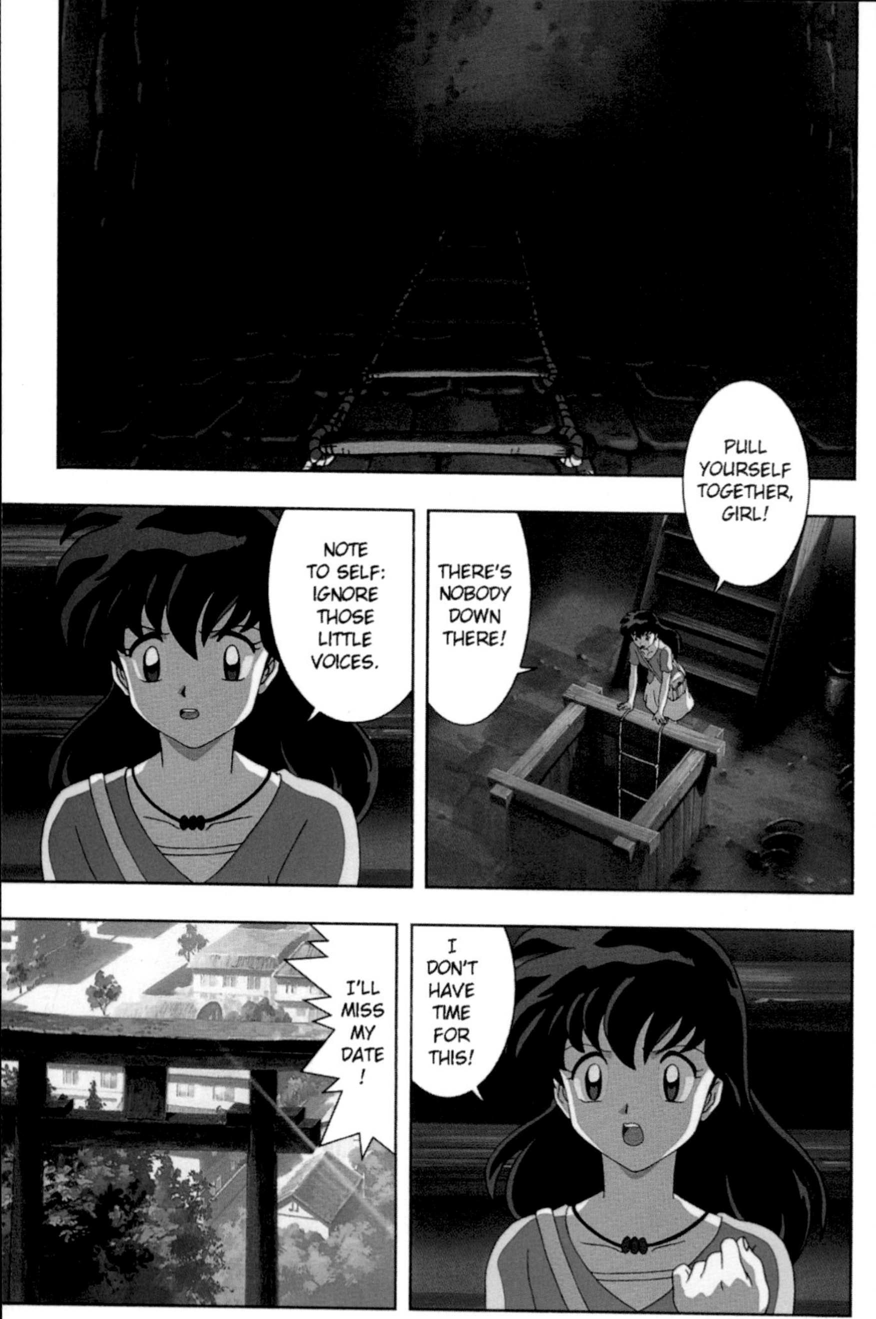
PULL YOURSELF TOGETHER, GIRL!
THERE'S NOBODY DOWN THERE!
NOTE TO SELF: IGNORE THOSE LITTLE VOICES.
I DON'T HAVE TIME FOR THIS!
I'LL MISS MY DATE!

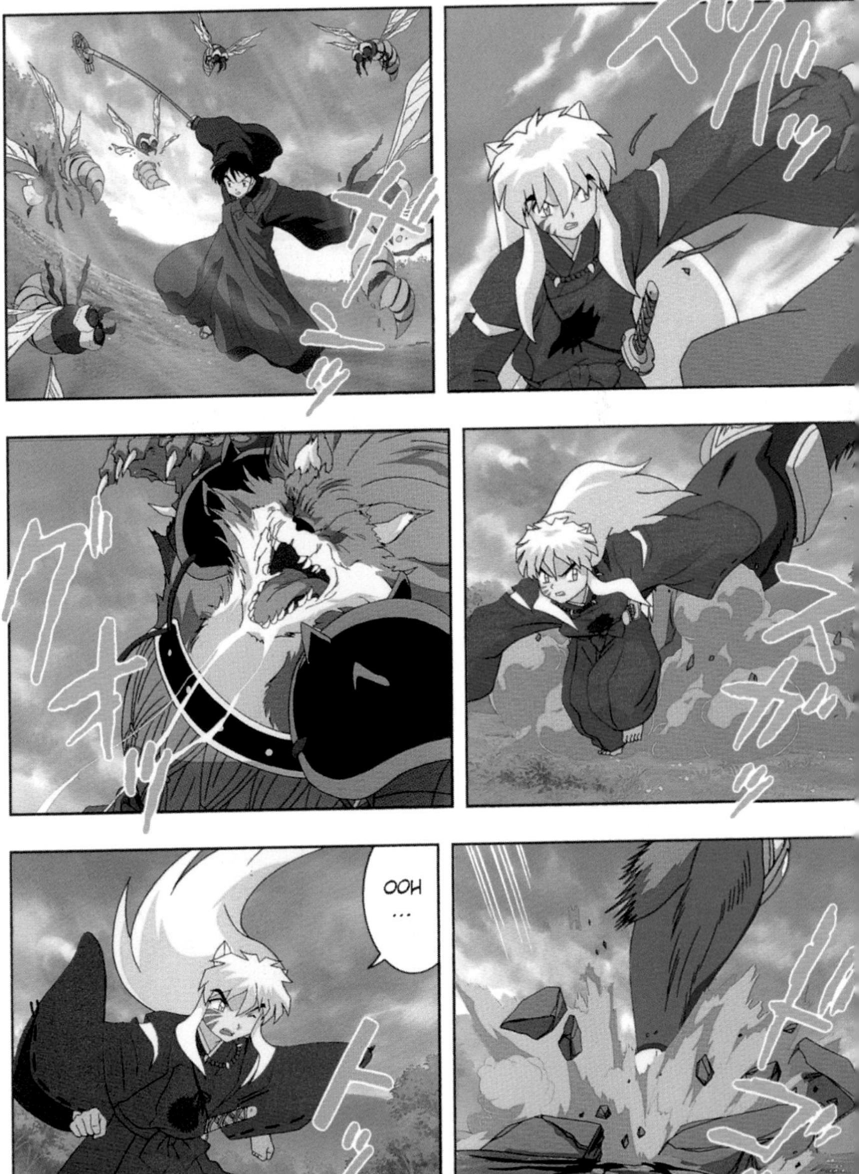
ズバッ
ザシュッ
ズザッ
グキッ
ドゴッ
OOH
...
トッ

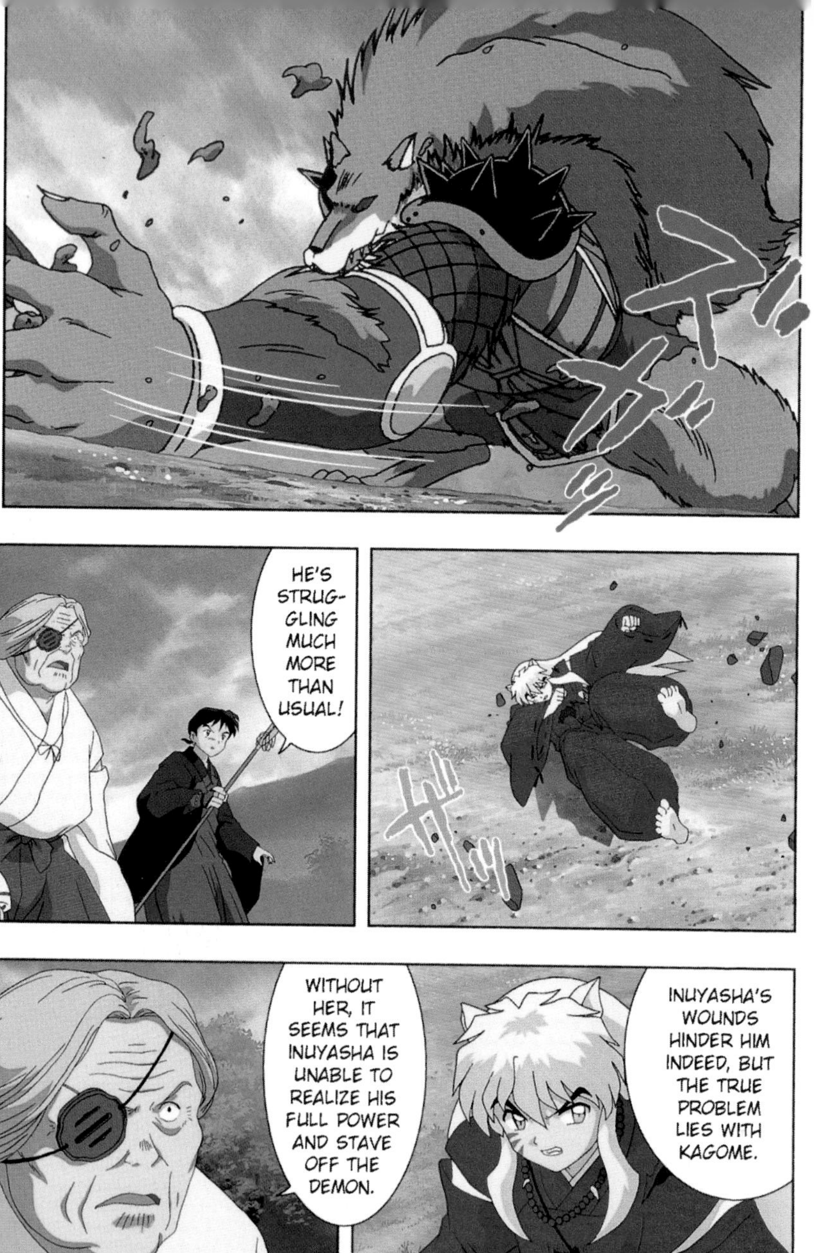
HE'S STRUG-GLING MUCH MORE THAN USUAL!
INUYASHA'S WOUNDS HINDER HIM INDEED, BUT THE TRUE PROBLEM LIES WITH KAGOME.
WITHOUT HER, IT SEEMS THAT INUYASHA IS UNABLE TO REALIZE HIS FULL POWER AND STAVE OFF THE DEMON.

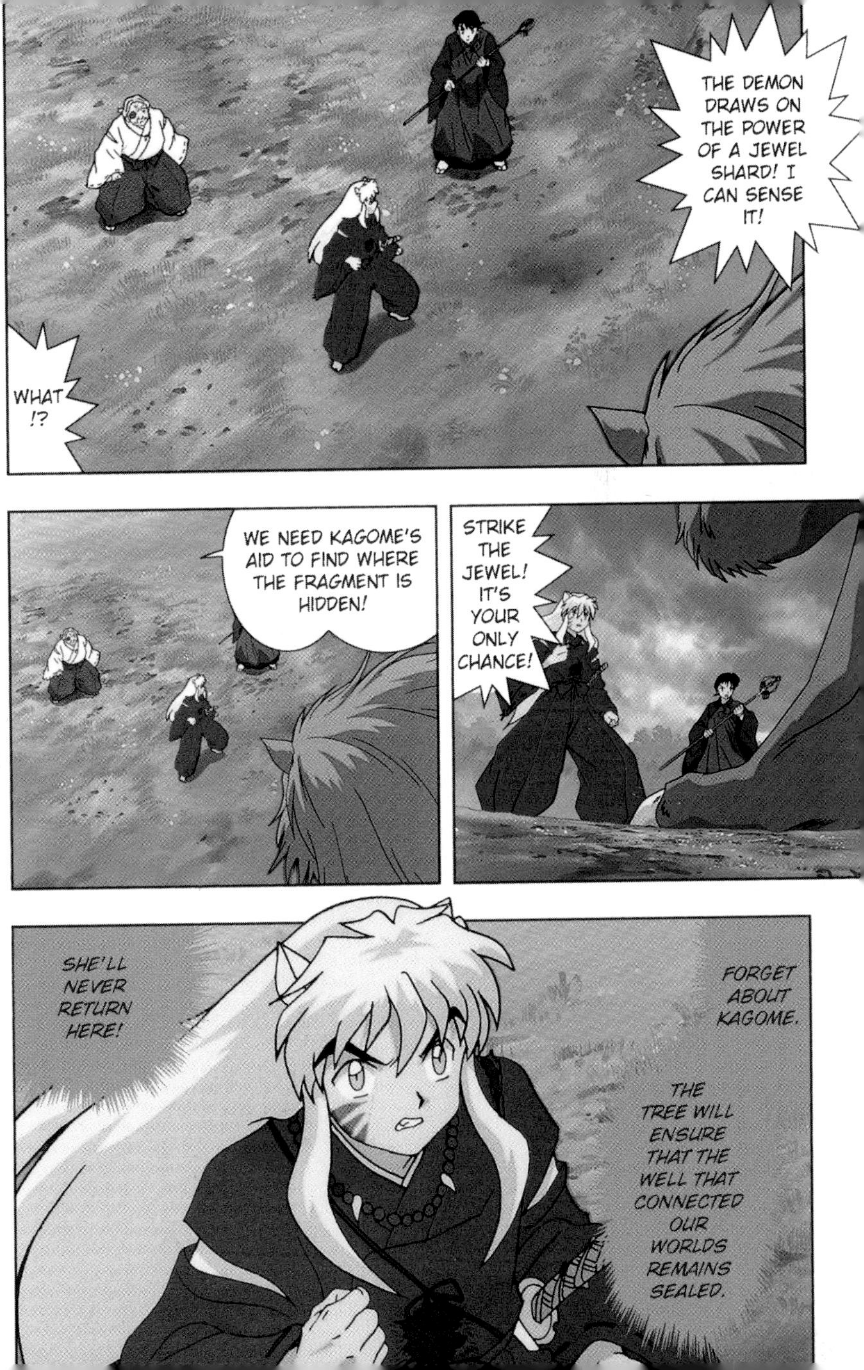
THE DEMON DRAWS ON THE POWER OF A JEWEL SHARD! I CAN SENSE IT!
WHAT!?
STRIKE THE JEWEL! IT'S YOUR ONLY CHANCE!
WE NEED KAGOME'S AID TO FIND WHERE THE FRAGMENT IS HIDDEN!
FORGET ABOUT KAGOME.
SHE'LL NEVER RETURN HERE!
THE TREE WILL ENSURE THAT THE WELL THAT CONNECTED OUR WORLDS REMAINS SEALED.

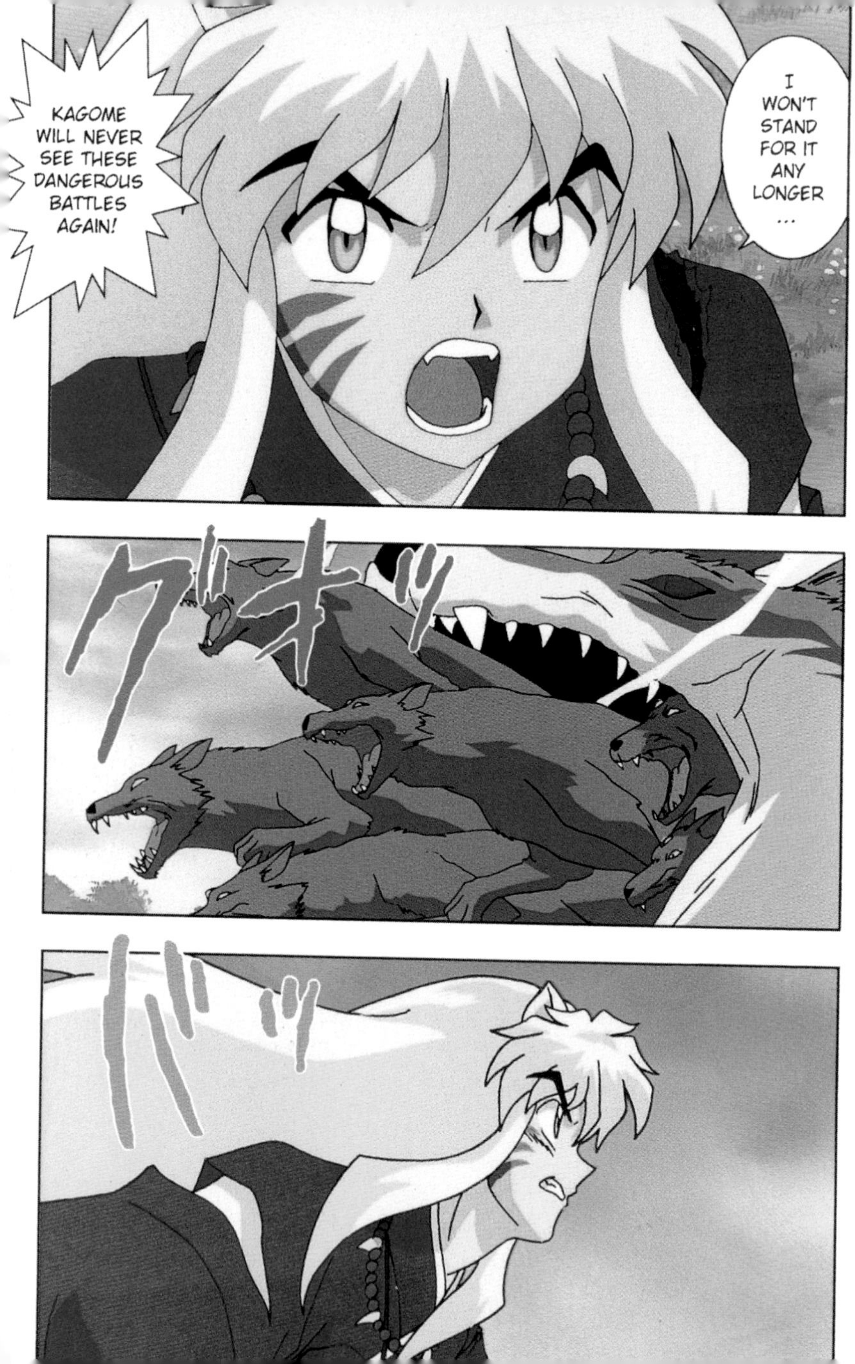
I WON'T STAND FOR IT ANY LONGER ...
KAGOME WILL NEVER SEE THESE DANGEROUS BATTLES AGAIN!
グオッ
バッ

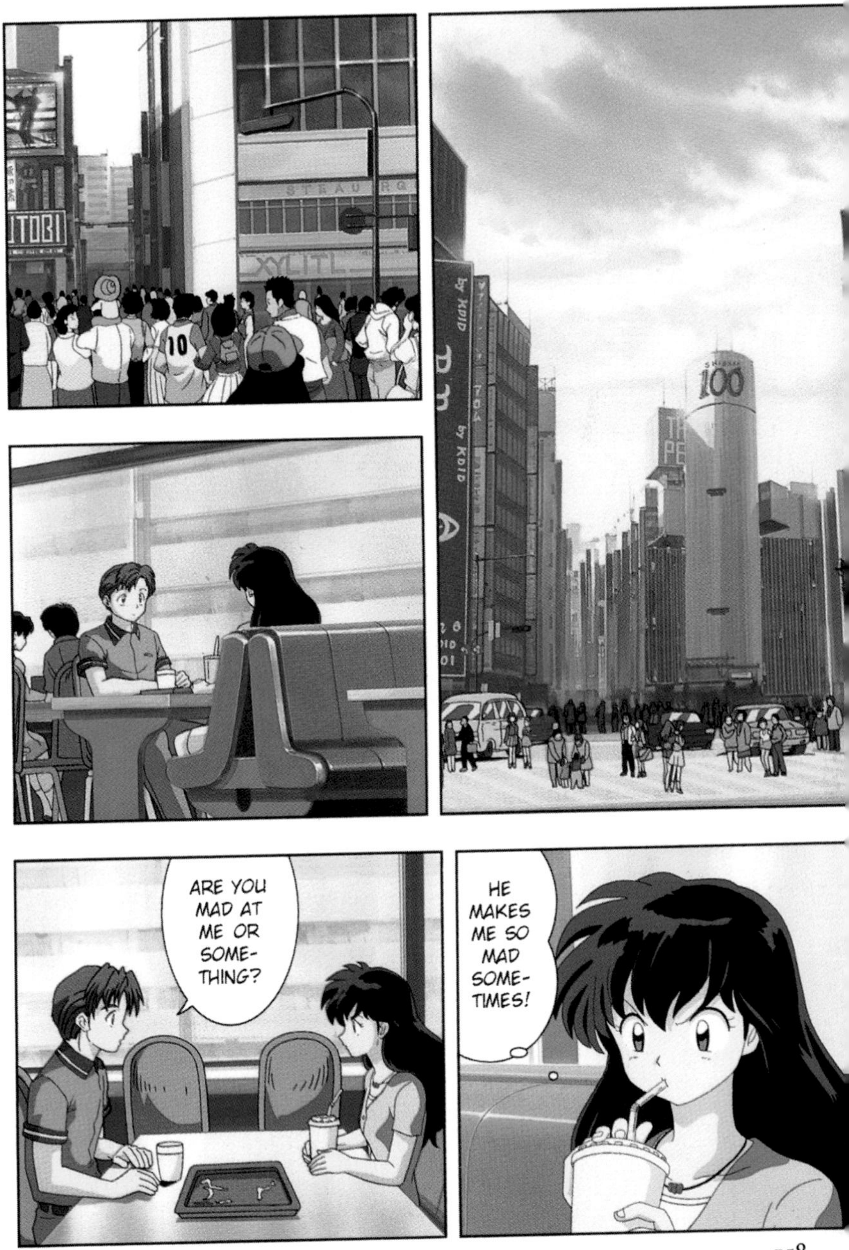
HE MAKES ME SO MAD SOME-TIMES!
ARE YOU MAD AT ME OR SOME-THING?

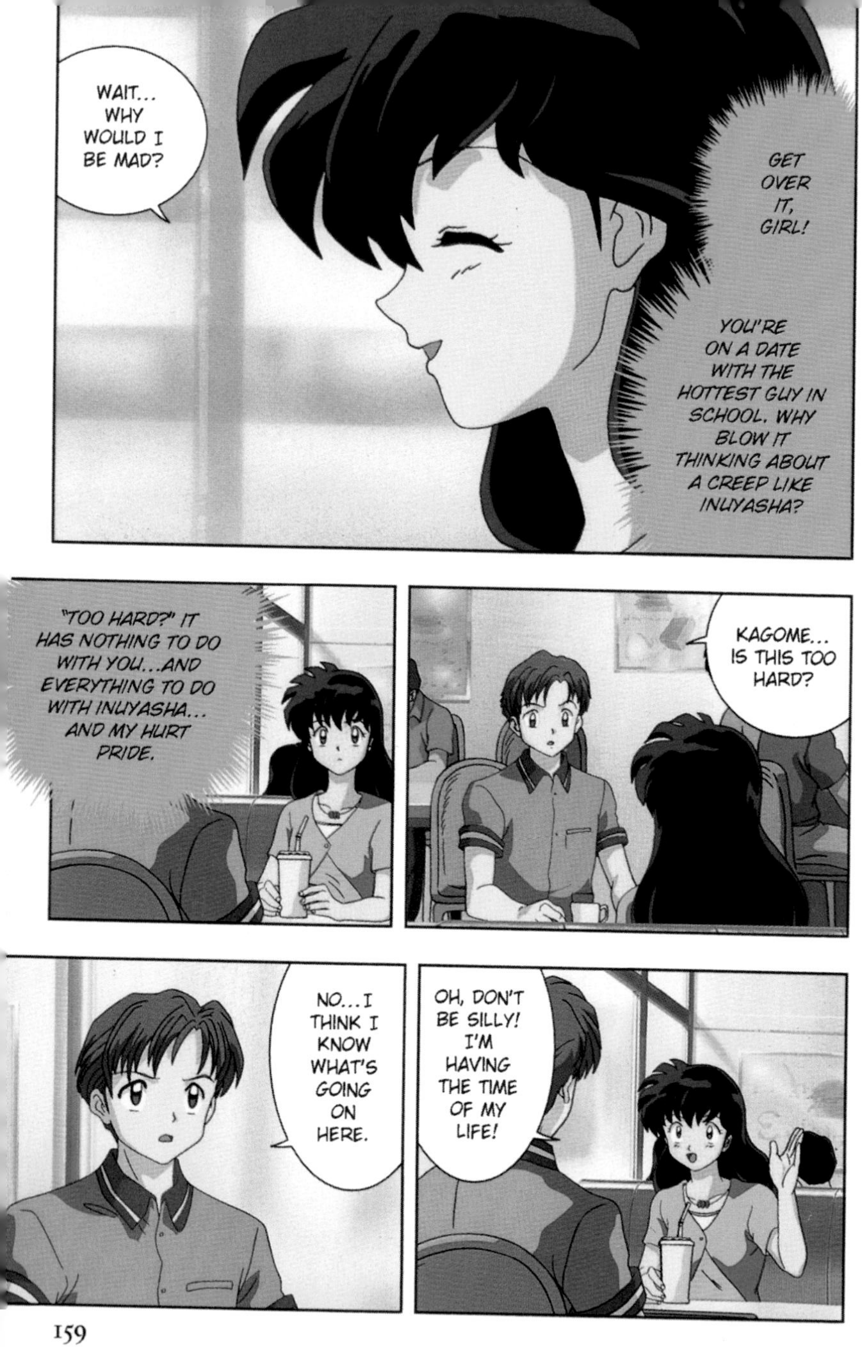
WAIT... WHY WOULD I BE MAD?
GET OVER IT, GIRL!
YOU'RE ON A DATE WITH THE HOTTEST GUY IN SCHOOL. WHY BLOW IT THINKING ABOUT A CREEP LIKE INUYASHA?
KAGOME... IS THIS TOO HARD?
"TOO HARD?" IT HAS NOTHING TO DO WITH YOU...AND EVERYTHING TO DO WITH INUYASHA... AND MY HURT PRIDE.
OH, DON'T BE SILLY! I'M HAVING THE TIME OF MY LIFE!
NO... I THINK I KNOW WHAT'S GOING ON HERE.

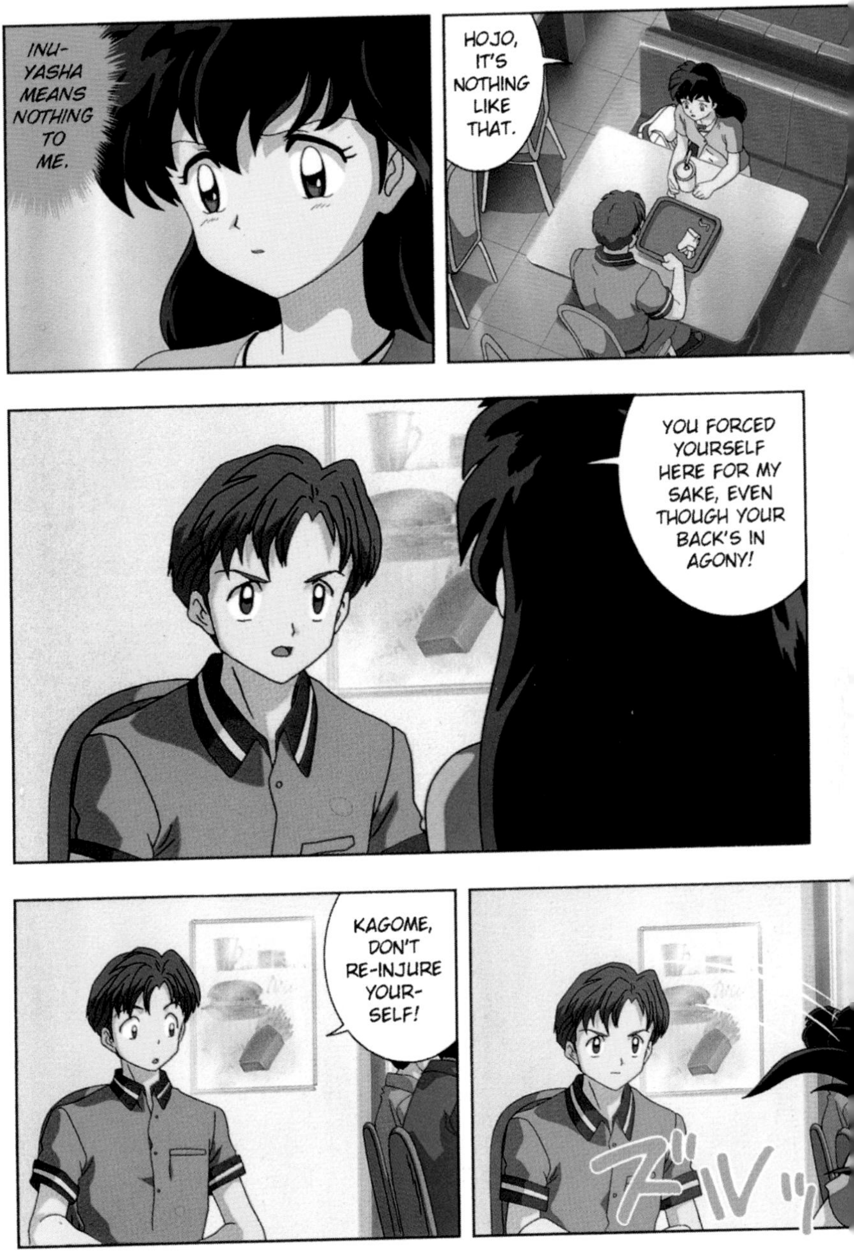
HOJO, IT'S NOTHING LIKE THAT.
INU-YASHA MEANS NOTHING TO ME.
YOU FORCED YOURSELF HERE FOR MY SAKE, EVEN THOUGH YOUR BACK'S IN AGONY!
KAGOME, DON'T RE-INJURE YOUR-SELF!

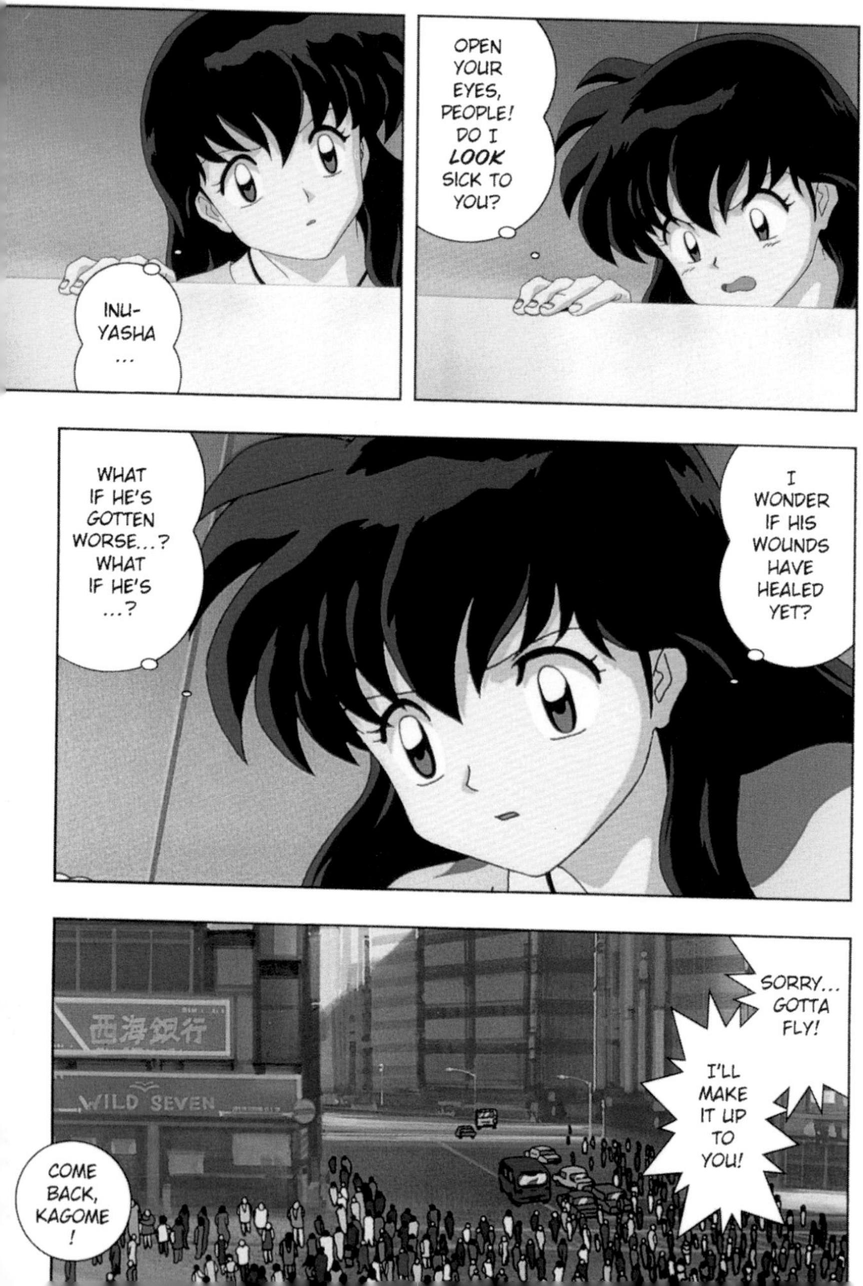
OPEN YOUR EYES, PEOPLE! DO I **LOOK** SICK TO YOU?
INU-YASHA ...
I WONDER IF HIS WOUNDS HAVE HEALED YET?
WHAT IF HE'S GOTTEN WORSE...? WHAT IF HE'S ...?
西海銀行
WILD SEVEN
SORRY... GOTTA FLY!
I'LL MAKE IT UP TO YOU!
COME BACK, KAGOME!

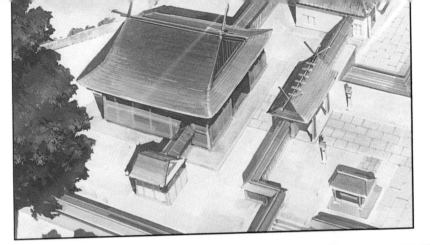

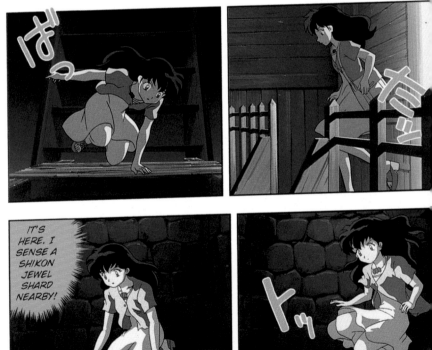

IT'S HERE. I SENSE A SHIKON JEWEL SHARD NEARBY!

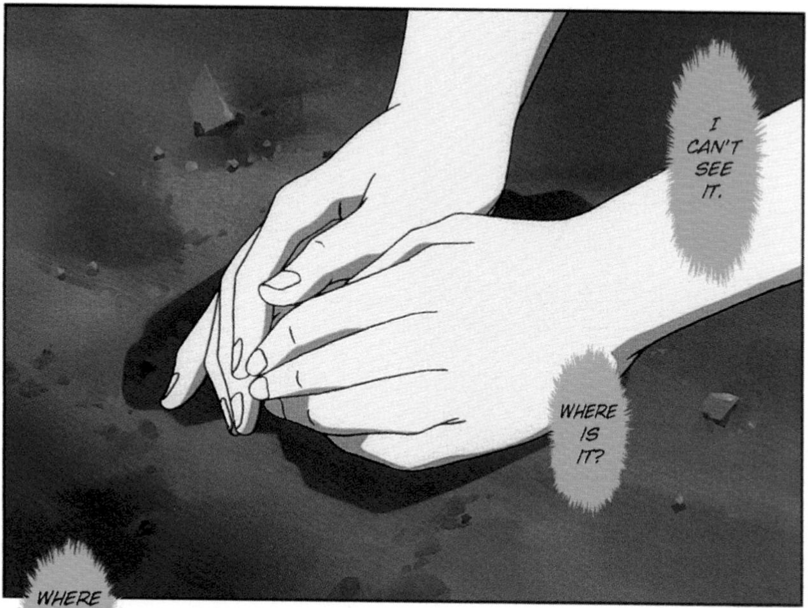
I CAN'T SEE IT.
WHERE IS IT?
WHERE IS THE JEWEL SHARD?
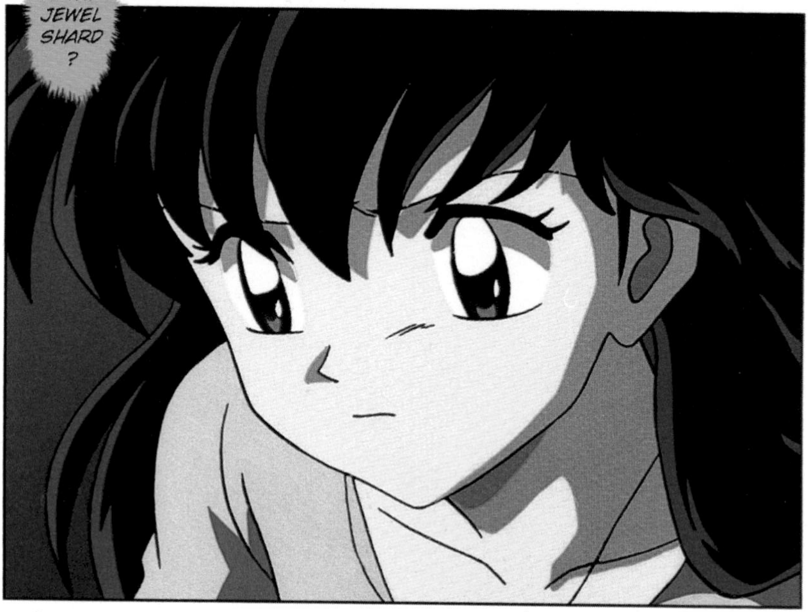

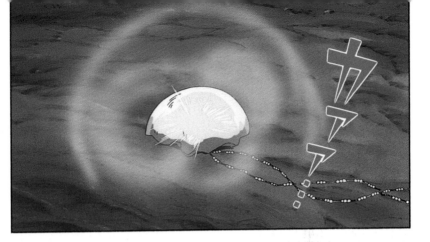

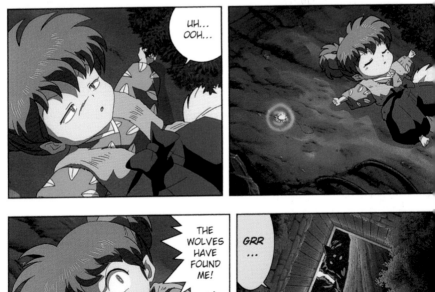

UH...
OOH...

THE
WOLVES
HAVE
FOUND
ME!

GRR
...

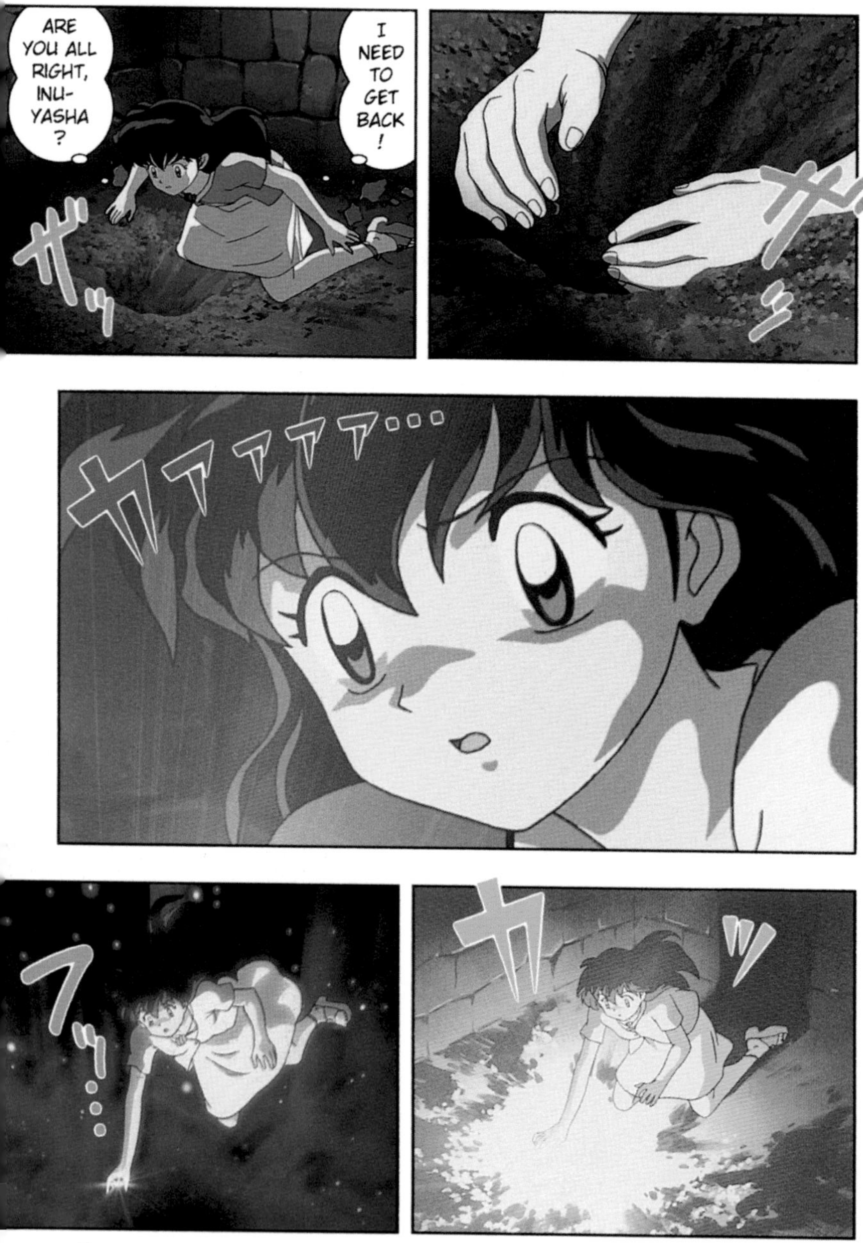
I NEED TO GET BACK!
ARE YOU ALL RIGHT, INU-YASHA?
ザッ
カァァァァ…
カッ
フッ…

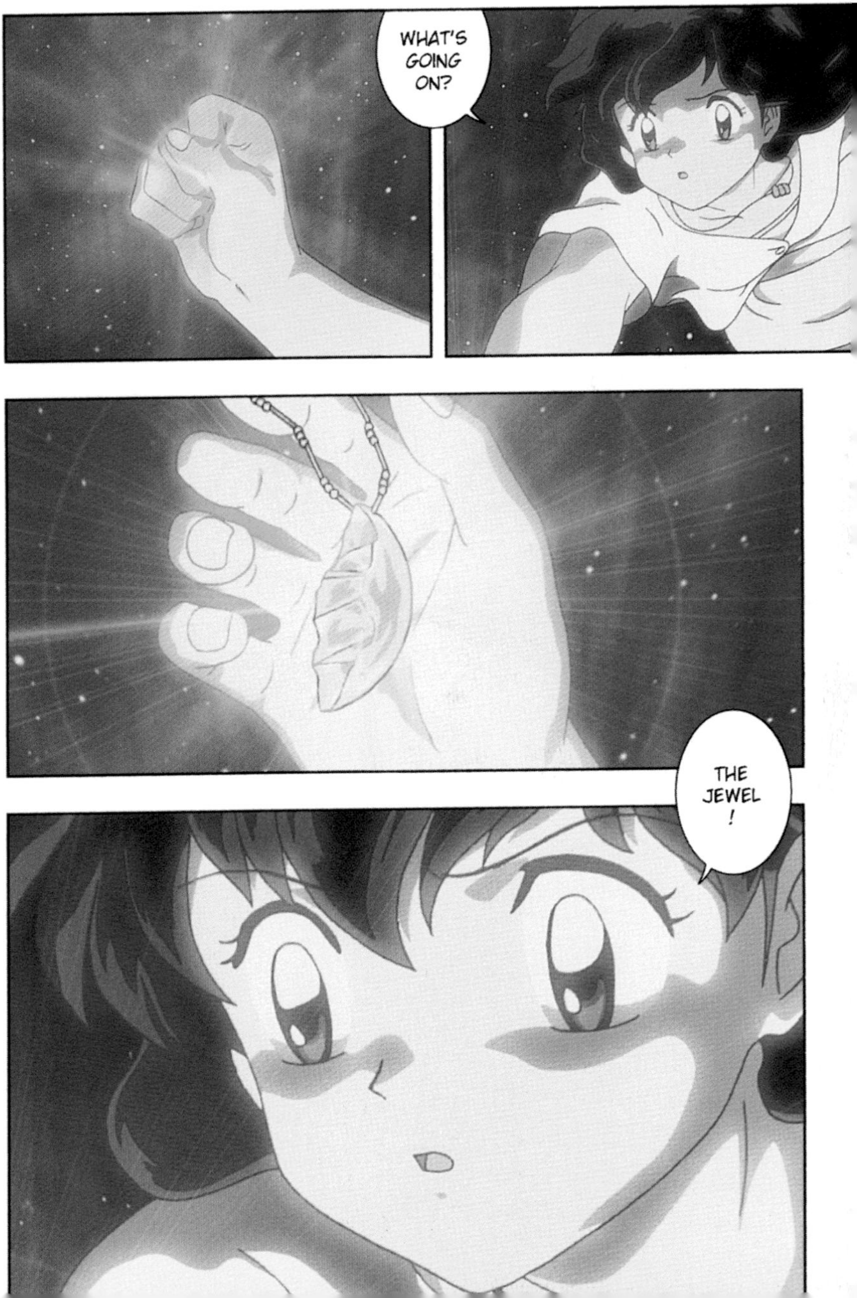
WHAT'S GOING ON?
THE JEWEL!

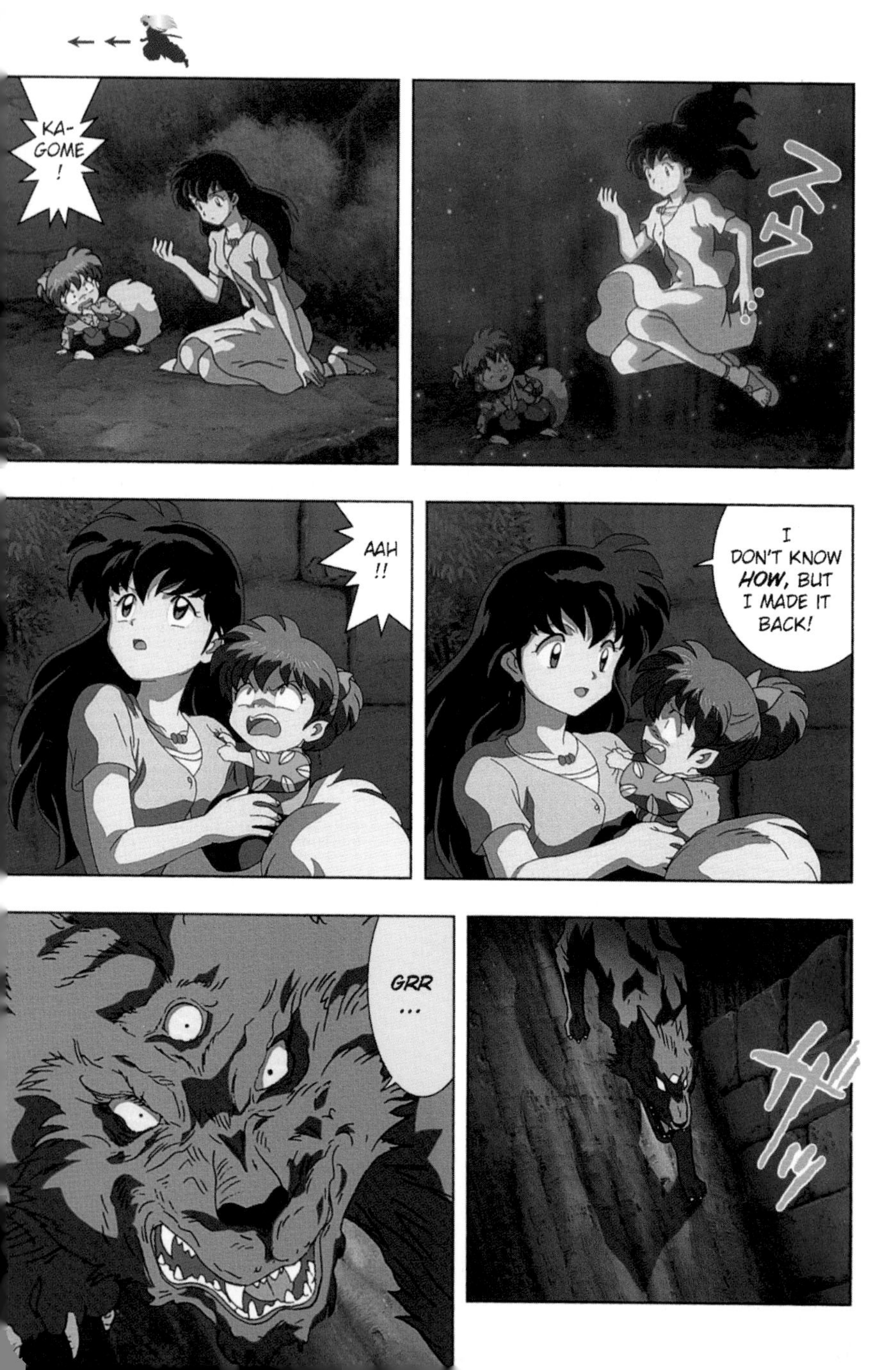
KA-GOME!
I DON'T KNOW *HOW*, BUT I MADE IT BACK!
AAH!!
GRR...

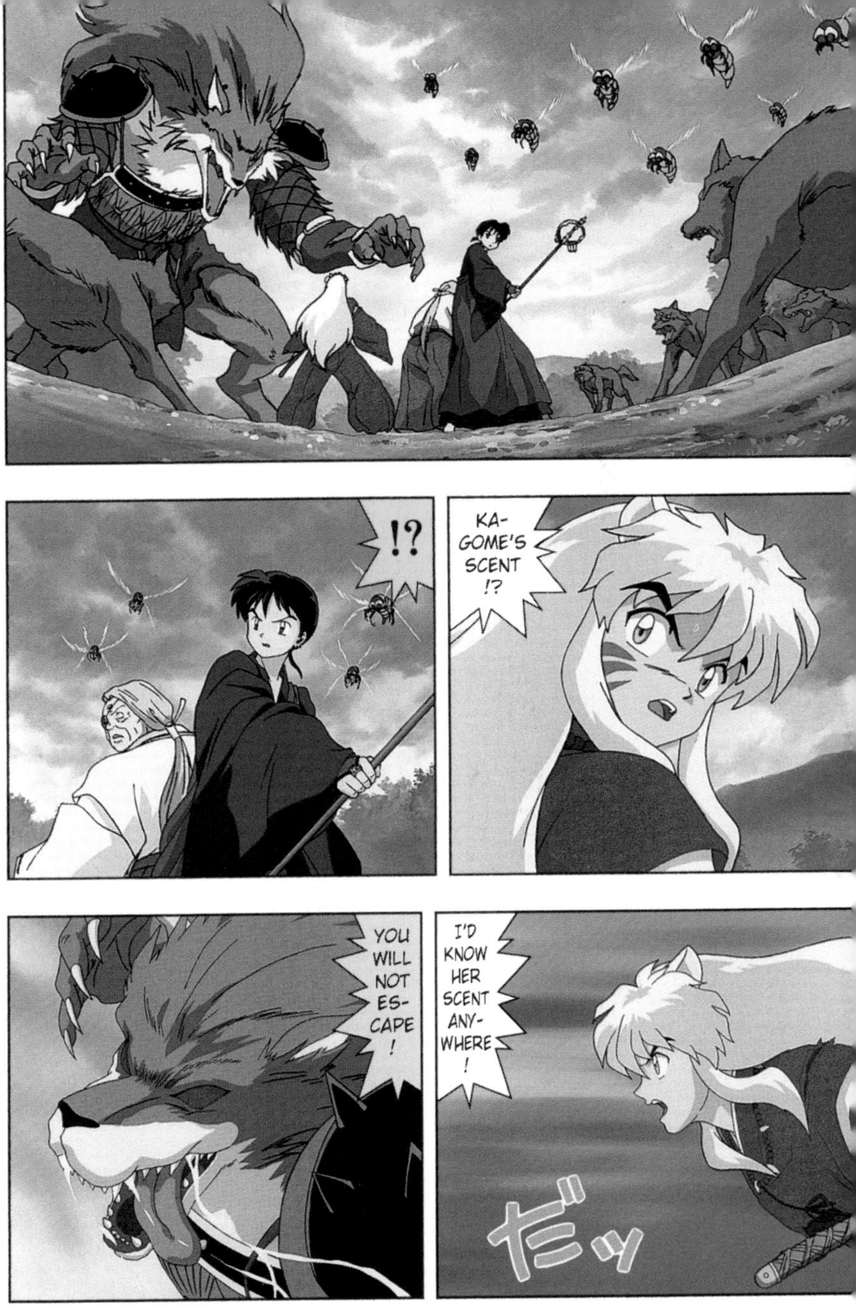
KA-GOME'S SCENT !?
!?
I'D KNOW HER SCENT ANY-WHERE !
ダッ
YOU WILL NOT ES-CAPE !

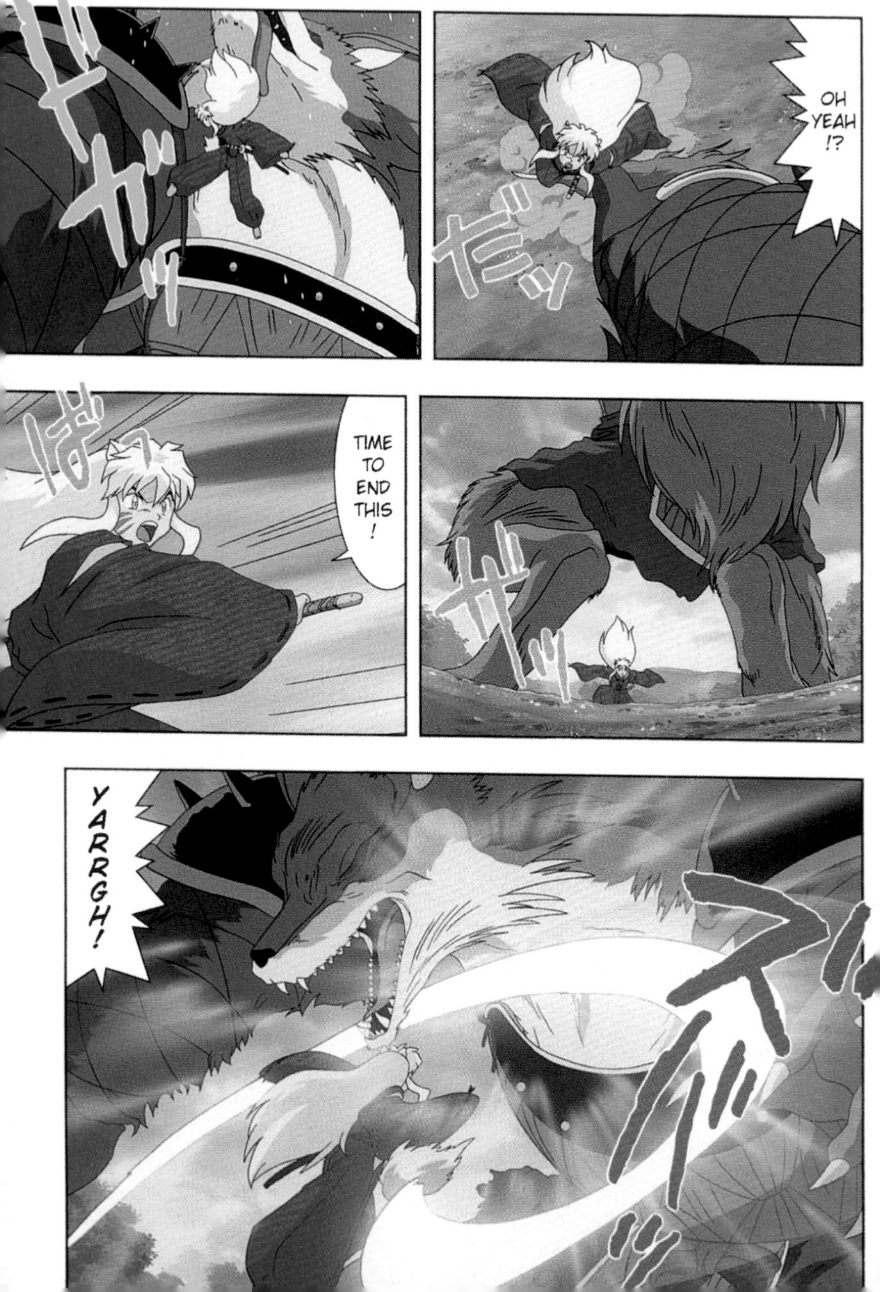
OH YEAH !?
TIME TO END THIS !
YARRGH!

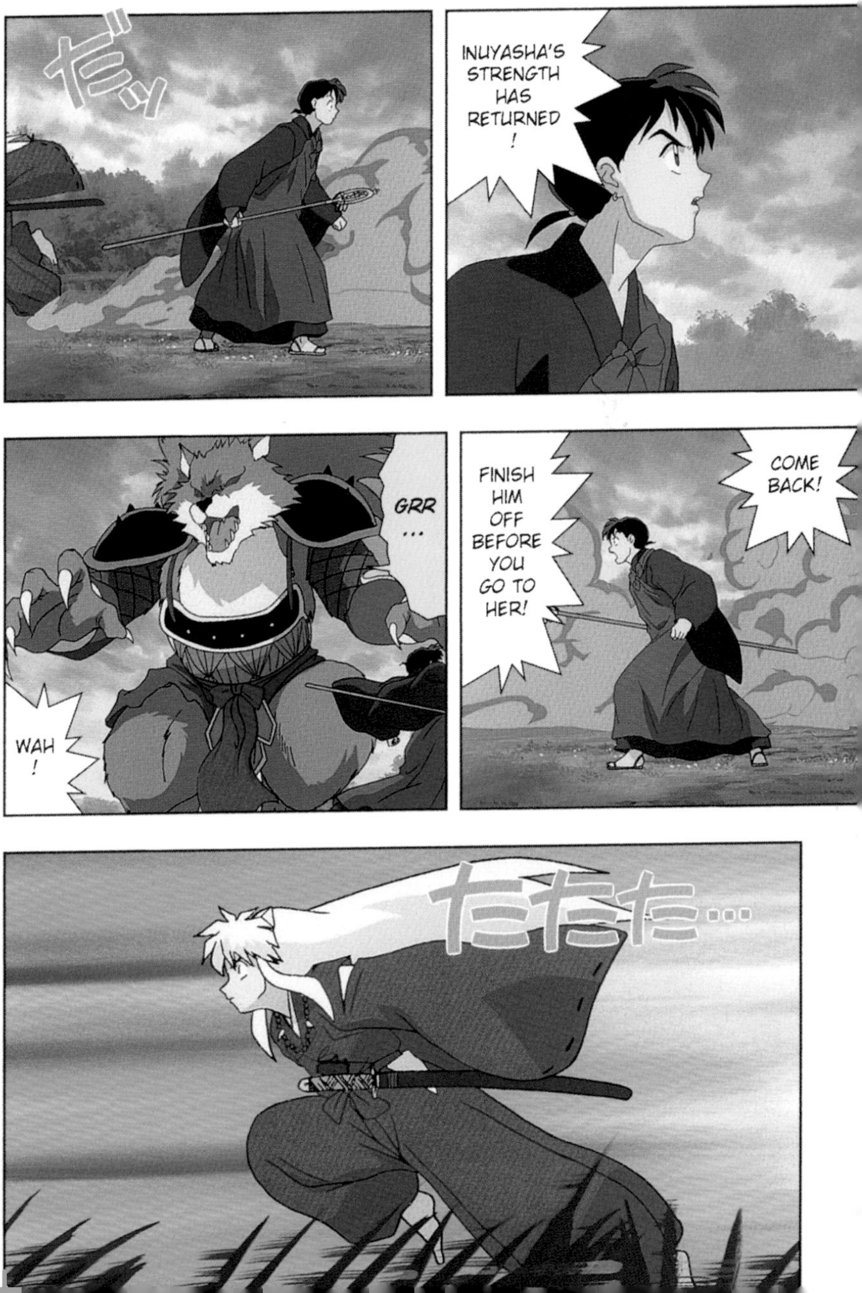

INUYASHA'S STRENGTH HAS RETURNED!
ダッ
COME BACK!
FINISH HIM OFF BEFORE YOU GO TO HER!
GRR...
WAH!
たたた...

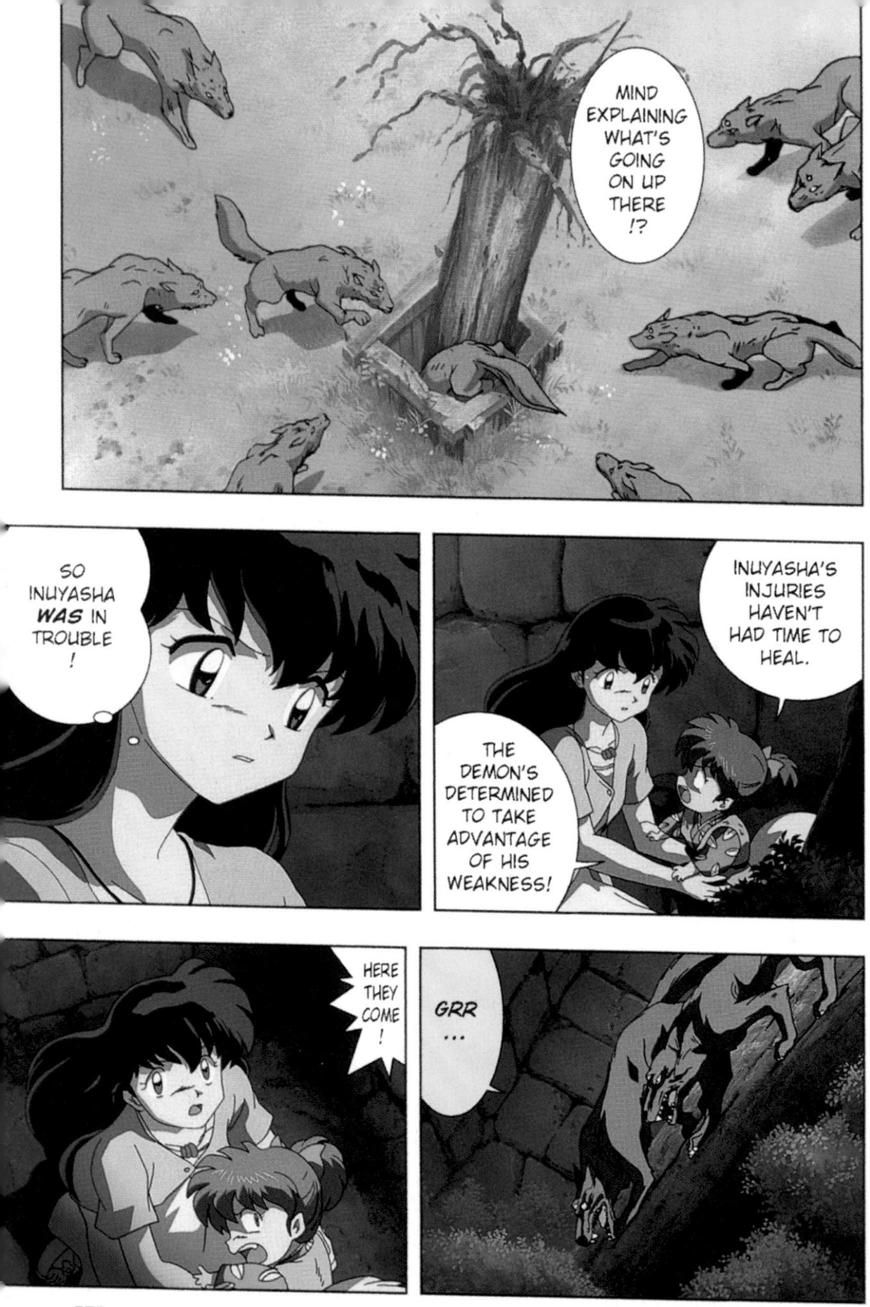
MIND EXPLAINING WHAT'S GOING ON UP THERE !?
INUYASHA'S INJURIES HAVEN'T HAD TIME TO HEAL.
THE DEMON'S DETERMINED TO TAKE ADVANTAGE OF HIS WEAKNESS!
SO INUYASHA WAS IN TROUBLE !
GRR ...
HERE THEY COME !

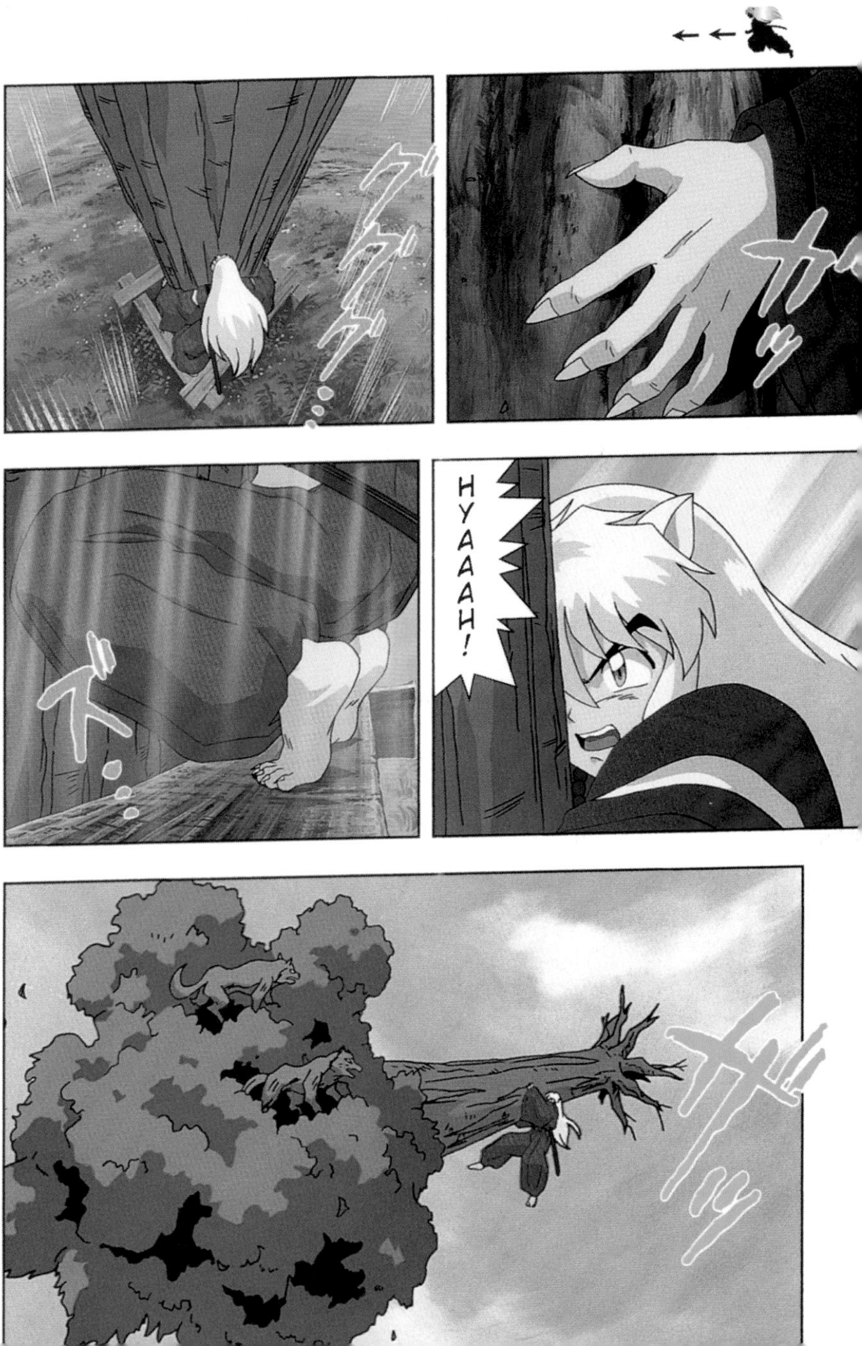
カッ
HYAAAH!

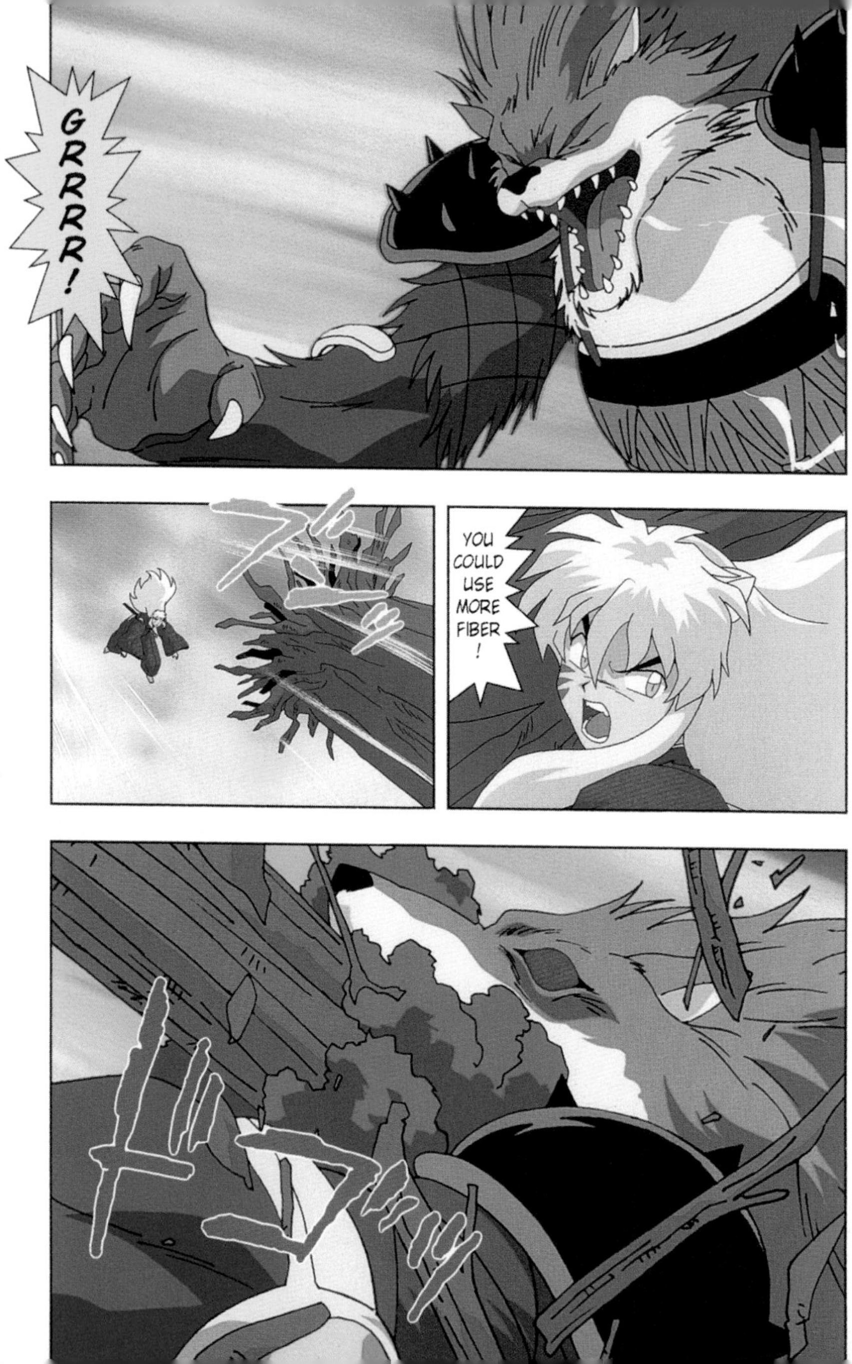
GRRRR!
YOU COULD USE MORE FIBER!

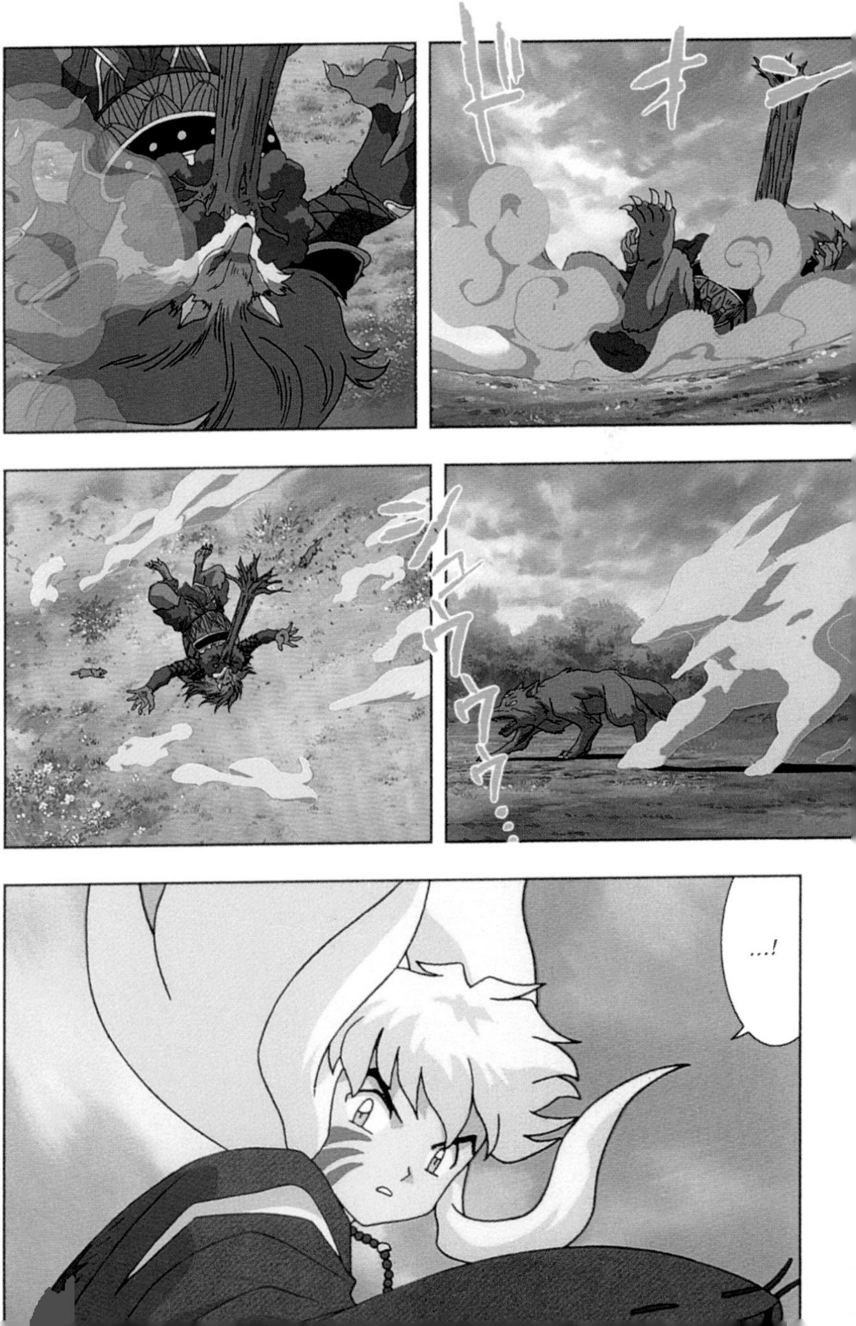
ドオー
シュウウウ…
…!

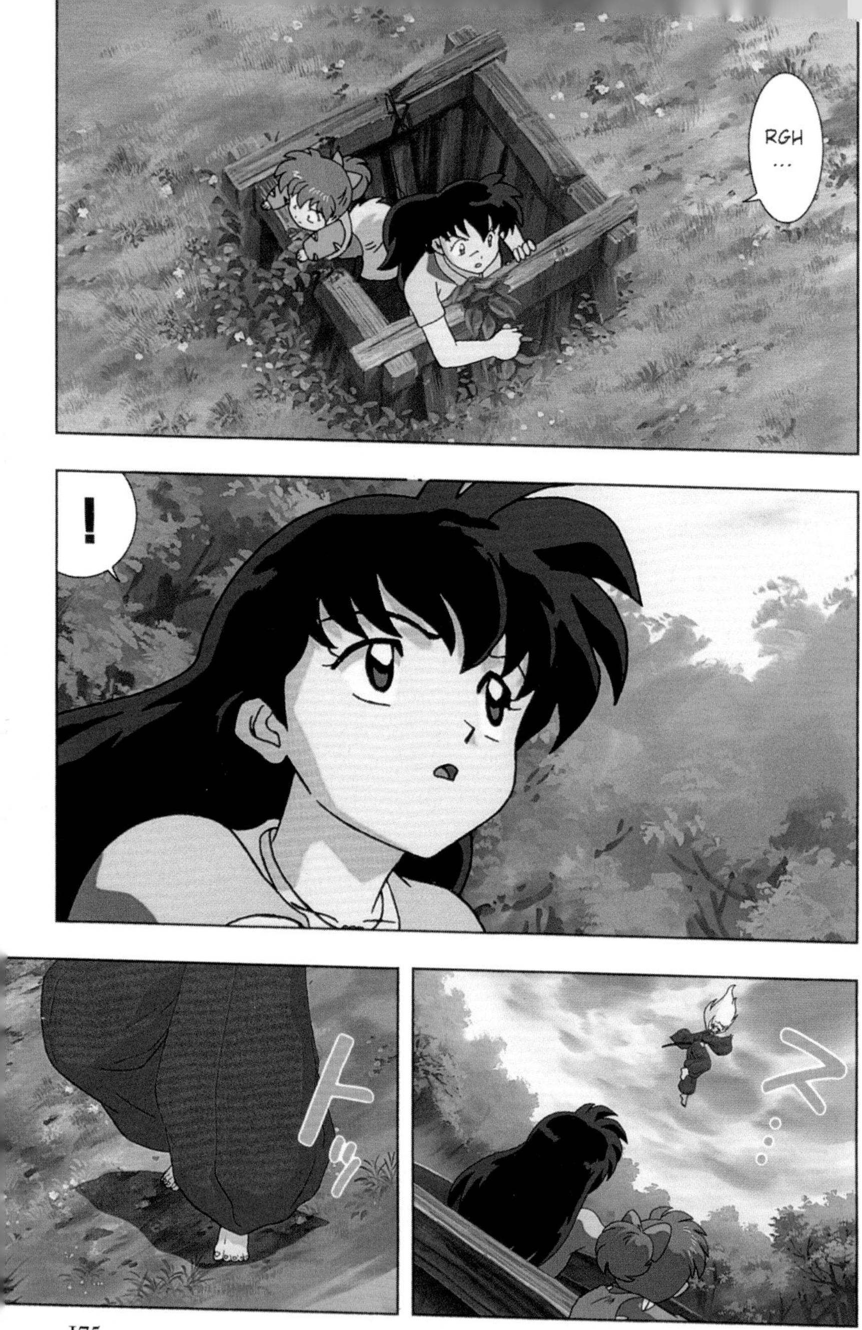
RGH ...
!
ス…
トッ

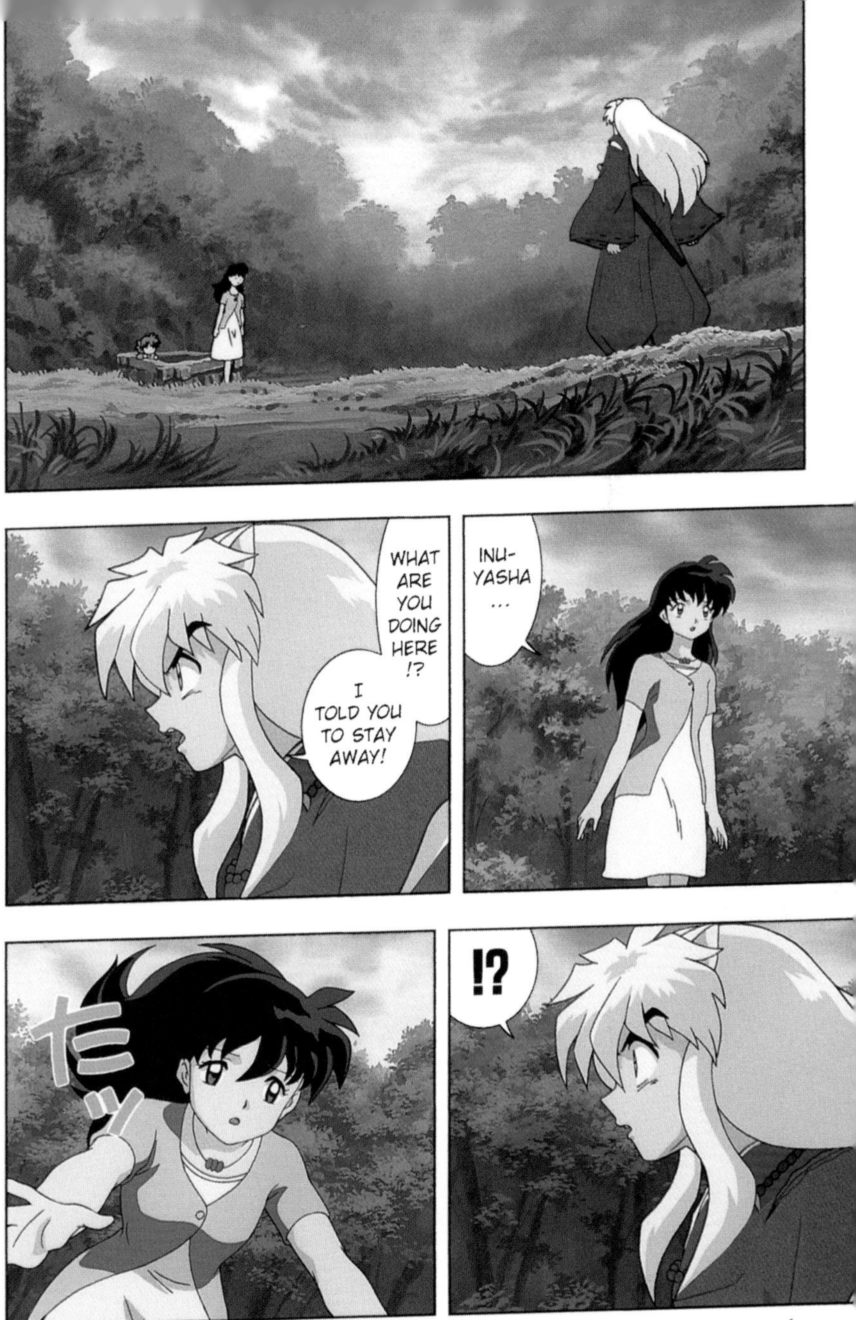
INU-YASHA ...
WHAT ARE YOU DOING HERE !?
I TOLD YOU TO STAY AWAY!
!?

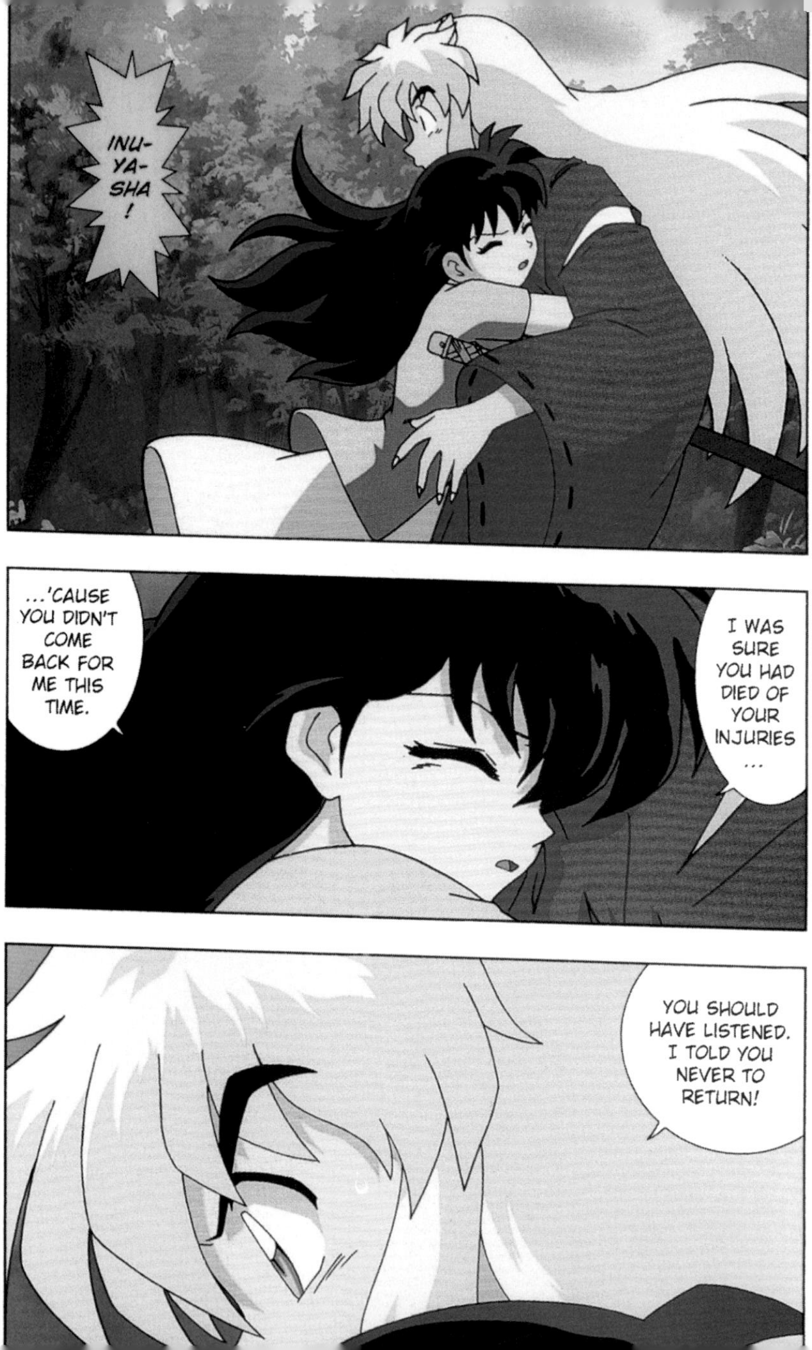
INU-YASHA!
I WAS SURE YOU HAD DIED OF YOUR INJURIES...
...'CAUSE YOU DIDN'T COME BACK FOR ME THIS TIME.
YOU SHOULD HAVE LISTENED. I TOLD YOU NEVER TO RETURN!

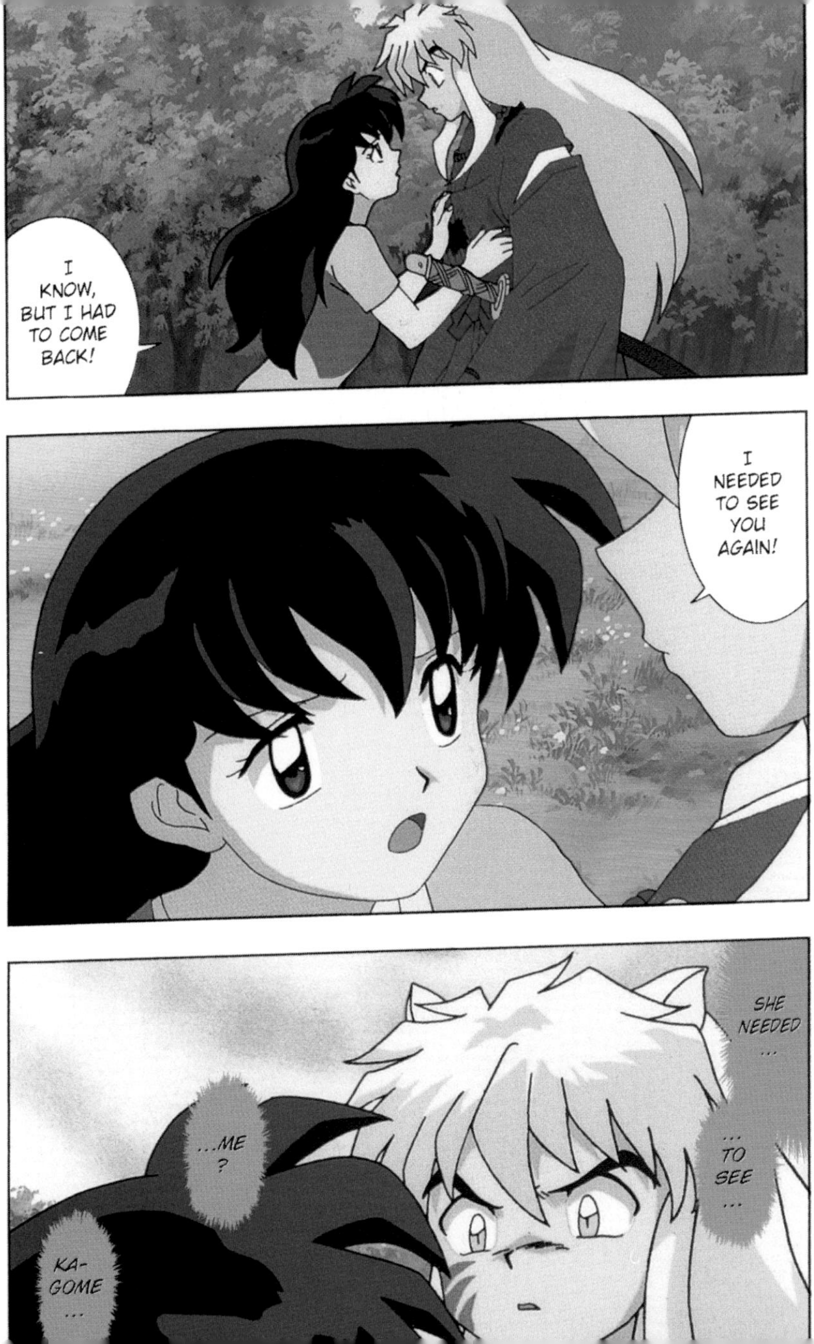
I KNOW, BUT I HAD TO COME BACK!
I NEEDED TO SEE YOU AGAIN!
SHE NEEDED …
… TO SEE …
…ME ?
KA-GOME …

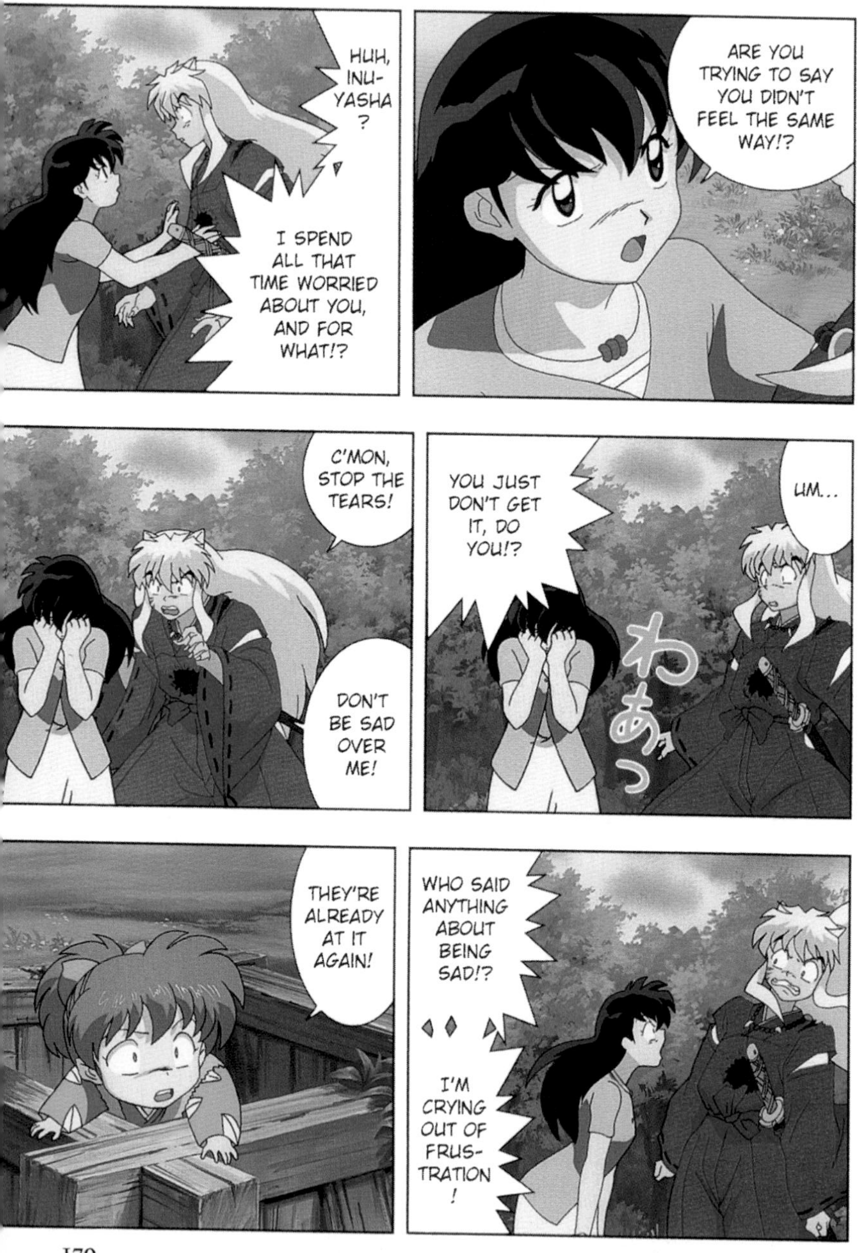
ARE YOU TRYING TO SAY YOU DIDN'T FEEL THE SAME WAY!?
HUH, INU-YASHA?
I SPEND ALL THAT TIME WORRIED ABOUT YOU, AND FOR WHAT!?
UM...
YOU JUST DON'T GET IT, DO YOU!?
わあっ
C'MON, STOP THE TEARS!
DON'T BE SAD OVER ME!
WHO SAID ANYTHING ABOUT BEING SAD!?
I'M CRYING OUT OF FRUS-TRATION!
THEY'RE ALREADY AT IT AGAIN!

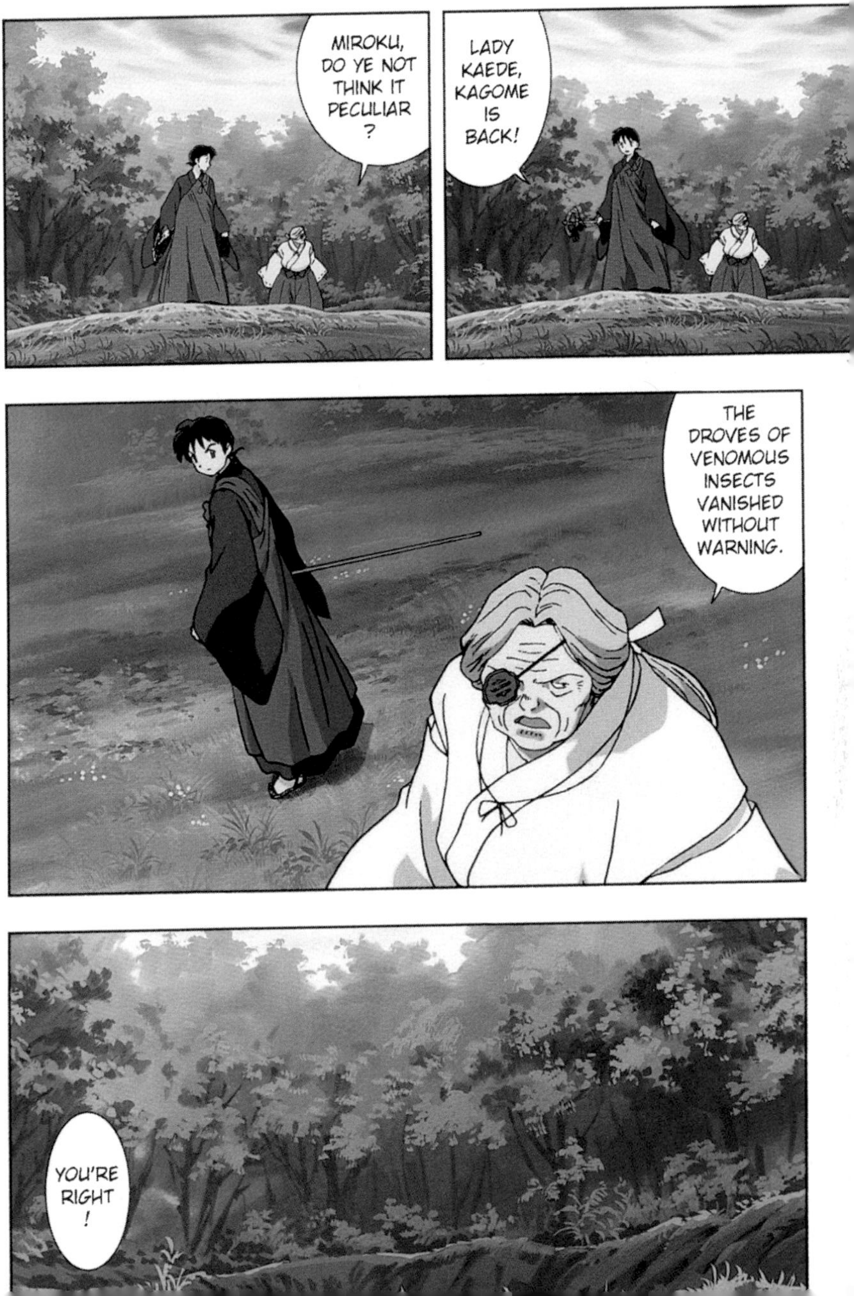
LADY KAEDE, KAGOME IS BACK!
MIROKU, DO YE NOT THINK IT PECULIAR?
THE DROVES OF VENOMOUS INSECTS VANISHED WITHOUT WARNING.
YOU'RE RIGHT!

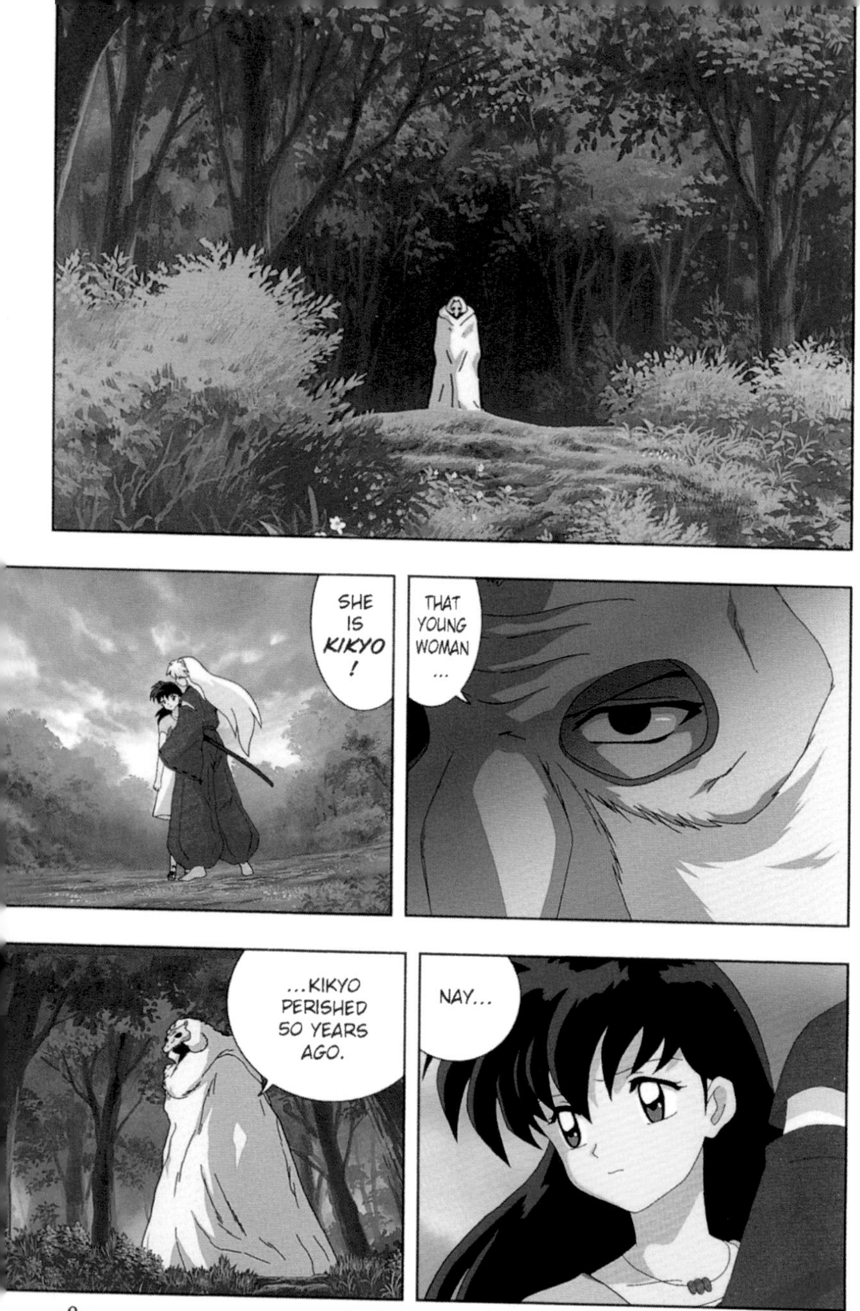
THAT YOUNG WOMAN ...
SHE IS *KIKYO* !
NAY...
...KIKYO PERISHED 50 YEARS AGO.

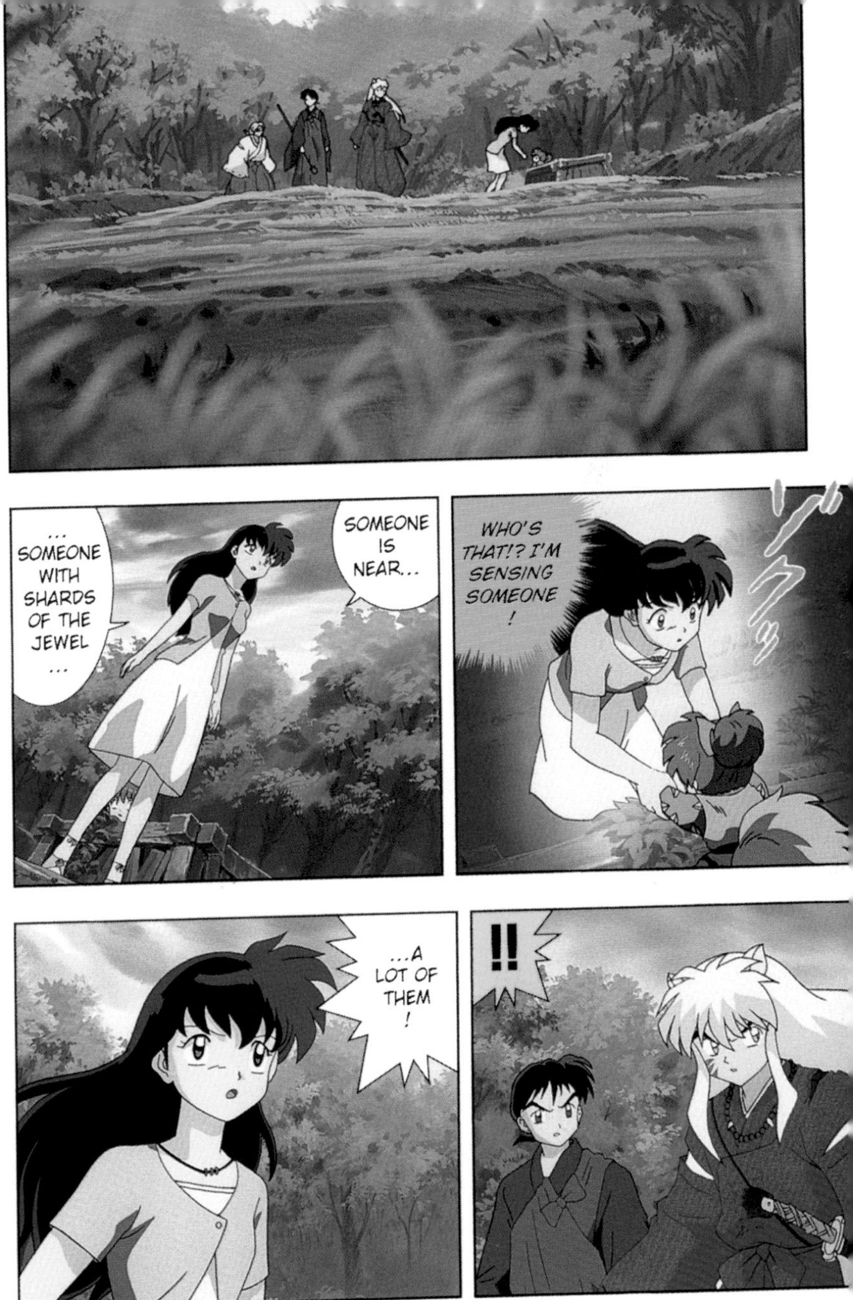

ゾクッ
WHO'S THAT!? I'M SENSING SOMEONE!
SOMEONE IS NEAR...
...SOMEONE WITH SHARDS OF THE JEWEL...
!!
...A LOT OF THEM!

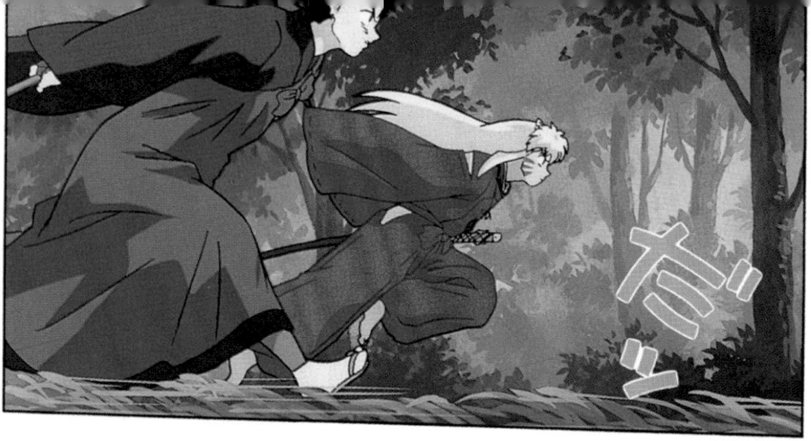

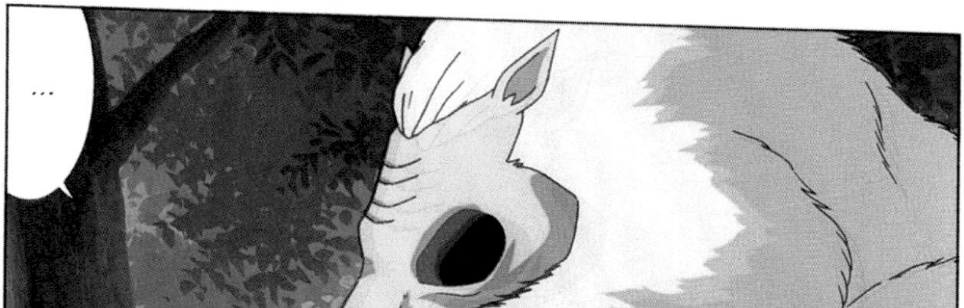
...

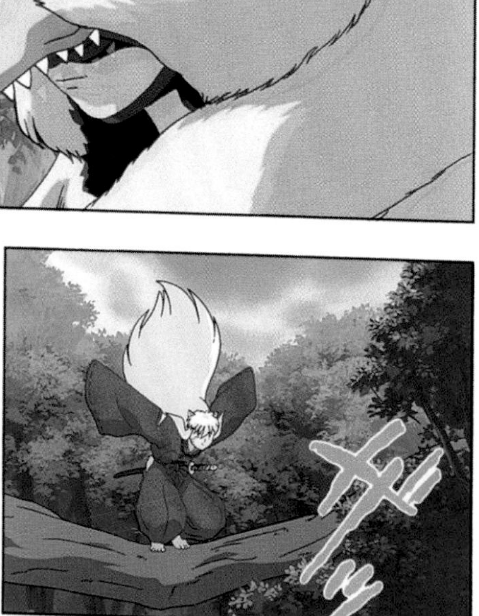

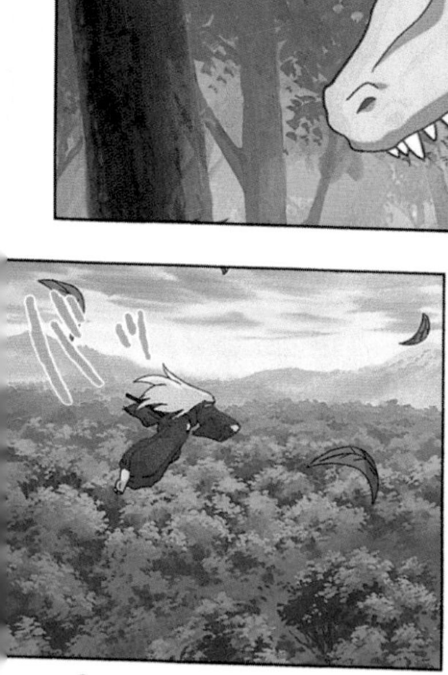

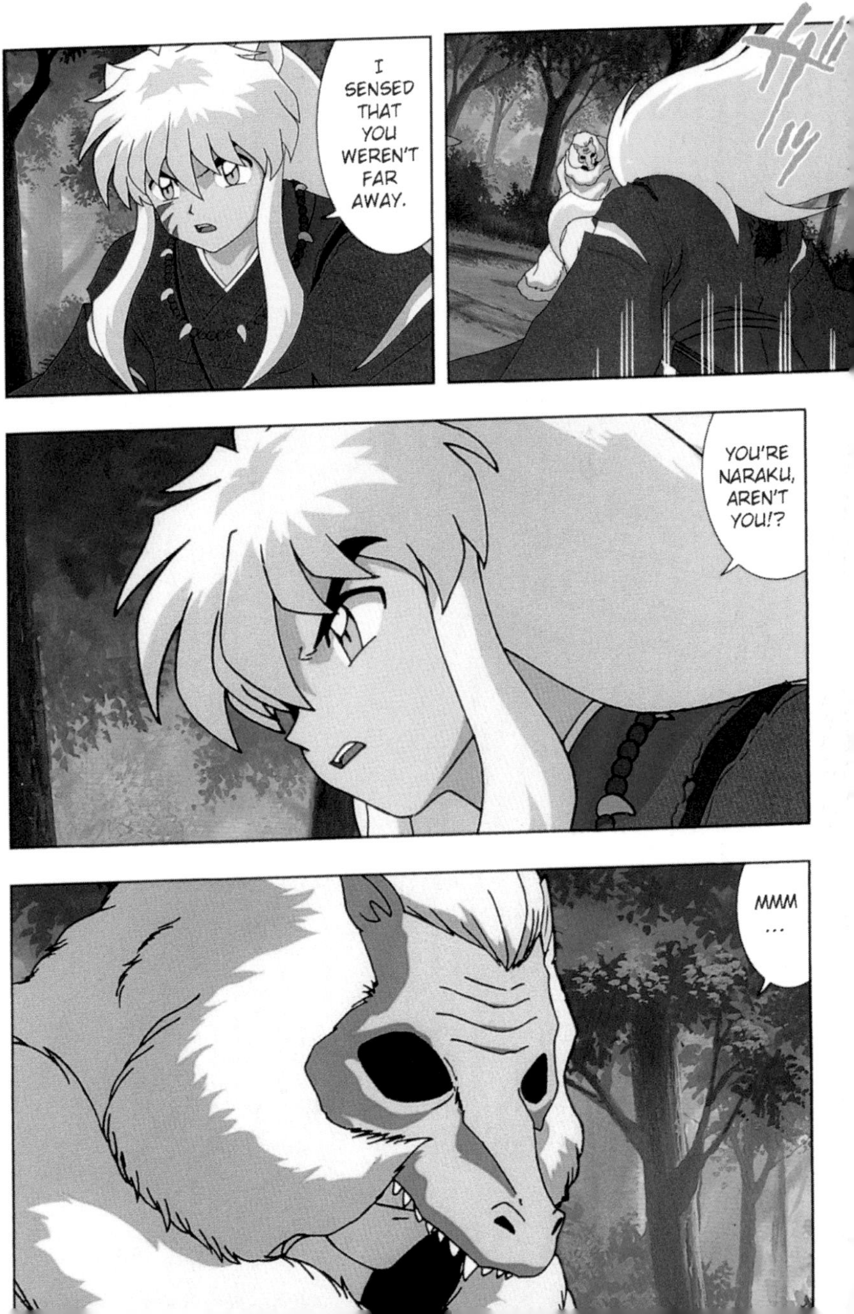
I SENSED THAT YOU WEREN'T FAR AWAY.
YOU'RE NARAKU, AREN'T YOU!?
MMM ...

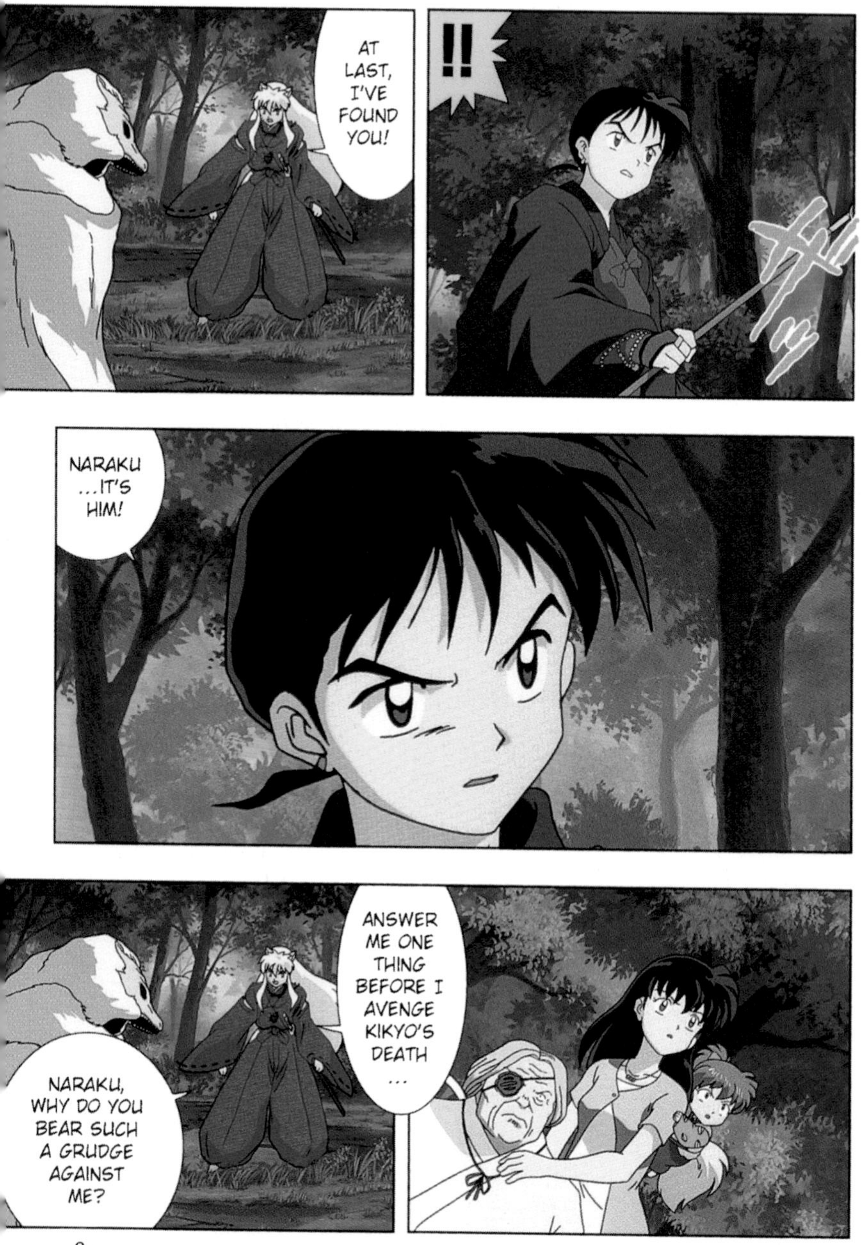
!!
AT LAST, I'VE FOUND YOU!
NARAKU ...IT'S HIM!
ANSWER ME ONE THING BEFORE I AVENGE KIKYO'S DEATH ...
NARAKU, WHY DO YOU BEAR SUCH A GRUDGE AGAINST ME?

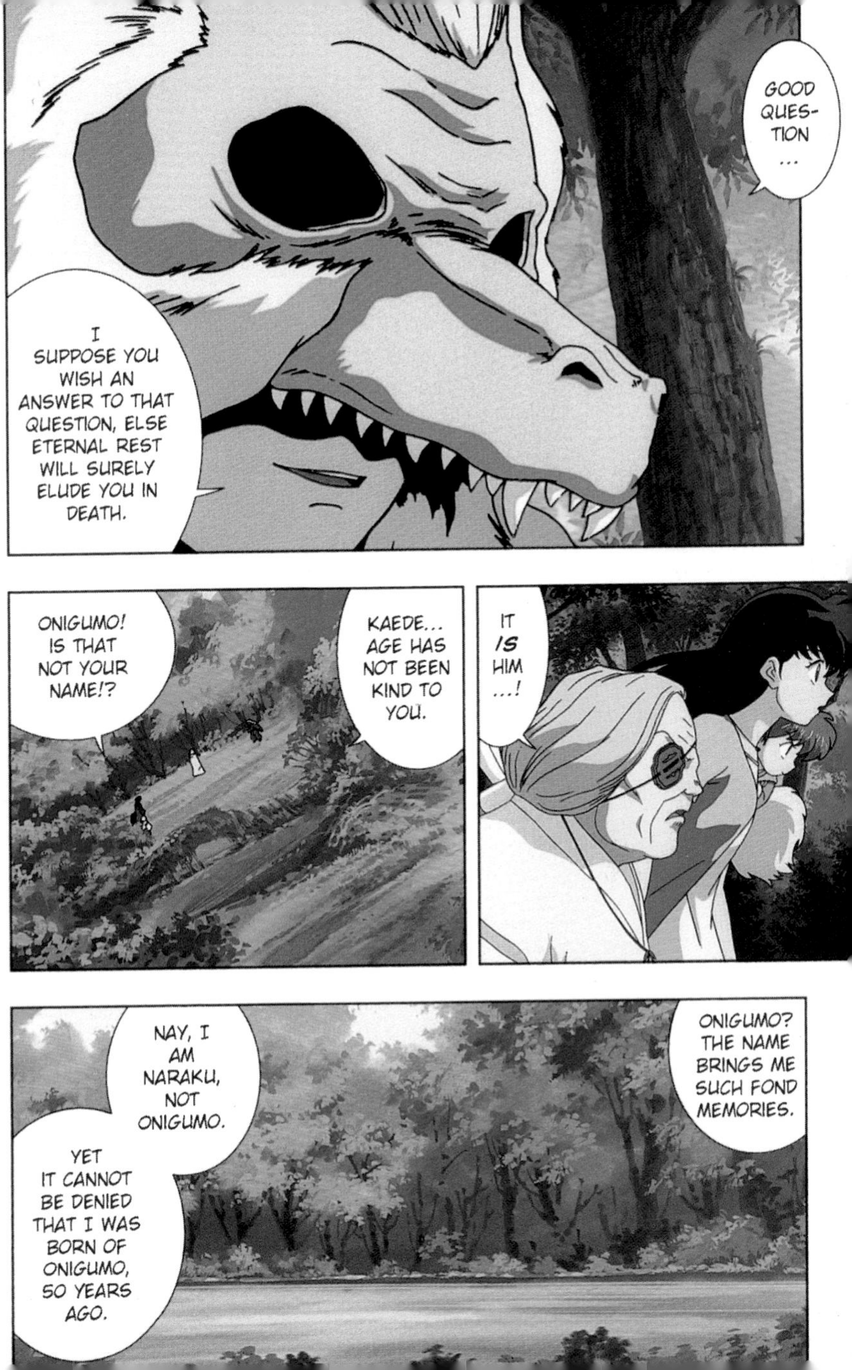
GOOD QUES-TION ...
I SUPPOSE YOU WISH AN ANSWER TO THAT QUESTION, ELSE ETERNAL REST WILL SURELY ELUDE YOU IN DEATH.
IT *IS* HIM ...!
KAEDE... AGE HAS NOT BEEN KIND TO YOU.
ONIGUMO! IS THAT NOT YOUR NAME!?
ONIGUMO? THE NAME BRINGS ME SUCH FOND MEMORIES.
NAY, I AM NARAKU, NOT ONIGUMO.
YET IT CANNOT BE DENIED THAT I WAS BORN OF ONIGUMO, 50 YEARS AGO.

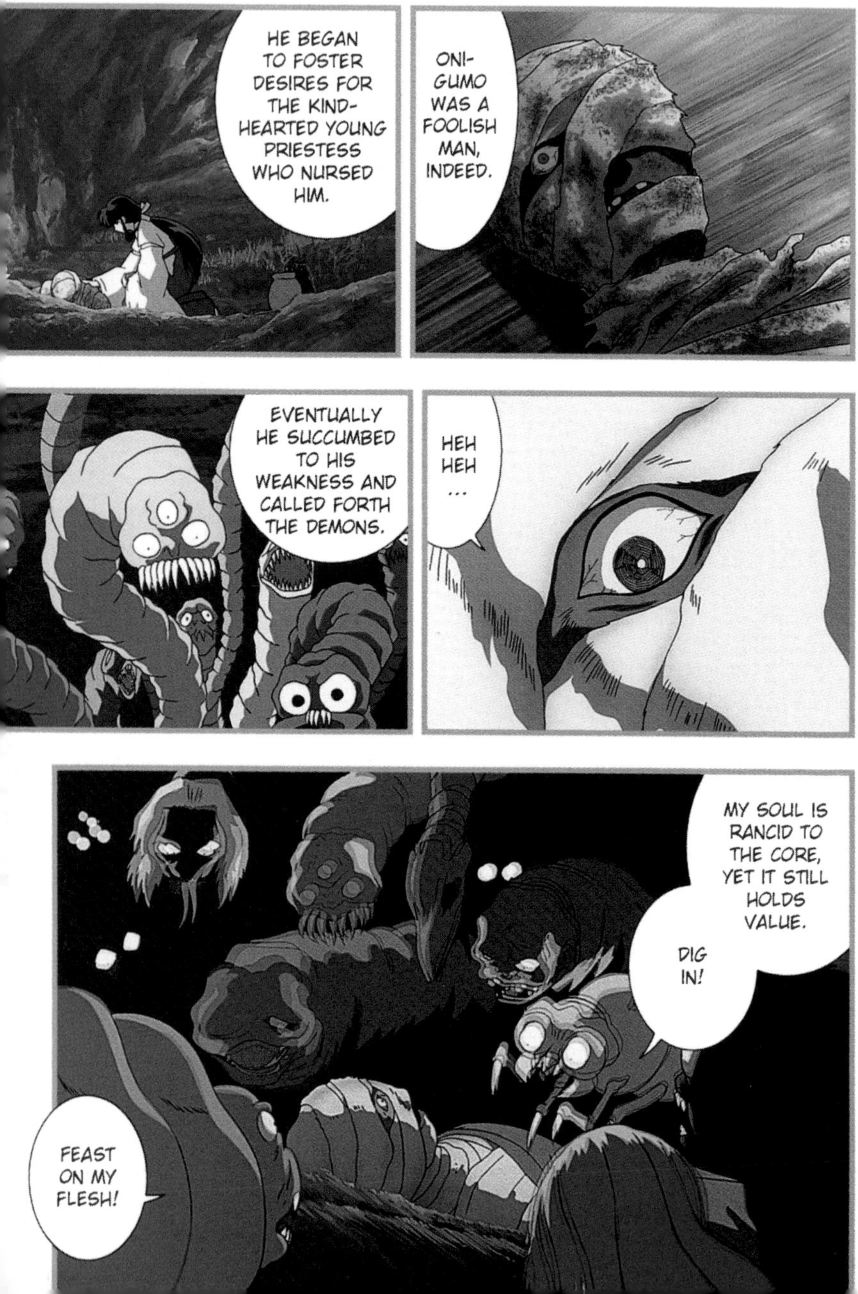
ONI-GUMO WAS A FOOLISH MAN, INDEED.
HE BEGAN TO FOSTER DESIRES FOR THE KIND-HEARTED YOUNG PRIESTESS WHO NURSED HIM.
HEH HEH ...
EVENTUALLY HE SUCCUMBED TO HIS WEAKNESS AND CALLED FORTH THE DEMONS.
MY SOUL IS RANCID TO THE CORE, YET IT STILL HOLDS VALUE.
DIG IN!
FEAST ON MY FLESH!

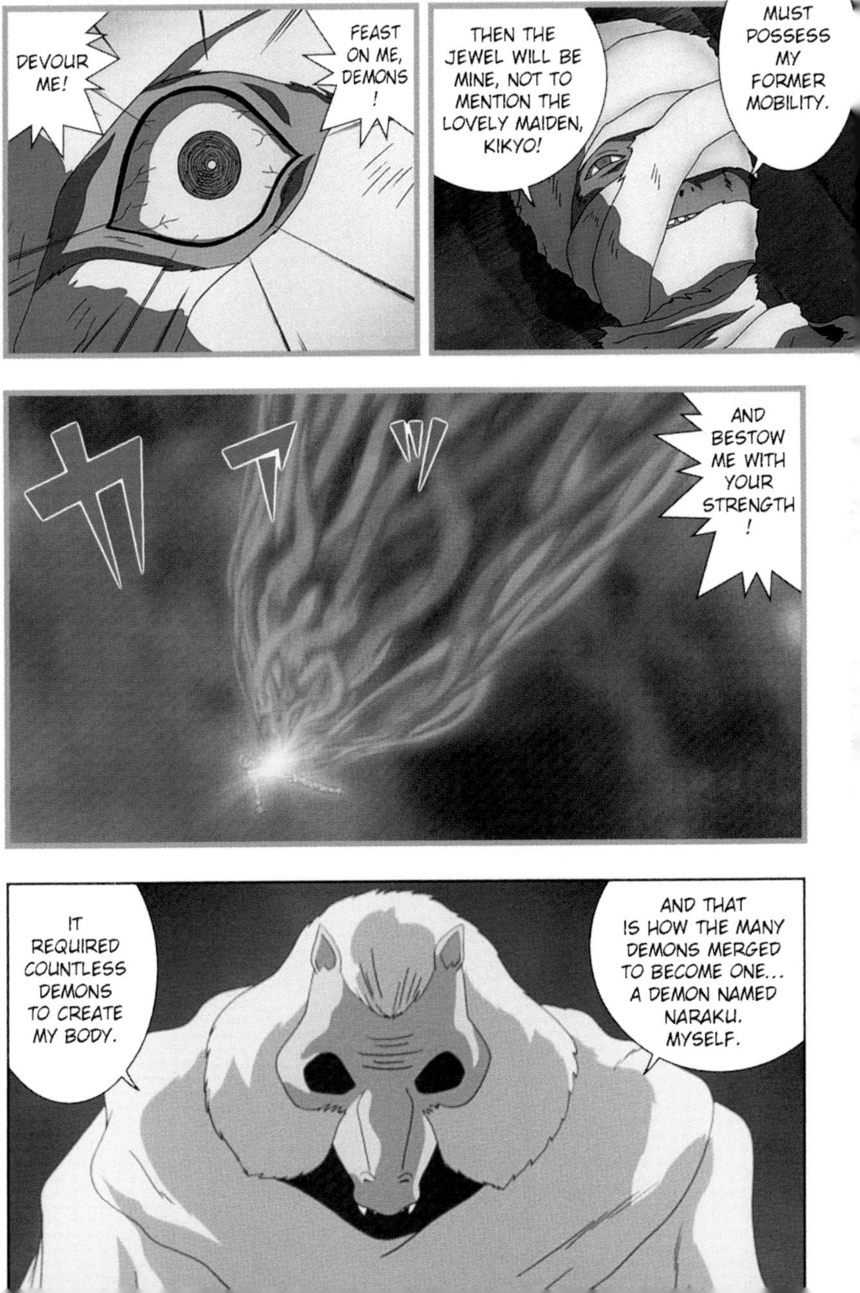
I MUST POSSESS MY FORMER MOBILITY.
THEN THE JEWEL WILL BE MINE, NOT TO MENTION THE LOVELY MAIDEN, KIKYO!
FEAST ON ME, DEMONS!
DEVOUR ME!
AND BESTOW ME WITH YOUR STRENGTH!
カァッ
AND THAT IS HOW THE MANY DEMONS MERGED TO BECOME ONE... A DEMON NAMED NARAKU. MYSELF.
IT REQUIRED COUNTLESS DEMONS TO CREATE MY BODY.

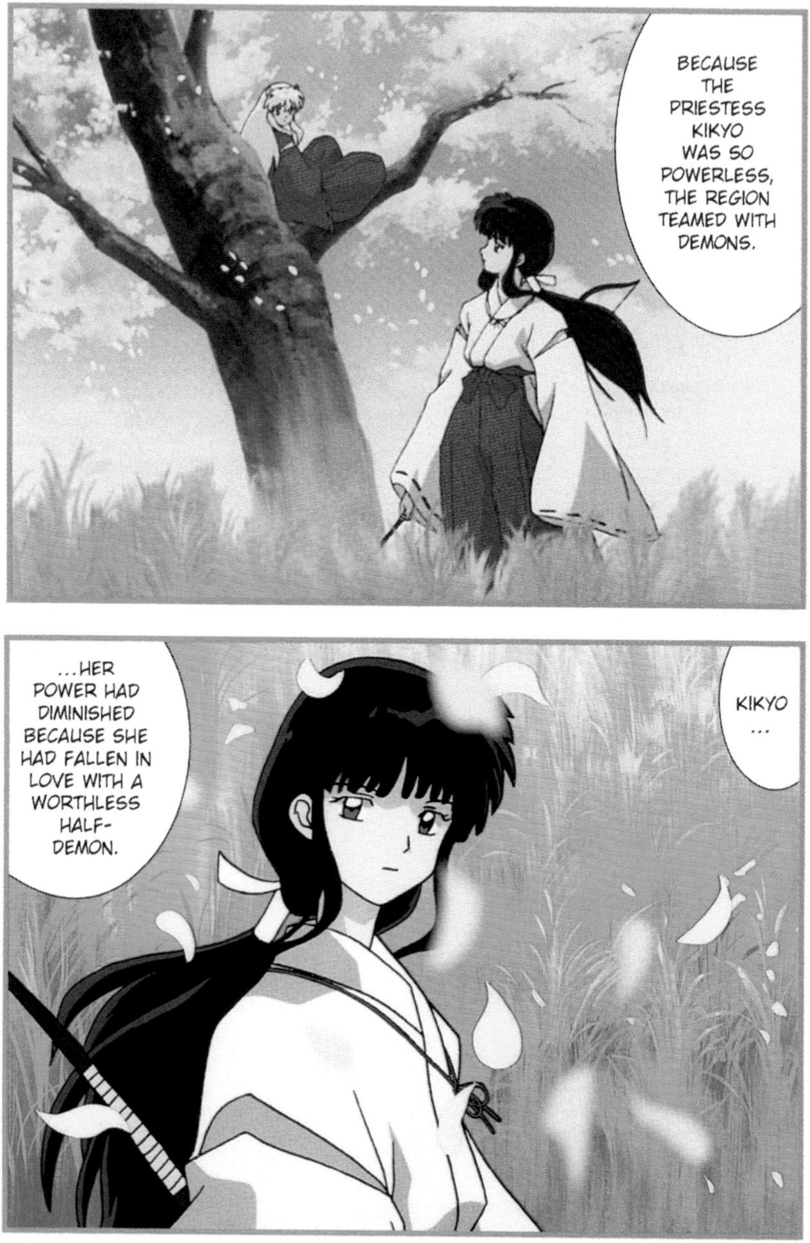
BECAUSE THE PRIESTESS KIKYO WAS SO POWERLESS, THE REGION TEAMED WITH DEMONS.
KIKYO ...
...HER POWER HAD DIMINISHED BECAUSE SHE HAD FALLEN IN LOVE WITH A WORTHLESS HALF-DEMON.

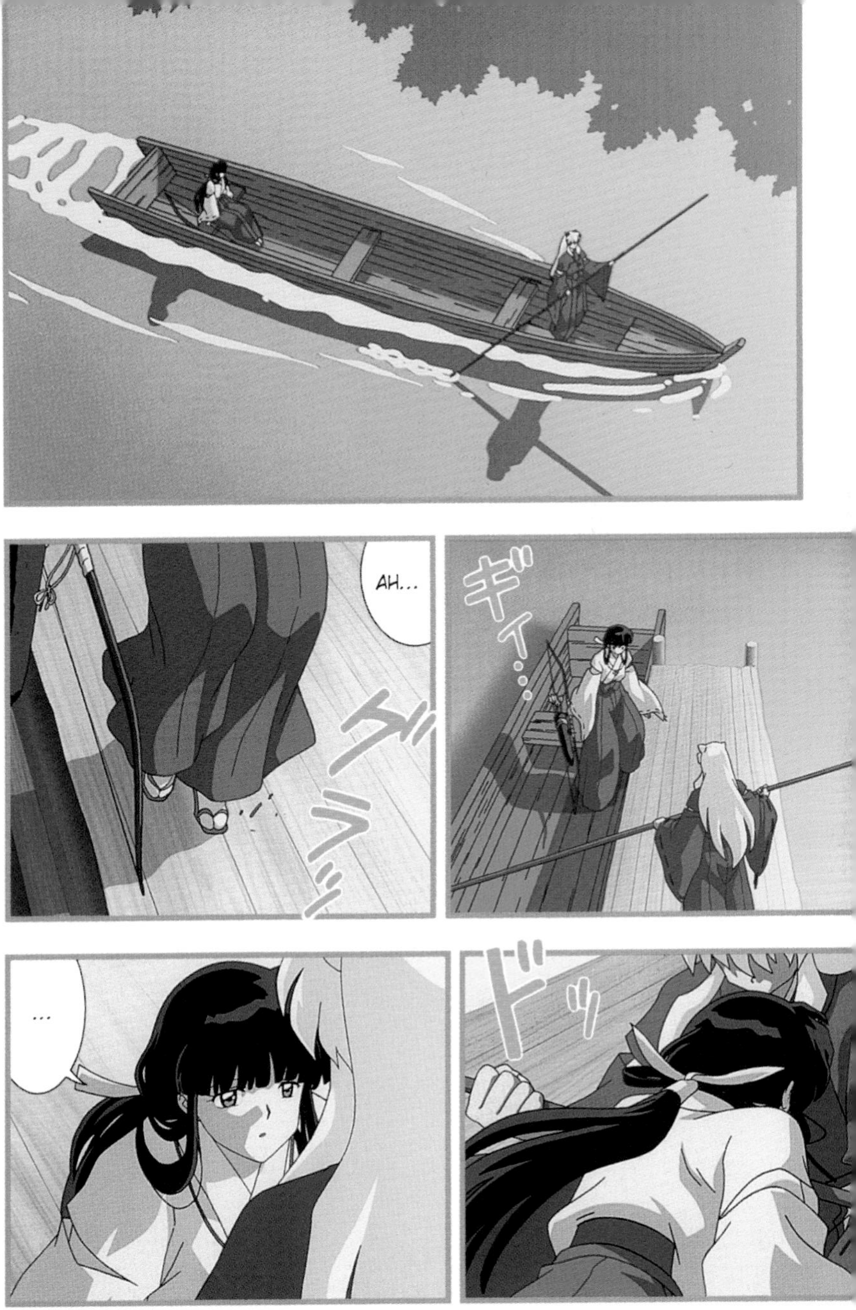
ギィ…
AH...
グラッ
ドッ
...

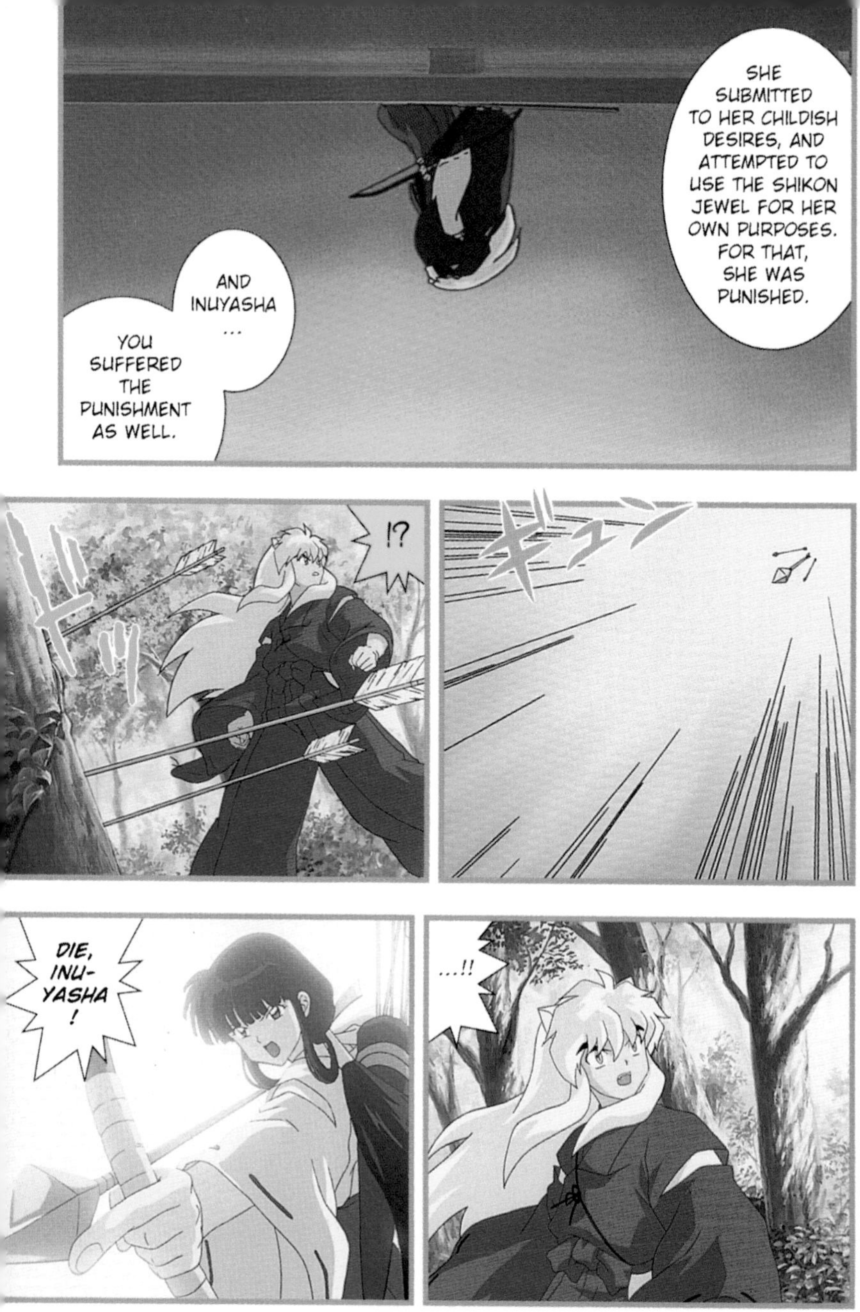
SHE SUBMITTED TO HER CHILDISH DESIRES, AND ATTEMPTED TO USE THE SHIKON JEWEL FOR HER OWN PURPOSES. FOR THAT, SHE WAS PUNISHED.
AND INUYASHA ...
YOU SUFFERED THE PUNISHMENT AS WELL.
!?
...!!
DIE, INU-YASHA !

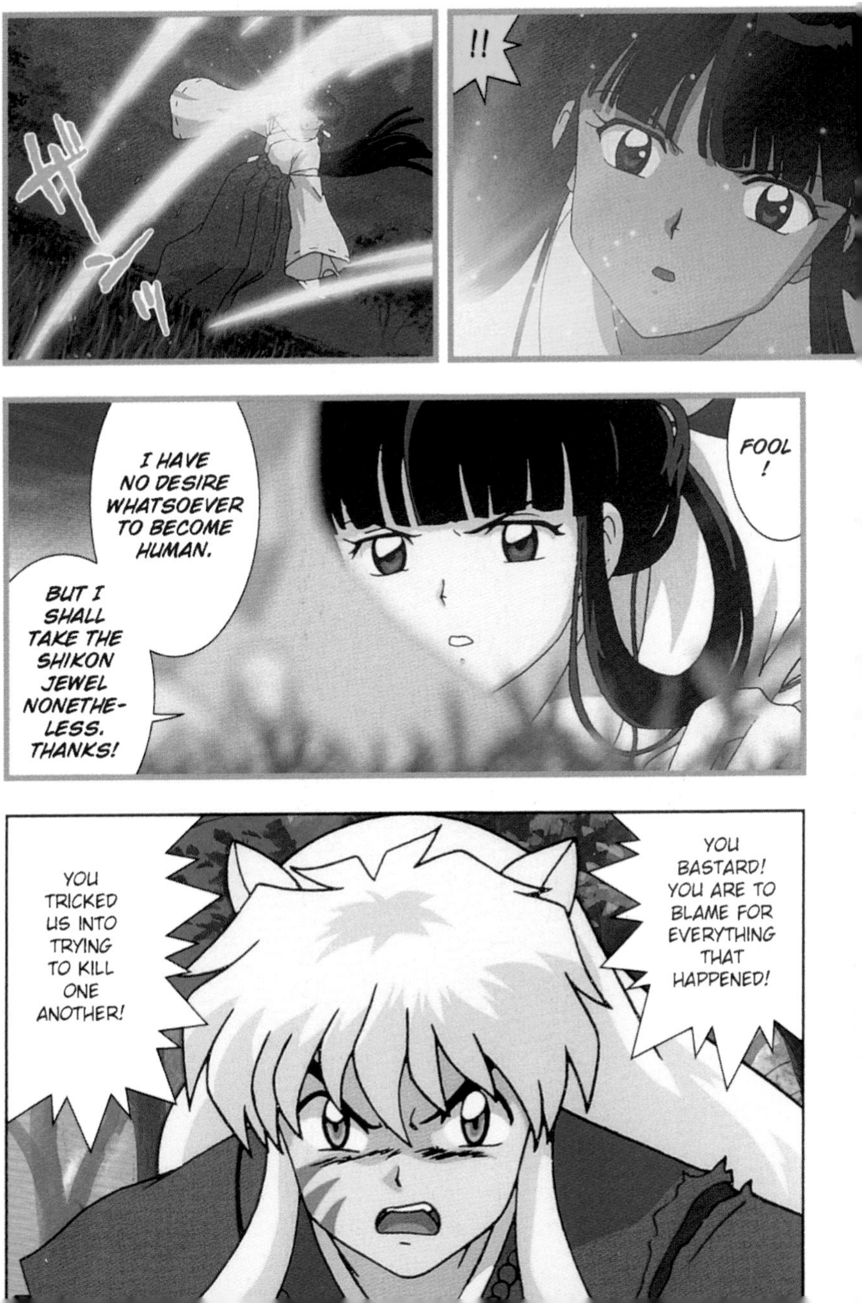
!!
FOOL!
I HAVE NO DESIRE WHATSOEVER TO BECOME HUMAN.
BUT I SHALL TAKE THE SHIKON JEWEL NONETHELESS. THANKS!
YOU BASTARD! YOU ARE TO BLAME FOR EVERYTHING THAT HAPPENED!
YOU TRICKED US INTO TRYING TO KILL ONE ANOTHER!

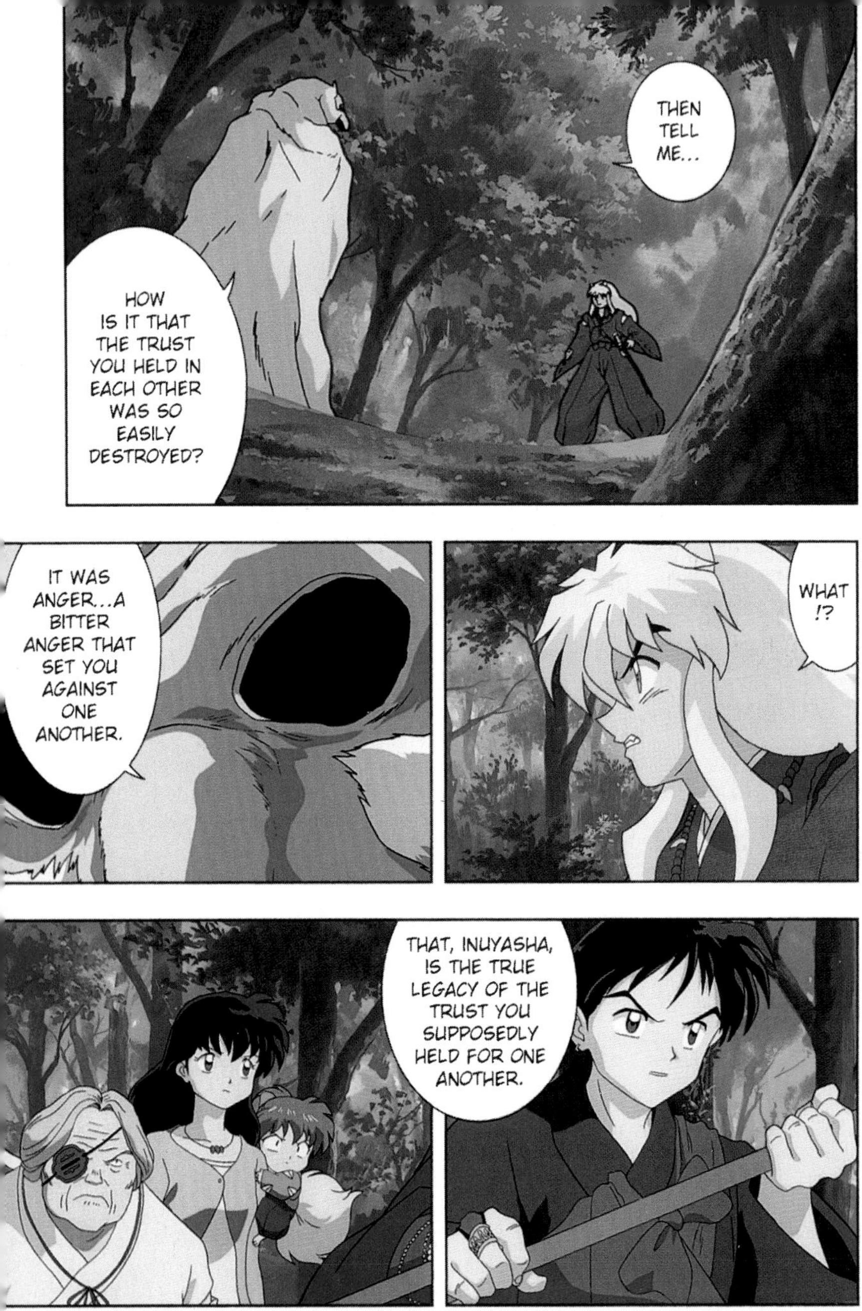
THEN TELL ME...
HOW IS IT THAT THE TRUST YOU HELD IN EACH OTHER WAS SO EASILY DESTROYED?
WHAT!?
IT WAS ANGER...A BITTER ANGER THAT SET YOU AGAINST ONE ANOTHER.
THAT, INUYASHA, IS THE TRUE LEGACY OF THE TRUST YOU SUPPOSEDLY HELD FOR ONE ANOTHER.

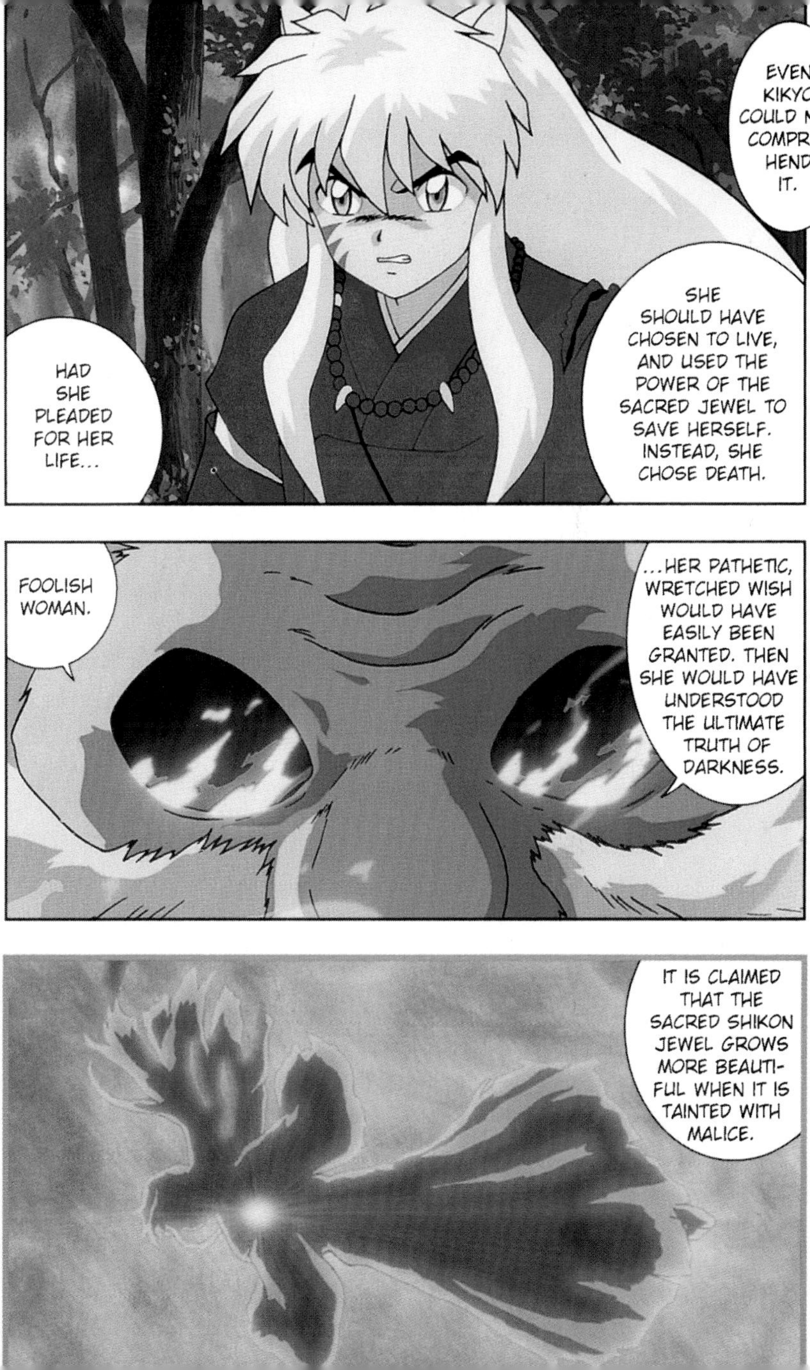
EVEN KIKYO COULD NOT COMPRE-HEND IT.
SHE SHOULD HAVE CHOSEN TO LIVE, AND USED THE POWER OF THE SACRED JEWEL TO SAVE HERSELF. INSTEAD, SHE CHOSE DEATH.
HAD SHE PLEADED FOR HER LIFE...
...HER PATHETIC, WRETCHED WISH WOULD HAVE EASILY BEEN GRANTED. THEN SHE WOULD HAVE UNDERSTOOD THE ULTIMATE TRUTH OF DARKNESS.
FOOLISH WOMAN.
IT IS CLAIMED THAT THE SACRED SHIKON JEWEL GROWS MORE BEAUTI-FUL WHEN IT IS TAINTED WITH MALICE.

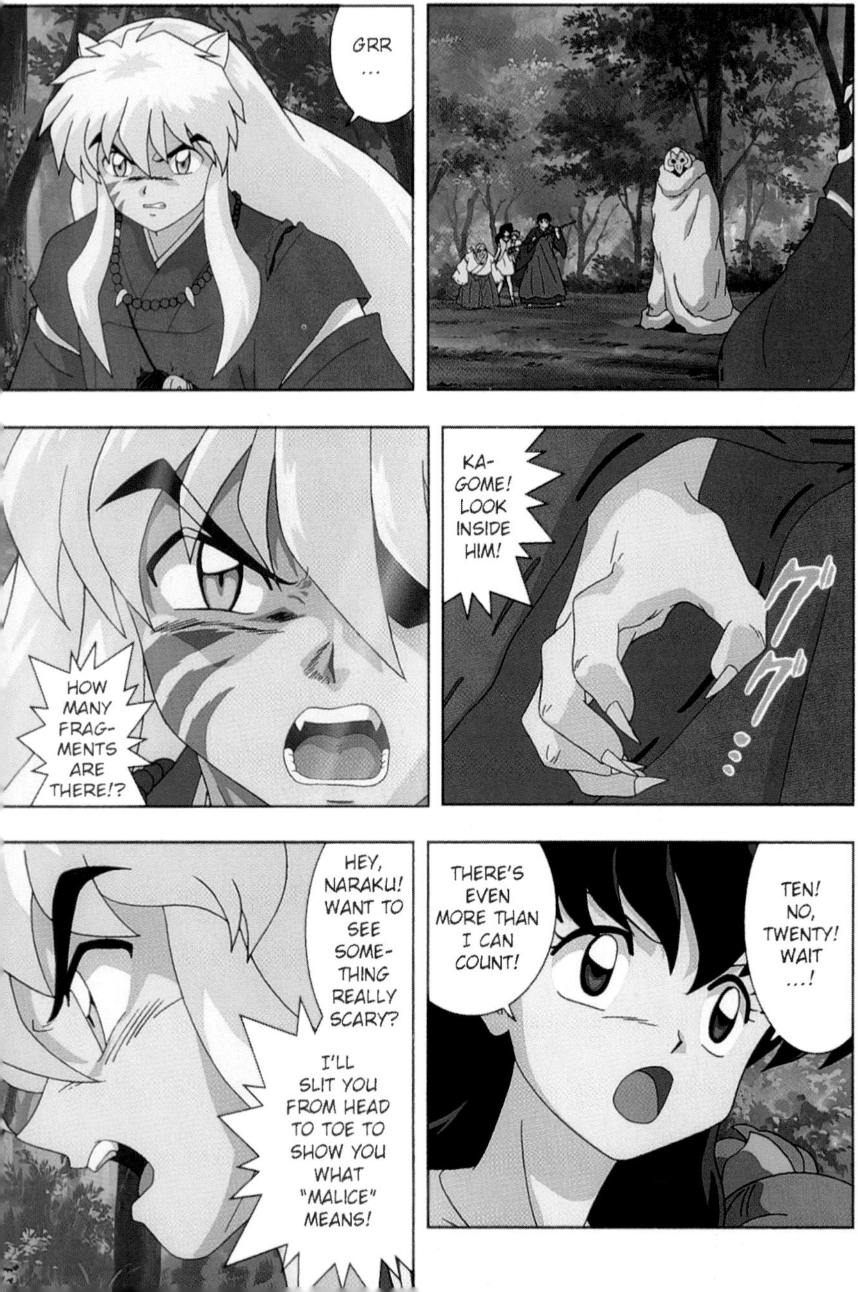

GRR ...
KA-GOME! LOOK INSIDE HIM!
ググ
HOW MANY FRAG-MENTS ARE THERE!?
TEN! NO, TWENTY! WAIT ...!
THERE'S EVEN MORE THAN I CAN COUNT!
HEY, NARAKU! WANT TO SEE SOME-THING REALLY SCARY?
I'LL SLIT YOU FROM HEAD TO TOE TO SHOW YOU WHAT "MALICE" MEANS!

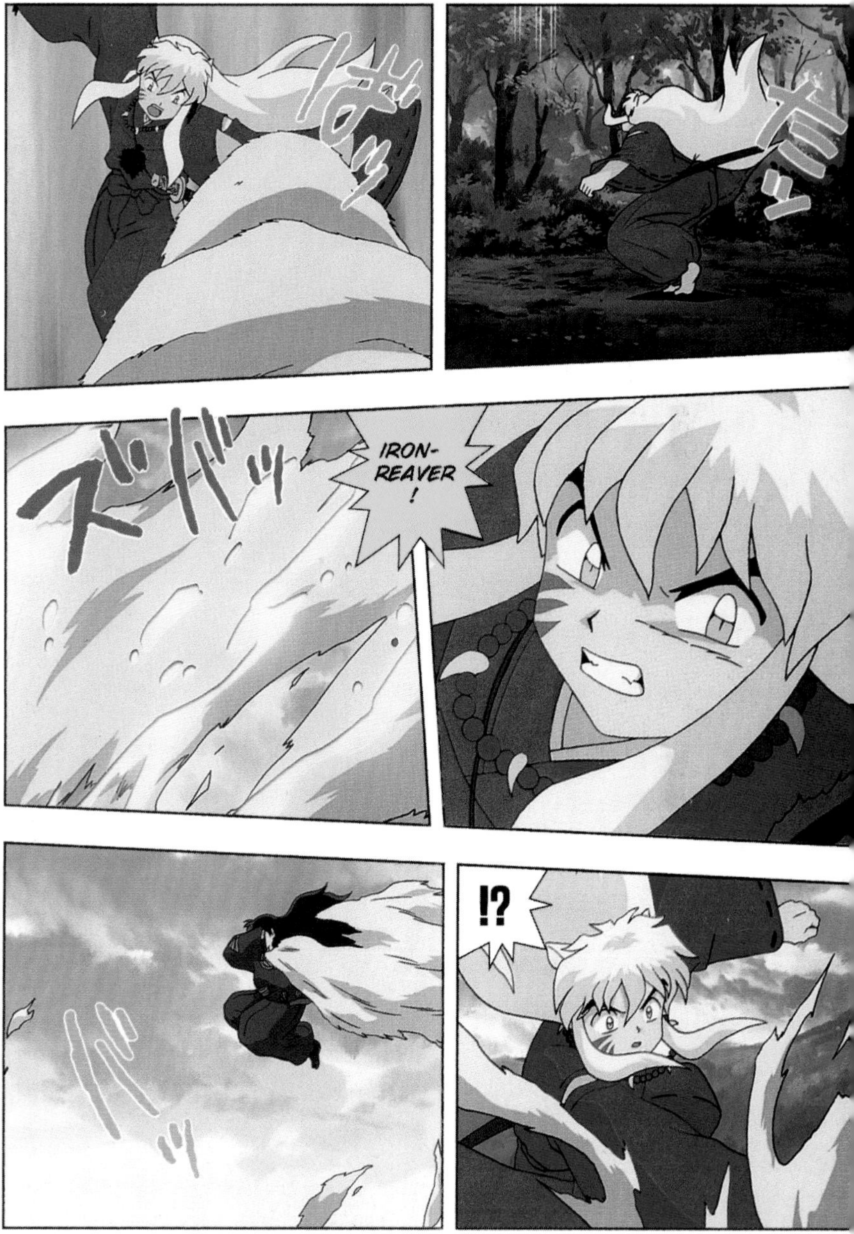
IRON-REAVER!
!?

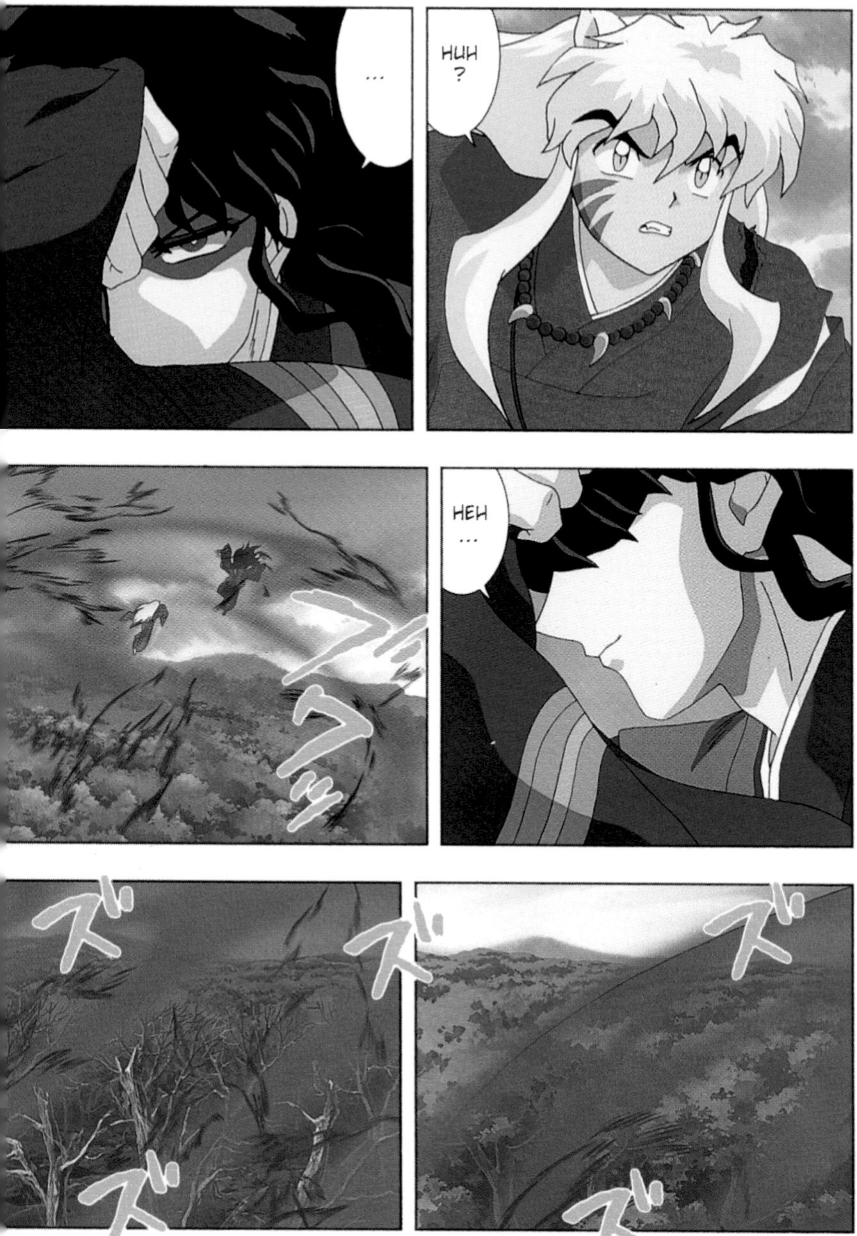
HUH ?
...
HEH ...
ズ
ズ
ズ
ズ
ズ

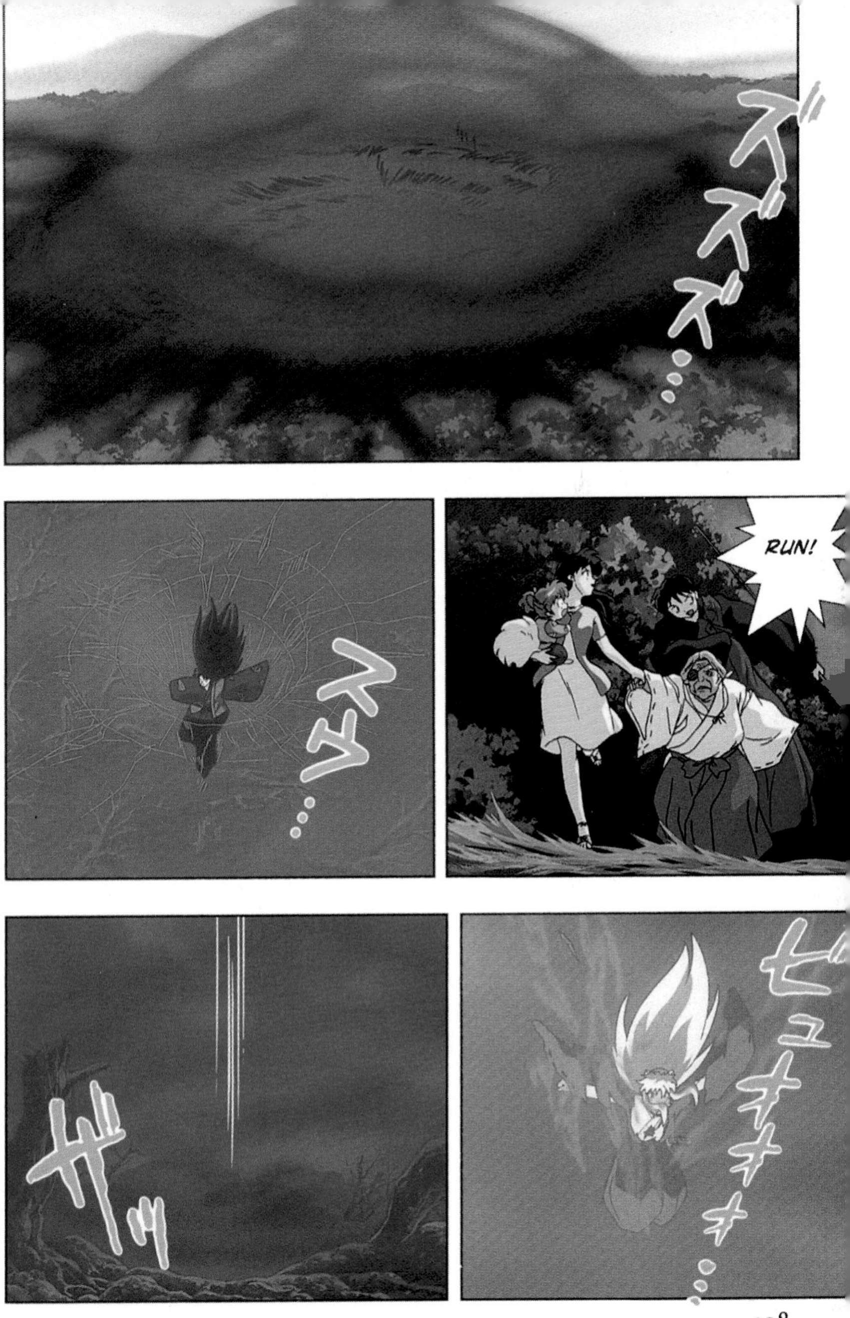
ズズズズ…
RUN!
スタ…
ビュオオオオ…
ザッ

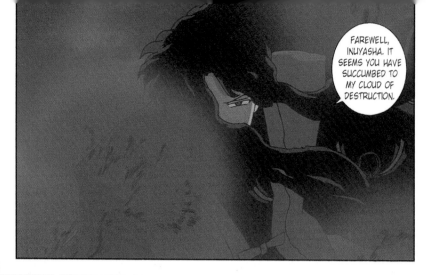

FAREWELL, INUYASHA. IT SEEMS YOU HAVE SUCCUMBED TO MY CLOUD OF DESTRUCTION.

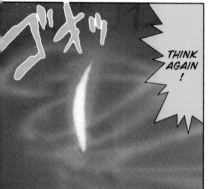

THINK AGAIN!

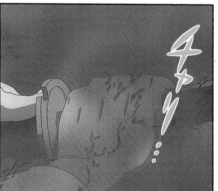

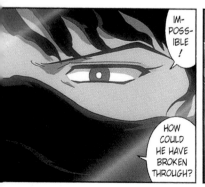

IM-POSS-IBLE!

HOW COULD HE HAVE BROKEN THROUGH?

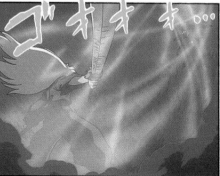

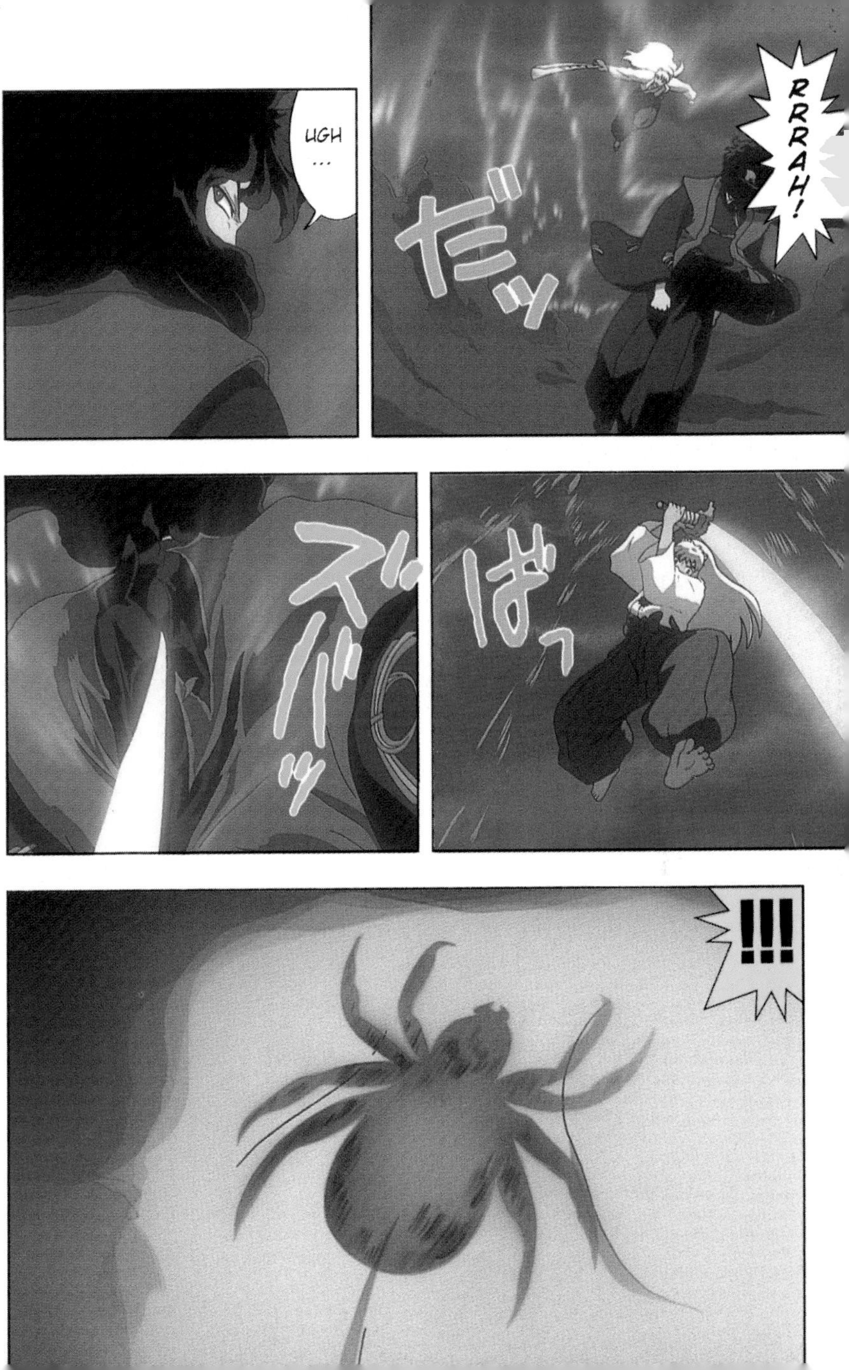
RRRAH!
だッ
UGH ...
ばっ
ズバッ
!!!

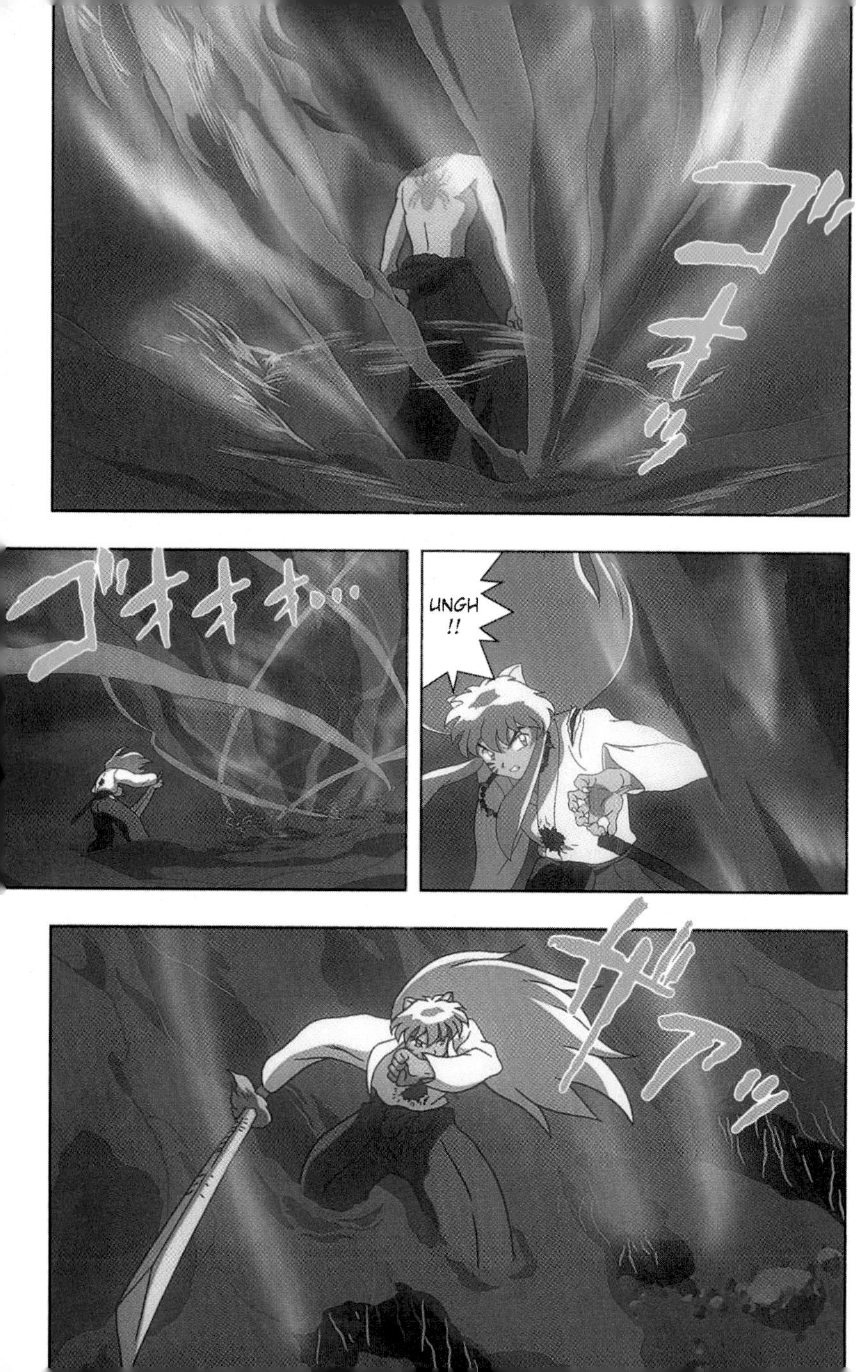
ゴオッ
UNGH !!
ゴオオオ…
ザアッ

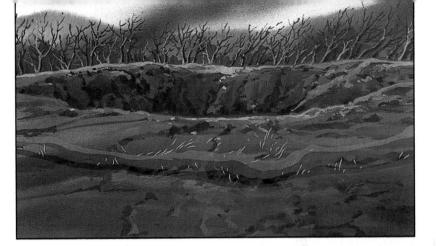

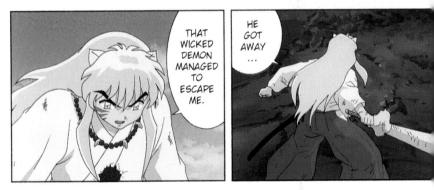

THAT WICKED DEMON MANAGED TO ESCAPE ME.

HE GOT AWAY ...

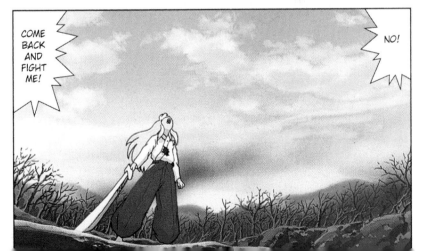

COME BACK AND FIGHT ME!

NO!

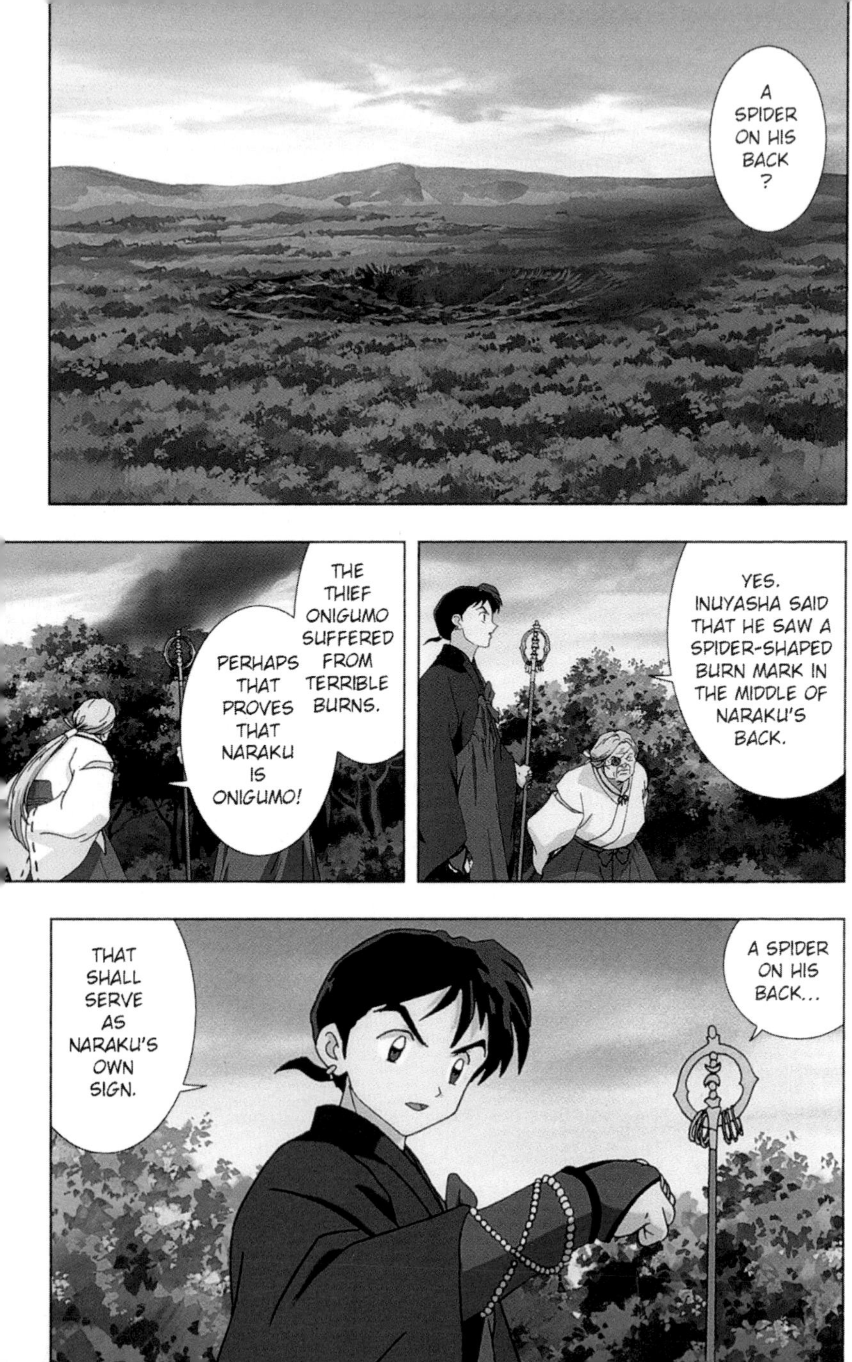
A SPIDER ON HIS BACK?
YES. INUYASHA SAID THAT HE SAW A SPIDER-SHAPED BURN MARK IN THE MIDDLE OF NARAKU'S BACK.
THE THIEF ONIGUMO SUFFERED FROM TERRIBLE BURNS.
PERHAPS THAT PROVES THAT NARAKU IS ONIGUMO!
A SPIDER ON HIS BACK...
THAT SHALL SERVE AS NARAKU'S OWN SIGN.

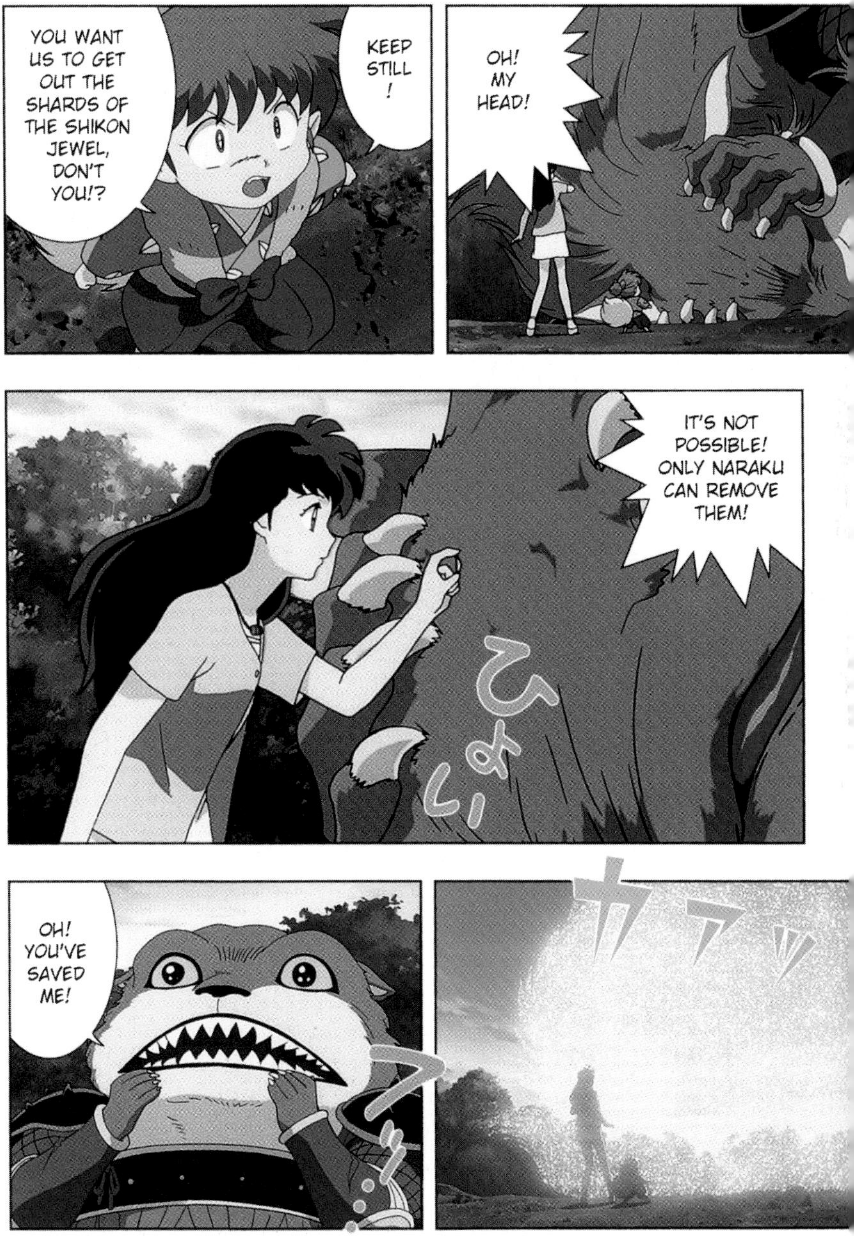
OH! MY HEAD!
KEEP STILL!
YOU WANT US TO GET OUT THE SHARDS OF THE SHIKON JEWEL, DON'T YOU!?
IT'S NOT POSSIBLE! ONLY NARAKU CAN REMOVE THEM!
ひょい
カァッ
OH! YOU'VE SAVED ME!
フッ

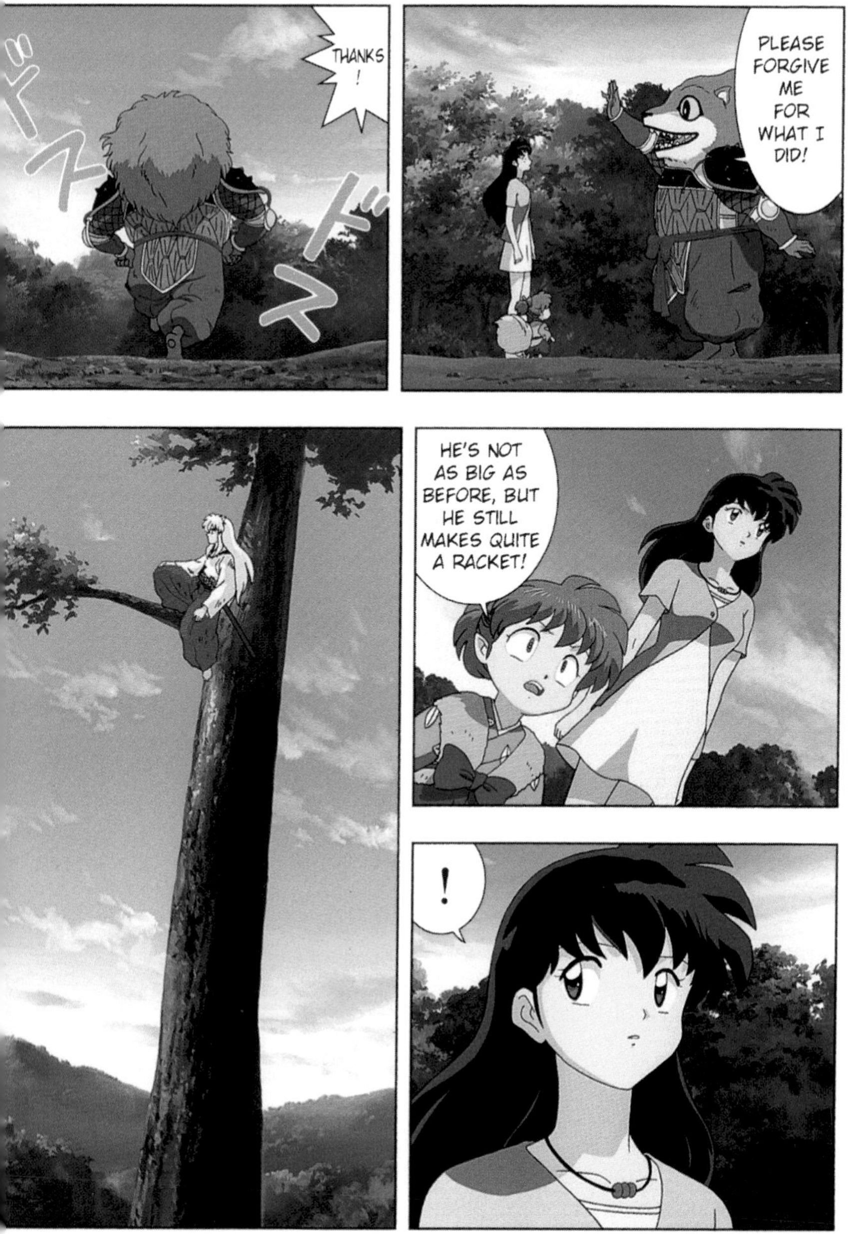
PLEASE FORGIVE ME FOR WHAT I DID!
THANKS!
ドスドス
HE'S NOT AS BIG AS BEFORE, BUT HE STILL MAKES QUITE A RACKET!
!

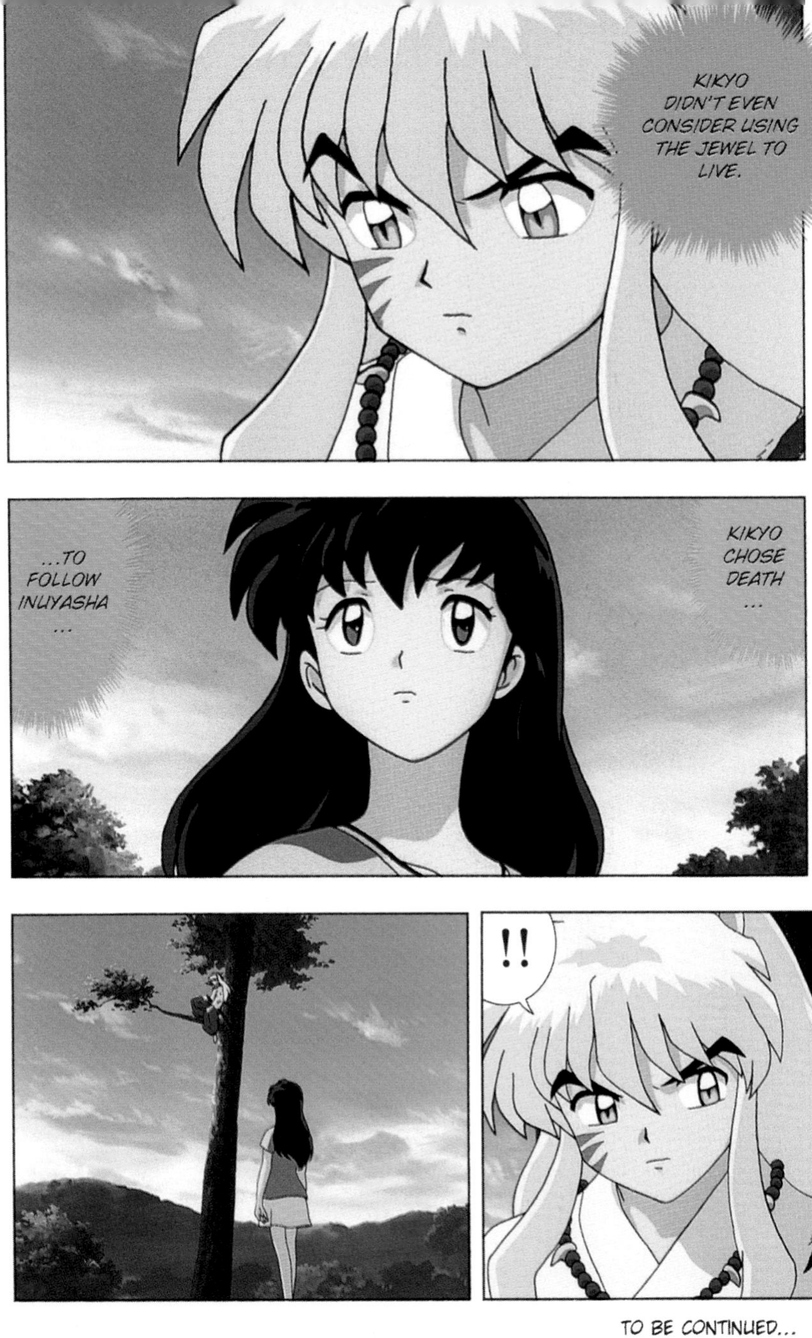
KIKYO DIDN'T EVEN CONSIDER USING THE JEWEL TO LIVE.
KIKYO CHOSE DEATH ...
...TO FOLLOW INUYASHA ...
!!

TO BE CONTINUED...

Glossary of Sound Effects

Each entry includes: the location, indicated by page number and panel number (so 3.1 means page 3, panel number 1); the phonetic romanization of the original Japanese; and our English "translation"—we offer as close an English equivalent as we can.

21.4 FX: Hyun (arrow files)
21.5 FX: Gohh (whoosh of arrow)

22.1 FX: Pashi (Sesshomaru catches arrow)
22.2 FX: Shuuuu… (arrow dissolves)

23.1 FX: Gohh (fire springs up)
23.2 FX: Da (running)
23.4 FX: Ba (Inuyasha catches Kagome in his arms)
23.5 FX: Gohhh… (flames)

24.1 FX: Zuzaza (Inuyasha and Kagome roll down slope)

25.1 FX: Kaaaa…(sword glimmers)
25.3 FX: Chari (metallic sword sound)
25.5 FX: Za (Miroku plunks down staff)

26.5 FX: Hyu (Inuyasha throws rock)

27.1 FX: Poto (rock lands)
27.2 FX: Bu bu bu (buzzing)
27.3 FX: Bu bu bu (buzz buzz buzz)

29.2 FX: Ba (slash)
29.3 FX: Gohh (flames whoosh)
29.4 FX: Bi (crackling sound from sword strike)
29.5 FX: Da (Inuyasha leaps)

30.1 FX: Gohhh… (explosion)
30.2 FX: Para para… (rocks and pebbles rain down)
30.5 FX: Gu gu… (Inuyasha chomps Sesshomaru's arm)

31.4 FX: Ta (running)
31.5 FX: Su (Sesshomaru raises hand to strike)

Chapter 19:
Go Home to Your Own Time, Kagome!

6.1 FX: Kiri kiri… (Kagome pulls bowstring)
6.2 FX: Giri… (Kagome pulls bowstring)
6.4 FX: Poh… (armor breaks)
6.5 FX: Hyun (arrow flies)

7.1 FX: Su (Sesshomaru dodges)
7.2 FX: Su (Sesshomaru jumps)
7.3 FX: Gohh (whoosh as Inuyasha jumps)
7.6 FX: Zuba (swipe)

8.1 FX: Toh (Sesshomaru leaps)

10.3 FX: Ga (smack)

17.1 FX: Da (running)
17.3 FX: Ba (missed strike)
17.4 FX: Za (swipe)
17.5 FX: Hyu (Sesshomaru's magic whip)

18.1 FX: Zan (crackle of strike)
18.2 FX: Ta (Inuyasha lands)
18.3 FX: Da (Inuyasha slides to stop)
18.4 FX: Hyun (rope swishes)
18.5 FX: Ta ta ta… (Inuyasha running)
18.6 FX: Tan (Inuyasha leaps)

19.1 FX: Bun (strike that misses)
19.2 FX: Guoh (power punch)
19.3 FX: Ga (Inuyasha punched in face)
19.4 FX: Za za za… (Inuyasha sent flying over rocky ground)

20.2 FX: Shururuthrough…(arrow flies)
20.3 FX: Ka (armor breaks)

51.1 FX: Za za za… (moving swiftly through grass)
51.2 FX: Za (moving through the grass)
51.4 FX: Zan (swipe)
51.5 FX: Doh (Kikyo lands in grass)

52.2 FX: Ga (fake Inuyasha steps on Kikyo's hand)

54.2 FX: Puku— (touchdown)
54.3 FX: Shuuuu… (slide to stop)
54.4 FX: Pon (Hachi turns back into a badger)

55.4 FX: Ta (Kagome runs off)

56.3 FX: Su… (Miroku follows)

63.3 FX: Gui (grab)

66.2 FX: Ba (Inuyasha forcefully pulls away)
66.3 FX: Doh (Kagome falls)

67.5 FX: Don (push)

68.3 FX: Da (Miroku runs to well)

70.3 FX: Ba (Kagome goes back into well)
70.4 FX: Za (Kagome smacks into bottom of well)

71.1 FX: Ki—n ko—n… (ringing of school bells)

Chapter 20:
Despicable Villain! The Mystery of Onigumo

74.1 FX: Doga (tree being stuffed in well)

78.4 FX: Shurururu… (arrow flies)
78.5 FX: Ka (arrow thunks into tree)

79.1 FX: Kiri kiri… (Kikyo pulls back bowstring)

84.2 FX: Gata
(Kagome stands up, slams hands on desk)

85.3 FX: Kaa… (light shines around Kagome)

86.2 FX: Zu zu… (slurp)
86.4 FX: Pon (Kaede slaps something on back)

32.1 FX: Zuba (big punch into Inuyasha's midriff)
32.3 FX: Zu zu zu… (Sessomaru's hand reappears)
32.4 FX: Ta ta ta… (running)

33.3 FX: Gui (grab)

34.1 FX: Zubo (Sessomaru withdraws hand)
34.5 FX: Gui (grab)

35.2 FX: Goto (arm falls off)

36.2 FX: Za (sinks to knees)

37.1 FX: Piku… (sword attacks)
37.2 FX: Goh (flames)

39.1 FX: Gohhh… (whoosh as Sesshomaru rises)
39.2 FX: Gohhh… (Sessomaru whooshes away)
39.3 FX: Buuuuu…n… (buzzing)
39.5 FX: Ta (running)

40.2 FX: Gura (Inuyasha starts to fall)
40.3 FX: Doh (Inuyasha lands face down)

41.1 FX: Bu bu bu (buzzing)

42.1 FX: Buchi (Sesshomaru removes arm)
42.2 FX: Ba (tosses arm to bugs)
42.3 FX: Shuuuu… (bugs devour arm for shard)
42.4 FX: Paku (bug gets jewel in pinchers)
42.5 FX: Buuuu…n… (bugs buzz away)

43.1 FX: Buuu…n… (bugs buzz off to Naraku)
43.1 FX: Su… (Naraku takes shard)
43.5 FX: Sa (Naraku turns around)

44.4 FX: Zan (Sesshomaru strikes)

45.1 FX: Zaa (skin collapses with nothing in it)
45.2 FX: Doh (skin plops to ground)
45.3 FX: Ga (Jaken kicks skin)
45.6 FX: Ba (Jaken tosses skin aside,
looking for Naraku)

47.1 FX: Gohhhh… (whoosh of flight)

94.1 FX: Pu… (Kikyo plucks flower)

95.3-4 FX: Gohhhhh… (flames roaring)

97.1 FX: Gu gu gu… (Shippo trying to lift out tree)
97.2 FX: Koron (tumbling to the ground)

98.5 FX: Zuu…n… (big feet plunk down)

99.1 FX: Gurururu… (growl)

102.1 FX: Da (running away)
102.3 FX: Zuzaza… (Shippo launches himself at Inuyasha)
102.4 FX: Doh doh doh doh… (galloping wolves)
102.5 FX: Da (Inuyasha throws his magic blades)

103.1 FX: Zuba (slash)
103.2 FX: Za (Shippo lands in Inuyasha's arms)
103.3 FX: Nuru… (dripping of blood on his paws)

105.3 FX: Dohh (wolves spewed forth)

106.1 FX: Guoh (Royakan's roar)
106.2 FX: Zuba (Inuyasha strikes)
106.3 FX: Ba (wolves leap)
106.4 FX: Ga (Miroku swings staff at wolves)
106.5 FX: Dohh (Royakan spews forth more wolves)

107.2 FX: Ba (wind tunnel opened)
107.3 FX: Gohhhh… (whoosh of wind tunnel)

108.1 FX: Doh (here come the wolves!)
108.2 FX: Doh doh doh (galloping wolves)

109.2 FX: Chari… (jewel shards sparkle)
109.3 FX: Zuba (Inuyasha's magic blades)
109.4 FX: Doh (wolf keels over)
109.5 FX: Gaku… (Inuyasha collapses to his knees)

110.1 FX: Gohhhh… (whoosh of wind tunnel)
110.4 FX: Ba (Miroku closes wind hole)
110.4 FX: Pashi (grabs staff)
110.6 FX: Ga (Royakan braces himself against wind tunnel)

111.1 FX: Gohh (whoosh of wind tunnel)
111.3 FX: Doga (Royakan smashes himself on ground brace himself against the tunnel)
111.4 FX: Gohhhh… (whoosh of wind tunnel)

112.3 FX: Fu… (Naraku levitates up and away)

113.6 FX: Fura… (Inuyasha gets up abruptly)

114.2 FX: Furaa… (Inuyasha collapses)
114.3 FX: Doh (Inuyasha passes out and hits the ground)

115.1 FX: Wa- wa- (buzz of distant voices)

118.1 FX: Bishi (Kagome is suddenly brought out of her reverie by her friend's accusation)
118.4 FX: Kuru (Kagome turns to face Hojo with resolve)

119.4 FX: Ba (Kagome jumps into well)
119.5 FX: Tan (ping from pulled muscle)

120.1 FX: Doga (kick)
120.2 FX: Don don (whack whack)

121.4 FX: Doga (kick)
121.5 FX: Gara (door opens)

122.3 FX: Gan (Inuyasha gets pinned to floor by Miroku's staff)

123.5 FX: Niko… (smile)

124.1 FX: Geshi geshi (kicking)

126.5 FX: Hyu (Naraku flicks shard at Royakan)

127.2 FX: Kaaa… (jewel shard shines)
127.3 FX: Da (running)
127.4 FX: Doh doh doh… (Royakan smacking into trees as he runs)

129.1 FX: Zawa… (sinister wind)
129.4 FX: Doh doh doh… (wolves approaching)

129.5 FX: Gu (Kaede and Miroku steel themselves against the approaching attack)

130.1 FX: Bachi (crackling as Royakan collides with spell energy)
130.2 FX: Zun… (Monster foot slams into ground)

131.3 FX: Bachi bachi (crackling of spell energy)

132.1 FX: Gyun (spear thrown)
132.2 FX: Goh (spear whooshes)
132.5 FX: Gin (deflects spear)
132.6 FX: Goh (whoosh)

133.1 FX: Ga (spear strikes ground harmlessly)
133.2 FX: Suu… (hut appears)
133.4 FX: Ba (demon leaps)
133.5 FX: Doga (slam into ground)

134.1 FX: Ba (slash)
134.2 FX: Za (Inuyasha lands on one knee in dirt)

135.1 FX: Guo (sword whooshes through air)
135.2 FX: Doga (strike)
135.3 FX: Goh (swoosh)
135.4 FX: Gashi (Royakan grabs blade between palms)

136.1 FX: Buo (smack that sends Inuyasha flying)
136.2 FX: Za (Inuyasha lands on ground)

137.1 FX: Karan… (jewel rolls)
137.2 FX: Doh doh doh (wolves running)
137.3 FX: Yoro… (Inuyasha unsteady on his feet)
137.4 FX: Sa (jewel snatched)
137.5 FX: Dogoh (big foot slams down)

138.1 FX: Ta ta ta… (Shippo running)
138.3 FX: Goh (Royakan spews forth wolves)
138.4 FX: Ta ta ta… (running)
138.5 FX: Doh doh doh… (galloping wolves)

139.3 FX: Buuu…n… (buzzing)
139.4 FX: Kyu (Miroku seals up hand again)

140.2 FX: Buuu…n… (buzzing)
140.4 FX: Doh doh doh doh (galloping wolves)

Chapter 21:
Naraku's True Identity Unveiled

142.3 FX: Ba (Kagome grabs phone)

143.2 FX: Ba (Kagome snatches away phone)

145.1 FX: Kacha kacha (sounds of Sota's fingers on game console)
145.2 FX: Ba—n (Sota's game character gets killed)
145.4 FX: Ta (footstep)

146.3 FX: Da (Kagome takes off)

150.2 FX: Za za za… (running wolf)
150.4 FX: Pon (pop)
150.5 FX: Guwa (wolf growl)
150.6 FX: Bon (illusion dissipates as wolf bites it)

151.1 FX: Koso (Shippo hops down)
151.2 FX: Za (Shippo slides)
151.3 FX: Ga (Shippo smacks into branch)
151.4 FX: Za (Shippo lands on head)
151.5 FX: Chari (shard falls on ground)
151.6 FX: Kaaa… (jewel shines)

154.1 FX: Zuba (smack)
154.2 FX: Zan (Miroku swings staff)
154.3 FX: Zuga (thump)
154.4 FX: Guoh (roar)
154.5 FX: Dogo (Royakan strikes)
154.6 FX: Toh (Inuyasha touches down)

155.1 FX: Zuga (swipe)
155.2 FX: Za (Inuyasha falls)

157.2 FX: Guo (Royakan vomits wolves)
157.3 FX: Ba (Inuyasha turns to strike Royakan)

160.4 FX: Zuru (Kagome falls over in disbelief)

162.2 FX: Ta (running)
162.3 FX: Ba (Kagome hops into well)
162.4 FX: Toh (Kagome lands in well)

164.1 FX: Kaaa… (jewel shining)

165.1 FX: Za (Kagome digging)
165.2 FX: Za (moving dirt out of hole)
165.3 FX: Kaaaaa… (jewel shining)
165.4 FX: Ka! (brightness, explosion)
165.5 FX: Fu… (Kagome falls into Inuyasha's world)

167.1 FX: Suu… (Kagome floats down to earth)
167.5 FX: Za (wolf approaches)

168.4 FX: Da (running)

169.1 FX: Da (Inuyasha jumps)
169.2 FX: Doga (Inuyasha kicks)
169.3 FX: Za (Inuyasha lands)
169.5 FX: Zuba (slash)

170.2 FX: Da (running)
170.5 FX: Ta ta ta… (running)

172.1 FX: Ga (Inuyasha grabs tree)
172.2 FX: Gu gu gu… (Inuyasha pulling tree out of well)
172.4 FX: Zu… (tree comes loose)
172.5 FX: Za (Inuyasha takes off with tree)

173.3 FX: Bun (Inuyasha hurls tree)
173.4 FX: Dogoh (tree hits Royakan in the mouth)

174.1 FX: Dohn (Royakan collapses)
174.3-4 FX: Shuuuu… (wolves turn into smoke)

175.3 FX: Su... (Inuyasha descends)
175.4 FX: Toh (Inuyasha lands)

176.5 FX: Ta… (running)

179.3 FX: Waa (sobbing)

182.2 FX: Zoku (realization)

183.1 FX: Da (running)
183.3 FX: Za (Inuyasha lands)
183.4 FX: Ba (Inuyasha jumps)

184.1 FX: Za (Inuyasha lands)

185.1 FX: Za (staff jingles)

188.3 FX: Kaa (jewel gleaming)

190.2 FX: Gii… (dock creaks)
190.3 FX: Gura (slipping)
190.4 FX: Toh (Kikyo falls into Inuyasha's chest)

191.2 FX: Gyun (arrow flies toward Inuyasha)
191.3 FX: Doh (thunk)

192.2 FX: Zan (swipe/strike)

195.3 FX: Gu gu… (Inuyasha making fist)

196.1 FX: Ta (Inuyasha lands)
196.2 FX: Ba (strike)
196.4 FX: Zuba (slash)
196.6 FX: Ba (Naraku escapes)

197.4 FX: Buwa (clouds gather)
197.5-6 FX: Zu zu zu zu zu (Naraku's cloud of destruction growing)

198.1 FX: Zu zu zu… (cloud continues to grow)
198.3 FX: Suu… (Naraku leaping about)
198.4 FX: Byuohh… (Inuyasha going after Naraku through cloud)
198.5 FX: Za (Inuyasha leaps)

199.2 FX: Chari… (Inuyasha draws sword)
199.3 FX: Gohh (swoosh of sword's power)
199.4 FX: Gohh… (more power of sword)

200.1 FX: Da (Inuyasha leaps)
200.3 FX: Ba (slash)
200.4 FX: Zuba (sword cuts Naraku's robe)

201.1 FX: Gohh (Naraku disappears)
201.3 FX: Gohhh… (whoosh of wind)
201.4 FX: Zaa (useless slash)

204.3 FX: Hyoi (Kagome removes jewel shard)
204.4 FX: Kaa (jewel shines)
204.5 FX: Fu… (Royakan shrinks back to pre-jewel shard self)

205.2 FX: Dosu dosu (Royakan walks off into sunset)

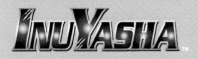

Rated #1 on Cartoon Network's Adult Swim!

In its original, unedited form!

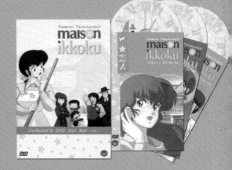

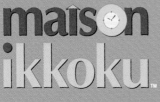

The beloved romantic comedy of errors—a fan favorite!

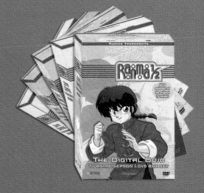

The zany, wacky study of martial arts at its best!

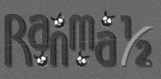

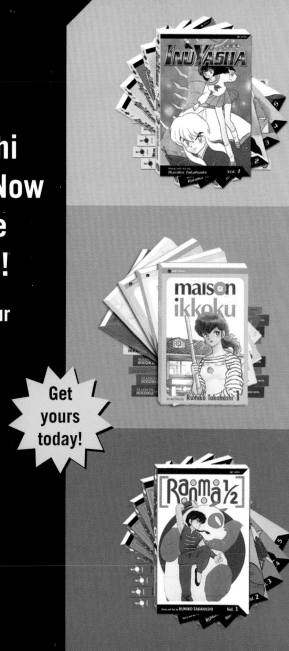

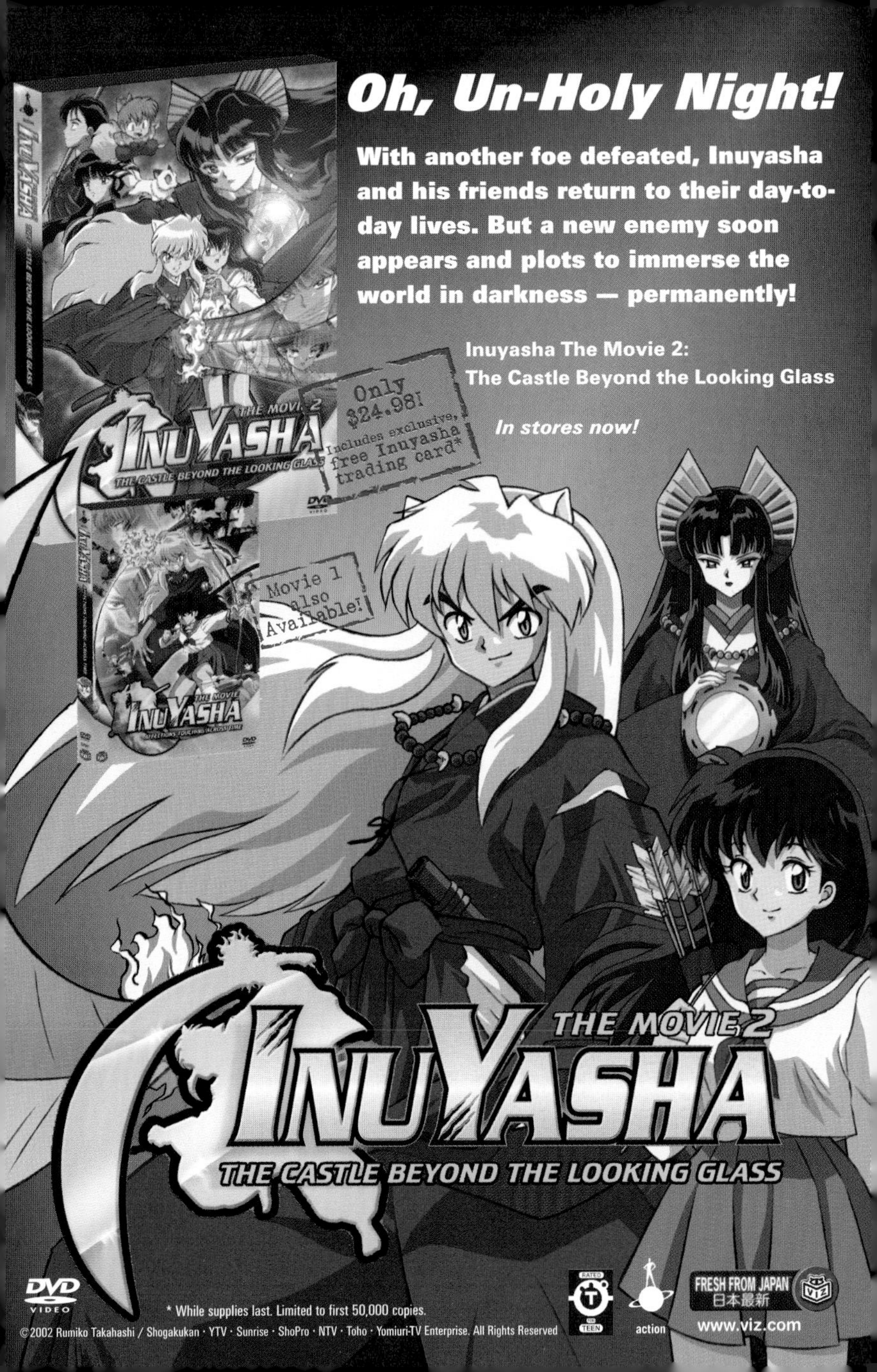
Oh, Un-Holy Night!
With another foe defeated, Inuyasha and his friends return to their day-to-day lives. But a new enemy soon appears and plots to immerse the world in darkness — permanently!
Inuyasha The Movie 2:
The Castle Beyond the Looking Glass
In stores now!
Only $24.98!
Includes exclusive, free Inuyasha trading card*
THE MOVIE 2
INUYASHA
THE CASTLE BEYOND THE LOOKING GLASS
Movie 1 also Available!
THE MOVIE
INUYASHA
THE MOVIE 2
INUYASHA
THE CASTLE BEYOND THE LOOKING GLASS
DVD VIDEO
* While supplies last. Limited to first 50,000 copies.
©2002 Rumiko Takahashi / Shogakukan · YTV · Sunrise · ShoPro · NTV · Toho · Yomiuri-TV Enterprise. All Rights Reserved
RATED T FOR TEEN
action
FRESH FROM JAPAN
日本最新
VIZ
www.viz.com

COMPLETE OUR SURVEY AND LET US KNOW WHAT YOU THINK!

☐ Please do NOT send me information about VIZ products, news and events, special offers, or other information.

☐ Please do NOT send me information from VIZ's trusted business partners.

Name: _____

Address: _____

City: _____ **State:** _____ **Zip:** _____

E-mail: _____

☐ Male ☐ Female **Date of Birth** (mm/dd/yyyy): ___ / ___ / ___ (Under 13? Parental consent required)

What race/ethnicity do you consider yourself? (please check one)

☐ Asian/Pacific Islander   ☐ Black/African American   ☐ Hispanic/Latino

☐ Native American/Alaskan Native ☐ White/Caucasian   ☐ Other: _____

What VIZ product did you purchase? (check all that apply and indicate title purchased)

☐ DVD/VHS _____

☐ Graphic Novel _____

☐ Magazines _____

☐ Merchandise _____

Reason for purchase: (check all that apply)

☐ Special offer   ☐ Favorite title   ☐ Gift

☐ Recommendation   ☐ Other _____

Where did you make your purchase? (please check one)

☐ Comic store   ☐ Bookstore   ☐ Mass/Grocery Store

☐ Newsstand   ☐ Video/Video Game Store ☐ Other: _____

☐ Online (site: _____)

What other VIZ properties have you purchased/own? _____

_____

How many anime and/or manga titles have you purchased in the last year? How many were VIZ titles? **(please check one from each column)**

ANIME	MANGA	
☐ None	☐ None	
☐ 1-4	☐ 1-4	
☐ 5-10	☐ 5-10	
☐ 11+	☐ 11+	☐ 11+

I find the pricing of VIZ products to be: **(please check one)**

☐ Cheap ☐ Reasonable ☐ Expensive

What genre of manga and anime would you like to see from VIZ? **(please check two)**

☐ Adventure ☐ Comic Strip ☐ Science Fiction ☐ Fighting

☐ Horror ☐ Romance ☐ Fantasy ☐ Sports

What do you think of VIZ's new look?

☐ Love It ☐ It's OK ☐ Hate It ☐ Didn't Notice ☐ No Opinion

Which do you prefer? **(please check one)**

☐ Reading right-to-left

☐ Reading left-to-right

Which do you prefer? **(please check one)**

☐ Sound effects in English

☐ Sound effects in Japanese with English captions

☐ Sound effects in Japanese only with a glossary at the back

THANK YOU! Please send the completed form to:

VIZ Survey
42 Catharine St.
Poughkeepsie, NY 12601

All information provided will be used for internal purposes only. We promise not to sell or otherwise divulge your information.